MUSICAL THEATRE

A History

MUSICAL
THEATRE

A History

John Kenrick

Bloomsbury Academic
An imprint of Bloomsbury Publishing Plc

B L O O M S B U R Y
NEW YORK · LONDON · NEW DELHI · SYDNEY

Bloomsbury Academic
An imprint of Bloomsbury Publishing Inc

1385 Broadway	50 Bedford Square
New York	London
NY 10018	WC1B 3DP
USA	UK

www.bloomsbury.com

BLOOMSBURY and the Diana logo are trademarks of Bloomsbury Publishing Plc

First published in 2010 by the Continuum International Publishing Group Inc
Reprinted 2011 (twice), 2012
Reprinted by Bloomsbury Academic 2013, 2015

Library of Congress Cataloging-in-Publication Data
Library of Congress Cataloging-in-Publication Data
Kenrick, John.
Musical theatre: a history/John Kenrick.
p. cm.
Includes bibliographical references (p.) and index.
ISBN: 978-0-8264-3013-7 (hardcover: alk. paper)
1. Musicals—History and criticism. I. Title.
ML2054.K46 2008
782.1'409—dc22 2007039005

ISBN: HB: 978-0-8264-2860-8
PB: 978-0-8264-3013-7

Printed and bound in the United States of America

*This book is dedicated to
Mary Pinizzotto Kenrick Marotta and Frank Crosio.
Neither my life nor this book would be possible
without their unfailing support.*

CONTENTS

ACKNOWLEDGMENTS

IT WOULD BE impossible for me to thank all the people who have inspired, assisted, and cajoled me in the process of creating this book, but a few curtain calls are in order. My first thanks goes to Hilary Cohen, whose eagle eye averted many a grammatical and factual disaster. Heaven be praised for Marty Jacobs, curator of the theatre collection at the Museum of the City of New York, who welcomed my offer to catalog George M. Cohan's eclectic archive. He then set me to work on the archives of Ethel Merman, Mary Martin, and so many others. Oh those joyous, dusty hours uncovering history! I am equally thankful for the existence of the Lincoln Center Library for the Performing Arts, which has been my home away from home since high school. I particularly thank Bruce Levy, whose friendship is even more priceless than his vast private collection of musical theatre recordings and memorabilia. Thanks also to those colleagues who have encouraged my efforts over the years, including Peter Filichia, Miles Kreuger, Kurt Ganzl, and Professor Meg Bussert.

A thousand thanks to the folks at Continuum Publishing for deciding that it was time for a new book on this subject, to the always elegant Ken Giniger for pursuing the idea, and to the York Theatre's dedicated and brilliant artistic director Jim Morgan for suggesting that these good people talk to me. The York is one of the true hopes for the future of musical theatre, and I am proud to be a friend and cheerleader for that resourceful company. I also thank my students at New York University's Steinhardt School and at Marymount Manhattan College. Their questions and enthusiasm made teaching a joy and helped to shape every chapter of this volume. It is *not* a very ancient saying, but it is a true and honest thought that "when you become a teacher, by your pupils you'll be taught." I can only pray that they learned half as much from me as I did from them.

All of the photos in this book come from materials in my personal archive, and every effort has been made to give proper accreditation. And just in case it needs to be said, as author, I take full responsibility for the contents of this book. Any questions or comments can be directed to me via my website, www.musicals101.com.

Introduction: "Let's Start at the Very Beginning ..."

... a very good place to start.

When I was a teenager, aging theatre buffs insisted that the Broadway musical's "golden age" ended in the 1950s. Recent books and documentaries speak of that era extending into the mid 1960s, and an upcoming generation of writers is pushing that "golden age" into the 1970s. Within a decade, someone will push it further, always pretending that the *really* good stuff happened about thirty years ago. Theatre is very much an art form of the now, here one moment and gone the next, so it is no surprise that many fans and professionals seem to think that the only theatrical events of any importance are those that have occurred within their theatregoing lifetime.

Musical Theatre: A History is an attempt to sidestep this trend. The fact is that musical theatre has enjoyed several golden ages, stretching back more than two thousand years to well before the time of Christ. Those golden ages are not relegated to the distant past, and the odds are that more are to come—why, a new one may be starting already. Each of these creative surges occurred under special conditions. History shows us that musicals thrive in cities that are the "happening place" at a given moment. These communities must meet four essential criteria:

1. A population large and prosperous enough to support an active theatrical culture.

2. A thriving artistic community that nurtures successive generations of creative and performing talent.
3. A shared sense of optimism in regards to the community and its future.
4. Freedom from extensive government censorship and/or political oppression.

This book traces the way that musical theatre's golden ages have taken it from place to place over the centuries in search of such environments, by examining how each of its hometowns has placed a unique stamp on the art form.

As an art form of the now, theatre defies second-hand appreciation. Photographs, films, videos, and sound recordings can preserve elements of a performance, but nothing yet invented fully captures the excitement, the visceral impact of live theatre. It is in the room with the audience, and each performance is unique—you are either there to share in it, or the opportunity is lost forever so that you can "do no more than guess" what it was like. In these pages, I cannot hope to bring long-lost performances back to life. If only there were some magical phrase that would allow us to whisk through time and attend the opening nights of Offenbach's *Les Brigands*, Gilbert and Sullivan's *The Mikado,* or Lerner and Loew's *My Fair Lady*! But we can go beyond cataloging the usual statistics and plot summations by actively examining the people and environments that gave birth to the great musicals of the past. With such knowledge, we can better appreciate what has led up to the musical theatre of our own time and make some educated guesses about the future of this powerful art form.

Theatrical history is littered with publicity and other forms of creative thinking that have gradually become accepted as fact through repetition and the passage of time. From Ziegfeld to David Merrick and beyond, denizens of the musical theatre have done much to revise and reshape reality. One of the Broadway producers for whom I worked made a point of revising his bio every few months, saying, "No one in this business can resist revising a script." Songwriter Jerry Herman explained this tendency when he had two of the characters in *Dear World* (1969) sing that when you wear false pearls, "little by little the pearls become real ... and isn't it the same with memories?" As much as possible, this book will stick to verifiable facts. Whenever a "pearl" is even slightly open to question but too interesting to overlook, this book classifies it as either legend or rumor.

What to Expect in the Pages Ahead

Although this book covers some topics found on my popular educational website Musicals101.com, this text is new and more detailed. It examines the artistic, business, and social forces in various cities and countries that helped to forge important new ideas and trends—a process that continues today in New York, London, and elsewhere.

The journey begins with a brief look at ancient Greece, where drama began as a form of musical theatre. The Romans later borrowed most of their theatrical conventions from the Greeks, adding a few tricks of their own, including the first tap shoes for dancers. The Middle Ages brought musical dramatizations of Bible stories and fables, which had been designed to make Church teachings readily accessible to a mostly illiterate populace. In time, these works led into a tradition of lighthearted pantomimes and comic operas that stayed popular across most of Europe for several centuries. By the time grand opera appeared in the 1700s, a separately evolved popular musical theatre was already thriving in much of Europe.

The musical as we know it first appeared in Paris during the 1840s, where composer Jacques Offenbach and a variety of collaborators turned operetta into an international sensation. After some developments in Vienna, the British revamped the form with the ingenious comic creations of playwright William Gilbert and classical musician Arthur Sullivan. Meanwhile, the United States developed its own slapdash but popular homegrown forms of musical theatre, as blackface minstrel shows were joined by such Broadway inventions as *extravaganza*. The rise of British music halls, vaudeville in the United States, and burlesque all contributed special elements to a form that England and America would both lay claim to—the musical comedy.

After some years of British dominance in the field, American musicals gained worldwide popularity in the twentieth century. The groundwork laid by George M. Cohan, Victor Herbert, and Jerome Kern made it possible for a succession of gifted songwriters and librettists to turn New York's Broadway into the world's primary source of musical entertainment. Cole Porter, the Gershwins, and the team of Richard Rodgers and Lorenz Hart brought musical comedy to new creative heights. Then Rodgers teamed with the gifted Oscar Hammerstein II to create the organically integrated musical play, a variation that enjoyed worldwide acclaim for several decades. Now acclaimed by many sources as "the golden age of the Broadway musical," this era came to an end with the rise of hard rock music in the 1960s. Before anyone realized what was happening, Broadway became a minor side street of popular culture— still profitable, but rarely noticed by an increasing percentage of the general population. Despite this dip in its fortunes, the musical theatre continues to thrive, on Broadway and beyond. The twenty-first century has brought a fresh wave of musical comedies and so-called *Pop-sicals* (musicals using already established pop songs), attracting new audiences to the theatre. For better or worse, public taste continues to change, and musicals must do so too.

This book discusses a few hundred essential works. If some of your favorite musicals are missing, my apologies; a chronicle of 2,500 years must of necessity be selective. My goal is to be informative, not exhaustive. For each musical discussed on the text, you will find the year of its premiere and the number of performances listed in parenthesis. Where necessary, I have also specified the city of origin.

What Is a Musical?

This is as good a time as any to clarify a few essential terms. Let's start off with a definition you will not find in any dictionary:

> *Musical (noun): a stage, television, or film production utilizing popular style songs to either tell a story or to showcase the talents of writers and/or performers, with dialogue optional.*

As with any other literary form, the primary job of a musical is to tell a story—or, in the case of a revue, to tell a number of brief stories via songs and skits. When all goes well, a musical's blend of song, dance, and the visual arts entertains, evoking an intellectual as well as an emotional response, but in order for any of those elements to matter, a musical must tell a compelling story in a compelling way.

An art form requires an artist, a medium, and eventually (one hopes) an audience. A popular or commercial art form requires the same trinity, with one crucial difference: there must be a paying audience that makes the act of expression profitable for the artist. When the art form is a collaborative, multidisciplinary one like musical theatre, it must also be profitable for all the auxiliary talents that help to bring an artist's conception to life (producers, director, designers, actors, investors, etc.—and, yes, intelligent investing is a talent). As in any commercial endeavor, the taste and attitude of the audience play a clear role in determining the development of the product; since suppliers must meet consumer demand, the demand helps to shape the supply.

As a commercial art form, musical theatre has reshaped itself continually over the centuries to meet ongoing changes in popular taste. In the last few decades, those changes have ranged from the superficial (electronic amplification, hydraulic sets, etc.) to the essential (recycled songs). While such innovations may or may not be motivated by a desire to reap greater financial profits, commercial successes are what spawn new trends and styles. Who in their right mind would emulate a financial failure?

Elements of a Musical

From a purely technical point of view, all musicals consist of certain key elements:

- Music and lyrics—The songs
- Book/Libretto—The connective story expressed in script or dialogue
- Choreography—The dance
- Staging—All stage movement
- Physical production—The sets, costumes, and technical aspects

Over the centuries, a great deal of creative energy has been spent in *integrating* these elements, making them all smooth-flowing parts of the storytelling process. Sung-through musicals (*The Phantom of the Opera, Les Miserables*) have led to all of the words—lyrics included—being referred to as the book or libretto. In dance-based musicals (*Contact, Movin' Out*), choreography and staging become synonymous.

But in defining the essential elements of a great musical, I gratefully borrow some imagery from MGM's *The Wizard of Oz*. Any great musical must have:

- Brains—Intelligence
- Heart—Emotional content and appeal
- Courage—The guts to do something in a fresh, new way

From *The Mikado* to *Oklahoma!* to *My Fair Lady* to *Crazy for You*, the best musicals—which do not always mean the biggest hits—all have these three qualities, and they must combine to generate a fourth key element: audience excitement.

It is not critics or awards that make a musical great. Even though the *New York Times* review is considered the holy grail for commercial success, condescending or blatantly negative *Times* reviews for *Cats, Les Miserables, Miss Saigon,* and *The Lion King* did not prevent those shows from achieving decade-plus Broadway runs. Since *Man of La Mancha* debuted in 1966, most critics have dismissed that play as an oversimplified bowdlerization of Cervantes's *Don Quixote*. However, the general public (which, by and large, has not read the original novel) has consistently cheered for this show, embracing its call to "reach the unreachable star." As of this writing, *Man of La Mancha* has returned to Broadway four times, the same number of revivals achieved by such mid-1960s critical darlings as *Hello, Dolly!* and *Fiddler on the Roof*. The intelligentsia may carp, but millions of theatregoers consider *Man of La Mancha* a great musical—and so, it is.

Great musicals enjoy the lasting acceptance of the ticket-buying public, and that popularity can last long after an original production is history. Several dozen musicals premiered on Broadway in 1927, but of them all, only *Show Boat* is still performed today. Of all the new musicals produced on Broadway in the "golden age" year of 1955, only *Damn Yankees* is still done. Two very different musicals, but by long-standing popular acclamation, they are among the greats. Am I suggesting that a flop cannot be great? Well, yes. A show without a large audience cannot have any tangible commercial or artistic impact. In rare cases, a musical that was ahead of its time has been revived years later with fresh energy, finally finding its audience—Bernstein's *Candide* died swiftly in 1956, but enjoyed a long run when creatively revived in 1974. Far more common are the old hits that are revived to shrugging ovations, making critics with short memories question how these shows ever impressed anyone in the first place.

Rich in stories of great shows and the people who made them happen, *Musical Theatre: A History* is a celebration of musical theatre, designed to delight new fans and veteran aficionados alike, a joyous book about a joyous form of entertainment. So curtain up and light the lights. We'll begin our story in an era when stage musicals were done without curtains or lights.

1

Ancient Times to 1850—
"Playgoers, I Bid You Welcome!"

Theatre is a communal activity where one or more people act out a story for an audience, so it is fair to suggest that musical theatre can trace its roots back to the religious rituals of prehistoric humankind. As practiced by still-existing primitive tribes, these ceremonies involve many elements that one expects in musical theatre, including costumes, makeup, props, choreography—and music, in the form of chants accompanied by drums and possibly other instruments. However, other than a smattering of cave paintings, little solid evidence exists as to what the earliest of these rituals looked or sounded like. (No doubt some prehistoric critic sat by the communal cave fire saying, "Ah, the old Manhood Ritual Dance ... they don't write 'em like that anymore!) So we will begin our discussion with the earliest form of musical theatre that left behind accessible literature.

"The Glory That Was Greece"

Anyone who thinks that *Oklahoma!* was the first integrated musical is off by a few dozen centuries. The dramas of ancient Greece used dialogue, song, and dance as integrated storytelling tools. In short, the early Greek dramas were musicals, and while they had little direct effect on the development of modern musical theatre, it is reassuring to know that the first theatre was musical—and that showtunes have been around for 2,500 years.

You didn't know that the classic tragedies and comedies of ancient Greece were musicals? Small wonder! Most histories of world drama hate to even note the existence of musicals, so the last thing that they would admit to is that drama began as a form of musical expression. Such snobbery is long overdue for debunking. Aeschylus, Sophocles, and Aristophanes were not only playwrights; they were also composers and lyricists. Call their works *lyric theatre* if you like; that's just another way of saying that they wrote musicals. When you envision the birth of musical theatre, don't picture the bright lights of Broadway or London's West End—think instead of a sun-drenched Athens hillside in the fifth century B.C.E.

By that time, Athens was a thriving city-state of approximately 100,000 souls. With trade ties reaching far and wide, it was also one of the Mediterranean's first cultural centers. Its history stretched back to the Stone Age, when humans first inhabited the Acropolis, a massive, flattopped rock that rises some five hundred feet above sea level and serves as the spiritual heart of the city. By the fifth century BCE, the Acropolis was adorned with a spectacular collection of temples and other public buildings, many built a century before during the reign of the military dictator Pericles. These architectural marvels included the first stone theatre ever built, a semicircular open-air structure cut into the southern base of the Acropolis. To the Athenians, theatre was not merely a place for entertainment, but a place to honor the gods, so they dedicated their theatre to the divine patron of agriculture, theatre, wine, and even joy itself—Dionysus.

The Greeks had a tradition stretching back to prehistoric times of honoring Dionysus with choral performances. These musical retellings of mythological tales were known as *dithyrambs*. The writings of Aristotle provide our only information on Thespis of Icaria, who may have been a writer-composer as well as a performer. Since Thespis was the first soloist to step out of a dithyramb chorus and enact specific roles by singing and speaking lines, he invented two things: the art of acting (which is why actors are sometimes referred to as "thespians"), and a new form of dithyramb that we call *tragedy*. When Athens held its first tragedy competition in 534 BCE, Thespis won. The contest was part of the annual five-day celebration of spring known as the City Dionysia, when Athens offered Dionysus a festival of athletic and artistic events. Imagine the Super Bowl, World Series, World

Cup, and Tony Awards all taking place within five days, and you have some idea of what this annual festival must have felt like.

Over time, tragedy became just one of three distinct types of drama, all of which involved music and dance:

- *Tragedy* was somber in tone, usually using stories taken from Greek mythology. The characters existed solely within their dramatic framework, never referring to current events. Dramatists were allowed to alter the details of established legends in order to make a point. Violence was never enacted, but would be described after occurring offstage.
- *Comedy* was lighter in tone and usually provided a happy resolution to the plot. Characters could openly address the audience, mentioning recent news events and current celebrities—even if the action was not set in the present. The Athens Dionysia added a comedy competition as of 487 BCE; by 440 B.C.E. a separate comedy competition became part of late January's Lenea festival. *Old* or *Attic Comedy* took aim at specific issues and individuals; *Middle Comedy* (starting about 404 B.C.E.) avoided political subjects and dropped the chorus; *Late Comedy* (from the mid-fourth century BCE onward) reflected its time by focusing on the cost of human foolishness and lax morality.
- *Satyr plays* involved mythological half-man/half-beasts who were closely associated with the worship of Dionysus. These male creatures lived in a state of perpetual sexual arousal, which made them perfect reflections of raw, impetuous human behavior. The content of these plays was not necessarily what we would call satirical. Long considered after-pieces to tragedies, satyr plays had a separate competition as of the mid-third century B.C.E.

Drama flourished in other city-states, but the annual Dionysia and Lenea competitions made Athens the center of theatrical activity in ancient Greece. Although these contests were founded as a form of religious worship, the Athenians of the fifth century B.C.E. saw them primarily as an expression of civic pride, of vital interest to every self-respecting citizen. The city government supervised the competitions. Before each festival, a magistrate selected a slate of dramatists. The number of contestants varied over the years but was eventually set at three for tragedy, five for comedy. Initially, it is believed that each dramatist served as his own director and leading actor, but over time those tasks went to separate men—in a society where the only women with public lives were either priestesses or prostitutes, it was unthinkable for a respectable woman to take part in theatre. Casts originally consisted of male volunteers drawn from the general public, but by the late fifth century B.C.E. the actors were unionized professionals paid by the state and assigned to productions by lot. (One wonders if they ever went on strike to get a seven and a half drachma raise.) The city also provided the theatre free of charge. All other production expenses fell to the chorus leader or *choregos*, a position the wealthiest men in Athens openly coveted, even though it involved shelling out thousands of drachmae. The winning dramatist collected bragging rights and a modest prize, and the victorious *choregos* won the right to build a triumphal column in his own honor. Such was the price of prestige.

Showtime in Ancient Athens

Depending on the city's finances in any given year, admission to the theatre festivals was either free of charge or at a small fee. The openair theatre sat below the south side of the Acropolis to allow maximum exposure to sunlight. Spending several hours under a blazing Mediterranean sun would have been pleasant in early spring when daytime temperatures hovered between the 50s and 60s.

In the Theatre of Dionysus, an ornate front row of stone seats was reserved for priests, magistrates, and other dignitaries. Behind them, 15,000 or more spectators filled benches that formed a bowl shaped semi-sphere around and above the flat, rectangular stone performance space known as the *orchestra*. This space could be accessed from corridors on the left and right. The original Theatre of Dionysus is long gone, its location now covered by the ruins of a replacement structure built in Roman times. But well-preserved amphitheatres dating from this period are acoustical marvels. A word spoken at conversational volume on the performance floor can be heard clearly in the last concentric row. Behind the orchestra stood the *skene*, a tent or stone cottage that actors used to change costumes and store props. It could also be used to represent a building in the play, and in later years supported painted scenic panels called *skenographia*.

During performances, actors wore full head masks to make it easier for the vast audience to tell one character from another. Since most
companies had no more than three actors, these masks also made it
possible for each actor to play multiple roles without confusing the
audience. None of these masks is known to have survived, but it is
believed that they included small megaphone-like cones to amplify the
voice. Since masks rendered facial features invisible, the actors relied
on vocal pitch and physical gestures to express emotion. Masks were
augmented with costumes, padded body suits, and props to depict the
physical characteristics of women, animals, and mythical creatures.

The chorus handled all the musical chores by singing, dancing, and
providing their own accompaniment using the harp, flute, and other
instruments. Since the audience consisted almost entirely of adult males,
there was no shortage of vulgar language and vivid sexual imagery. Bawdy
jokes, bathroom references, and giant phalluses were common features
in these plays. While it is possible that some Greek dramatists interpolated existing songs into their scripts, such masters as Aeschylus and
Sophocles composed their own. Songs allowed the chorus to comment
on the play and to sometimes take direct part in the dramatic action.
Musical solos were rare but not unheard of. In most cases, stretches of
monologue (one speaker) or *dialogue* (two or more) were interspersed
with choral numbers. Since songs were often used to advance the plot
and develop characters, it is fair to suggest that some early Greek dramas
can be classified as integrated musicals. We do not know if there was
anything like a curtain call, but it seems safe to assume that the end of a
play was marked by some sort of audience response.

During festival competitions, several plays were offered each day.
The competitions were judged by ten *kritai*, male citizens selected
by lot who were not necessarily experts on the theatre (appropriate
namesakes for critics, no?). The *kritai* wrote out their choices on tablets that were placed in an urn, and to give the gods a say in the decision, only five of the ten tablets were drawn to select a winner.

After the decline of Athens, some four dozen texts survived, thanks
primarily to the efforts of educated Greeks who continued to study
and perform these plays through the Roman era and beyond. Of more
than seventy-five plays credited to Aeschylus, only seven full-length
texts exist today. Aristophanes fared somewhat better, with eleven of
his forty plays surviving. Some papyrus evidence of ancient Greek

musical notation has been discovered, but the melodies used in the surviving plays are long lost, so we can only guess what these songs sounded like. Since the lyrics had to be audible to an audience of thousands, it is reasonable to suggest that the tunes lent themselves to vocal projection and that the accompanying instrumentals were relatively simple.

The Birds

In 414 B.C.E., Aristophanes (448–385 B.C.E) offered *The Birds*, a play that made reference to current events without using them as comic targets. At age thirty-four, he was already a past winner of the Dionysia and one of the most famous men in Greece. His works are the best examples that we have of Old Comedy, giving us some idea of how music was used in early Greek drama.

In this lighthearted fantasy, common citizens Euelpides and Pisthetaerus are fed up with life in Athens. They seek out Epops, a mythological king who transformed himself into a bird, and offer a bold proposal: since birds rule the skies that sit between earth and the gods, why not build a wall separating the two and then demand tribute from both sides? The birds (played by the chorus) appear, and in an example of self-referential humor, promise not to attack if the judges will grant this play a unanimous victory in the Dionysia! The birds agree to the wall plan, and a nightingale proclaims their newfound power over humankind. The nightingale appears in the form of a flutist who plays an introduction to the *parabasis*, a feature unique to Old Comedy in which the chorus offered three songs, alternating with three speeches. These speeches might be integrated into the action of the play or be major departures from it. In this case, the birds tell the creation story from their point of view, claiming that their origin was much older than that of the gods on Olympus. Their song then assures humankind:

> *If you recognize our divine power,*
> *We shall be your guide and inspiration.*
> *Through us you will know*
> *The winds and the seasons,*
> *Summer, winter, and the temperate times.*
> *We shall not withdraw like Zeus to distant clouds,*

But shall be among you to give
You and to your children
And your children's children,
Health and wealth, long life, peace,
Youth, laughter, songs and feasts;
In short, you will all be so happy
That you will be exhausted with pleasure.

Euelpides and Pisthetaerus are magically given wings and feathers as the massive walls of Nephelococcygia ("Cloud-cuckooland") are erected. When Pisthetaerus sets himself up as dictator, Euelpides returns to earth in disgust. The Olympian gods miss their earthly sacrifices and send Poseidon and Hercules to offer Pisthetaerus a chance to marry Zeus's beautiful handmaiden Basileia. Pisthetaerus accepts, realizing that this marriage will give him power over both gods and mortals. The play ends as the birds offer an *epithalamium*, a hymn of praise sung to a bride en route to her nuptial chamber.

Oh, you golden flashes of lightning!
Oh, you heavenly shafts of flame,
Shot forth by Zeus!
Oh, you rolling thunders
That herald the rain!
Now it is by the order of OUR king
That you will make the earth tremble!
Oh, Hymen! Through you
He now commands the universe
As he makes Basileia, stolen from Zeus,
Take her seat at his side.

What brought the golden age of Athenian musical theatre to an end? In the late 450s B.C.E., the city enjoyed fifteen years of peace and prosperity under the leadership of Pericles. During that time, Athenians developed an unhealthy sense of superiority that helped bring on the Peloponnesian War, a devastating series of conflicts between Athens and a coalition of other Greek states led by Sparta, which lasted for twenty-seven years. Athens was ultimately defeated in 404 B.C.E., and its fortunes never recovered. The city was ruled by a series of dictators, and fear of reprisals by these oppressive regimes soon terrorized the life out of the theatre. By the time Philip II of Macedon conquered the city sixty-six years later, Athenian drama was essentially a thing of the past.

The Roman Empire

The ancient Romans were not above borrowing good ideas, especially from Greece. In particular, they co-opted various theatrical conventions, adjusting them to fit Roman tastes. The mixture of dialogue, song, and dance was retained. Like the Greeks, Romans produced plays as part of festivals to honor the gods, but there was no governmental involvement. In fact, for several centuries, the Roman establishment saw theatre, with its suspension of reality and reversals of social norms, as a potentially dangerous influence.

Eventually, attitudes changed, and the Romans built permanent open-air theatres following the Greek example. But for most of the empire's history, Roman dramas were performed in temporary wooden structures that could be built and dismantled within a day, usually near the temple of the god being honored. It is believed that prominent citizens had priority seating, with the general public scrambling for bench space or settling for standing room. The performing area was a raised wooden platform, with no space separating spectators from the stage. However, there was a drop curtain, which was lowered into a trough at the front of the stage to signify the start of a performance. There was no chorus, so casts were smaller, and there could be much direct interplay between actors and their frequently rowdy audiences. Spectacle was left to the more violent entertainments of the arena; the Roman theatre was a more intimate pleasure. To make dance steps audible, actors attached metal chips (*sabilla*) to their footwear, creating precursors of modern-day tap shoes. Initially, all of the actors in Roman theatre were men, so a simple visual costume code was developed to make it instantly clear who was who. Wig color signified age or status (black=young, white=old, red=slave), a yellow robe indicated a woman, and the addition of a yellow tassel indicated a god. Over time, female slaves took on the women's roles, but the wig and costume codes remained in common usage.

Plautus (b. 254 B.C.E.?) is the best remembered Roman playwright. His comedies included song, dance, and instrumental accompaniment.

Plautus borrowed ideas, characters, names, and settings from Greek theatre, reinterpreting them in his own terms. In some cases, he pieced together elements from two or more old Greek works to create something new. What he wound up with was not just a copycat adaptation, but a form with its own personality. Plautus used conversational Latin, as opposed to the more formal language found in high poetry. He reinterpreted and then perpetuated stock characters that became lasting stereotypes in western theatre. If you have ever seen or read the twentieth-century musical comedy *A Funny Thing Happened on the Way to the Forum* (1960), you may find these characters familiar:

- Pseudolous: the clever slave who could outwit his Roman masters. Although clever slaves had been seen in Greek drama, Plautus moved them from supporting roles to the forefront.
- Senex: the ridiculous, aging girl-chaser
- Miles Gloriosus: the vain, bragging soldier
- Mulier: the respectable wife of a citizen
- Courtesan: an unmarried woman without social status

By the time the empire collapsed, Roman theatre had become so tawdry that the Catholic Church condemned it as a corrupt and sinful influence. The Church's influence was such that professional theatre ceased to exist in Europe for several centuries.

The Middle Ages: Saints & Clowns

During the Middle Ages, traveling minstrels and roving troupes of performers crisscrossed Europe, offering popular songs and simple slapstick comedy in exchange for coins, or for food and lodging in the castles of wealthy nobility. In the twelfth and thirteenth centuries, the Catholic Church saw new possibilities in theatrical performances, and actively encouraged the development and presentation of liturgical music-dramas. At a time when an overwhelming majority of the populace was illiterate, these musical plays supposedly made key Bible stories more accessible—but since the texts were in Latin, the lowest classes might not have found performances particularly instructive. In an unintentional echo of ancient Greece, these church dramas were often presented in conjunction with major religious festivals. The cast consisted of clerics, choir boys, and in at least some instances, nuns. Originally performed in church to augment the mass or evening prayer, these plays eventually moved to outdoor stages where more vernacular content was acceptable. By that time, members of local craft guilds had taken an active role in the performance and production of these plays.

There were various types of music-drama, each defined by specific content:

- *Mystery plays* were dramatizations of Bible stories.
- *Miracle plays* involved the lives (true or fictional) of saints.
- *Morality plays* were allegories illustrating the seven deadly sins.
- *Folk plays* involved popular myths, such as the legend of Robin Hood.

Some of these works have survived, including *The Play of Herod* and *The Play of Daniel*, which are occasionally performed today. The texts are quite serious, with no hint of comedy. These plays are sung throughout, although the surviving musical notation is often crude. Instrumentation included recorder, harp, bagpipe, and rebec (a type of fiddle). Although the stage technology was crude, the medieval period did introduce one promising innovation. In situations where the outdoor stage could not be positioned to take full advantage of natural daylight, polished metal bowls were sometimes used to reflect sunlight on key performers—in effect, the first follow spotlights.

In the 1400s, *commedia dell'arte* developed in Italy, where it remained popular for the next four centuries, but commedia-style troupes were soon found all over continental Europe. Always on the move, these companies used no written scripts. Instead, they improvised performances using a core group of stock characters to enact hundreds of stock scenarios. A typical plot would involve a pair of young lovers (*innamorati*) thwarted by one or more elders (*vecchi*), but eventually outsmarting them with the help of a sympathetic servant (*zanni*) such as Harlequin or Columbina. Actors would mix traditional jokes with topical references to current events, and there was a great deal of broad physical humor. Battles or beatings would be simulated using a *slapstick*, a pair of hinged boards that created a loud "whack" without anyone actually being hit. The characters and conventions of *commedia dell'arte* would live on in many forms of western comedy, including pantomimes, musical comedies, and television sitcoms—and although the slapstick has fallen out of use, it has given its name to knockabout physical humor.

During the Renaissance, Italians rediscovered ancient Greek drama and, seeing the extensive use of choral verse, assumed that these plays were originally all sung-through. Based on this well-meaning error, Monteverdi and the Camarata Fiorentina made Greek drama the model for what we now know as opera. So contrary to the widely held belief that musical theatre is a descendant of opera, it turns out that opera is actually an accidental descendant of musical theatre!

William Shakespeare included the occasional song in his plays, but none of these works could be fairly described as a musical. In France at the end of the 1600s, Molière turned out several comedies with songs for Louis XIV's court at Versailles, using music provided by no less than Jean Baptiste Lully. Their joint output included *Le Mariage Forcé* (1664), *L'Amour Médecin* (1665), and *Le Bourgeois Gentilhomme* (1670). However, these musical entertainments inspired no trends and soon passed out of style.

Comic and Ballad Opera

During the Age of Enlightenment, the first stirrings of popular musical theatre occurred in England, Germany, Austria-Hungary, and France. Each of these countries enjoyed different degrees of prosperity and cultural renewal during this period, which, coupled with the gradual growth of cities, created a ready-made audience for new and more sophisticated types of entertainment. Grand opera enjoyed widespread popularity, but primarily among the upper and newly formed middle classes. Other forms of stage entertainment enjoyed a popularity that crossed traditional lines of class, appealing to rich and poor, highborn and low alike.

In the 1700s, a typical theatrical evening included several works of varying lengths and styles. After a brief one-act curtain raiser came some kind of full-length play, followed by a shorter afterpiece. Any of these offerings might be a musical. Producers and publishers described musical stage works of this period with many conflicting names, a practice that has led to some confusion among scholars. *Comic opera* became an all-purpose classification for any form of eighteenth- or nineteenth-century stage entertainment that included songs. However, we can identify at least three separate genres of musical theatre that developed during this period:

- *Comic opera* used operatic conventions and compositional styles to amusing effect, usually involving a heavy dose of romance. Michael Balfe's *The Bohemian Girl* (1845) told the story of an Austrian noblewoman kidnapped in infancy who, ignorant of her heritage, falls in love with the Polish aristocrat who carried her off. The melodic score included "I Dreamed I Dwelt in Marble Halls," which became a longtime staple in the soprano concert repertory. *The Bohemian Girl* was frequently revived and toured well into the twentieth century. *Comic opera* was a clear precursor of *operetta*, a form that would come into its own in France during the mid-1800s (see chapter 2).
- *Pantomime* included songs and dialogue, dance, physical comedy, acrobatics, special effects, and such *commedia dell'arte* clown characters as Harlequin. Despised by serious critics, these comical works were extremely popular with audiences. The U.S. pantomime tradition would reach its peak on Broadway in the 1870s (see chapter 3). A somewhat different form of pantomime evolved in England, where such shows are still presented as Christmas holiday entertainment for children.
- *Ballad operas* used existing popular ballads and operatic arias, usually in such a way that the original title or lyrics of a song added to their meaning.

The first ballad opera ever written is still frequently discussed and even occasionally performed today. In the eyes of some, it is the great-grandfather of modern-day English-language musical theatre. That designation is an exaggeration, but only because governmental oppression stifled this new art form in its cradle.

The Beggar's Opera

People can react to losing a job in very different ways. The world might be a far happier place if more people followed the example of

John Gay (1686–1732), whose thwarted job hunt inspired him to pick up a pen and invent a new kind of musical theatre. English writers of the early 1700s saw little income from their creative efforts and were dependent on political appointments and the patronage of wealthy aristocrats. As the youngest son of a youngest son, Gay came to London at age twenty-two with no title, no money, and only a few useful contacts. Thanks to a witty mind and an eloquent pen, he soon made friends among London's literati, including Alexander Pope and Jonathan Swift. Gay hoped his connections would lead to a position in Queen Anne's royal court, the clearest route to wealth and power for a man of limited means. In time, Gay got to know London and the inner workings of government, and found rampant corruption at almost every turn. Administrative posts were available to the highest bidder, regardless of ability. Once in a job, purchasers felt entitled to profit on their investment by whatever means necessary. For example, the Keeper of Newgate Prison paid approximately five thousand pounds to obtain his job, so he felt quite justified in openly charging prisoners hundred of pounds for lodging in the only cells with adequate light and air. All but the richest inmates had to settle for darkness and squalor.

Among London's intellectuals and courtiers, grand opera was all the rage. Gay viewed this Italian invention with skepticism. Foreign composers and singers were imported at great cost, earning far more than their British counterparts. Feuding sopranos Francesca Cuzzoni and Faustina Bordoni each earned 2,000 pounds or more for a single season in London. The town anticipated fireworks when both women were cast in the premiere of *Alessandro* (1726), but the wily German composer George Friderick Handel balanced their roles so perfectly that neither singer could claim superiority.

Gay's close allegiance to the Tory party brought him some unfortunate enemies, including the powerful Whig politician Robert Walpole, who quietly blocked the young man's advancement for two decades. When Gay finally realized that his hoped-for career would never be, he set to work on a theatre piece designed to comically skewer the corrupt system that had denied him any share in its spoils. It was widely believed that Walpole enriched himself at the nation's expense. If government administrators were no better than common thieves, Gay reasoned, then respectability was nothing more than the pretense of the powerful. Why not use the format of opera, so beloved by the upper class, to illustrate that class's resemblance to the lowest criminals?

The Beggar's Opera (1728) opens with a beggar explaining that he has written an opera that follows the required forms without being "unnatural, like those in vogue." In a snide reference to recent events, he states, "I have observed such a nice impartiality in our two ladies that it is impossible for either of them to take offence." The plot involves Macheath, a professional thief and murderer who goes by the title "captain" and is described as being "as good as a Lord." This charming demon has secretly married Polly, the not-so-innocent daughter of Peachum, a "respectable" businessman who fences stolen goods—an offense punishable by death at that time. Anxious to annul the marriage, Peachum learns that Lucy, the daughter of the jailer Lockit, is already pregnant with Macheath's child. Peachum and Lockit arrange for Macheath's arrest, knowing that his long list of crimes guarantees that he will hang. In jail, Macheath pays Lockit a hefty bribe to obtain a better cell and complains: "The fees here are so many, and so exorbitant, that few fortunes can bear the expense of getting off handsomely, or of dying like a gentleman."

When four additional women appear claiming that Macheath is the father of their babies, the scoundrel tells the executioners that he is ready to die. But the beggar-author character suddenly reappears, and when scolded that "an opera must end happily," he admits that "in this kind of drama, 'tis no matter how absurdly things are brought about." And so, Macheath receives a pardon, swears to find partners for the women he has wronged, and publicly confirms his marriage to Polly even while calling her a "slut."

Of sixty-nine songs in *The Beggar's Opera*, forty-one used melodies that had been taken from popular tavern ballads, and the rest were taken from operas and other sources. Although the melodies were borrowed, Gay's lyrics were original and quite specific to the characters and plot. Take this scene, in which Mr. and Mrs. Peachum discover that their daughter has secretly married Macheath. The elder Peachums are in no position to condemn their new son in law—aside from their own criminal activities, the Peachums aren't even legally married! The melody Gay used in this excerpt comes from "Grim King of the Ghosts," a ballad about a vain girl forced to marry a horrifying specter. The original was quite familiar in 1728, so audiences would have appreciated the connection between Polly's situation and that of the girl in the original ballad.

> MR. PEACHUM: Married! The captain is a bold man, and will risk anything for money; to be sure, he believes her a fortune. Do you think your mother and I should have lived comfortably so long together if ever we had been married? Baggage!
>
> MRS. PEACHUM: I knew she was always a proud slut; and now the wench hath played the fool and married, because forsooth she would do like the gentry. Can you support the expense of a husband, hussy, in gaming, drinking, and whoring? Have you money enough to carry on the daily quarrels of man and wife about who shall squander most? There are not many husbands and wives who can bear the charges of plaguing one another in a handsome way. If you must be married, could you introduce nobody into our family but a highwayman? Why, thou foolish jade, thou wilt be as ill-used, and as much neglected, as if thou hadst married a lord!
>
> MR. PEACHUM: Let not your anger, my dear, break through the rules of decency, for the Captain looks upon himself in the military capacity, as a gentleman by his profession. Besides what he hath already, I know he is in a fair way of getting, or of dying; and both these ways, let me tell you, are most excellent chances for a wife. Tell me, hussy, are you ruined or no?
>
> MRS. PEACHUM: With Polly's fortune, she might very well have gone off to a person of distinction. Yes, that you might, you pouting slut!
>
> MR. PEACHUM: What, is the wench dumb? Speak, or I'll make you plead by squeezing out an answer from you. Are you really bound wife to him, or are you only upon liking? (Pinches Polly.)
>
> POLLY: (Screaming) Oh!
>
> MRS. PEACHUM: How the mother is to be pitied who has handsome daughters! Locks, bolts, bars, and lectures of morality are nothing to them—they break through them all. They have as much pleasure in cheating a father and mother, as in cheating at cards.
>
> MRS. PEACHUM: Why, Polly, I shall soon know if you are married, by Macheath's keeping from our house.

AIR (To the tune of "Grim King of the Ghosts"):

POLLY: *Can love be controlled by advice?*
Will cupid our mothers obey?
Though my heart were as frozen as ice,
At his flame 'twould have melted away.
When he kissed me so closely he pressed,
'Twas so sweet that I must have complied:
So I thought it both safest and best
To marry, for fear you should chide.

MRS. PEACHUM: Then all the hopes for our family are gone for ever and ever!

MR. PEACHUM: And Macheath may hang his father and mother-in-law, in hope to get into their daughter's fortune.

POLLY: I did not marry him (as 'tis the fashion) coolly and deliberately for honor or money. But I love him.

MRS. PEACHUM: Love him! Worse and worse! I thought the girl had been better bred.

At a time when London stage productions were lucky to run for a week, *The Beggar's Opera* broke all precedent by lasting for an astounding sixty-two performances, making it the world's first long-running musical stage hit. It seemed that everybody of consequence in London society saw it, and its lyrics were repeated in every ale house and side street. So were its jokes, including a reference to "Bob Booty" that everyone understood to be a personal slap at the corrupt Robert Walpole.

The Whig establishment was being laughed at and did not appreciate it. When Gay announced plans for a sequel called *Polly*, Walpole used his influence and had it banned. The disheartened author soon withdrew from London to live quietly on a benefactor's country estate. Four years after the premiere of *The Beggar's Opera*, John Gay died at forty-seven. As in ancient Greece, political repression had squelched creativity, and the ballad operas that followed in Gay's wake avoided political content. Lacking any lasting interest, none of these later works are performed or studied today.

Despite Walpole's efforts, *The Beggar's Opera* found its way into the repertory of many theatre troupes in Great Britain and its North

American colonies, becoming one of the most frequently performed English stage works of the eighteenth century. It was rediscovered in a 1923 London production that ran for three years, and has been filmed twice, with the role of Macheath sung by Laurence Olivier on the big screen in 1953, and by rock star Roger Daltry in a 1983 BBC-TV version. The text provided the inspiration for Bertolt Brecht and Kurt Weill's *Die Dreigroschenoper/The Threepenny Opera* (1928), which would update the action to modern times but keep the basic plot and major characters.

Aside from its ongoing life on stage and screen, *The Beggar's Opera* set a precedent for musical theatre in the English-speaking world. British and U.S. audiences have continually shown an affinity for musicals that tweak the establishment's nose and sing about social hypocrisy. Except for Brecht and Weill's brief flowering in pre-Nazi Germany, such works have not thrived in other languages. A long list of writers and composers from Gilbert and Sullivan to Mel Brooks can look back on John Gay as an artistic forefather.

Such are the earliest roots of musical theatre. While some of these works are occasionally performed today, the modern musical's family tree formally reaches no further back than the 1840s, when a new strain of lyric drama appeared in Paris.

2

Continental Operetta (1840–1900) — "Typical of France"

T he French would like to believe that everything of value in western culture originated in France. Well, drama and cuisine were first cultivated in Greece, opera was invented in Italy, electric light was developed in the United States, and attitude was perfected by Asians before the Gauls had figured out how to build mud huts. But what we know as the modern musical was born and raised in Paris, for which fans of the genre can be eternally grateful. The composer most responsible for developing this new genre was not a born Frenchman. From the very start, the modern musical theatre showed signs of being an international art form.

Paris

The Romans were the first to raise a settlement on the island that sits where the River Seine transects with a major trade route. The collapse of the Roman Empire brought a brief decline, but things improved when the first Frankish kings made the city their capital. A Viking invasion and various civil upheavals did their worst, but Paris gradually spread out to either side of the river in a confusing jumble of streets and neighborhoods. Realizing that an uprising would be almost impossible to control in such a city, many French monarchs preferred to spend most of their time at a safe distance. Theatre thrived in Paris by the 1600s, thanks in part to the encouragement of the royal court—and as we've already mentioned, Molière and Lully offered several musical theatre pieces. Theatre survived when the poor of Paris exercised their mob power with a series of riots in the late eighteenth century, culminating in the overthrow of King Louis XVI and the prolonged upheavals of the French Revolution (1789–1799). In the bloody years that followed, the guillotine rose and fell, as did a series of governments, but Paris remained a center of the arts, including theatre.

Napoleon Bonaparte, who crowned himself Emperor of France in 1804, had disposed of various European monarchs and promptly installed his relatives on the empty thrones. When Bonaparte was forced out of power in 1815, his relatives soon lost their titles. His illegitimate nephew Louis, who had been prince of Holland, resented the demotion. When the Revolution of 1848 forced the formation of a new French republic, Louis was elected president by a landslide margin. Bored by constitutional limitations, he staged a bloodless coup in 1851, and after one year as dictator, arranged a national referendum that granted him the title of Emperor. Out of respect to Napoleon I's dead son, who had technically ruled France for a few weeks following his father's abdication, Louis Bonaparte declared himself Napoleon III. History knows his eighteen-year reign as the Second Empire.

Napoleon III instituted a series of reforms, modernizing the French economy and encouraging widespread industrialization. These changes created new jobs for the working class and new fortunes for entrepreneurs. The Emperor also gave Paris a radical facelift, with ancient neighborhoods demolished to make way for parks and wider boulevards—not only beautiful, but designed to offer better crowd control if the poor ever rioted again. Few complained as his regime censored all dissension in the press, rendered the legislature powerless, and placed the performing arts under a slew of picayune regulations. Fortunately, these rules did almost nothing to regulate the content or subject matter of stage entertainments. Theatre and opera had long been part of Parisian life, and both drew expanded and enthusiastic audiences in this era of renewed prosperity.

Offenbach: "Entrez, Messieurs, Mesdames!"

In 1833, a fourteen-year-old Jewish native of Cologne arrived in Paris to study the cello. Preferring the excitement of making music to the tedium of taking classes, he soon dropped out of the Conservatoire to perform full time in a series of orchestras, developing a reputation as a soloist and composer. Determined to be as French as possible, he converted to Catholicism and changed his first name from Jakob to Jacques to become Jacques Offenbach (1819–1880). His professional goal was to create a new kind of musical entertainment that would offer more fun than grand opera while retaining a high degree of musical sophistication.

Others were already attempting this feat, with limited degrees of success. Adolphe Adam (1803–1856) is best remembered for composing the ballet *Giselle*, but he also wrote music for several early comic light operas, including *Pierre et Catherine* (1829). He opened his own Opera National in 1847, where he offered a series of such works written by himself and others. In *Don Quichotte et Sancho Panca* (1847), the role of Quixote was played by the multitalented composer of the piece, church organist Florimonde Ronger, who composed and acted using the name Hervé (1825–1892). The revolution of 1848 forced the financially strapped Opera National to shut down. In 1854, Hervé became director of the tiny Folies-Concertantes, which he soon renamed the Folies-Nouvelles. There he presented more than thirty of his own musicals, and also showcased several early pieces by Offenbach.

In 1855, Napoleon III presented an *Exposition Universelle* to show the world that France was thriving under his rule. Realizing that this world's fair would attract countless visitors to Paris, Offenbach resigned his well-paid position as musical director of the Comedie Francaise and leased a small, fifty-seat, wooden theatre just off the Champ Elysees. The Theatre des Bouffes Parisiens may not have looked like much, but it was near the fairgrounds and just the right size for the intimate musical productions that Offenbach was planning. He would have preferred to work on a larger scale, but imperial law forced him to keep it small. To prevent competition with government-sponsored operatic productions, musical works at independent theatres were limited to one act in length and no more than three singing characters—a silent character could be added by special license. Operating on the principle that bigger is not necessarily better, Offenbach and a small team of librettists set out to turn this handicap into an asset. The first program at the Theatre des Bouffes-Parisiens opened on July 5, 1855, consisting of four new one-act works, all with music by Offenbach but each representing a different genre:

- Prologue: *Entrez, Messieurs, Mesdames!*
- Operetta: *Une Nuit Blanche* (*A Sleepless Night*)
- Pantomime: *Arlequin Barbier* (with melodies adapted from Rossini's opera *Il Barbiere di Siviglia*)
- Bouffonerie musicale: *Les Deux Aveugles* (*The Two Blind Men*)

Les Deux Aveugles, with its story of two Parisian beggars pretending to be blind as they bicker over a prime begging spot, was the clear hit of the evening. Although called a "bouffonerie musicale," it was an example of the new, tuneful genre Offenbach was developing—*operetta*. In opera, the music is always paramount; in *operetta*, the words and music are ideally of equal value. There would be a wide range of works classified as operettas over time, so Offenbach's style, which combined opera-sized singing with zany comic plots, is specifically referred to as *opera-bouffes*. The music was lighter than the sort of bombast one heard in grand opera but still quite demanding, requiring a higher caliber of vocal training than popular street ballads. The overall tone of *Les Deux Aveugles* was decidedly comic and appealed to the contemporary point of view, allowing Parisians to laugh at themselves—which is probably the only thing they have always enjoyed more than laughing at others. Offenbach soon dropped pantomimes from the repertory and concentrated on one-act opera-bouffes. His shows turned into the must-see events of the Exposition season, and everybody who was anybody made a point of attending, including members of the imperial court.

Playwright Ludovic Halévy (1834–1908) was a civil servant who held onto his government job by day and wrote stage works by night. He penned *Entrez, Messieurs, Mesdames!*, the opening prologue to Offenbach's first night at the old Bouffes, and would co-author the librettos for many of Offenbach's hits.

Because Offenbach's opera-bouffes had only the most refined hints of sexual innuendo and were staged with unfailing good taste, respectable women could attend, with or without their husbands. Hervé presented similar works that year, but his efforts were soon eclipsed by Offenbach's amazing popularity. The Exposition had been a great political success for Napoleon III, but as far as France's popular culture was concerned, the most lasting legacy of that summer was the triumphant introduction of Offenbach's opera-bouffes.

When the Exposition shut down in the autumn, Offenbach leased a far larger theatre in the Passage Choiseul and spent a fortune renovating the 668-seat auditorium that he promptly rechristened with a familiar name, calling it the Théâtre des Bouffes-Parisiens. On December 29, 1855, Offenbach opened the new house with *Ba-ta-Clan*, the story of Alfred and Virginie, two Parisians shipwrecked in the fictional Asian kingdom of Che-i-noor, where they have become members of the royal court. They want nothing more than to return to France, but King Fe-ni-han wants Alfred to succeed him, thwarting the royal ambitions of Ko-ko-ri-ko, the ambitious captain of the royal guard— who, in keeping with the three-character limit, is never seen. Alfred and Virginie eventually discover that Fe-ni-han is a fellow stranded Frenchman who wound up ruling this Asian country even though he doesn't speak its language. Ko-ko-ri-ko turns out to be a Frenchman too, and informs the others (via letter) that he is willing to take the throne so that the rest of them can return to France. This bit of tuneful nonsense kept the new Bouffes Parisiens packed as tightly as its tiny predecessor.

Offenbach composed with astonishing speed, providing his audience with an ever-changing repertory. In 1856 alone, he wrote and produced seven new one-acts. The plots were decidedly on the silly side but always rooted in social satire, such as *Le 66* (1856), in which a peasant thinks he holds wining lottery ticket 66, only to find out that he's actually got number 99. Offenbach's melodies delighted all classes of society, with his music equally at home in seedy taverns, middle class parlors, and royal ballrooms. Tourists visiting Paris brought these melodies home with them, and Offenbach's songs soon swept Europe, with productions of his operettas sprouting up in Brussels, Berlin, and other theatre centers. Offenbach's troupe toured the continent in 1857, bringing his works to Vienna and London, where local translations became standard fare for years to come. In a shrewd move designed to garner fresh publicity, the composer held a contest for operettas written in his style, offering the winner 1,200 francs and a guaranteed production. There was a tie for first place, and although both entries flopped with the public, composers George Bizet and Charles Lecocq would both would go on to tremendous careers.

The Offenbach "Bounce"

Serving as his own producer, Offenbach refused to economize, pouring all of his profits into lavish new productions. Despite excellent ticket sales, the Bouffes Parisiens kept falling into debt. By the time the French government dropped the ludicrous three-character restriction in 1858, Offenbach was in desperate need of a money-making hit. Halévy and fellow librettist Hector Crémieux conceived a full-scale burlesque of the ancient Greek legend of Orpheus, well known to theatregoers of that time thanks to several operatic versions, including a particularly popular one by Gluck. With a long list of characters, it was the perfect choice for Offenbach's first two-act operetta, *Orphée aux Enfers/Orpheus in Hell* (1858, 228 performances in Paris). As in the original myth, the ancient Greek musician Orpheus goes into the dreaded land of the dead to bring back his deceased wife Eurydice, but in this version he loathes his spouse and only makes the trip in order to placate a nagging character named "Public Opinion." Throughout the piece, Offenbach and his collaborators spoofed the original myth as well as the various grand operas based on the tale. Taking things a step further, the gods of Olympus were depicted as vain and capricious, serving as a satiric reflection of Napoleon III's imperial court. However, the intention was to evoke laughter, not to incite rebellion or, worse yet, to preach. In the world of opera-bouffes, nobody is perfect, and everyone can afford to laugh at everyone else.

Offenbach contracted the artist Gustave Doré to design *Orphée's* original sets and costumes. Initial response to the music was positive, but critics complained about the irreverent libretto, and it seems no one recognized that something new and exciting was taking place. About six weeks into the run, with ticket sales falling and financial failure imminent, a major critic published a newspaper article vigorously condemning the show for "profaning sacred antiquity." Offenbach wrote a witty reply that appeared in a competing paper, and the public wanted to see what inspired this journalistic ruckus. Ticket sales soared, and *Orphée* ran for an unprecedented seven months, at which point the exhausted cast demanded a break. After all, it was positively unnatural for a production to run so long! (Imagine how they would react to the twenty-year runs that hit musicals enjoy today.) Before long, *Orphée* was reintroduced into the repertory at the Bouffes. Its "infernal gallop" became the most famous cancan melody ever written and a universally recognized symbol of French culture.

Offenbach's melodies are sophisticated but never pretentious. His "up" tunes have a particular quality that I call "the Offenbach bounce," an infectious, heady lilt that offers the sonic equivalent of drinking a few glasses of really good champagne—minus any resulting hangover. In *Orphée aux Enfers*, the god Mercury's *rondo saltarelle* ("Eh hop! Eh hop! / Look out! Look out!") is just such a merry tune, one that sets feet tapping and makes audiences smile on the first or one hundredth hearing. Offenbach may not have invented such melodies, but as far as we can tell, he was the first to bring them to the musical stage. Sprinkled throughout his best operettas, these sprightly tunes are a key to their composer's lasting popularity, and the "Offenbach bounce" would remain a standard feature in European operetta right into the twentieth century.

Orphée aux Enfers marked the beginning of more than a dozen golden years for Offenbach. While maintaining an artistic home at the Bouffes, he also produced hits in larger houses such as the Palais Royal and the Théâtre des Variétés. He composed literally dozens of operettas, the best of which followed triumphs in Paris with comparable success throughout Europe. The lack of international copyright laws made Offenbach's scores irresistible to U.S. producers, who staged translations of his works without paying any royalties. Throughout the 1860s and 70s, it was not uncommon for ten or more Offenbach revivals to be played in New York during any given year; these productions would then tour the states with the claim that they came "Direct from Broadway." The composer was not overly concerned about the lack of royalties from the United States. After all, new hits kept pouring out of his pen.

Beginning in 1864, playwright Henri Meilhac (1831–1897) teamed up with Halévy to create librettos for Offenbach. With the composer referring to his collaborators as "Mel" and "Hal," the trio created a series of works that dominated the world's musical stages:

- *La Belle Hélène* (1864): the legendary beauty Hélène is married to the boring King Ménélas of Sparta. At the behest of the gods, she is seduced and eventually carried off by Prince Paris of Troy.

- *La Vie Parisienne* (1866): two Parisian rakes set out to seduce a visiting Swedish baroness. During a party where servants masquerade as aristocrats, a series of mistaken identities leads the baroness into her loving husband's arms.
- *La Périchole* (1868): a lovely Peruvian street singer must choose between marrying a poor artist or the powerful Spanish viceroy.
- *Les Brigands* (1869): a band of Italian thieves plans to rob the womanizing Duke of Mantua, who unintentionally echoes *The Beggar's Opera* by nonchalantly observing that "one steals in accordance with one's rank."

Meilhac and Halévy are among the most rarely credited heroes of musical theatre. Offenbach's melodies didn't just appear from thin air—he was inspired to create them by funny, well-crafted librettos. These were not just plays ornamented with songs, but true integrated musicals that used songs as part of the storytelling process. Without outstanding scripts, Offenbach's musicals would never have become international favorites. The words truly were as important as the music.

La Grande-Duchesse de Gérolstein (1867) was arguably the apex for Offenbach, Meilhac, and Halévy, and the crowning achievement of the opera-bouffes style. The story takes place in a minor duchy ruled by a coquettish noblewoman. Her weakness for men in uniform is expressed in the suggestive "Ah, que j'aime les militaire" ("Oh, How I Love the Military!"):

> *Ah! How I love the military.*
> *Their cocky uniforms,*
> *Their moustaches and their little plumes …*
> *I would like to be their canteen girl!*
> *I'd always be with them,*
> *And I would intoxicate them!*
> *With them, valiant and heady,*
> *I would launch into battle.*

The "little plumes" used on military uniforms tended to be stiff and upright, a subtle phallic reference. As one of the few females in a battle zone, a canteen girl would have been the only eligible female among thousands of lonely, frightened men, leading to obvious sexual opportunities. Such tastefully packaged innuendo delighted the Parisians, but was always expurgated from early English translations.

Attracted to the handsome Private Fritz, the Grand Duchess impetuously promotes him to lead her army into war. This promotion distresses the Grand Duchess's tutor Baron Puck, her acoustically named General Boum, and her long-ignored fiancé Prince Paul. After Fritz pulls off a surprise victory by getting the enemy drunk before attacking, the Grand Duchess sings the seductive "Dites-lui" ("Tell Him"), explaining to Fritz that a woman of the court is in love with him, and clearly suggesting that she is the woman. But the simple country boy fails to get the hint and asks the Duchess for permission to marry his girlfriend Wanda. Frustrated, the Duchess sends Fritz off to get married.

At this point, the Duchess falls for Prince Paul's tutor, the handsome Baron Grog, who arrives to encourage the long-delayed royal marriage but can only stick around if she marries the Prince. The wedding is quickly arranged, and with the Duchess freshly distracted, her ministers set out to humiliate Fritz by sending him off to face a nasty ambush. When the Grand Duchess strips Fritz of his rank, he happily gives up army life. With all threats gone, Grog reveals that he is happily married, and the now-married Duchess accepts her fate, observing that "when you cannot have what you love, then you must love what you have."

The premiere of *La Grande-Duchesse de Gérolstein* took place at the Théâtre des Variétés on April 12, 1867, carefully timed to coincide with Napoleon III's second Exposition Universelle. World leaders flocked to Paris—Tsar Alexander II of Russia, England's Prince of Wales, and Germany's Kaiser Wilhelm I and his "Iron Chancellor," Otto Von Bismark—and all of them made a point of attending *La Grande-Duchesse.* Worried that the operetta might cause offense, Napoleon III's government had forced a few minor changes, but the male rulers of Europe enjoyed what they saw as a satire of the dangers posed by women in positions of power. However, most audiences understood that the authors were comically decrying how the fate of nations and soldiers often rested on the personal whims of rulers, regardless of gender. The show became a hit.

In the title role, Hortense Schneider (1833–1920) enjoyed the greatest success of her career. She had made her Paris debut at the Bouffes in Offenbach's *Le Violoneux* (1856), and over the next decade became a full-blown star at competing theatres before accepting the title role in *La Belle Hélène*. At her peak, Schneider was one of the most celebrated women in Paris, with newspapers following her adventures both on and off the stage. Because she attracted a bevy of wealthy admirers, including some with royal titles, gossips dubbed her "le passage des princes." Photos show that she was amply proportioned and not exactly a classic beauty, but sex appeal is as much a question of personality as anything else, and Schneider had enough personality to fill any theatre. In her professional life, she played the role of diva with relish, terrorizing coworkers with tantrums and punishing uncooperative managers with walkouts. She battled frequently with Offenbach, who had a hot temper of his own. Since both seemed to realize that they owed their success to each other, hatchets were usually buried in time for opening nights. That ended when Schneider refused the role intended for her in *Les Brigands*. She went off to work for other managers, only to find that no one else could give her the kind of hits Offenbach had.

Offenbach continued to turn out new works, and his career was going full steam in 1870, the year that Napoleon III moronically declared war on Prussia. Within months, the French army suffered a devastating defeat, the Emperor was sent into exile, and a new republican government quickly announced a surrender. Extremists in Paris refused to accept defeat and declared the city an independent commune. The Communards barricaded the city and held out until May 1871, when the French army retook the town, borough by borough. By the time the fighting was over, 18,000 Parisians were executed for treason, and much of the city had been devastated by fire. Paris was soon rebuilt, but remained under martial law for the next five years. In the wake of so much civic trauma, the gaiety of Offenbach's opera-bouffes rang hollow.

In an effort to accommodate changing tastes, Offenbach offered a fantasy extravaganza of the sort that was already the rage in New York and London. *Le Roi Carotte* (*The Carrot King*, 1872) involved a penniless prince who is deposed by a magically empowered government of vegetables. After this success, the composer endured a series of frustrating failures before introducing a four-act version of *Orphée aux Enfers* in 1874 at the Théâtre de la Gaîté. With a chorus of

180, this massive production made a handsome profit. Jules Vernes's fantastic stories of interplanetary travel inspired Offenbach to compose another lavish extravaganza, *Voyage Dans le Lune* (*A Trip to the Moon*, 1875), which did well. Hortense Schneider had a much harder time of it. When her performance in Hervé's indelicately titled 1875 operetta *La Belle Poule* (*The Old Hen*) led some critics to comment that she looked old, the forty-two-year-old diva took the hint and left the stage. She remained a prominent and respected figure in Parisian society until her death in 1920.

Offenbach refused to give up. Aside from his insatiable artistic ambition, the extravagant budgets for several unsuccessful productions had left him with mounting debts, and his only source of income was new work. His final hits were *Madame Favart* (1878), which built a fictional 1700s adventure around the famed actress Justine Favart, and *La Fille du Tambour Major* (*The Drum Major's Daughter*, 1879). At the time of Offenbach's death in 1880, he was hard at work on his final composition, the grand opera *Les Contes des Hoffmann*. There have been various editions of this piece, some with additional music by other composers. Ironically, this grand opera is now Offenbach's most widely performed work. Except for occasional stagings in France, his operettas are rarely performed, and that lack is a great pity. There are many fine audio recordings, and several inventively staged productions are now available on home video. Fans of musical theatre should treat themselves to a taste of Offenbach—they may find him as intoxicating as ever.

Other French composers carried on the operetta tradition, but none matched Offenbach's output. Charles Lecocq (1832–1918), one of the winners of Offenbach's operetta competitors, developed a slightly more sober style that some classify as *opera comique*, but by any name it was still operetta. His most popular work was *La Fille de Madame Angot* (1872), the story of Clairette, an orphan girl who spurns the offer of a middle class marriage in hopes of winning her true love. While competing for that love with a former schoolmate, she somehow gets entangled in a revolutionary plot. This piece premiered in Brussels, where a long run led to successful productions worldwide. It offered a melodic score, several witty plot twists, and two stellar prima donna roles for the title character and her schoolmate. Several particularly catchy melodies helped to keep this work a favorite through the end of the century. Lecocq's other hits included *Les Cent Vierges/The 100 Virgins* (1872), *Giroflé-Girofla* (1874) and *Le Petit Duc/The Little Duke* (1878).

Vienna

Offenbach certainly made frequent use of the waltz, but no place was as closely identified with this sound as imperial Vienna. By the late nineteenth century, the waltz was the city's life beat, heard in every café and ballroom, whistled on every street corner. The capital of the Austro-Hungarian Empire had a long history as a cultural center. Its numerous theatres, concert halls, ballrooms, and cafés were in constant need of new music to entertain one of the most diverse and sophisticated civic populations in the world. Viennese operetta three-quarter-timed its way into being when a theatre owner couldn't afford performance rights to Offenbach's imports.

A handful of Vienna's theatres concentrated on musical works, offering grand operas, burlesques, and farces. There was also *singspiele,* a form of musical theatre that combined spoken dialogue with operatic arias, ensembles, and popular-style ballads. This form may sound suspiciously similar to the megamusicals of the late twentieth century, but the bulk of the singing in singspiele was so vocally demanding that these works pass as operas and are only performed by opera companies today. Mozart's *Die Entführung aus dem Serail/Abduction from the Seraglio* (1782) and *Die Zauberflöte/The Magic Flute* (1791) are among the best know examples of the genre. In these works, the music and stellar singing were usually given far more importance than plot and character development.

Franz von Suppé (1819–1895) was Austria's most popular singspiele composer. Of Belgian descent but raised in Italy, he worked as a conductor and composer at several of Vienna's leading theatres. By 1860, he already had more than a hundred and twenty singspiele, farces, and other musical stage works to his credit. He eventually began composing operettas, his most famous being *Die Schöne Galathée/The Beautiful Galatea* (1865), which stole its plot and characters from a French comedy based on a Greek legend. It told the story of the sculptor Pygmalion, who creates a beautiful statue of a woman, names it Galatea, and begs the gods to bring it to life. The wish is granted, but Galatea proves to be a handful. She ignores Pygmalion, flirts with his young assistant, drinks to excess, and makes a general nuisance of herself. Galatea finally decides that human life is too complicated, and gets the gods to change her back into lifeless marble.

Adding merry melodies to an already funny plot, *Die Schöne Galathée* became an immediate sensation. Productions were mounted in all major German-speaking cities, and the following decade saw successful stagings in London and New York. No one had the nerve to present this work in Paris, where a foreign-born operetta would have faced a merciless critical firing squad. Other musicals about statues coming to life would do well in years to come (*Adonis, One Touch of Venus*), as would a mid-twentieth-century musical based on a variation of the Pygmalion legend (*My Fair Lady*). Suppé's operettas had no extended life outside the German-speaking world, and today are remembered primarily for their overtures, several of which are staples in the classical concert repertory.

In the late 1800s, Johann Strauss II (1825–1899) was the world's best-known composer of popular music. His dance music fueled an international craze for waltzes and polkas, earning him the nickname "The Waltz King." Since similar music was a staple in Offenbach's stage works, it seemed only natural that Strauss should try his hand at the operetta form. The two men openly admired each other's work, and legend has it that the Frenchman encouraged his Austrian colleague to give it a go. Strauss began writing operettas in 1871, but his early stage works all had embarrassingly short runs. Strauss was able to recycle melodies from those flops as popular dance tunes, so his music was clearly not at fault. What he needed was a solid libretto.

Franz Geneé obliged with a German-language adaptation of *Le Réveillon*, a French play by no less a team than Halévy and Meilhac. The extremely convoluted plot of *Die Fledermaus/The Bat* (1874, 16 performances in Vienna) involved Dr. Valke, a Viennese gentleman who seeks revenge for the night that a friend left him beside a suburban road, drunk and dressed as a bat. The perpetrator was Alfred von Eisenstein, who happens to be facing a brief stint in jail for insulting a minor official. Valke persuades Eisenstein to put off jail for one night and come to a gala ball being thrown by the wealthy Russian expatriate Prince Orlofsky. Eisenstein agrees, accepting the suggestion that he masquerade as a marquis. The catch is that Valke has also invited Eisenstein's wife Rosalinda (who comes masked) and house-maid Adele (who hopes to become an actress), as well as Herr Frank, governor of the city jail where Eisenstein is set to spend time.

At the party, Orlofsky warns that any guest who appears bored will be thrown out, so each must find their own pleasure ("*Chacun a son gout!*"). Eisenstein unwittingly tries to seduce his masked wife, and becomes his incipient jailer's new drinking buddy. Throw in a few unplanned twists, like Rosalinda's onetime lover Alfred (an aria-spouting Italian tenor) barging into her house and getting arrested in her husband's place, and you have enough mistaken identities to fill an evening with merry chaos. The next morning at the jail, everything is sorted out. Eisenstein is incarcerated, his wife's thwarted infidelity is overlooked, Orlofsky becomes Adele's patron, and everyone blames their behavior on "His majesty, King Champagne."

This feast of silliness inspired Strauss to turn out a giddy, melodic score filled with Offenbach-style bounce. Highlights include Adele's lilting waltz "Mein Herr Marquis," sometimes referred to as "The Laughing Song." When Eisenstein accuses Adele of being his maid, she treats it as a jest. The laughter is, of course, an excuse for colora-tura fireworks:

> *My hand, I dare say, is so fine, ha, ha, ha, ha, ha!*
> *My foot is so dainty and childlike, ha, ha, ha, ha, ha!*
> *My way of speaking, my self-command,*
> *My waistline, my figure.*
> *You'll never detect these in a ladies maid!*
> *You must admit it's a laughable mistake.*
> *Yes, a funny story, ha, ha, ha,*
> *What a cause to ha, ha, ha,*
> *So funny, you'll excuse me, ha, ha, ha,*
> *If I laugh, ha, ha, ha!*

The original Vienna production of *Die Fledermaus* was so plagued by misfortunes that some sources have unfairly labeled it a failure. It closed after just sixteeen performances because the Theatre an der Wein had another booking lined up. Soon after the piece reentered the theatre's repertory, the actress playing Orlofsky forced cancellations when she fell ill. When the original Dr. Falke fell dead on stage in mid-performance, the ill-starred production shut down at sixty-eight performances.

Die Fledermaus was soon performed in most of the world's major theatre centers, but only Berlin received the show with immediate acclaim. It was not until the early twentieth century that better translations and changing tastes made this piece a staple in operatic repertories worldwide. In both Europe and the United States, it has become customary for opera companies to offer *Die Fledermaus* on New Year's Eve, with special guest performers brought in to entertain during Orlofsky's party scene. Strauss composed a dozen more operettas, with varying degrees of success, but *Die Fledermaus* remains his landmark stage hit.

Vienna's composers kept churning out operettas, but most of these works found little audience outside of German-speaking nations. Every now and then, one broke through to an international audience. Carl Millöcker (1842–1899) did it with *Der Bettelstudent/The Beggar Student* (1882), a tuneful farce involving a poor college student passing himself off as a wealthy nobleman. Likewise, Carl Zeller's (1842–1898) *Der Vogelhändler/The Birdseller* (1891) used irresistible melody to sell the story of a small-town bird catcher who seeks a better job and winds up working for fraudulent royalty. Occasionally heard in Germany or Austria, these works are no longer performed in Britain or the United States. By the end of the nineteenth century, many assumed that the golden age of Viennese operetta had passed, but it would return again in the early twentieth century with the sensation surrounding Lehar's *The Merry Widow* (1905).

By that time, a new city had become a creative epicenter for the musical theatre. In fact, the world would eventually identify this city and one of its avenues as the primary home of the genre. So it is ironic that New York stumbled through its first century before seeing any professional stage productions, and would wait a good deal longer before developing what we would recognize as a Broadway musical.

3

American Explorations (1624–1880) — "The Music of Something Beginning"

W hat was the first Broadway musical? There is no clear answer, but one thing is certain: it was not *The Black Crook*. That much-talked-about show was the result of a series of accidents, more of a business achievement than an artistic one. The American musical theatre was already thriving, with companies offering a wide assortment of imported and homegrown entertainments. The United States had even evolved a genre that had no European antecedents: minstrelsy, which helped established the commercial theatre nationwide. *The Black Crook* simply proved how profitable "the show business" could be. To borrow a phrase from the title song of *Ragtime*, "it was the music of something beginning."

Broadway's Early Years

The high ridge that runs along the length of Manhattan Island had long been used by the native Lenape tribe as a trade route. When the Dutch establish New Amsterdam as a trading post in 1624, that ridge became the settlement's main thoroughfare, earning the logical name of High Street. In 1664, the British navy forcibly took over the colony and renamed it New York in honor of the King's brother, the Duke of York. Since High Street was the widest boulevard in town, the English called it "Broadway." Plays and comic operas were regularly performed in other British colonial centers, including Charleston, Philadelphia, and Williamsburg. However, the mostly

Dutch population of New York considered stage entertainment sinful, and with no audience, there can be no theatre. Broadway had to wait until the following century to see its first theatrical performances.

In 1732, a professional troupe from London presented a repertory of plays in a jerry-rigged Manhattan storeroom, but records do not indicate what was performed. The first documented professional performance of a musical in New York took place on December 3, 1750, when a resident company presented John Gay's *The Beggar's Opera* in a simple wooden theatre that stood east of Broadway on Nassau Street. In 1767, a more elaborate theatre opened nearby on John Street, and served as the city's primary performance space for the next thirty years. The British army occupied New York City during most of the War for Independence. With professional troupes forced into extended exile, army volunteers staged performances at the Theatre on John Street. In the rest of the thirteen states, the Continental Congress officially discouraged playgoing, and several states issued an outright ban on public performances. After the war, President George Washington frequently attended theatrical performances in both New York and Philadelphia, helping to lift the stigma. Anti-performance laws were gradually repealed, and professional companies either visited or set up residence in major U.S. cities.

In a promising development, the Theatre on John Street hosted *The Archers* (1796), a comic opera that some scholars point to as the earliest American-born musical. Sadly, *The Archers* gave only a handful of performances and set off no trends. Most of the musical works performed on U.S. stages during the early years of the new republic were British imports. These were the same ballad operas, comic operas, and pantomimes enjoyed by their estranged English cousins. Theatre companies paid little attention to genre definitions, so musical stage works were indiscriminately publicized as "masques," "burlettas," or "parlor operas." No one took these shows to be serious art. Like most of what is seen on modern day television, popular stage entertainments of the early 1800s were designed to be disposable—enjoyed today, then eclipsed by something else and forgotten tomorrow.

As the population of Manhattan Island spread northward, Broadway served as the community's commercial and cultural spine. The importance of any business or entertainment venue in the city was measured by its proximity to Broadway. To be anywhere other than "there" meant that you were nowhere. The ticket buying power of the upper classes eventually set the tone for most of the entertainment found on Broadway. The working and lower classes found their pleasures on the Bowery, a somewhat scruffier avenue that sat on the eastern side of the island. With a jumble of theatres, taverns, and brothels, the Bowery became a haven for entertainment aimed at "the common man." One genre born on the Bowery would enjoy international popularity for more than half a century.

Minstrelsy

Blackface performers were around several decades before the first minstrel shows evolved. Such acts were common features in circuses and traveling shows from the 1790s onward. In the 1820s, white entertainer Thomas Rice caused a nationwide sensation with a blackface song and dance act that burlesqued negro slaves. A native New Yorker, Rice traveled the country as a sort of one-man show, offering songs and humorous stories. Having little if any direct knowledge of plantation life, he supposedly got the idea for his groundbreaking routine from a black stable hand (some versions say it was a street performer) who danced a simple jig while singing:

> First on de heel tap, den on de toe
> Every time I wheel about I jump Jim Crow.
> Wheel about and turn about en do j's so.
> And every time I wheel about, I jump Jim Crow.

Over the years, Rice named several northern cities as the location for this fateful encounter. We can only guess if the former slave's name really was "Jim Crow," but it is clear that a character soon took shape in Rice's mind. Using burnt cork to blacken his features and costumed in ragged old clothes, he added topical verses to the song and filled out the routine with a comic dance and some "plantation-style" banter. In a society that constitutionally defined negro slaves as property, few people considered either the song or the character offensive. Rice's "Jim Crow" routine won ovations all across the United States, including his old home turf at New York's Bowery Theatre. By that time, there were so many people copying the act that Rice had to bill himself as "the *original* Jim Crow."

Although solo blackface acts were soon common, it was not until 1843 that a troupe of four unemployed white performers joined forces to present a full-length show. Taking a cue from a Mitteleuropean "Tyrolese minstrel" family that had just toured the United States to surprising acclaim, the new troupe called themselves the Virginia Minstrels. Billy Whitlock, Frank Pelham, Dan Emmett, and Frank Brower donned blackface and sat in a semicircle with a tambourine player on one end and a "bones" player (using either real cow ribs or wooden replicas to "clack" out a rhythmic accompaniment) on the other. This first-ever minstrel program consisted of songs and dances interspersed with comic skits and seemingly improvised "plantation-style" patter. Performing in the Bowery Amphitheatre (just across the avenue from where Rice had offered "Jim Crow"), the Virginia Minstrels could not have realized that they were launching the first indigenous form of musical theatre in the United States of America.

Within three years, New York City had ten resident minstrel companies, and within a decade that number doubled. Innumerable troupes toured the United States, including the Christy Minstrels, the Ethiopian Serenaders, and the Virginia Vocalists. Companies ranged in size from half a dozen to more than a hundred, with wagon-born troupes reaching even the smallest towns. The production and marketing of minstrel shows marked the beginning of American show business, with a nationwide complement of producers, managers, writers, and theatre personnel relying on minstrelsy for part or all of their income.

Minstrel shows soon developed a standard, three-part format. After an overture came:

1. The first part or "Minstrel Line," with the cast seated on a semi-circle of chairs stretching across the stage. In the center sat an interlocutor (often the only performer not in blackface) who served as the dignified master of ceremonies. He tailored each performance on the spot, cutting short any joke or routine that seemed to fall flat. A rousing opening chorus number ended with the interlocutor's ritual cry, "Gentlemen, be seated!" after which the ensemble launched into a loosely structured series of songs and jokes. The main burden of amusing the crowd fell to the endmen. Brudder Tambo (playing the tambourine) and Brudder Bones (playing the bones) were seated on

the left and right ends of the line, using their namesake instruments and providing funny chatter, frequently egged on by the interlocutor. The rest of the line consisted of singers, instrumentalists, and specialty performers, all dressed in the most lavish uniforms that the management could provide. After an intermission came ...

2. The "Olio," a variety show featuring members of the company offering their specialties—songs, dances, comedy skits, juggling, etc. It was not unusual for olio performers to slip off their gloves, proving that they were really white skinned. The olio traditionally included a stump speech, in which one of the endmen mocked the ostentatious political orations of white politicians. Only clean, family-friendly material was allowed, which has led some to suggest that the olio was a precursor of vaudeville, albeit with blackface conventions. All or part of the olio could be performed "in one" (in front of a closed curtain) to allow stagehands to set up for the final feature.

3. The "Afterpiece" was a one-act play with songs. Initially, these were sentimental, comic tales of plantation life, but in time minstrel afterpieces became burlesques of popular topics, novels, or plays. Two stock characters were almost always involved—"Jim Crow," the shiftless country bumpkin ripe for humiliation, and "Zip Coon," the conniving city slicker whose self-assurance often led to his comic comeuppance. These roles were usually played by the two endmen. On occasion, the afterpiece parodied popular novels and stage works. When the Offenbach craze hit the United States in the 1860s, one minstrel troupe staged a spoof entitled *The Grand Dutch S.* The afterpiece traditionally ended with a walkaround, a thrilling cakewalk dance involving the entire company. Performed with an arched back and high strutting steps, cakewalks had developed on southern plantations, where negro slaves tried to imitate the way their white masters cavorted at formal balls. According to tradition, early competitions involving this dance offered a cake as first prize, giving the dance its name.

This three-part structure provided audiences and performers with a reliable template, within which an infinite range of variations and specialties could be accommodated. So every minstrel show was both familiar and new. It was the first completely American-born musical entertainment, one that did not have any clear European ancestors.

Here is a sample of the sort of comic dialogue traditionally used in the first part, or Minstrel Line.

BONES: Mr. Interlocutor, I had a narrow escape from the devil.

INTERLOCUTOR: Tell us all about it, Mr. Bones.

BONES: Last Saturday night, I started backslidin'. The tempter came and put an empty sack in my hand and started me toward Mr. Smith's chicken coop.

ALL: Amen, Amen.

BONES: I done my best to fight off temptation, but the tempter said, "Go on, go on," and I kept getting closer and closer to that chicken coop.

ALL: Glory be, glory be.

BONES: But, praise the Lord. Just as I was climbing the fence to get to that chicken coop, I see a possum up in the apple tree.

ALL: Halleluiah, halleluiah.

BONES: And then the moon comes out, and I see Mr. Smith behind that chicken coop holdin' a big shot gun.

ALL: Praise the Lord.

BONES: Quick as a flash, I yell to Mr. Smith to shoot that possum, and he hits that possum with both barrels.

ALL: Go on, brother.

BONES: All I can say is that when the tempter shows us where there is a chicken coop—

ALL: Yes, yes.

BONES: We is lucky if Providence shows us a possum in a tree.

ALL: Amen.

During the 1850s, when the United States was being torn apart by the debate over negro slavery, minstrel shows offered reassuring images of negroes either gratefully enjoying life with "massah," or stuck in some northern city ruefully wondering why they had ever sought freedom. Abolitionists opposed to slavery grumbled, and a few minstrel comics tried to depict blacks in a more positive light, but most white U.S. citizens accepted these stereotypes as wholesome family entertainment.

Minstrelsy's most lasting artistic legacy was its songs. As they criss-crossed the United States, minstrel troupes became the first entertainment medium that could give songs relatively quick national exposure. The Christy Minstrels turned Stephen Foster's (1826–1864) "Oh, Susannah" into an immediate hit in 1848, and the young composer followed this hit with "Ring, Ring the Banjo," "Camptown Races," "Old Black Joe," "Beautiful Dreamer," and "Old Folks at Home." Each became a staple in the minstrel repertory, and the successful publication of these songs made Foster the first American songwriter to earn a living from his craft.

Dan Emmett, one of the original Virginia Minstrels, composed such minstrel standards as "Turkey in the Straw," "Jimmy Crack Corn," and "Dixie," a tuneful mock plantation ode that enjoyed tremendous popularity.

> Oh I wish I was in the land ob cotton.
> Old times there are not forgotten,
> Look away, look away,
> Look away, Dixieland.
> In Dixie land where I was born in
> Early on one frosty morning,
> Look away, look away,
> Look away, Dixieland.
>
> I wish I was in Dixie—hooray, hooray!
> In Dixieland I'll take my stand
> To live and die in Dixie,
> Away, away, away down south in Dixie.
> Away, away, away down south in Dixie.

A devoted abolitionist, Emmett was appalled when "Dixie" became the battle hymn of the Southern Confederacy during the American Civil War (1861–1865).

Aside from specific songs, minstrelsy left the United States of America with a lasting musical institution: the barbershop quartet. It was standard procedure for minstrel troupes to include a male quartet, which is why many minstrel songs, including those of Stephen Foster, were originally written and published in four-part harmony. In communities all across the United States of America, men hanging out at the local barbershop would pass the time by harmonizing *a capella* on these songs. Thousands of men and women of all races keep this tradition alive today.

After the war, the mass migration of southern negroes to northern cities gave minstrelsy a new comic focus. Newly transplanted "northern negroes" were depicted as either preening dandies or shiftless blockheads, ripe targets for exploitation at the hands of the unscrupulous. These new stereotypes reassured white audiences that liberated blacks posed no serious social or economic threat. In reality, the only real threat was the one faced by African Americans as the same bigotry that had allowed the existence of slavery now manifested in new forms of social and legal oppression. White-hooded members of the Ku Klux Klan organized cross-burnings, beatings, lynchings, and execution-style murders to keep blacks terrorized. Borrowing a phrase from minstrelsy, states that had belonged to the Southern Confederacy now passed a series of so-called "Jim Crow" laws, formalizing the social segregation of blacks in schools, restaurants, and other public places. Among other oppressive features, these laws barred African Americans from appearing on stage.

Of course, there has never been an effective way to outlaw talent. Black performers got their first taste of mainstream theatrical success appearing in supposedly all-white minstrel shows. Troupes frequently included black performers who were light skinned enough to pass as whites when offstage. All-black troupes were touring in the north as early as 1855, and the trend really caught on after the Civil War, when newly emancipated slaves swelled the minstrel ranks as "authentic darkies." After some years, the Jim Crow laws were adjusted, and all-black troupes (billed as "Colored minstrels") became almost as common as white troupes in blackface (billed as "Nigger minstrels"). Unfortunately, the presence of real negroes did not effect any viable changes in the conventions or content of minstrelsy. Thanks to the unnatural glow of gas-fueled lighting, most negroes had to darken their skins with burnt cork in order to look "black enough" on stage, establishing a tradition that lasted well into the next century. Worse yet, the presence of black performers gave greater credibility to the old comic minstrel stereotypes.

By the early 1900s, racism was still endemic throughout the United States, but tastes and attitudes were shifting so that professional minstrel troupes were gone by 1910. However, echoes of minstrelsy lived on in North American popular music and in the use of blackface on Broadway and in Hollywood films. Al Jolson and Eddie Cantor are remembered for "blacking-up" their faces in films, but so did Bing Crosby, Irene Dunne, Joan Crawford, Fred Astaire, Mickey Rooney, and Judy Garland. One of the last uses of blackface in mainstream entertainment occurred when the radio series *Amos 'n Andy* moved to television in the 1950s, its title characters direct descendants of Jim Crow and Zip Coon.

A sense of historical perspective is essential in any discussion of blackface or the other aspects of minstrelsy. Blackface is now universally and deservedly condemned as a hateful practice, but suggesting that all performers using it were automatically racist is comparable to saying that any man who wears drag must be a homosexual. Blackface was a widely accepted convention of stage and screen up to the early 1940s. Most performers who used it were just trying to entertain, not make a racial comment. That does not make the results less offensive today, but contemporary critics might consider investing less time in attacks on the past and concentrating instead on the living echoes of minstrelsy. Jim Crow and Zip Coon are still appearing in movies and television sitcoms where black performers depict the shiftless fool or the conniving dolt. Perhaps these characters are so deeply ingrained in the America's cultural subconsciousness that we will never fully escape them.

American Variety

It may have begun as a cheap rip-off of minstrelsy's olio, or perhaps its origins lie in school pageants, talent contests, medicine shows, or even circuses. Although variety's beginnings are obscure, there is no question that it had a tremendous impact on American entertainment and, in particular, on the development of musical theatre.

By the mid-1800s, saloon keepers in cities and towns of every size latched onto the idea of providing entertainment to keep customers coming back for more. Performances might take place on a makeshift elevated stage or in the middle of a barroom floor. The bill of fare typically included comedians, acrobats, clowns, jugglers, animal acts, specialties, and an occasional singer—all of the smaller acts one would have expected to see in a traveling circus of that era. Musical accompaniment might be provided by a small orchestra, but was more often handled by a club-thumbed pianist who took at least part of his pay in liquid form. Acts had to perform several times a day, with performances running from early afternoon through the middle of the night. The actual number of performances varied from place to place, as did the number of acts. The content of a variety show could be adjusted from day to day, deleting anything that audiences did not like and adding more of the things they approved of. And variety audiences definitely expressed their opinions. As the booze flowed freely, testosterone levels ran high in these smoke-filled halls, where heckling, fistfights, and even gunfire were common. Performers put up with the rowdiness to earn about fifteen dollars a week, and in the mid-1800s that was more than most farmers earned in a month.

Because saloon clientele was exclusively male, variety shows always featured underdressed ladies with their legs in tights. These seemingly amiable damsels danced and sang in the show and then wandered the room, encouraging customers to buy more rounds of overpriced drinks. The more liquor the men bought, the more commission the girls collected from the owners. Uninitiated customers often assumed that the dancers and "waiter girls" were selling themselves along with the liquor, but such was rarely the case. Customers in search of sex were passed off to prostitutes who worked on the premises or in nearby brothels. In rougher halls, such as those found on New York's Bowery, naïve customers would be drugged, pickpocketed, and left in a nearby alley to sleep it off. The local police, who routinely received bribes from saloon owners, saw to it that these crimes went unreported.

While the dancing girls were always a surefire hit, comedy had a hell of a time getting noticed. The content of songs and skits was coarse. One comic number widely performed in late variety was "Such a Delicate Duck":

> I took her out one night for a walk,
> We indulged in all sorts of pleasantry and talk.
> We came to a potato patch, she wouldn't go across;
> The potatoes had eyes and she didn't wear no drawers!

Note the use of a rhyme (across/drawers) requiring the singer to mispronounce both words. Of course, the men in a variety saloon audience would have paid scant attention to lyrical craftsmanship. All they might have noticed was the risqué joke. Latenight variety performances sometimes included racy acts, staged long after any plainclothes law officers had either gone home or gotten too drunk to care. A common variety skit involved a young, scantily clad farm girl crossing the stage and stepping behind a haystack. A succession of men would then join her, one or more at a time, departing in increasingly disheveled condition and drawing knowing hoots from the randy audience.

In the 1850s, showman P. T. Barnum (1810–1891) offered a different approach to variety at his American Museum, which stood on the southeast corner of Broadway and Ann Street in New York City. After seeing his collection of bizarre sideshow exhibits, customers could enjoy a selection of clean acts in a handsomely appointed auditorium, without a beer or whiskey bottle in sight. Exchange a tent for the theatre, and it amounted to a precursor of the blend Barnum would use three decades later in his circus shows. By labeling the performances as "moral lectures," he attracted the sort of family audience that normally steered clear of variety halls. When it became clear that many customers were touring through the facility several times on just one admission, the shrewd Barnum posted a sign saying TO THE EGRESS—and many did not realize "Egress" meant "Exit" until they found themselves on the sidewalk. The sign soon drew so much publicity that few were actually fooled by it. Despite several fires and relocations, Barnum's Museum remained one of New York's top attractions for more than a decade.

Inspired by Barnum's success, some of the larger variety saloons evolved into well-appointed theatres, but always with that added and highly profitable element, a bar. As more venues opened in the years following the Civil War, it became feasible for variety performers to tour for months at a time, and the prospect of steady, well-paid employment drew better talent.

There was no set standard in variety. From one town to another—and in some larger cities, from one block to another—variety venues were as diverse as the audiences that they catered to. They went by various names: at one end of the spectrum stood "music halls" and "dime museums," while at the other stood "slabs" and "dives," the last so named because customers could expect to see someone "take a dive" before an evening was over. Two New York City variety halls of the early 1880s illustrate the differences. Well-heeled locals and tourists watched the finest acts in the business at Koster & Bial's Concert Hall on 23rd Street. When a new ordinance banned the sale of alcoholic drinks in all Manhattan theatres, Koster & Bial's replaced their stage curtain with a huge folding fan, insisting that a curtain-less space could not be classified as a theatre. The bar stayed open, and Koster & Bial's thrived. Downtown on the Bowery, working class stiffs packed Miner's, a far less elegant establishment where audiences could heckle hopeful unknowns competing for prizes in New York's first "amateur nights."

By the mid-1880s, variety was replaced by a cleaner, more family-friendly genre called vaudeville—a change examined in chapter 5. Variety passed on two legacies to the earliest Broadway musicals: underdressed showgirls in tights and the concept of adjusting content to meet audience demand.

Broadway Musicals of the Pre-Civil War Years

One of the advantages of the multi-act format of variety and minstrelsy was that shows could be tailored to please any particular audience by adding or deleting bits, changing the running order, or dropping ineffective bits. So it is not surprising that American musicals of the mid-nineteenth century were constructed in the same flexible hodgepodge manner.

Advertisements and playbills used various terms to describe musical shows, but no one had yet stumbled on the idea of calling a show with songs "a musical." *The Magic Deer* (1852, 5 performances) advertised itself as "A Serio Comico Tragico Operatical Historical Extravaganzical Burletical Tale of Enchantment," just to make sure that potential ticket buyers understood that it was a play with songs. In the mid-nineteenth century, most Broadway theatres maintained resident stock companies who offered an ongoing repertory, so musicals of this period rarely played more than a week or two of continuous performances.

The longest New York run of the 1850s was *The Elves* (1857, 50 performances), presented by Laura Keene (1826–1873), one of the first women to excel as an actor-manager in the theatre in the American theatre. She had her own theatre at 622 Broadway, where she racked up seven years of extraordinary success. As renowned for her talent as for her business prowess, Keene starred in many of her own productions, including the occasional musical. Her longest running musical hit was the "burletta" *The Seven Sisters* (1860, 253 performances), which involved seven female demons who leave hell to take a sightseeing tour of New York City. A score was cobbled from existing songs, with "Dixie" thrown in to provide a surefire finish. As long as the audience was entertained, who cared whether or not the songs had any connection to the plot or characters? Best of all, there was a socko transformation scene that used the latest handcranked stage technology to change a set in full view of the audience. *The Seven Sisters* kept folks coming for almost nine months, dwarfing any other stage run up to that time on either side of the Atlantic.

Soon afterward, America's Civil War had a disastrous effect on New York's economy, so Keene sold off her theatre and toured with a repertory of her biggest hits. Since *The Seven Sisters* involved so much stage machinery, it could not travel. Instead, Keene toured comedies like her acclaimed production of *Our American Cousin*, which she performed at Ford's Theatre in Washington, D.C., on the night that John Wilkes Booth assassinated President Abraham Lincoln in 1865. Keene's name became so firmly linked with that tragedy that she was soon forced to retire from the stage, and her record-setting success with *The Seven Sisters* soon faded from memory. With its magical themes and special effects, it was the clear precursor of a show that many incorrectly hail as the first Broadway musical. It is almost impossible to overestimate the importance of timing.

The Black Crook: "We're Midnight Fairies Roaming"

After the Civil War ended in 1865, New York City grew bigger and richer than ever, as new residents poured into the city and new businesses proliferated. There were dozens of theatres in town, but only two had state-of-the-art stage facilities: the ritzy Academy of Music on East 14th Street and the more egalitarian Niblo's Garden at the northeast corner of Prince Street and Broadway. William Wheatley (1816–1876) served as the producing actor-manager of Niblo's. An experienced actor, he occasionally appeared in his own productions, offering varied seasons that ran the gamut from Shakespeare to comic opera to melodrama. He aimed at the mostly upper and middle class

audience that frequented Broadway houses. In his productions, sensation was welcomed but vulgarity was not. Since Niblo's stage equip-
ment was second to none, with a series of mechanized trapdoors that
made it possible for people and things to appear or vanish on cue, and
state-of-the-art riggings that made swift set changes a breeze, Wheatley looked for material that would benefit from special effects and
generous doses of visual spectacle.

In the summer of 1866, Wheatley optioned *The Black Crook* (1866,
474 performances), a new melodrama by the relatively unknown
actor-playwright Charles M. Barras. At some point, Wheatley must
have realized that this four-act melodrama was a cliché-ridden stinker,
with a tortured plot that stole elements from Goethe's *Faust*, Weber's
Der Freischütz, and several other well-known plays and operas. It is
set sometime around the year 1600 in Germany's Hartz Mountains,
where the evil Count Wolfenstein realizes that he will never win the
affection of the lovely peasant Amina so long as her handsome sweetheart Rodolphe is in the way. Wolfenstein calls in Hertzog, an aging
crook-backed master of *black* magic (hence the show's title) who
stays alive by annually providing the Devil with fresh souls. Hertzog agrees to make Rodolphe his next victim, but while the unknowing hero is being led to a hellish fate, he selflessly saves a wounded
dove from a snake attack. The bird magically turns out to be Stalacta,
Fairy Queen of the Golden Realm. (Are you still following this?) The
grateful Queen whisks Rodolphe to safety in her utopian kingdom,
and gives him a ring—if kissed, it will summon her aide. The young
man returns home. When Wolfenstein's guards try to kill Rodolphe,
he summons Stalacta's army, and the young lovers escape. Act two
begins six months later, the day before Rodolphe and Amina are to
wed. Here is a taste of the dialogue, which was clunky even by the
standards of the 1860s:

AMINA: There seems to be a lurking danger in the air—a cloud between
us and the coming light.

RODOLPHE: Fear not—here in the deep seclusion of our forest home
we are safe from all pursuit. (Distant horn, and echo at back.) Hark, 'tis
Greppo calling in the huntsmen. Let's go on to meet them. (Music. They
are crossing stage when they are suddenly confronted by HERTZOG,
WOLFENSTEIN, and WOLFGAR, who enter quickly. Chord.)

WOLFENSTEIN: Ha—ha—ha. At last, we meet!

RODOLPHE: (Starting back and drawing his sword.) Entrapped! Fly Amina—seek safety with our people. My arms shall bar pursuit.

AMINA: No, Rodolphe, we will die together.

WOLFENSTEIN: Alive—take him alive! Yield!

RODOLPHE: He who takes my sword must win it.

HERTZOG: Put up thy blade; she whom thou would'st invoke is powerless to aid.

RODOLPHE: False wretch, but that another's life hangs on the slender thread of mine, and though coward numbers swarmed on every side, I'd try this issue with my single sword. But know thou, thou still art juggled with the power I once invoked, potent still. (Music. He kisses ring. STALACTA springs from the thicket in glittering full armor with DRAGONFIN.) Behold, we meet on equal ground!

WOLFENSTEIN: Though environed by a thousand fiends, my hate would find a way to reach you.

(Music. Grand triple sword combat. RODOLPHE and WOLFENSTEIN, STALACTA and HERTZOG, DRAGONFIN and WULFGAR. HERTZOG, wounded and dismayed, flies. AMINA, who during the combat has knelt in prayer, throws herself into the arms of RODOLPHE. They both kneel at the feet of STALACTA. DRAGONFIN indulges in grotesque exultation over the bodies of WOLFENSTEIN and WULFGAR.)

Soon afterward, gleeful demons drag the evil Hertzog into the flames of hell, and Rodolphe and Amina are reunited.

The production of this murky four-act play was still in its planning stages when promoters Henry C. Jarrett and Harry Palmer appeared at Wheatley's door. They had arranged for a Parisian ballet troupe to perform at the Academy of Music, which had just burned to the ground—an all-too-common problem in an era of wooden theatres. Stuck with a shipload of imported sets, costumes, and ballerinas, Jarrett and Palmer wondered if they might lease out Niblo's for the fall season. Conflicting versions of what happened next make it impossible to say who first thought of merging the ballet with the Barras play, but Wheatley grabbed the idea and ran with it. He later claimed that he lavished some $25,000 on additional sets, costumes, and special effects. If true, it was far more than anyone had spent on a Broadway production up to that time. When Barras protested that it was madness to turn his "serious" play into a spectacle, a $1,500 bonus bought his disgruntled silence.

Wheatley pepped up the proceedings with a stack of songs by a variety of composers. Some numbers fit the plot, but others were specialties designed to showcase specific cast members. When British music hall star Millie Cavendish was cast in the relatively minor role of Amina's maid, Wheatley arranged for a showcase solo, "You Naughty, Naughty Men," with music by G. Bicknell and lyrics by T. Kennick. In scene four, the maid offers a meandering monologue about her mistress's upcoming marriage, finishing with the rather obvious song cue, "I declare, I am so happy I could sing for a month!" Cavendish then went into her bit:

> *I will never more deceive you,*
> *Or of happiness bereave you,*
> *But I'll die a maid to grieve you,*
> *Oh, you naughty, naughty men.*
> *You may talk of love and sighing,*
> *Say for us you're nearly dying,*
> *All the while you know you're trying*
> *To deceive, you naughty men.*

After an encore or two, Cavendish left the stage, and the story resumed. The song had nothing to do with the plot, but no one cared. In 1866, anything that added to a show's sense of fun was considered a plus. The few plot-based numbers weren't nearly as enjoyable. In one scene, dozens of fleshy ballerinas bounced about in a moonlit grotto while singing "The Song of the Amazons":

> *Gaily welcome from deep and dark blue sea,*
> *And lightly we march through the world.*
> *We're midnight fairies roaming to music of the waves,*
> *And gaily wander 'til morning.*

The lyrics didn't make much sense, but at least it involved fairies singing about what it's like to be fairies.

The visual spectacle of *The Black Crook* swept all other concerns from the audience's mind, but took a harsh toll on their nether extremities. The September 12 opening night lasted a bottom-numbing five and a half hours. One dazzling set followed another as the action switched from a country cottage to an evil magician's laboratory to a wooded glen to a castle dungeon. Instead of just one transformation scene, there were several. In one, a mountain forest turned into "the Grotto of the Golden Stalactites," with fairies sleeping on jewel-studded rocks beside a lake of sliver. Another took the audience into the depths of Hell itself, with Satan seated on an illuminated throne of skulls and surrounded by the Miltonic-sounding "vistas of Pandemonium, teeming with infernal life and wreaths of flame." The greatest effect was saved for the final moments, described in the original libretto as:

> Music. An elaborate mechanical and scenical construction of the Realms of Stalacta, occupying the entire stage. This scene must be of gradually developing and culminating beauty, introducing during its various transformations STALACTA, the entire host of fairies, sprites, water nymphs, amphibians, gnomes, etc., bearing treasure. RODOLPHE, AMINA GREPO and CARLINE. Calcium lights, brilliant fires, and slow curtain.

Grand as such scenes were, they didn't cause as much fuss as the hundred ballerinas of the ensemble. The ballets staged by choreographer David Costa were considered eye-filling, but attention soon focused on the dancers themselves. Surviving photos of the original *Black Crook* chorines may puzzle the modern viewer. These ladies were most definitely not skinny little things. They had the amply proportioned, well-fed look that was in vogue at the time. Why did audiences go berserk over the sight of legs in tights? It is worth remembering that this was an era when women's dresses covered every bit of skin except the hands and face, and that Victorian fashions tried to obscure the natural contours of the female figure with bustles, corsets and other frillery. A stage filled with young ladies in tights and form-fitting bodices was a revelation. Even the wealthier classes who frequented classical ballet had never seen so many underdressed women in one place at one time. Not long before this, wives would have avoided such a leggy stage display, but after running businesses and hospitals during the Civil War, many women were no longer easily shocked.

By 1866, the novelty of the unveiled, glamorized female form was of equal interest to both sexes.

At first, most newspaper critics dismissed *The Black Crook* as harmless nonsense. When word of mouth kept the show running month after month, the novelty was suddenly perceived as a threat to public morality. Ministers began condemning the show from their pulpits, and a few bluenosed journalists joined the righteous chorus. Luckily for William Wheatley, controversy sells tickets, especially when the promise of seeing something sexy is involved. People who rarely went to Broadway shows now made a point of seeing *The Black Crook*. Torn between propriety and the lure of scandal, some women attended the show while hiding beneath heavy veils. Propriety be damned, they were not going to miss out on this one.

The Black Crook became the first stage production in world history to run for more than a year. Wheatley periodically added new songs and scenic effects to please legions of repeat customers—at a time when travel was still challenging and Broadway audiences consisted almost entirely of New Yorkers. Marie Bonfanti, the company's attractive prima ballerina, became an instant celebrity at age nineteen, and was embraced by even the most respectable social circles. Wheatley presented Bonfanti in a blatant follow-up called *The White Fawn* (1868, 176 performances), which managed a good run but was no match for its predecessor. Soon afterward, Wheatley retired a wealthy man. After years of struggle, playwright Charles Barras should have enjoyed the success of *The Black Crook* more than anyone, but his creation was not what he intended it to be, and misfortune dogged his private life. When his beloved wife died and his own health faltered, mounting royalties proved to be cold comfort. Six years after *The Black Crook*'s premiere, Barras died at fifty-three in an accident that many considered a suicide.

If *The Black Crook* was not the first Broadway musical, and wasn't even Broadway's first long-running musical hit, why is it hailed as a landmark? Simple: it was the first Broadway musical to become a nationwide hit. Just six years before, it had not been feasible for Laura Keene to take the elaborate *Seven Sisters* on tour. During and after the Civil War, America's railroad system underwent aggressive expansion and improvement, making train travel safer, faster, and more affordable. In a calculated gamble, *The Black Crook* went on tour with most of its mechanized sets and a massive cast. Wherever the railroads went, companies of *The Black Crook* followed. The physical production was the real star, and it packed theatres all across the country. The profits were astounding, and the American musical theatre was suddenly seen as an industry with vast, untapped economic potential. Productions of *The Black Crook* toured profitably for the next three decades. Broadway would see more than a dozen revivals, with the score and staging changing radically each time. The spectacle was what mattered most. A bizarre six-person off-Broadway production in 2006 proved that without visual dazzle, *The Black Crook* is a deadly bore.

For years to come, similar spectacles with fantasy themes, known as *extravaganzas*, played on Broadway and in the provinces. The songs had little to do with the stories, which always involved whimsical trips to fairyland with plenty of girls in tights. But the best of these early musicals provided relatively clean family entertainment. With millions of dollars to be made, these newfangled musicals turned what was then referred to in the United States as "the show business" into big business.

Early Burlesque: Thompson's British Blondes

At its most basic, *burlesque* means to make fun of something, and this intent was true of the various theatrical formats described by the term. By the twentieth century, burlesque was a rundown form of variety that flaunted sexual mores and relied on the pelvic bumps and grinds of female strippers to sell tickets. But burlesque started out as a form of legitimate musical theatre that spoofed Victorian society's rigid perceptions of gender.

As early as the 1840s, Broadway had a homegrown genre of full-length productions that burlesqued popular plays and operas of the day. Shakespeare's *Merchant of Venice* was sent up in *Shylock: A Jerusalem Hearty Joke* (1853, 4 performances), and Verdi's *Il Trovatore* inspired something called *Kill Trovatore!* (1867, 30 performances). Such spoofs usually played for a week or two and were then discarded. No scripts are known to survive, so we are not exactly sure about the contents, but surviving reviews give no indication that gender-based or sexual comedy was involved. A decade later, word reached America of a new kind of burlesque that was all the rage in London. These musical shows poked fun at popular legends or hit novels, but added a new dimension by letting women handle all the major roles while clad in revealing tights. Thanks to *The Black Crook*, Broadway audiences were accustomed to seeing women in tights, but only as fantasy female characters. In these British "leg shows," women played men, and acted as bold sexual aggressors. That potentially scandalous sight was something many American men and women were interested in seeing.

At age thirty, Lydia Thompson (1838–1908) was the most renowned purveyor of London burlesque, starring in productions that she also produced and managed. After an avalanche of advance publicity, Thompson and her troupe of "British Blondes" made their Broadway debut at Wood's Museum in *Ixion* (1868, 104 performances), the story of a mythological king who faced eternal torture after flirting with the wife of the god Jupiter. Thompson played the title role, and, as with *The Black Crook* chorines, she was not a remarkable beauty. However, she captivated audiences with a charismatic stage persona and was a master of the new burlesque form, which involved a freewheeling combination of planned gags, improvisation, and borrowed music. Best of all, Thompson and her British Blondes openly interacted with members of the audience, offering seemingly improvised asides. This impertinent yet amusing challenge to society's male-dominated status quo drew capacity audiences, and the initial critical response was favorable.

That all changed when Thompson's British Blondes moved their repertory from Wood's Museum to that bastion of respectability, Niblo's Garden. Self-appointed guardians of public morals broke out their *Black Crook* bromides and suddenly filled their pulpits and editorial columns with vehement protests, depicting the British Blondes as artistic invaders offering a brazen display of filth that threatened everything America held sacred. Once again, indignation did wonders for ticket sales. By the time Thompson and her troupe went off to tour the rest of the United States, she had grossed an estimated $370,000 and was a household name. During a run in Chicago, one journalist slandered Thompson so viciously that she tracked him down and publicly horsewhipped him. The small fine she paid was nothing compared to the mountain of resulting publicity, much of which was sympathetic to a woman defending her own honor.

Copycat burlesques soon appeared. Thompson and her imitators did not bother to hire composers. Instead, they recycled melodies from operatic arias and popular songs of the day and added new lyrics. To discourage unauthorized productions, the scripts from these early burlesques were not published. The material changed often, sometimes from night to night, and these productions all predate the development of stage photography. So we can only guess at the exact content and appearance of these shows, but it is clear that audiences of the 1860s were delighted.

Within a few years, men took over the management of burlesque troupes, and the form lost its transgressive edge. It became another form of variety, with respectably underdressed showgirls as the only remaining hint of what had once made the form a hot ticket. As Thompson's style of "high" burlesque fell out of fashion, her career fizzled out. An initially successful stint as a West End producer ended in financial failure, and several benefits were eventually held to restore her security. Forty years after her first Broadway triumph, Thompson died of pneumonia at age sixty, with many still cherishing the memory of the world's first burlesque star.

Burlesques of the Late 1870s–1880s: The Birth of "The Formula"

Broadway soon spawned a different kind of burlesque musical. The prime mover behind this new genre was Edward Rice (1849–1924), who produced, directed, and wrote songs for a series of popular hits. While Rice was inspired by Thompson, his shows did not challenge any popular notions about gender roles. Plenty of high-kicking showgirls in tights were on hand, but only as ornamentation. The main point was to offer easily digestible fun designed for family audiences.

Billed as "an American Extravaganza," *Evangeline* (1874, 14 performances) was loosely based on an epic poem by Longfellow. The title character and her lover Gabriel (played by a woman in tights) seek each other in a series of locales, ranging from Newfoundland to Africa to the American Wild West. The musical also featured a dancing cow (two men in an animal suit), a spouting whale, and a seriocomic silent character called "The Lone Fisherman"—none of whom are found in Longfellow. Confusing as all this sounds, it gave audiences a great deal of pleasure. Rice provided a completely original score, with lyrics by his colibrettist, J. Cheever Goodwin. This score was a major change from the recycled songs found in burlesque up to that time, and *Evangeline* was one of the first American musicals to have an entire score by one native-born songwriting team. None of the songs proved to be lasting hits, but audiences appear to have been impressed enough to keep the show touring profitably for almost thirty years.

Swiftly thrown together to fill a two-week midsummer gap in the schedule at Niblo's Garden, *Evangeline* returned repeatedly to New York between tour engagements, eventually racking up several hundred Broadway performances. At a time when genre labels were still hazy, this play was one of the first American hits to refer to itself in some publicity materials as a "musical comedy."

Rice put together seventeen more Broadway productions in the years that followed, and his touring companies crisscrossed the United States with highly profitable results. His most successful burlesque was inspired by the legend of Pygmalion, but with a twist. *Adonis* (1884, 603 performances), which billed itself as "a disrespectful perversion," was the story of a handsome male statue that comes magically to life. In the title role, handsome Henry E. Dixey (1859–1943) spoofed burlesque tradition by appearing in tights. Dixey's muscular legs delighted feminine viewers, making him one of Broadway's first musical matinee idols. Men enjoyed watching Adonis elude his various romantic pursuers by assuming various comic disguises. Like *Pygmalion*'s Galatea, Adonis finally tires of "this life of care and strife," and chooses to turn back into stone, asking that a placard be placed on him saying "Hands Off."

The songs for *Adonis* were composed by Rice and John Eller, with lyrics by Dixey and William F. Gill. Critics spoke highly of the score in its day, but as with *Evangeline*, none of the songs in *Adonis* enjoyed lasting popularity. The libretto was published, and the dialogue by William Gill is laden with puns and wisecracks. Groaners abound in this scene where two sisters quiz the newly humanized statue about what he has learned:

ADONIS: Now for Astronomy, all you have to do is slip on a piece of orange peel and you'll see all the stars the astronomers ever dreamt of.

PATTIE: Arithmetic? If you hire a plumber at ten shillings a day for twenty days, what will he have at the end of the time?

ADONIS: Your house and lot.

NATTIE: Music!

ADONIS: Ah, music hath charms to soothe the savage beast—that's why they put a brass band around a dog's neck.

NATTIE: In 3/4 time, how many beats are there in a bar?

ADONIS: That depends on the quality of the free lunch—and that concludes the first part of my entertainment.

Adonis was a precursor of American musical comedy, embodying a formula for success that would remain viable for the next six decades. During that period, almost every major musical hit on Broadway abided by this formula:

- A story—or casting gimmick—with intriguing comic possibilities: timeworn plot ideas could be revitalized by creative casting.
- One or more extraordinary performers, the more the better: while established stars were good to have, amazing new talent could be equally effective.
- Star vehicles (designed around the unique talents of a particular performer) could work, but only so long as the original star was on hand.
- An abundance of jokes, wisecracks, and sight gags was required to keep the action flowing between songs.
- The score had to be easy on the ear and have no offensive content. Hit songs were helpful at the box office, but not essential.
- Any relation between the plot and songs is unnecessary.

As far as we know, no one formalized these principles at the time, but people in show business intuited them and lived by them. Hollywood would unquestioningly abide by these principles when screen musicals came along in the late 1920s. Now and then, some writers and composers tried their damnedest to go beyond the standard formula. Most of these innovators didn't get very far, but those who succeeded opened the way to new developments in musical theatre.

Full-Length Pantomime

Lighthearted one-act pantomimes had been a regular feature on American stages since colonial times. Wordless clowning made the action easily accessible to children and the less literate, and some intellectual critics embraced the simplicity of the physical comedy. For a brief period in the mid-1800s, pantomime thrived as a popular form of full-length stage entertainment. The unchallenged master of this extended format was George L. Fox (1825–1877), whose breakout hit *Humpty Dumpty* (1868, 483 performances) ran on Broadway for more than a year, toured with extraordinary success, and enjoyed an ongoing series of revivals, sequels, and imitations.

Aside from wearing a baldpate and white facial makeup, Fox made no attempt to look like the walking egg in the classic nursery rhyme. A realistic egg costume would have interfered with the physical comedy that pantomime required. Audiences understood this convention. They also understood that pantomimes had no formal plotline. In the show, Humpty Dumpty and his Mother Goose playmates are transformed into harlequinade clowns, and then go aimlessly romping through such diverse settings as a candy store, an enchanted garden, and Manhattan's costly new City Hall building. With a lavish ballet staged by David Costa (choreographer of *The Black Crook*), there was plenty of visual spectacle to offset the knockabout humor. The score was sometimes credited to "A. Reiff Jr.," but it was a mish-mosh of recycled Offenbach and old music hall tunes. No one paid much attention to the songs, which were not even listed in the program— Fox's buffoonery was the main attraction.

In the published libretto to *Humpty Dumpty*, a brief introductory dialogue is followed by page after page of detailed stage directions, interrupted by the occasional song cue. In most musical stage librettos, dialogue and stage directions are kept separate, but in this case dialogue was so minimal that it was just inserted in the stage directions to save room. For example, at one point, the nursery rhyme hero Tommy Tucker asks Humpty to share an apple:

> HUMPTY bites off a very little piece and goes to put it in TOMMY's hand—thinks a second and concludes it is too big—bites another piece off the small piece, and lays it in TOMMY'S hand with an air of satisfied generosity. TOMMY looks at it and says, "Is this for me?" HUMPTY says, "Yes." TOMMY says, "Who is that big piece for?"— meaning the apple in HUMPTY's hand. HUMPTY says, "For me," and bows. TOMMY repeats, "This little piece for me?" HUMPTY laughs.

TOMMY draws back hand and fires piece of apple in HUMPTY's eye. HUMPTY picks piece of apple out of his eye and goes to throw it away. On second thought puts it in his mouth and chews away.

TOMMY tells OLD ONE TWO, who says, "We will fix him"—so he gives each one [of the villagers] a stuffed club. He gets at the head of the line—they all follow as close as possible. They advance to HUMPTY, who sees them coming, and just as OLD ONE TWO goes to hit him, HUMPTY jumps up very quick and runs off with big steps, laughing. With the force of the blow OLD ONE TWO falls across the chair. TOMMY and VILLAGERS mistake him for HUMPTY and they all commence to beat him unmercifully. He finally gets up off chair and beats and fights them all, off-takes chair up stage and goes in the cottage, rubbing his back and shaking his fist.

Fox made this nonsense work with his extraordinary physical dexterity and a colorful gallery of facial expressions. Whether lit up with joy or burdened with sorrow, his face made his emotions easy to see in even the largest theatres. Children and adults found him irresistible, and other pantomime troupes shamelessly boasted about how closely their lead clowns resembled and imitated Fox. He was happily married and well known for leading an abstemious private life, so colleagues were shocked when the great clown began showing signs of advanced syphilis. He started to interrupt performances with unexplained emotional breakdowns and incoherent monologues. Although family and friends tried to blame this behavior on the long-term effects of the harsh chemicals in Fox's white makeup, colleagues and the public soon caught on. After violently pelting an audience with props in November 1875, Broadway's first great comic star was forced into retirement. He died two years later at age fifty-two.

While many other performers imitated Fox, no one could replace him, and full-length pantomime soon disappeared from the American stage. However, Fox's unbridled style of low physical comedy survived in the routines of many American vaudeville and burlesque comics, keeping his spirit visible on musical theatre stages—and most memorably on silent screens—right into the next century.

4

Gilbert and Sullivan (1880–1900)—"Object All Sublime"

Few who saw Richard D'Oyly Carte (1844–1901) walking along London's Strand in 1875 would have guessed that he was planning a revolution. Walking was one of his favorite pastimes, and he did a lot of it. Flawlessly groomed and attired in a well-tailored suit, astrakhan-collared overcoat, and silk top hat, he looked like any other reputable British businessman. So what if his business was the theatre? He was a man of driving ambition, and such men were drawn to London at that time.

In the thirty-three years since Victoria had ascended the British throne, an aggressive foreign policy had expanded her domains until it could be honestly boasted that "the sun never sets on the British empire." At home, England spearheaded the industrial revolution, creating enormous wealth for the lucky few, newfound comfort and leisure for a burgeoning middle class, and newfound depths of squalor for the teeming working and under classes. The resulting social upheavals were reflected in British literature, where the ruthless social minuets of Jane Austen were replaced by the much harsher urban realities of Charles Dickens.

For all their power and wealth, the British seemed content with a rather low standard of musical-stage entertainment. As in the United States of America, extravaganzas and burlesques dominated the scene with improbable plots, leggy showgirls, and recycled popular songs. For musicals with original scores, one had to look almost exclusively to the imported works of Jacques Offenbach, which were popular despite clumsy translations and actors who considered it their duty to interpolate whatever comic business they could devise. Since London stage productions rarely ran for more than a few weeks, budgets were small and artistic standards were pathetic. Critics occasionally called for something better, but the few producers who attempted to oblige were unable to make any serious headway. The time was ripe for an artistic revolution—exactly the sort that Carte was contemplating.

A well-established booking agent for lecturers and concert artists, Carte was as meticulous in his business dealings as he was in matters of dress. His adeptness at negotiations won him the nickname "Oily Carte," and as a sometime composer, he had a natural empathy for people with artistic temperaments. In 1871, Carte attended a performance of *Thespis*, a Christmas season specialty hurriedly thrown together by the popular playwright William S. Gilbert (1836–1911) and England's most promising classical composer, Arthur S. Sullivan (1842–1900). The plot, which involved the aging gods of Olympus taking a vacation and temporarily handing their powers over to a troupe of actors, was very much in the Meilhac-Halévy *opera-bouffe* mode, but the presence of leggy chorus girls in tights suggests that it was also a burlesque. Critics reacted to the under-rehearsed production with little more than a shrug. When *Thespis* closed after a respectable sixty-three-performance run, Gilbert and Sullivan went their separate ways, thinking so little of *Thespis* that all copies of the score were lost.

Carte was convinced that this unsuccessful show pointed the way to a new British form of comic operetta, one that could match and even eclipse the continental version. In the wake of the Franco-Prussian War, the flow of hits from Paris was drying up. An enthusiastic British audience still existed for such works, so why not offer them a homegrown alternative?

Carte had individually approached both Gilbert and Sullivan to discuss his concept of a new kind of British musical theatre, and it seems that they were interested, but the pull of other commitments and a lack of ready funds kept this potential collaboration in limbo. Opportunity struck in 1875 when Carte was hired to manage a London production of *La Perichole*. At only two-acts, it was too short for the sort of full-length evening London theatregoers expected. Along with an afterpiece, a one-act "curtain raiser" was required. So Carte had a stage and a budget, but he also had an intimidating deadline. Could Gilbert and Sullivan come up with a new piece in just three weeks?

As it happened, Gilbert had a libretto ready to go. For some years, he had been publishing a series of comic poems in magazines, using his childhood nickname "Bab" as a *nom de plume*. One of these so-called Bab Ballads involved a jilted bride suing her former fiancé for "breach of promise of marriage"—a common legal proceeding in a society where most women relied on marriage as their only possible source of livelihood. Gilbert had already adapted his poem into a one-act libretto. While reading the text to Sullivan, Gilbert persuaded himself that the composer hated it, when in fact the opposite was true. To Gilbert's surprise, Sullivan accepted the piece, and the collaboration was on.

Three frantic weeks later, *Trial by Jury* (1875, 131 performances) premiered at the Royalty Theatre on March 25. At Gilbert's insistence, instead of typical stage costumes, the court officials appeared in genuine court robes, the bride wore a real wedding gown, and the courtroom setting was authentic in every detail. In this unusually realistic frame, Gilbert unleashed all sorts of outrageous behavior. The defendant flirts openly with every woman in the courtroom, and the jilted plaintiff shamelessly throws herself at the all-male jury. The judge has no qualms about telling the jury that he only rose to judicial prominence thanks to a propitious marriage "to a rich attorney's elderly, ugly daughter" who "may very well pass for forty-three in the dusk with the light behind her." When the litigants prove uncooperative, the judge settles the bothersome case by marrying the unwanted bride himself. This realistic piece turned reality upside down!

Barely thirty-five minutes in length, *Trial by Jury* is the only sung-through piece in the Gilbert and Sullivan canon, but it established several themes and basic character traits that would often appear in the team's future collaborations:

- *Topsy-turvydom*: the plot places accepted reality on its ear, to great comic effect.
- Realistic settings and costumes are used to make the topsy-turvydom all the funnier.

- Unqualified men have wheedled their way into high public office.
- The course of true love not only never runs smooth, but often runs in surprising directions.
- There is an appalling disdain for women over forty years of age.
- There is at least one word-heavy *patter song* for the lead comedian.
- Gilbert makes an unprecedented use of creative rhyme.

From the start, Gilbert's main characters are refreshingly human, well beyond the one-dimensional comic figures that filled musical stages at that time. Gilbert saw reality as an uneasy blend of sense and nonsense, and felt that the ridiculous was far more amusing when depicted in a realistic context. This viewpoint not only meant that the sets and costumes had to look like (or actually be) the real thing, but that the characters themselves had to have at least some of the contradictions and complexities of human beings. Consider the Judge in *Trial by Jury*, who has no real command of the law but obtains his position through marital influence. Such stories were not uncommon in Victorian England, where the right connections could make a career regardless of ability or experience. (Can we honestly pretend things are all that different today?) When this realistic character does the unthinkable and resolves the case by marrying the plaintiff, Gilbert ushers audiences into a topsy-turvy world only slightly removed from so-called reality.

Trial by Jury's jabs were so clean and good-natured that no one took offense. In an uncertain, repressive society, a musical spoofing the justice system would have been quickly silenced. Victorian Britain was at its political and financial peak, and could readily afford to laugh at itself. What John Gay began, Gilbert was able to fulfill, primarily because he could make fun of the system without directly attacking or angering those in power. Any government minister or Member of Parliament could enjoy a good chuckle over a fictional breach of promise case, as could any judge or attorney. Word of mouth kept business at the Royalty brisk for months. Many people came just to see this opening one-act, so to prevent *La Perichole* from playing to a half empty theatre, Carte moved Gilbert and Sullivan's piece to the end of the evening.

Carte cobbled together sufficient funds to form a producing partnership, but both Gilbert and Sullivan were very much in demand, a fact that would always put a strain on their attempts to work together.

Two and a half years after *Trial by Jury*, Carte took out a lease on
the Opera Comique, a handsomely appointed but peculiarly situated
London theatre that could only be entered via underground tunnels.
There, Gilbert and Sullivan's first full-length comic operetta *The
Sorcerer* (1877, 178 performances) opened to favorable notices. When
diminutive comic actor George Grossmith (1847–1912) was offered
the title role and protested that it should go to a "fine actor with a fine
voice," Gilbert replied, "That's precisely the sort of actor we don't
want." Grossmith's performance as John Wellington Wells, "a dealer
in magic and spells" hired to unleash a love potion on the inhabitants
of a small British village, made him a lasting, central figure in Carte's
repertory company. He was particularly adept at handling Gilbert's
challenging lyrics. As the magical Wells, he describes his business
this way:

> *We've a first-class assortment of magic;*
> *And for raising a posthumous shade*
> *With effects that are comic or tragic,*
> *There's no cheaper house in the trade.*
> *Love-philtre—we've quantities of it;*
> *And for knowledge if any one burns,*
> *We're keeping a very small prophet, a prophet*
> *Who brings us unbounded returns:*
> *For he can prophesy*
> *With a wink of his eye,*
> *Peep with security*
> *Into futurity,*
> *Sum up your history,*
> *Clear up a mystery,*
> *Humour proclivity*
> *For a nativity—for a nativity;*
> *He has answers oracular,*
> *Bogies spectacular,*
> *Tetrapods tragical,*
> *Mirrors so magical,*
> *Facts astronomical,*
> *Solemn or comical,*
> *And, if you want it, he*
> *Makes a reduction on taking a quantity!*

Gilbert's lyrics are always motivated by plot and character, but he used creative rhyme as no lyricist had before in English or any other language. His words are not just tools, but playthings that give the listener delight while simultaneously helping to tell the story. Sullivan set the above lyric to a catchy jiglike tune. All his melodies were designed to fit the dramatic needs of each scene and character. He certainly knew how to give his music the Offenbach-style bounce, but he could also command a tonal luster one did not usually find outside of grand opera. The resulting sound was rich, varied, and thoroughly entertaining.

The Sorcerer's healthy four-month run encouraged its authors to continue their collaboration with *H.M.S. Pinafore* (1878, 571 performances), a merry send-up of the British class system set on a naval warship. Gilbert was aware that many Victorians who shed sentimental tears whenever melodramas suggested that "love levels all ranks" would howl with outrage if a member of their own family actually considered marriage with someone from a lower social class. Once again taking inspiration from his Bab Ballads, Gilbert concocted the story of Captain Corcoran, a naval social climber who is delighted to arrange a match between his unwilling young daughter Josephine and the elderly Sir Joseph Porter, First Lord of the Admiralty and "ruler of the Queen's Navy." So long as Corcoran's daughter is "marrying up," he insists that love levels all ranks. However, he demands vengeance when his daughter tries to elope with the lowly sailor Ralph Rackstraw. True love's cause seems lost until it is revealed that the captain and the sailor were accidentally switched at birth. They instantly exchange their naval ranks, and since the First Lord will not stoop so low as to marry a common sailor's daughter, the girl is now free to marry the man whom she loves. In so doing, she will still manage to raise her rank a notch above her father's.

Contrary to legend, *Pinafore* opened to excellent notices, but a prolonged summer heat wave kept audiences away. With ticket sales averaging forty pounds a night, the cast took a thirty percent salary cut in an attempt to keep the show going. By a happy coincidence, Sullivan was conducting the popular Promenade Concert series at Covent Garden's Royal Opera House. Making practical use of a legitimate opportunity, he included a medley of tunes from *Pinafore* that scored an immediate success. The resulting boost in ticket sales, spurred on by a break in the weather, gave the show's box office a much-needed boost. *Pinafore* not only survived that long summer but carried on profitably through the next one—an astounding run for that time.

Gilbert and Sullivan's nautical nonsense did well in England, but that was nothing compared to the unexpected sensation it caused in the United States. While it must have been gratifying to know that there were dozens of American productions, the infuriating fact was that the show's creators saw none of the resulting profits. Due to the lack of international copyright agreements, American producers could stage a British show without paying royalties. These pirated productions could take unlimited liberties with the material, adding and deleting numbers and characters at will. But in spite of such revisions, Americans could not get enough of *H.M.S. Pinafore*. At one point, eight productions were simultaneously running on Broadway, and it is estimated that some fifty more appeared all across the United States— and no two were exactly alike. However, the songs and jokes became familiar all across the country, and one line in particular was quoted ad nauseam by Americans in every walk of life. When *Pinafore*'s Captain Corcoran sings that he's "never ever" sick at sea or prone to use foul language, his knowing crew asks:

CREW: What, never?

CAPTAIN: No, never.

CREW: What, never?

CAPTAIN: Well, *hardly* ever.

According to legend, one newspaper editor in New York called in his staff, pointed out that the "hardly ever" punch line had appeared twenty times in the previous day's paper, and angrily ordered, "Never let me see that line again." A reporter asked the inevitable, "What, never?" and the defeated editor replied, "Well, *hardly* ever."

In an attempt to beat the American theatrical pirates at their own game, Carte brought over Gilbert, Sullivan, and a full company to introduce New York to the original version of *H.M.S. Pinafore*. While there, they also planned to debut the team's newest work simultaneously in the United States and England, establishing clear legal copyright in both countries. Partway across the Atlantic, Sullivan discovered he had left his musical sketches for the first act at home, and so he was forced to reconstruct the score from memory. Back in Britain, Carte's touring company staged what must have been a fascinating single performance of the new operetta in the town of Paignton, using costumes and props from *Pinafore*. Although *The Pirates of Penzance* (1888, 91 performances in New York; 363 performances in London) debuted on opposite sides of the pond in slightly different versions, the discrepancies did nothing to dampen audience enthusiasm.

Sometimes called "*Pinafore* on land," *Pirates* is actually a more sophisticated work that aims its barbs at grand opera, social pretension, and the much-abused principle of duty. Frederic is an apprentice pirate who at age twenty-one strikes out on his own, announcing that he is bound by his social duty to wipe out his former comrades in nautical crime. The Pirate King accepts this, dismissing any suggestion that he give up his illegal profession because, "contrasted with respectability, it is comparatively honest." Finding a bevy of beautiful, young maidens on a beach, the pirates attempt to kidnap and marry the lot, but this plan is foiled by the girls' adoptive father, Major General Stanley. Later on, when it looks as if Frederic may actually succeed in exterminating his old friends, the Pirate King points out that the young man was apprenticed until his twenty-first birthday—and since he was born on Leap Year Day (February 29), he is technically duty-bound to remain their apprentice for another sixty years. The pirates handily defeat a band of timid policemen, but surrender meekly when the police sergeant invokes the authority of Queen Victoria, to whom all Englishmen—pirates included—owed duty.

Gilbert's dialogue could have as much fun with the English language as his well-rhymed lyrics. In the following exchange, the Pirate King and Major General Stanley stumble over the similar pronunciation of two common words:

GENERAL: I ask you, have you ever known what it is to be an orphan?

KING: Often!

GENERAL: Yes, orphan. Have you ever known what it is to be one?

KING: I say, often.

PIRATES: (Disgusted) Often, often, often! (Turning away)

GENERAL: I don't think we quite understand one another. I ask you, have you ever known what it is to be an orphan, and you say "orphan." As I understand you, you are merely repeating the word "orphan" to show that you understand me.

KING: I didn't repeat the word often.

GENERAL: Pardon me, you did indeed.

KING: I only repeated it once.

GENERAL: True, but you repeated it.

KING: But not often.

GENERAL: Stop! I think I see where we are getting confused. When you said "orphan," did you mean "orphan," a person who has lost his parents, or "often" frequently?

King: Ah! I beg pardon. I see what you mean. Frequently.

GENERAL: Ah, you said "often" frequently.

KING: No, only once.

GENERAL: (irritated) Exactly, you said "often" frequently, only once.

Unlike the forced puns found in most nineteenth-century stage dialogue, this word game still wins laughs from today's audiences.

How They Worked

Gilbert and Sullivan were both established masters in their separate fields, and both were therefore accustomed to getting their way. A sense of professional good will usually prevailed between them, with each creatively deferring to the other. On occasion, more serious disagreements developed, and Richard D'Oyly Carte or his secretary Helen Lenoir would act as mediators. The one creative authority that Gilbert and Sullivan recognized was the audience. After opening nights, they would still make substantial changes, deleting or revising material that did not clearly delight the public. They did not care if a performer lost a prized moment—in Gilbert and Sullivan's operettas, the only real star was the show itself.

William Gilbert was the son of a successful surgeon, raised in comfort and decently educated. An unsuccessful barrister, his comic writing began as a sideline but quickly became his life's work. His translations and original plays made him one of the most popular young playwrights in England. Gilbert spent weeks and sometimes months developing story ideas in leather bound notebooks, several of which are preserved at the Pierpont Morgan Library in New York City. These fascinating volumes show Gilbert starting with outlines that look very much like legal briefs, and then laboriously working out plot twists and characterizations in detailed notes that run on for dozens of pages. His dialogue and lyrics underwent frequent and sometimes radical revisions. He was never reluctant to toss out material that he felt was substandard.

Serving as his own director, Gilbert reinvented the art of stage direction for the musical theatre. Before he came on the scene, staging was usually handled by star performers out to glorify their own performances regardless of the material—librettos were considered disposable formalities. Gilbert took a more practical, text-based approach. Before rehearsals began, he worked out scenes on a model stage using small blocks of wood to represent the performers. By knowing exactly what he wanted in advance, Gilbert avoided the chaos found at standard rehearsals, and was able to give greater attention to dramatic and technical detail. Gilbert's most radical notion was that comic actors had to be serious no matter how ridiculous the material. For his brand of topsy-turvy to work, the performers had to act naturalistically.

Rehearsals for Gilbert's productions took six weeks, lasting from 11:00 A.M. until 4:00 P.M.—a challenging schedule for actors who were often simultaneously appearing in another production at night. He was demanding and energetic, and his natural sarcasm sometimes got the better of him. When a hefty actress tripped and landed on her rump during a rehearsal, Gilbert reportedly bellowed, "I knew you'd make an impression on the stage one day!" In most cases, he was more civil, and showed great patience in training cooperative performers to achieve the effects he desired. However, he sternly corrected any unauthorized attempts to add dialogue or stage business during a run. Gilbert always demanded clear diction, knowing that one missed word could kill a crucial laugh. He would sit in the upper gallery and make the cast rehearse a number or scene until every word came through clearly. Experienced actors were initially confused by this sort of whip cracking, previously unheard of in the slapdash world of British musical theatre.

Arthur Sullivan was born in Lambeth, the heart of cockney London. His father became bandmaster for the Royal Military College at Sandhurst, which proved to be the family's ticket out of poverty. As a boy, Arthur sang in the Chapel Royal choir and then studied at the Royal Academy of Music and the Leipzig Conservatory before launching his professional career as a composer and conductor. In his collaborations with Gilbert, he normally did not begin composing until the libretto was completed. Sullivan's genius was unquestioned, but he loved hobnobbing with the rich and powerful. The distractions of an active social life frequently interrupted his work, as did a series of chronic kidney and bladder ailments. However, the pressure of an impending premiere would inspire Sullivan to bursts of brilliant last-minute productivity. Some of his giddiest melodies were created while he suffered agonizing physical pain. Whatever condition he was in, Sullivan liked to conduct opening night performances, and on at least one of these occasions barely got through except thanks to heavy doses of coffee and morphine.

As a conductor, Sullivan set a new professional standard for musical performances in Great Britain. Trained on the continent, he knew the value of exact adherence to tempo, orchestration, and harmony, and demanded it from musicians and singers alike in a firm but courteous tone. If such standards were new to Britain's classical musicians, they were a genuine shock to anyone working in the theatre. Sullivan was the first person in England to take light music seriously, and he demanded the same of everyone playing or singing in productions of his works. However, he knew what it was like to struggle for a living and treated musicians and performers with the same gracious manners he affected when weekending with the aristocracy. Sullivan's gift for melody made him the foremost British composer of his day, and many critics and colleagues urged him to drop comic operetta and devote his time to "serious" composition. Although Sullivan instinctively agreed with such advice, his classical efforts brought only a small fraction of the income he received from his work with Gilbert. Having become accustomed to an expensive lifestyle, Sullivan was compelled to keep turning out light operas. Whatever his personal misgivings, millions of fans could not have been more delighted.

Glory Years: "Object All Sublime"

Gilbert and Sullivan hit their stride in the 1880s, with Carte providing almost as much innovation offstage as his authors did before the
footlights. During the year-plus run of *Patience* (1881, 578 performances), which poked fun at the more self-indulgent aspects of the
aesthetic movement, Carte moved his troupe into the newly built
Savoy Theatre, the first auditorium in Great Britain to feature electric lighting. As a precaution, gaslight was also installed. At the first
public performance, the auditorium's gas jets were lowered as the new
filament bulbs came on, giving a warm, noiseless, odorless glow that
delighted the audience. However, since electrical stage lighting was
still being developed, the cast of *Patience* continued to perform under
gaslight. In another revolution, Carte placed specific seat numbers on
all tickets, ending the age-old problem of customers scrimmaging for
unreserved seats.

Gilbert got his first chance to experiment with electrical stage
lighting in *Iolanthe* (1882, 398 performances in London), probably the most "English" of all the Gilbert and Sullivan operettas.
In it, an Arcadian shepherd defies the Lord Chancellor of England
to claim the hand of the chancellor's lovely young ward. This defiant act puts the chancellor and Britain's House of Peers at odds with
the shepherd's relatives, a platoon of female fairies. If this sounds like
The Black Crook, that's because Gilbert was deliberately spoofing the
use of fairies and other magical characters in pantomimes and extravaganzas. He took this gag all the way, having the fairy chorus wear
crowns of stars powered by hidden battery packs. There is a bit of
genuine sentiment when Iolanthe, the shepherd's fairy mother, risks
death by revealing that as she is the chancellor's long-lost wife, the
shepherd is consequently his son. The entire fairy chorus then con-
fesses that they have broken their magical law by marrying Peers. In a
final topsy-turvy touch, the fairy queen and chancellor join forces to
resolve the crisis, giving Gilbert a fresh chance to skewer his former
profession:

> QUEEN: You have all incurred death; but I can't slaughter the whole
> company! And yet (unfolding a scroll) the law is clear—every fairy
> must die who marries a mortal.

CHANCELLOR: Allow me, as an old Equity draftsman, to make a suggestion. The subtleties of the legal mind are equal to the emergency. The thing is really quite simple—the insertion of a single word will do it. Let it stand that every fairy will die who *doesn't* marry a mortal, and there you are, out of your difficulty at once.

QUEEN: We like your humor. Very well!

The fairy queen immediately marries a strapping guardsman and turns the Peers into fairies; then the entire cast flies off to Fairyland.

When Sullivan began complaining about Gilbert's "topsy-turvy" plots, the playwright took a very different approach with *Princess Ida* (1885, 246 performances in London), which was based on his already successful stage parody of a poem by Alfred Lord Tennyson. The dialogue was in verse form, and the plot involved a medieval princess eschewing the company of men in order to run a college for women. Hilarion, the foreign prince betrothed to Ida at birth, demands her hand, and a bloodless battle ends with the royal couple in love. The lush score was one of Sullivan's best, but critical carping and a punishing heat wave combined to make this show a disappointment at the Savoy box office. *Princess Ida* remains the caviar of Gilbert and Sullivan operettas, unknown to most but dearly admired by a dedicated and enlightened few.

Gilbert then offered yet another plot involving a *Sorcerer*-style magical lozenge, and a disgruntled Sullivan announced that he was no longer willing to write for the Savoy. Sullivan had received a knighthood in 1883 and was under greater pressure than ever to concentrate on so-called serious compositions. This high-handed attitude did not go over well with Gilbert, who refused to write librettos "on approval." The equal importance of words and music in operetta had led each collaborator to accommodate the other, and little resentments had accumulated over time. Carte was unable to effect a reconciliation, and for a few weeks it appeared that the partnership of Gilbert and Sullivan was over.

Legend suggests that Gilbert found inspiration when a Japanese ceremonial sword fell from the wall of his study. Taking advantage of the then-current craze for the culture and fashions of Japan, he came up with an extraordinary libretto. In *The Mikado* (1885, 672 performances in London), an imperial law that punishes flirting with a sentence of death inspires the residents of the Japanese town of Titipu to elevate Ko-Ko (a lowly tailor convicted for flirting) to be their Lord High Executioner—on the theory that he "cannot cut off another's head until he's cut his own off." When the Mikado demands an execution, Ko-Ko plans to behead Nanki-Poo, a wandering musician who has fallen in love with Ko-Ko's young ward, Yum-Yum. (Stick with me; this summary will make sense in the end.) Ko-Ko was planning to marry the girl himself, but he puts self-preservation first and lets the young lovers wed for a month, after which Nanki-Poo will be executed. Then it turns out that Nanki-Poo is actually the Mikado's son and has been masquerading to avoid marriage with Katisha, an unscrupulous and repellently ugly woman of the royal court who has falsely accused him of flirting. When Ko-Ko reluctantly wins Katisha's affections, Nanki-Poo is free to marry Yum-Yum, and everyone makes it to the final curtain in one piece.

Why did this giddy nonsense prove to be Gilbert and Sullivan's most popular work, and why has it retained that distinction for so many years? Gilbert's characters are improbable and yet entirely believable, providing a faux Japanese mirror that reflects Victorian Britain's social and political hypocrisies—many of which are familiar to every era and nation. For example, when all the other town officials of Titipu resigned to protest Ko-Ko's appointment, Pooh-Bah ("a nobleman of the highest rank") took on all their titles—and by this seemingly selfless act managed to collect all their salaries, as well as all the illegal payoffs that those positions attract. At one point, Ko-Ko asks for advice on how to pay for his upcoming wedding to Yum-Yum, and Pooh-Bah responds:

> Certainly. In which of my capacities? ... Speaking as your Private Secretary, I should say that, as the city will have to pay for it, don't stint yourself, do it well.... Of course you will understand that, as Chancellor of the Exchequer, I am bound to see that due economy is observed.... Oh, as your Solicitor, I should have no hesitation in saying "Chance it," if it were not that, as Lord Chief Justice, I am bound to see that the law isn't violated.... Of course, as First Lord of the Treasury, I could propose a special vote that would cover all expenses, if it were not that, as Leader of the Opposition, it would be my duty to resist it, tooth and nail. Or, as Paymaster General, I could so cook the accounts that, as Lord High Auditor, I should never discover the fraud. But then,

as Archbishop of Titipu, it would be my duty to denounce my dis-
honesty and give myself into my own custody as first Commissioner
of Police.... I don't say that all these distinguished people couldn't be
squared; but it is right to tell you that they wouldn't be sufficiently
degraded in their own estimation unless they were insulted with a very
considerable bribe.

Ko-Ko apologizes for Pooh-Bah's pompous behavior by saying,
"Don't laugh at him, he can't help it—he's under treatment for it"—a
line as timely in the twenty-first century as it was in the late nineteenth. Gilbert's lyrics are equally ageless, such as Ko-Ko's list of
likely victims for beheading:

> *As some day it may happen that a victim must be found,*
> *I've got a little list—I've got a little list*
> *Of society offenders who might well be underground,*
> *And who never would be missed who never would be missed!*
> *There's the pestilential nuisances who write for autographs—*
> *All people who have flabby hands and irritating laughs—*
> *All children who are up in dates, and floor you with 'em flat—*
> *All persons who in shaking hands, shake hands with you like that—*
> *And all third persons who on spoiling tête-à-têtes insist—*
> *They'd none of 'em be missed—they'd none of 'em be missed!*

Aside from strong characterization and lyrical wit, *The Mikado* boasts
one of Sullivan's richest outpourings of melody, from the breezy
opening men's chorus "If You Want to Know Who We Are," through
the egotistical introspection of Yum-Yum's solo "The Sun Whose
Rays Are All Ablaze," right through the triumphant grand finale
"For He's Gone and Married Yum-Yum." Every melody is a specific
tonal expression of the sentiments expressed in the lyrics. A particular highlight is the title character's sadistic comedy aria, explaining
that his "object all sublime" is "to let the punishment fit the crime" for
all evil-doers—including society gossips, quack physicians, amateur
singers, and even those who endlessly play billiards. Gilbert thought
so little of the song that he cut it after the final rehearsal, but an appeal
by the ensemble led him to restore it in time to stop the show on opening night at the Savoy. *The Mikado* became a permanent fixture of
the musical stage in Great Britain and the United States, and by 1900

translations had been produced in German, Danish, French, Russian, Hungarian, Czech, and Italian.

Whatever Gilbert and Sullivan offered immediately after such a tremendous success was doomed to suffer by comparison. Although *Ruddigore* (1887, 288 performances in London), a mock-melodrama featuring family curses and vampirism, was not their most brilliant work, it did not deserve the opening night cries from the upper balcony of "Bring back *The Mikado*!" Happily, no such complaints plagued *The Yeoman of the Guard* (1888, 423 performances in London), the most serious of the Savoy operettas. It is set in the Tower of London during the bloody reign of Henry VIII. Strolling player Jack Point loves fellow performer Elsie Maynard, but she falls for Colonel Fairfax, a condemned prisoner in the Tower. Plots and mistaken identities abound until a pardoned Fairfax marries Elsie, and Point collapses from heartbreak. Grossmith originally played the ending for laughs, giving a twitch to assure audiences that his character was quite alive, but when later actors chose to depict Point as dead, Gilbert approved, saying "the end of the opera should be a tragedy." Both Gilbert and Sullivan described this work as a personal favorite.

In 1889, Richard D'Oyly Carte introduced another innovation. Over the years, customers had complained that it was difficult to find a decent meal anywhere near the Savoy Theatre. Since the best dining establishments of that era were found in hotels, D'Oyly Carte built a hotel right next to the theatre. His plans called for so many bathrooms that the architect asked if amphibious guests were expected. The Savoy Hotel set new standards for luxurious accommodation, and its restaurant became home to the first after-theatre dinners. As of this writing, both the hotel and its restaurant remain world class institutions.

Just months after the hotel opened, the Savoy Theatre premiered *The Gondoliers* (1889, 554 performances). The plot involves two newlywed Venetian gondoliers being dragged away from their wives to rule an island kingdom. It seems one of them was born to be king of this revolution-torn country, and until a rather grand Spanish Inquisitor verifies who is who, both gondoliers must act as coregents. The true king (whichever one he is) was betrothed in infancy to marry the daughter of the Duke of Plaza Toro, an impoverished Spanish nobleman who finds extraordinary wealth by incorporating himself.

Thanks to a "switched at birth" gimmick reminiscent of *H.M.S. Pinafore*, the Duke's lowly drummer (who coincidentally loves the Duke's daughter) turns out to be the true king, and the relieved gondoliers are restored to their wives. *The Gondoliers* played a private command performance at Windsor Castle for Queen Victoria, who must have enjoyed the merry first act paean to the joys of being "a grand and glorious queen."

The Savoy operettas had the benefit of being tailored for Carte's repertory troupe, all handpicked by Gilbert. He mixed trained singers with actors who had little if any musical experience—claiming such people had "less to unlearn." Patter comedy roles were all fashioned for George Grossmith (Ko-Ko, Jack Point). Comic parts that required stronger singing went to character baritone Richard Temple (Dick Deadeye, the Pirate King, the Mikado) or the more physically imposing Rutland Barrington (Captain Corcoran, Pooh-Bah). Churlish matrons like Katisha or the Duchess of Plaza Toro were originally played by soprano Rosina Brandram, who got a rare chance to show off her natural beauty when she played Iolanthe. The younger female leads went to Jessie Bond, Leonora Braham, and an ongoing succession of new talents. Scotsman Durward Lely created many of the major tenor roles, including Nanki-Poo.

Final Bows and an Artistic Legacy

The tensions simmering in Gilbert and Sullivan's partnership finally exploded in 1890, when a worn section of carpeting in the Savoy Theatre's lobby had to be replaced. In accordance with their contract, Carte charged Gilbert and Sullivan for part of the cost. Gilbert refused to pay, Sullivan sided with Carte, and the ensuing discussion soon turned into a bitter quarrel. Over a question of five hundred British pounds, the collaboration that had given new life to the English musical theatre was snuffed out. Revivals kept Gilbert and Sullivan's hits before the public. After several years, hatchets were buried, and the teams turned out two more works. While *Utopia, Limited* (1893, 245 performances) and *The Grand Duke* (1896, 123 performances) had definite charms, neither attained anywhere near the popularity of the team's classic successes.

Weakened by years of poor health, Sullivan succumbed to severe bronchitis in 1900, dying at age fifty-eight. Gilbert enjoyed renewed popularity in the new century, finally receiving a long-awaited knighthood in 1907. In 1911, a seventy-four-year-old Gilbert suffered a fatal heart attack while saving a young woman from drowning in a pond on his country estate. After many years of illness, Richard D'Oyly Carte died in 1901. The D'Oyly Carte Opera Company continued first under the shrewd management of his wife Helen, then under his son Rupert and granddaughter Bridget. The company revived the best of Gilbert and Sullivan through most of the twentieth century in a repertory format, making frequent tours of Britain and the United States, and creating complete recordings of every work in "the canon." Financial woes forced the company to shut down in 1983, but Bridget D'Oyly Carte's will left seed money for a new troupe using the family name. Since 1988, the new company has staged popular revivals of Gilbert and Sullivan's works in Britain.

Gilbert and Sullivan's operettas were frequently revived on Broadway right through the twentieth century. In the 1930s, Broadway saw a battle between two jazz updates of a Gilbert and Sullivan favorite: *The Hot Mikado* and *The Swing Mikado*. In 1981, Kevin Kline, Rex Smith, Linda Ronstadt, and George Rose headed a thrilling centennial production of *The Pirates of Penzance* that ran on Broadway for more than a year, using new orchestrations and interpolating two songs from other works in the canon. A hyperkinetic but otherwise faithful Canadian staging of *The Mikado* garnered Tony Award nominations in 1987. The surprising thing about all of these acclaimed productions was that they left the original words and music essentially intact. After more than one hundred years, the works of Gilbert and Sullivan could still be thoroughly enjoyed in the form that the authors intended.

After Gilbert, the craft of lyric writing would never be the same. Many of the great lyricists of the future found crucial inspiration in his work. P. G. Wodehouse, Lorenz Hart, Cole Porter, Ira Gershwin, Alan Jay Lerner, E. Y. Harburg—all freely admitted that they studied Gilbert's lyrics and emulated his playful use of rhyme. Stephen Sondheim included an homage to Gilbert in *Pacific Overtures* (1976). The stage version of *Thoroughly Modern Millie* (2002) turned *Ruddigore*'s 115-year-old patter song "My Eyes Are Fully Opened" into a fresh showstopper.

The legacy of Gilbert and Sullivan reaches far beyond the realm of the professional stage. From the 1880s onward, Carte made performance rights for their works available to schools and amateur groups in the United States of America and the British Empire. This availability simultaneously encouraged the development of amateur musical theatre and set a high standard for the types of works such groups could present. In the twenty-first century, amateur groups continue to present hundreds of Gilbert and Sullivan productions annually in all English-speaking countries. Whenever young actors rediscover *The Pirates of Penzance* or *The Mikado*, it is a fitting living tribute to Gilbert, Sullivan, and Carte—the first men in the English-speaking world to take the art of musical theatre seriously.

Aftermath

In the United States, the success of Gilbert and Sullivan raised audience expectations. Wit and melodic sophistication were now demanded, and a number of writers and producers sought to blatantly imitate the Gilbert and Sullivan model. John Phillip Sousa turned his hand to composing comic operettas, most notably *El Capitan* (1896, 112 performances), which is primarily remembered for its popular march. Unfortunately, Sousa's works were saddled with mediocre librettos, and soon faded into obscurity.

Composer Reginald DeKoven (1861–1920) and librettist Harry B. Smith (1860–1936) enjoyed modest success with *The Begum* (1887, 22 performances), which offered a Gilbert-style topsy-turvy plot and featured characters like "Myhnt-Jhuleep" and "Howja-Dhu." The same team found a more lasting hit with *Robin Hood* (1891), an operetta based on the popular legend of a British Saxon nobleman who steals from the rich Normans and gives to the poor. Frequently revived for the next half century, its sentimental ballad "Oh Promise Me" became a favorite at weddings. Although DeKoven was the first American to attain substantial wealth composing for the musical stage, his shows and songs have been largely forgotten. Smith remained a leading librettist and lyricist for decades to come. He was not a great poet, but wrote with amazing speed, making him a prized collaborator at a time when Broadway needed dozens of new musicals each season. His credits eventually included more than a hundred and twenty Broadway musicals, including collaborations with Victor Herbert and Jerome Kern, so you will find more on this man's work in chapters to come.

In London, manager George Edwardes (1855–1915) interrupted the usual schedule of burlesques at his Gaiety Theatre to present *Dorothy* (1886, 931 performances), a comic operetta about a young noblewoman who disguises herself as a milkmaid to win the affections of a rakish aristocrat. With a tuneful score by Carte's longtime musical director Alfred Cellier (1844–1891), *Dorothy* managed a then-astounding two-and-a-half-year run, far outdistancing all of Gilbert and Sullivan's original productions. However, despite a tuneful score, this work is no longer performed today.

Six years later, Edwardes stumbled upon a slightly different formula for theatrical success. Beginning with *The Gaiety Girl* (1893, 413 performances)—which by an ironic twist was not presented at the Gaiety Theatre—he produced a series of book musicals that alternated between two basic plots: either an impoverished young woman loves an aristocrat and wins him against all odds, or a young woman of means tries to escape an unwanted marriage and leads other characters on a chase through some colorful locale. Everything was always resolved happily just before the final curtain. The scores bore a certain tuneful but forgettable resemblance, as did the titles—*The Shop Girl, The Geisha, The Quaker Girl, My Girl, The Circus Girl, The Utah Girl, A Runaway Girl* ... each a variation on the same basic theme. And that is exactly the way the critics and public in Britain wanted it. Since Edwardes presented most of these "Girl" shows at his home theatre, they are sometimes referred to as "The Gaiety Musicals."

Edwardes called these shows *musical comedies*, leading some scholars to incorrectly credit him with inventing something that others (under the label *musical farce*) had already established on Broadway a decade earlier. But although the "Girl" shows proved to be profitable on both sides of the Atlantic, the first creators of musical comedy were American lads whose shows were so specifically attuned to a New York audience that they had little appeal outside of that city.

5

The Birth of Musical Comedy (1880–1899) — "It Belong'd to My Father Before I Was Born"

W hat's in a name? Offenbach called his works "operettes" and "opera-bouffes" while Gilbert and Sullivan referred to their creations as "comic operas." Early American musicals were advertised as everything from "burlettas" to "extravaganzas." Indistinct labels can cause confusion, even among theatre historians, some of whom claim that British producer George Edwardes invented *musical comedy*. To support this view, these scholars insist that the 1891 Broadway hit *A Trip to Chinatown* does not count, nor does a popular series of New York shows that starred Ned Harrigan and Tony Hart in the 1880s. After all, those works were labeled "musical farces," which means they were not musical comedies, right?

If we take the phrase *musical comedy* at its face value—literally, a comic drama that makes substantial use of original songs as a storytelling element—then there is no quantifiable difference between Edwardes's *The Geisha* (1896) and Harrigan and Hart's *Mulligan Guard's Picnic* (1878). Both use original, popular-style songs (as opposed to the more ambitious operatic-style melodies found in operetta) to help dramatize comic stories. Some productions before Harrigan and Hart billed themselves as musical comedy, but as of this writing no scripts have been found to verify the classification. Working from the evidence in hand, it seems that Harrigan, Hart, and composer David Braham were the first to establish musical comedy as a genre. They were also the first people to inject mainstream musical theatre with the comic energy of variety and its descendant, vaudeville. So let's start with a brief examination of vaudeville and the contribution it would make to the development of musical theatre.

Vaudeville

In the last two decades of the nineteenth century, the United States was not yet a world-class power, but it was on a breathtaking ascent. The Industrial Revolution born in Europe had ignited change all across America, hurtling that nation's economy into previously unimagined growth and drawing hopeful multitudes to new jobs in major cities. As of the 1880s, the majority of Americans lived in large towns and cities. New York City is just one example. According to official census figures, between 1880 and 1910, the population skyrocketed from 1.2 million to 4.7 million. Those new millions included not only masses of immigrants from all over the world, but millions of rural Americans happy to abandon the crushing drudgery of farm life. Urban life was no panacea, but with all its new challenges came one major advantage: after toiling all week long in offices, sweatshops, and factories, many for the first time in their lives had weekly leisure time and a few disposable dollars.

A large portion of this growing urban audience consisted of women, and whether they were factory girls, office staffers, or housewives, these ladies did not consider saloons and honky-tonk variety shows a viable option. The entertainment industry was only too happy to cater to this new paying audience, even going so far as to evolve a new genre to meet the demand.

On October 24, 1881, veteran variety performer Tony Pastor (1832–1908) presented the first commercially successful "clean variety" bill at his theatre on New York's Fourteenth Street. Pastor offered a new selection of acts each week, with reserved seats going for fifty cents. He often appeared onstage himself, singing such sentimental favorites as "The Band Played On." Pastor held all acts to a rigorous standard of decency, and word of mouth soon attracted a large, devoted audience that included all classes and age groups—and most importantly, all sexes. In a major break with variety tradition, booze was banned from the premises. Women attended without fear of offense and brought along the children for matinees. Pastor's theatre was located near Union Square, the city's premiere theatre and shopping district at that time, and a suitable destination for even the most proper spectators.

It was inevitable that such a promising business idea would attract copycats. In 1883, Boston entrepreneurs Benjamin F. Keith and Edward F. Albee took the fortune that they had accrued from staging unauthorized productions of Gilbert and Sullivan hits and opened a theatre that boasted a clean variety program presented several times a day. They called this *vaudeville* (French slang meaning "songs of the town") and would forever insist that they invented the genre—but contemporaries knew better. Pastor's mistake was that he stuck to one small theatre in New York. Keith and Albee spread out from Boston, building or buying a chain of theatres in cities all across the northeastern United States.

Soon, other major vaudeville chains were built all across the country by such managers as Alexander Pantages, Sullivan and Considine, and Marcus Loew. More than 25,000 people performed in vaudeville over its fifty-plus years of existence, working their way through the three levels defined by the trade newspaper *Variety:*

- *Small time*: small-town theatres and cheaper venues in larger towns. Performers made as little as $15 a week, but eventually up to $75. These often-crude theatres were the training ground for new performers, or a place where old-timers on the skids could eke out a few final seasons.
- *Medium time*: good theatres in a wide range of cities, offering salaries of up to a few hundred dollars a week. Performers seen here were usually either on the way up or on the way down. Some performers insisted that "medium time" was a fiction, and that there was only small time or ...
- *Big time*: the finest theatres in the best cities, using a two-performance-a-day format. Most big time acts earned hundreds per week, with headliners commanding a thousand dollars or more.

The number of performances per day varied from circuit to circuit, ranging from two a day in the big time theatres to six or more in some small time dives. These circuits generated an ongoing demand for performers who traveled the nation for months at a time. Women, uneducated immigrants, the poor—anyone with determination and a talent to entertain could earn a respectable living. In 1919, when the average factory worker earned less than $1,300 a year, small time Keith circuit performers playing a standard forty-two-week season could easily make $3,150. A few big time stars could make that much in a single week. Even before the introduction of income tax, deductions had to be made. Ten percent of each performer's salary went to his or her agent, with managers and booking agents taking further cuts. Over time, Keith and Albee bullied their way into controlling the bookings for most of the major vaudeville circuits, and every performer had to pay Keith and Albee an added booking fee for each engagement—the equivalent of employees giving the boss a kickback for the privilege of being hired. This centralization gave Keith and Albee extraordinary power over all aspects of the genre. Performers who complained or misbehaved could be blacklisted out of the business.

B. F. Keith, a man of few words, is remembered for one quote: "I never trust a man I can't buy." Even so, he was almost benign compared to Albee, who took full control of the Managers Association after Keith's retirement in 1909. Albee ruled vaudeville's golden age with an iron hand. No one could afford to have him as an enemy, and no one considered him a friend.

A vaudeville show could be almost any length, but the ideal big time show consisted of approximately eight acts presented in two and a half hours. Acts could be anything from song and dance routines to various specialties such as jugglers, plate spinners, regurgitators, and so on—in short, anything that might beguile an audience for fifteen minutes or so. Every Monday morning, theatre managers placed a billboard in front of the house, listing the featured performers for the upcoming week. The top slot on the "bill" went to the star or "headliner," with all other acts listed in order of perceived popularity. Over time, the order of appearance in a vaudeville performance came to follow a set order:

1. The first spot usually went to a nonverbal or "silent" act (acrobats, animal tricks, etc.) that would not compete with the bustle of the audience as it settled in.
2. Next came a set of singing sisters (the Gumm Sisters) or dancing brothers (the Nicholas Brothers). Some of these acts were genuine siblings, and some just pretended to be.
3. Third spot was a skit or one-act play. This could be the work of an unknown or a top writer, and it was not unusual for top actors

such as Sarah Bernhardt, Ethel Barrymore, or Walter Hampden to tour the vaudeville circuits.

4. A novelty act (sword swallower, eccentric dancer, etc.) would be thrown in to change the pace.
5. The first half ended with either a rising or falling star act, followed by an intermission.
6. The second act opened with a "big act" that required an elaborate set or bandstand, such as a choir or novelty orchestra.
7. The crucial "next to closing" spot went to the star act whose name headlined the billboard. These headliners were usually vocalists or comedians, and the most famous of them became show business legends.
8. When the star act was done, the closing spot was reserved for a boring short film or a particularly annoying live act (one man bands, etc.) that might encourage patrons to leave and open up seats for the next performance.

Vaudeville provided a template for the Broadway revues of the early twentieth century. More importantly, vaudeville's comedians, dancers, and singers would play a direct role in reshaping the musical theatre. After all, who knew audiences and the ways of the theatre as vaudevillians did? Their classroom was the stage itself, where they had learned by doing. Two or more shows a day taught performers how to evoke anything from laughter to tears, and competition forced them to grab an audience's attention quickly and hold it as long as possible. Vaudeville's performers and writers had to contend with a nationwide audience, one that stretched far beyond New York's city limits. That is why variety and vaudeville veterans shaped Broadway's earliest musical comedies as populist entertainment aimed at the common man and woman, giving the new, vast working class a cultural voice.

Harrigan and Hart

In 1870, two variety comics met while having their shoes polished at a sidewalk stand in Chicago. Edward "Ned" Harrigan (1844–1911) was a seasoned veteran looking for a new act, and Anthony J. Cannon was a reform school escapee trying to get a start in the business. The two sensed a common bond, and the conversation soon moved to Harrigan's rooms, where they compared jokes, sang a few songs, and decided to form a comedy team. Anxious to make a fresh start, Cannon changed his name to Tony Hart (1855–1891).

From the start, Hart's youthful, charismatic exuberance played well against Harrigan's technical expertise. Audiences responded to the duo with such enthusiasm that Harrigan, who had little previous experience as a writer, was inspired to turn out a series of sketches that allowed the team to spoof various classes and racial groups. They struck pay dirt with their ten minute "Mulligan Guard" routine, which lampooned the paramilitary volunteer militias that had plagued major American cities since the mid-nineteenth century. Ostensibly formed so that men could practice the arts of marching and shooting during peacetime, many of these groups became little more than weekend drinking clubs, with politicians providing members with free liquor in exchange for their support at election time. "Drills" often ended with drunken units staggering through the streets and causing general mayhem. Since many public officials relied on the votes of militia members, little was done to curb this behavior.

Harrigan cast himself as the lone trooper of such a brigade, with Hart as its commander. Both used broad Irish brogues and sported ill-fitting uniforms. In a classic "dumb and dumber" combination, Hart spouted befuddled drill instructions that Harrigan responded to with disgruntled wisecracks and inebriated ineptitude.

> TONY: Attention, by the left, no, no I mean the right. (Pulls out book.) What the devil does the manual say about it. Shoulder arms. (NED drills awkwardly.) You haven't it, you haven't it. Put it down, put it down.
>
> NED: It's not the way we drilled last year.
>
> TONY: It's the new style.

The act climaxed with "The Mulligan Guard March," which described a typical day of drilling on Manhattan's Lower East Side:

> *We shouldered arms, and marched and marched away,*
> *From Baxter Street, we marched to Avenue A.*
> *With drums and fifes how sweetly they did play*
> *As we marched, marched, marched in the Mulligan Guards.*

Harrigan's lyrics may not look like much, but the ear-catching tune by composer David Braham (1938–1905) and the physical antics provided by Harrigan and Hart made the song and the act a sensation. After months of acclaim on the road, they brought the act to Harrigan's home turf in New York City, where popular demand turned a one-week variety engagement into an open-ended run. Harrigan provided new sketches and characters, but audiences always demanded and got "The Mulligan Guard March" before the show was done. Over time, Harrigan's sketches grew in length and scope, featuring songs with music by Braham. The forty-minute long *Mulligan Guard Picnic* (1878, 40 performances) ran at Broadway's Theatre Comique for a full month, a healthy commercial run for that time. It became the first in what would be a series of farcical musical comedies starring Harrigan and Hart.

Aside from performing, the versatile Harrigan produced, directed, and wrote the book and lyrics for these shows. There was no sign of the girls in tights one found in burlesque. The action in Harrigan's musicals was realistically set on the scruffy streets of downtown Manhattan, with the author playing politically ambitious Irish saloon owner Dan Mulligan and Hart winning praise in a variety of supporting roles, including the African American washerwoman Rebecca Allup. The series followed the misadventures of Mulligan and his Irish cronies, who inevitably found themselves at odds with German butcher Gustav Lochmuller (whose son forms a *Romeo and Juliet*–style romance with Mulligan's daughter Cornelia) or the African-American Skidmore Guard. These clashes often come to a head in open brawls that Harrigan's scripts indicate with a simple one-word stage direction—"melee."

Harrigan took things a step beyond mere stereotype by investing his characters with touches of genuine humanity. The plots focused on such real-life problems as interracial tensions and political corruption. Since every major ethnic group was treated as fair game, nobody took offense, and there was always enough physical humor to keep everyone laughing. *The Mulligan Guard Ball!* (1879, 152 performances) launched the team onto a new level of popularity. Their shows were embraced by New York's immigrant-based lower and middle classes, who loved seeing themselves depicted realistically on stage. Powerful politicians anxious to curry the favor of lower class voters made a point of showing up too, turning Harrigan and Hart's opening nights into major social events.

While Harrigan's dialogue relied on puns and ethnic dialect to win laughs, his lyrics featured a timely mix of street smarts and blatant sentiment. The songs had no more than a peripheral connection to the plot, so favorites from previous productions could be interpolated, particularly the ever-popular "Mulligan Guard March." But Harrigan and David Braham kept new hits coming. In *Cordelia's Aspirations* (1883, 176 performances), "My Dad's Dinner Pail" glorified a working man's lunch box. Note the use of an Irish-American dialect in the lyrics:

> *Preserve that old kettle, so blacken'd and worn,*
> *It belong'd to my father before I was born,*
> *It hung in a corner, beyant on a nail,*
> *'Twas an emblem of labor was Dad's dinner pail.*
>
> *It glisten'd like silver, so sparkling and bright,*
> *I am fond of the trifle that held his wee bite.*
> *In summer or winter, in rain, snow or hail,*
> *I've carried that kettle, my Dad's dinner pail.*

Ned and Tony rarely took their productions on tour because they aimed exclusively at an audience of 1880s working-class New Yorkers, using street slang and topical humor that would be confusing outside of the city and indecipherable to most modern day listeners. Although songs and scenes from Harrigan and Hart's shows retain a great deal of period charm, the shows themselves are not revivable.

Over the course of seven years, Harrigan and Hart became a New York institution, but the "merry partners" were such inherently different men that severe disagreements were perhaps inevitable. The budget-conscious Harrigan was appalled at Hart's habit of spending every dollar the moment it was made. Harrigan's habit of hiring relatives left Hart resentful, and there were the inevitable squabbles over the size of roles. When the Theatre Comique burned down in late 1884, it was discovered that no one had bothered to take out fire insurance. Harrigan and Hart's troupe quickly resumed performing elsewhere, but a bitter blame game went on behind the scenes. Months later, no official reason was given when Hart announced that he was striking off on his own. The public outcry was such that the mayor tried to personally mediate the dispute, but the decision proved irrevocable, and Harrigan and Hart shared their final joint bow in the summer of 1885.

Tony Hart's career was soon cut short by the unmistakable effects of advanced syphilis, a disease that was all too common among actors at that time. Forced into an asylum, he died at age thirty-six. Ned Harrigan remained popular until his retirement from the stage in 1892, and although he had penned dozens of dramas and comedies, he would always be best remembered for the seventeen "plays with music" he wrote and costarred in with Hart. At the time, no one seems to have noticed that Harrigan and Hart had given birth to a new genre. Farcical musical comedies remained popular over the next decade as a steady stream of them reached Broadway.

Hit Songs and Great Clowns

By the 1890s, most of the music publishing firms in New York City had set up shop on a small stretch of West 28th Street. On warm days when windows were left open, the sound of countless songwriters pounding away on worn-out pianos raised a din that one journalist compared to the sound of a thousand housewives banging tin pans in their kitchens. This neighborhood thus came to be known as Tin Pan Alley, a nickname that came to symbolize American popular music for decades to come.

In the late nineteenth century, farcical musical comedy followed Harrigan's model, with loose plots involving ordinary people (as opposed to aristocrats or fantasy figures), using plenty of sight gags and pun-filled dialogue. It was not unusual for several teams of songwriters to contribute to any given score. Some shows seemed to be built as showcases for hit songs, strengthening the obvious relationship between the theatre and the music publishing industry. After all, it didn't take a genius to see that hit songs helped to sell tickets to musicals, and vice versa. When *A Trip to Chinatown* (1891, 657 performances) was in rehearsal, producer-playwright Charles Hoyt (1860–1900) realized that his flimsy story of a widow who inadvertently maneuvers several young suburban couples into a big city restaurant where a rich man loses his wallet before true love wins out (did someone say *Hello, Dolly!*?) was little more than a series of vaudeville gags masquerading as a libretto. It needed great songs to boost its audience appeal. Hoyt and composer Percy Gaunt contributed "Reuben and Cynthia" ("Reuben, Reuben, I've been thinking") and "The Bowery," a musical recollection of a night on New York's most infamous avenue:

> *I had walk'd but a block or two,*
> *When up came a fellow, and me he knew;*
> *Then a policeman came walking by,*
> *Chased him away, and I asked him why.*
> *"Wasn't he pulling your leg?," said he.*
> *Said I, "He never laid hands on me!"*
> *"Get off the Bow'ry, you Yap!," said he.*
> *I'll never go there anymore.*
>
> *The Bow'ry, the Bow'ry!*
> *They say such things,*
> *And they do strange things*
> *On the Bow'ry! The Bow'ry!*
> *I'll never go there anymore!*

Sometime after the show opened, Hoyt called on veteran Tin Pan Alley songwriter Charles Harris, who provided "After the Ball"—a song that became so synonymous with the 1890s that it would be reprised thirty-six years later in *Show Boat*. As these three songs became immediate favorites, their popularity helped *A Trip to Chinatown* set a long-running record, which would stand unchallenged on Broadway for more than two decades. Those songs are still heard occasionally today, which is more than can be said for any of the "sophisticated" songs heard in imported British musical comedies of that era.

Since it has always been impossible to guarantee a hit-laden score, musical comedies of this period also relied on the popularity of comic stars. When the British-born *Erminie* (1885, 154 performances in London) came to Broadway (in 1886, for more than 680 performances), its tale of two thieves who kidnap a young bride for ransom and thereby inadvertently save her from a dreaded marriage did not prove to be as appealing as the performance of Francis Wilson (1854–1935) as one of the hapless thieves. Unlike most stage clowns of the time, Wilson relied on detailed characterization as well as physical buffoonery. The producer kept underestimating *Erminie*'s popularity with New York audiences, and repeatedly sent it out on tour only to bring it back again after a few months. This piecemeal run eventually totaled well over six hundred performances. Even though *Erminie*'s score included no lasting hits, the show was revived as often as Wilson was willing to return in his original role, which he played into the 1920s. Much loved by his colleagues, Wilson helped organize the Actors Equity Association and served as the union's first president.

One of the first American stage hits to travel successfully to Britain was *The Belle of New York* (it ran in 1897 in New York through 56 performances, and in London in 1898 played through 697 performances). This story of a Salvation Army girl who must save her millionaire boyfriend from being disinherited ran for a disappointing seven weeks on Broadway. With minor tweaking and American actress Edna May still in the lead, a London production ran for nearly two years. The British so thoroughly took the show to their hearts that it received nine West End revivals over the next four decades. The tuneful songs, popular in their day, are now forgotten, and the show never found an audience in the United States. This is the kind of show many people think of as "Gay 90s" entertainment—lighthearted musical comedy with a touch of innocent romance, all designed to showcase lovely young women in lavish but at times moderately immodest costumes.

Far more typical were a series of spoofs starring Broadway's reigning musical clowns of the 1890s, Joseph Weber (1867–1942) and Lew Fields (1867–1941). They met as schoolboys on New York's Lower East Side, formed a comedy team, and worked on various variety and vaudeville circuits. Weber and Fields became vaudeville's definitive "Dutch" act (a corruption of "Deutsch") playing a pair of bewhiskered German immigrants with broad accents, bristling whiskers, and garish clothes, with the diminutive, heavily padded Weber as simpleminded "Mike," and the taller Fields as the conniving "Meyer." The act invariably began with Fields pushing his partner onto the stage, with Weber squealing, "Don't pooosh me, Meyer, don't pooosh me!" Both characters spoke fractured English—

WEBER: I am delightfulness to meet you!

FIELDS: Der disgust is all mine!

Some sources credit Weber and Fields with originating the classic joke:

> WEBER: Who vas dat lady I seen you wid last night?

> FIELDS: Dat vass no lady! Dat vass mine vife!

In the course of their banter, one would offend the other, and verbal insults quickly turned into all-out physical battles. After becoming one of the most imitated acts in vaudeville, Weber and Fields opened their own Broadway Music Hall in 1896, where they produced a popular series of musicals burlesquing theatrical hits and current events. The scores used parodies of existing songs, augmented by some original tunes, so there is some disagreement as to whether these productions should be classified as burlesques or musical comedies. The full-length Weber and Fields send-ups included such titles as *Cyranose de Bric-a-brac* (1899), and *Quo Vass Iss.* These comical parodies did so much to strengthen ticket sales for their comic targets that producers openly encouraged Weber and Fields to mock the hits. It helped that the team often worked with Julian Mitchell (1854–1926), the first important director and choreographer of Broadway musicals. A former chorus dancer, Mitchell was forced to give up performing when he lost his hearing. As a director, he became known for coordinating people, props, settings, and movement to create compelling stage pictures. Unfazed by deafness, he would sit on a piano to sense the beat of a song, and stand shoeless on a stage to feel the rhythm of his dancers. A cruel and probably apocryphal story tells of a set piece crashing backstage during a rehearsal, prompting Mitchell to shout, "Which one of you girls is off the beat?"

Weber and Fields also produced a series of shows that combined one-act musical spoofs with a collection of vaudeville acts. With nonsensical titles like *Hoity Toity* (1901, 225 performances) and *Higgeldy Piggeldy* (1904, 185 performances), these events—which fans and journalists sometimes referred to as "the Weberfields shows"—offered the duo in their trademark slapstick routines while showcasing all-star lineups of musical comedy headliners, including comic baritone DeWolf Hopper (1858–1935), feisty contralto Fay Templeton (1865–1939), and the legendary soprano Lillian Russell (1861–1922). Already a major operetta star, Russell reached the height of her popularity in these zany musicals. Surviving recordings suggest that her popularity rested on something other than her uncertain soprano voice. Her generous hourglass figure and exquisite facial features made her one of the first "professional beauties" of the new photographic age. Americans thrilled to stories of Russell's colorful nightlife, dressed to the nines and eating mammoth meals at Rector's, Luchow's, or other Broadway eateries while hefty socialite "Diamond" Jim Brady drank champagne from her slipper.

While Russell thrilled the public with her offstage glamour, she was still expected to give audiences their money's worth on stage, and that required a constant stream of new high-quality material. For *Whirl-a-Gig* (1899, 264 performances), Weber and Fields called on songwriter John Stromberg, who had already written several hit numbers for Russell. Stromberg repeatedly delayed delivery of the star's big solo, insisting that it wasn't ready. Shortly before the opening, the composer, who was suffering from an agonizing illness, was found dead by his own hand, supposedly with the completed song in his pocket. The press made much of this now-legendary incident. When Russell broke down on opening night while singing the song, "Come Down My Evenin' Star," she won the audience's sympathy and a new set of headlines. It's impossible to say whether this collapse was genuine emotion or at least partially calculated, but the public was so entranced that for the rest of Russell's career, her stage appearances were not complete until she reprised the song.

With a relatively small theatre and several hefty star salaries to pay, Weber and Fields could only make so much from their string of burlesque musical hits. The team broke up in 1904, and each enjoyed a lucrative series of successes before staging a final reunion in *Hokey Pokey* (1912, 108 performances), which also marked Lillian Russell's last Broadway run. Weber and Fields independently carried on as performers and producers of musical comedies, recognizing that there was no longer a place on Broadway for their kind of burlesque. A new attitude now prevailed in musical theatre, one attuned to the increasing speed of a new century.

"The Show Business" Becomes Big Business

From its inception, American entertainment had been what is now described as a cottage industry. Theatres were individually owned and managed, with small town managers relying on booking agents in

New York to keep their stages filled from week to week. This system was rather chaotic, but if a performer had a bad experience with any particular theatre owner or booking agent, there were still many others to work for. This system changed with the appearance of Abraham Lincoln Erlanger (1860–1930) and Marcus Klaw (1858–1936), who saw how corporate monopolies profited from a centralization of power and resources, and came up with a similar scheme for theatrical bookings. In August 1896, Klaw and Erlanger joined with theatre managers Charles Frohman, A. I. Hayman, S. F. Nixon, and J. F. Zimmerman to organize the Theatrical Syndicate, which controlled the bookings for more than seven hundred legitimate theatres all across the United States. A few hearty souls managed to resist the syndicate, including Weber and Fields, who performed exclusively in the few remaining independent venues.

Erlanger's flair for handling the complexities of nationwide bookings made him the dominant partner, as well as the most powerful man in the American commercial theatre for the next two decades. Producers, agents, writers, and actors relied on his tender mercies for their livelihood. Anyone who challenged his authority or protested at his harsh tactics was forced out of the business. Small in stature, Erlanger liked to draw comparisons between himself and Napoleon Bonaparte, but people in the business tended to describe him in less flattering terms. Librettist Guy Bolton later offered this description:

> "It was as though nature had said to itself, 'I'll make a toad,' and then halfway through had changed its minds and said, 'No, by golly, I'll make a czar of the American theatre.'"

Klaw and Erlanger's shameless greed made them countless enemies. On the upside, they built some of Broadway's finest theatres, including the New Amsterdam and the St. James (originally called the Erlanger), and played vital roles in financing early productions by George M. Cohan and Florenz Ziegfeld. It seems even the most hateful people can prove useful when there's a profit to be made.

Early Black Musicals

Several pioneers managed to establish an African-American presence on Broadway during the late nineteenth and early twentieth centuries.

Up until that time, minstrelsy had been America's only professional stage outlet for black talent, so it made sense that the earliest black musicals came out of the minstrel tradition, bringing along minstrelsy's exuberance and melody, as well as some of its racist conventions. The first noteworthy black musical seen in New York was *The Creole Show* (1890), an all-black minstrel troupe that featured a female interlocutor, as well as several women in what would traditionally have been an all-male ensemble. Relatively little is known about this landmark show, which is often overlooked by historians because it played in a theatre outside of the established Broadway theatre district.

Inspired by the success of *A Trip to Chinatown*, black songwriter Bob Cole (1861–1911) created *A Trip to Coontown* (1898, 8 performances), the story of con artist Jimmy Flimflammer's attempts to steal an old man's pension. The first full-length New York musical comedy written, directed, and performed exclusively by blacks, this show—like its title—was saddled with minstrel stereotypes. It toured extensively and enjoyed two brief runs at Manhattan's Third Avenue Theatre. Four years later, Cole's most memorable hit song, "Under the Bamboo Tree," was introduced by white vaudeville star Marie Cahill in *Sally in Our Alley* (1902), and reprised by Judy Garland and Margaret O'Brien in the 1944 MGM film *Meet Me in St. Louis*.

Another black composer used sheer nerve to get a black musical into a Broadway theatre for the first time. Will Marion Cook (1869–1944) and his cast walked into the Casino Theatre (in its pre-Shubert years) to audition for a booking. Producer Edward Rice was shocked to find negros performing on his stage, but was practical enough to put business ahead of bigotry and gave *Clorindy, the Origin of the Cakewalk* (1898) a brief run in the Casino's rooftop summer theatre. Because the outdoor venue made dialogue inaudible, the libretto was jettisoned, leaving only the songs and some physical gags. Despite these last minute deletions, Cook's ragtime score delighted an all-white audience.

A few years later, Cook was the natural choice to provide a score when black vaudevillians George Walker (1873?–1911) and Bert Williams (1874–1922) turned their popular song and dance act into full-length musical comedies. The premise always involved a variation of minstrelsy's Jim Crow and Zip Coon, with the slick Walker talking the dull-witted Williams into a fresh get-rich-quick scheme. *In Dahomey* (1903, 53 performances in New York) packed its plot, dialogue, and lyrics with the usual stereotypes. The story involved several African Americans finding a pot of gold and using their fortune to travel back to Africa. Once there, Williams (the bumbling "Shylock Homestead") and Walker (the conniving "Rareback Pinkerton") maneuver through several plot twists and are crowned rulers of Dahomey, where:

> Evah dahkey is a King.
> Royalty is jes' de ting.
> If yo' social life is a bungle,
> Jes' you go back to the jungle,
> And remember dat you daddy was a king.
> White fo'k's what's got dahkey servants,
> Try and get dem everything.
> You must never speak insulting.
> You may be talking to a king.

Williams and Walker interpolated a song they had coauthored with James W. Johnson, which reached beyond racial barriers, expressing the universal experience of imminent bankruptcy:

> When it's all goin' out, and nothin's comin' in,
> That is the time when your troubles begin.
> Money's gettin' low, people say, "I told you so,"
> And you can't borrow a penny from any of your kin,
> When it's all goin' out, and nothin's comin' in.

After an eight-week run in New York, *In Dahomey* traveled to London later that same year (251 performances), where it became a novelty sensation, drawing royalty and the cream of British society. Williams and Walker starred in several more musicals that made it to Broadway, but their partnership was cut short when illness forced Walker into early retirement in 1908. Williams embarked on a solo vaudeville career, which quickly led to stardom in Ziegfeld's *Follies*, as discussed in our next chapter. When Williams moved into mainstream projects, the black musical lost its primary proponent and the newborn form went into a quick decline. More than a decade would pass before black musicals found new life on Broadway, thanks in large part to the rise of jazz.

In the meantime, white talent continued to dominate Broadway, creating entertainment that was designed to please the widest possible audience.

6

A New Century (1900–1913) — "Whisper of How I'm Yearning"

In 1900, ambitious young women of limited circumstances found that the most direct route to attracting the attention of wealthy, powerful men was the stage. With dozens of musical productions reaching New York each season, it was easy enough for a girl with good looks, a modicum of talent, and determination to land a chorus job, and many chorines succumbed to the enticements of jewels and midnight rendezvous. A classic period anecdote tells of a backstage chat between two ladies of the ensemble. When one exclaims that she found a pearl in an oyster at a restaurant, her companion replies, "That's nothing! I got a string of pearls off an old lobster at Rector's last week."

The acclaimed British musical comedy *Florodora* (455 performances in London in 1899) proved to be an even bigger hit on Broadway (where it ran for 553 performances in 1900). Its story of an heiress seeking the restoration of a stolen inheritance and finding love along the way is long forgotten, but the show's primly dressed female sextet is not. Each standing five foot four and weighing a uniform 130 pounds, these six comely young ladies caused a sensation by singing the flirtatious "Tell Me Pretty Maiden," with a decorous line of chorus boys in morning coats and top hats:

MEN: *Oh tell me, pretty maiden, are there any more at home like you?*

GIRLS: *There are a few, kind sir, but simple girls, and proper too.*

MEN: *Then tell me pretty maiden what these very simple girlies do.*

GIRLS: *Kind sir, their manners are perfection and the opposite of mine.*

In their fashionable floor-length gowns, the attractive "*Florodora* sextet" looked nothing like the showgirls in tights who had dominated Broadway since the 1860s. Adding to the hoopla, the New York production's entire original sextet married wealthy men.

In a far more sensational development, *Florodora*'s featured gypsy dancer Evelyn Nesbit had a prolonged affair with eminent architect Stanford White before she married Pittsburgh millionaire Harry K. Thaw. In 1906, the deranged Thaw shot White to death during a performance at Madison Square Garden's rooftop theatre—claiming this "beast" had ruined his wife. Thaw's murder trials stretched over several years while Evelyn made a great show of standing by his side. Press coverage stressed the seamy connection between high society gentlemen and young women in "the show business," and such scandal only made the theatre more forbiddingly attractive to the general public. Thaw was finally found not guilty by reason of insanity. After a brief incarceration in a mental hospital, he promptly divorced Evelyn, who was forced to make a living dancing in vaudeville. Her story would be recalled in E. L. Doctrow's novel *Ragtime*, which was later dramatized for the screen and musical stage.

It was the end of America's Gilded Age, an era when great fortunes were made with astonishing speed, even as crushing urban poverty became more widespread than ever. In 1898, Manhattan had joined with four surrounding counties to form Greater New York City. The resulting improvements in public transportation (the first subway opened in 1904) expanded Manhattan's potential theatre audience by hundreds of thousands, as did an ever-increasing flow of tourists. This increase meant that Broadway could support more productions and longer runs. By 1900 there were more than thirty legitimate theatres on Broadway, and dozens more would rise over the next two decades as the theatre district moved up from Union Square to the city's new transportation hub at 42nd Street and Broadway—an area known as Longacre Square. When the *New York Times* built new headquarters there, politicians curried journalistic favor by renaming the district Times Square. This intersection became New York City's physical and psychological heart, as well as the center for popular entertainment.

But popular entertainment was not limited to Broadway. Vaude-ville houses sprang up in almost every neighborhood of the city's five boroughs. Edison's motion pictures were still just a novelty, and the rise of commercial radio was decades away, so those who wanted entertainment in the early 1900s still had to get it live. For the time being, big time show business meant only one thing—the stage.

Family-oriented shows had long been a staple during the Christ-mas season, but in the new century, such shows became year-round attractions. Children's novelist L. Frank Baum served as librettist and co-lyricist for a musical stage adaptation of his popular children's book *The Wizard of Oz* (1903, 293 performances). Some changes were made to the story. Since a dog would be hard to see from a balcony seat, this version had Dorothy travel to the magical land of Oz with her faithful cow Imogene, played by two men in an animal costume. The libretto was no masterpiece, but at a time when musical scripts tended to be forgettable, it was up to the actors to supply the missing magic. Acrobatic vaudeville clowns David Montgomery (1870–1917) as the Tin Woodman and Fred Stone (1873–1959) as the Scarecrow brought Baum's beloved characters to vivid life, their contortioned cavorting delighting every age group. They also interpolated several comedy songs that had no relation to Baum's story, such as "Pimlico Malinda" ("a cockney negro song"), and a nautical nonsense show-stopper entitled "Hurrah for Baffin's Bay." *The Wizard of Oz* also benefited from a creative staging by Julian Mitchell, who used stere-opticon projections to depict the famous cyclone, and wowed audi-ences with a fully realized field of magical red poppies. *The Wizard of Oz* toured for years, making Montgomery and Stone major stars of the legitimate stage. Although none of the songs became lasting hits and there was no attempt to bring this distinctly American creation to London, it made such a hefty profit that it inspired numerous child-friendly imitators—the best of which became a classic in its own right, mostly due to a score by Broadway's leading composer.

Victor Herbert: "Ah, Sweet Mystery of Life"

Born in Ireland, then raised and trained in Germany, cellist Victor Herbert (1859–1924) came to the United States in 1886 when his wife was contracted to sing at New York's Metropolitan Opera House.

Within fifteen years, Mrs. Herbert had faded from the public eye, but her husband rose from playing in the Met's orchestra to conducting the prestigious Pittsburgh Symphony. In the meantime Herbert's gift for writing sophisticated yet accessible, ear-pleasing classical compositions led to invitations to write operettas for the popular stage. After several promising commercial failures, he received good notices for *The Serenade* (1897, 79 performances) and *The Fortune Teller* (1898, 40 performances), both with lyrics and librettos by Harry B. Smith. Although Smith's work was considered state of the art in his time, his declamatory dialogue and sometimes grandiose rhymes sound dated today. Such was the case with most of Herbert's theatrical collaborators. As a result, most of his shows are no longer performed, and his melodies have often been left to survive on their own.

Several of Herbert's musicals have managed to last. *Babes in Toyland* (1903, 192 performances) was an obvious attempt to imitate the success of *The Wizard of Oz*, but Herbert's glorious melodies put it in a separate class. Director Julian Mitchell was on hand again to make fresh use of color, sound, and movement. A group of schoolchildren (played by adult actors) performed "I Can't Do the Sum," which makes fun of the convoluted math problems found in elementary school textbooks (lyric by Glen MacDonough):

> *If a steamship weighed ten thousand tons and sailed five thousand*
>   *miles*
> *With a cargo large of overshoes and carving knives and files,*
> *If the mates were almost six feet high and the bos'n near the same,*
> *Would you subtract or multiply to find the captain's name?*

Mitchell armed the "children" with the small blackboards and chalk that were standard issue in schoolrooms at that time. While singing the refrain, the cast used the chalk to clack out a bouncy rhythm on the boards:

> *Put down six and carry two,* (clack, clack, clack—clack, clack, clack)
> *Gee, but this is hard to do.* (clack, clack, clack—clack clack, clack)
> *You can think and think and think*
> *Till your brains are numb,*
> *I don't care what teacher says,*
> *I can't do the sum.*

There was also "The March of the Toys," which set a stage filled with fantasy figures into motion with Herbert's catchy martial melody. Aside from periodic revivals, *Babes in Toyland* would be filmed twice. Despite revisions, the best of the score remains familiar, including the ballad "Toyland," with its bittersweet warning that once you leave childhood's borders "you can never return again."

Herbert discovered that increasing popularity brought him greater creative leverage, thereby allowing him to offer more ambitious scores. On its face, *Mlle. Modiste* (1905, 202 performances) is a rather conventional Cinderella story about Fifi, a Parisian shop girl who rises to operatic stardom, winning the love of a handsome young nobleman along the way. But Herbert's winning melodies give this neglected gem a timeless appeal. Lyricist Henry Blossom provided the composer with better than average words, including the comic proclamation of an aging roué, "I Want What I Want When I Want It." Viennese soprano Fritzi Scheff proved a sensation in the title role, particularly when singing "If I Were on the Stage," a trio of songs that culminates in the romantic "Kiss Me Again." Scheff revived the role frequently over the next twenty-five years, and continued singing "Kiss Me Again" for the remainder of her career. In the late twentieth century, an off-Broadway revival by the Light Opera of Manhattan proved that *Mlle. Modiste* is a needlessly neglected gem.

Rather than limit himself to romantic operettas, Herbert was willing to branch out into musical comedy. *The Red Mill* (1906, 274 performances) was the story of an American vaudeville comedy team stranded in Holland, where they help a young girl whose romance with a local boy is opposed by her father, the burgomaster. With Montgomery and Stone as the vaudevillians, physical gags were guaranteed, such as Stone making his entrance by falling down an eighteen-foot ladder. Herbert provided the young lovers with operetta-style love songs like "The Isle of Our Dreams" and "Moonbeams," but gave Montgomery and Stone the pure musical comedy showstopper "The Streets of New York." Blossom's lyrics had a distinct Ned Harrigan flavor:

> *In old New York! In old New York!*
> *The peach crop's always fine!*
> *They're sweet and fair and on the square!*

The maids of Manhattan for mine!
You cannot see in gay Paree,
In London or in Cork!
The queens you'll meet on any street
In old New York!

Victor Herbert refused to limit himself to any genre, working simultaneously on musical comedies, operettas, and even grand operas. He bridged all three forms in *Naughty Marietta* (1910, 136 performances), a work commissioned by opera impresario Oscar Hammerstein I, and tailored to the talents of two Metropolitan Opera stars. Emma Trentini played Marietta d'Altena, an Italian who avoids an unwanted marriage in 1780 by escaping to New Orleans, where she falls in love with American privateer Dick Warrington, played by Orville Harrold. Both characters must contend with the local governor's son, a murderous pirate out to seduce Marietta, but all is resolved when Warrington completes Marietta's unfinished dream melody, "Ah, Sweet Mystery of Life." Herbert's rapturous tune accompanied some heavy poetic language by lyricist Rida Johnson Young:

Ah, sweet mystery of life at last I've found thee!
Now at last I know the secret of it all.
All the longing, seeking, striving, waiting, yearning,
The burning hopes, the joy and idle tears that fall.
For 'tis love, and love alone, the world is seeking;
And it's love, and love alone, that can reply;
'Tis the answer, 'tis the end and all of living,
For it is love alone that rules for aye!

No one has ever spoken English this way. While such high-falutin' lingo may have been acceptable to theatregoers in 1910, it makes this song—and most of Herbert's operettas—sound hopelessly dated to twenty-first-century ears. "Ah, Sweet Mystery of Life" has suffered the further misfortune of becoming a campy joke thanks to its comic use in Mel Brooks's film *Young Frankenstein* (1974). As a result, it is now almost impossible for modern day audiences to take the song seriously. The screen and stage versions of *Thoroughly Modern Millie* won a quick laugh by quoting the opening lines of the song, but the 2002 Broadway staging then segued to Herbert's "I'm Falling in Love with Someone"—another florid ballad from *Naughty Marietta*, but one that has not been identified as camp. The result was one of the few genuinely touching moments in a laugh-packed twenty-first-century musical comedy.

Just as *Adonis* established a long-standing formula for successful American musical comedy, Herbert and Blossom's *Naughty Marietta* instituted a formula that American operetta would stick to for the next two decades:

- The plot requires a historic and/or exotic setting.
- The music rules.
- Both the music and lyrics should be flowery and poetic.
- Romance is the main ingredient, not sex.
- The heroine must be indecisive; the hero, stalwart and macho.
- A class difference (real or imagined) between the leads is preferred.
- Productions should be handsome and lavish.
- Comedy is a spice that must be used sparingly.
- Wit? Never heard of it. Whatever it is, it need not apply.

Although Herbert outlived his heyday, he always remained in demand, writing special material for several editions of the Ziegfeld *Follies*, and contributing to the same 1924 jazz concert that marked the debut of George Gershwin's "Rhapsody in Blue." A copious drinker with a trencherman's appetite, Herbert had solid business sense and served as a cofounder of the American Society of Composers, Authors, and Publishers (ASCAP), the first organization ever formed to protect the often-overlooked rights of songwriters. Although his shows are passing into silence, his music is still worth hearing. It serves as a reflection of his time, and its combination of European sophistication with an all-American spirit provided a crucial bridge between the once-separate worlds of operetta and musical comedy. Where he led, future giants Jerome Kern, Richard Rodgers, and Frederick Loewe would soon follow.

George M. Cohan: "I Am That Yankee Doodle Boy"

Herbert was easy for critics and the public to agree on, because he had melodic talent and foreign training—a useful combination in a country still uncertain about its own claims to cultural greatness. It wasn't so easy for George M. Cohan (1878–1942), who had plenty of talent but whose only training was a lifetime performing on hundreds of stages all across the United States. His parents, Jerry and Nellie, were New Englanders of Irish decent who toured the old variety circuits in their own song and dance act. Their daughter Josie joined the act as a junior skirt dancer, and little George (who contrary to legend was born on the 3rd of July) handled small roles and even played the violin when forced to. By the time he was fifteen, George was a seasoned professional with more experience in vaudeville than most adult performers. His confidence sometimes turned into arrogance, earning him an early reputation as a smart aleck, but his parents and sister remained supportive at all times. The Four Cohans were a tight and loving clan, acting as one both off stage and on. As George's mother later put it, "we were sufficient unto ourselves."

By age fifteen, George wanted the family act to take a shot at performing in New York, but Jerry insisted that the Four Cohans were a "road" act, not the sort that had a chance on Broadway. Only when George attempted to run away did his father relent, not wanting anything to split up the family.

George's hopes for their 1893 Broadway debut at Keith's Union Square Theatre were ruined when the stage manager broke the family act into separate units. Young George complained so angrily that his song and dance solo was banished to the dreaded opening spot on the bill, where in vaudeville parlance, he "died" at every performance, four shows a day for a seemingly endless week. Josie's solo dance act was such a success that she played a string of major New York engagements, paying the family's bills for the rest of the year. Adding to George's chagrin, word that he was a "troublemaker" made it temporarily impossible for him to find bookings. This difficulty taught Cohan that emotions could be dangerous, and from this point forward, he usually kept his deepest feelings private. With the rest of the family performing, George made good use of his free time by writing skits for other vaudeville performers and getting his first songs published by Tin Pan Alley. The easygoing Jerry then put his hard-driving teenage son in charge of the act, which went back out on the road and quickly became the most highly paid "four hand" in vaudeville.

An argument with Keith and Albee over improper billing led the Four Cohans to permanently leave vaudeville and move to the legitimate stage. George expanded two of his vaudeville sketches into full-length musical comedies, for which he wrote the words and music, produced, directed, choreographed, and played the dance-happy male leads. *The Governor's Son* (1901, 32 performances) and *Running for Office* (1903, 48 performances) were filled with an all-American jingoistic energy that found a cold reception in New York, where critics saw Cohan as a vaudeville upstart. Some simply could not accept the radically new idea of a tap-dancing leading man. Before Cohan, leading men in musicals did little if any dancing. His dances were masculine, straightforward, and exciting, setting a new professional standard. However, both shows prospered on the road where they toured for a year or more.

Realizing that he was onto something, Cohan wrote his next musical expressly for Broadway. In *Little Johnny Jones* (1904, 52 performances), George starred as the title character, an American jockey who has the nerve to compete in the English Derby. Brimming with confidence, he arrives in London singing "Yankee Doodle Boy":

> *I'm a Yankee Doodle Dandy,*
> *Yankee Doodle do or die,*
> *A real live nephew of my Uncle Sam,*
> *Born on the Fourth of July.*
> *I've got a Yankee Doodle sweetheart,*
> *She's my Yankee Doodle joy.*
> *Yankee Doodle came to London*
> *Just to ride the ponies,*
> *I am a Yankee Doodle Boy.*

Professional gambler Anthony Anstey (Jerry Cohan) offers Jones a fortune to throw the race, but the honorable Jones refuses. Anstey arranges for Jones to lose anyway and then falsely accuses the jockey of throwing the race. Forced to stay in England until his name is cleared, Jones goes to the pier to bid farewell to a shipload of friends bound for New York. Notice that this lyric flows like everyday conversation, with no hint of grand poetic language:

> *Give my regards to Broadway,*
> *Remember me to Herald Square,*

Tell all the gang at Forty-second Street
That I will soon be there.
Whisper of how I'm yearning
To mingle with the old-time throng.
Give my regards to old Broadway
And tell them I'll be there 'ere long.

As it happens, Anstey is on the same ship, along with a detective who has promised to fire off a skyrocket if he can find hard evidence of the gambler's deceit. Dusk falls, and as the now distant ship sails along the horizon, a brilliant skyrocket zooms heavenward (a state-of-the-art special effect for 1904) and Jones tap-dances across the pier in triumph. Jones returns to America, unmasks Anstey's illegal activities, and reclaims his "Yankee Doodle sweetheart," played by Ethel Levy. Cohan called this play "an old fashioned comedy melodrama 'all dressed up' in songs and dances." He directed the show at a fast pace, offering his definition of musical comedy performance: "Speed! Speed! And lots of it! That's the idea of the thing. Perpetual motion." New York's critics reacted with a shrug, and the Broadway run of *Little Johnny Jones* ended after just six weeks. Cohan then took the show on the road and toured for three profitable years, revisiting Broadway several times until the show had racked up 205 New York performances. For the first time, "the road" told Broadway what was good.

With his credentials established, Cohan was finally in demand. Theatre owner Abe Erlanger asked if Cohan could write a show without a flag, and George responded that he could write a show "with nothing but a pencil." He came up with *45 Minutes from Broadway* (1906, 90 performances), the story of Mary, a housemaid in suburban New Rochelle, who renounces a millionaire's inheritance to keep the love of Kid Burns, a wisecracking New Yorker. Once again, most critics savaged the show, so Cohan closed it after three months, cleaned-up on tour and returned to Broadway in victory. Both "Mary's a Grand Old Name" and the catchy title tune became sheet music best-sellers. Cohan would have been the perfect choice to play Kid Burns, but he was busy starring in *George Washington Jr.* (1906, 81 performances) as an American who refuses to marry the British aristocrat whom his socially ambitious father has selected for him, choosing instead to be renamed after the father of his country. The musical highlight was "You're a Grand Old Flag."

The New York critics clearly considered Cohan anathema, but his critical failures were making him a wealthy man. Cohan was irked enough to publish rebuttals, but he wasn't about to change his style. He went right on writing for folks in "the sticks," and in so doing he attuned the New York theatre to a national mindset, exuding an optimism and sense of pride that were rampant in a nation just beginning to recognize its own possibilities. Crafted singlehandedly by Cohan, these musical comedies had a coherence of style and content that was very unusual on Broadway at the time, and his lyrics had a conversational ease that fell comfortably on the ear, standing in stark contrast to the poetic language found in most songs of the era.

Cohan's success continued. Since critics who are out of touch with popular taste are soon out of work, Cohan gradually found himself transformed from vaudeville upstart to critic's darling. With his multitudinous talents, he became one of the most popular and powerful individuals in the American theatre. As longtime friend and fellow actor William Collier put it:

> George is not the best actor or author or composer or dancer or playwright. But he can dance better than any author, compose better than any manager, and manage better than any playwright. And that makes him a very great man.

Cohan's book musicals were at their best when he was on hand to direct and perform in them. Attempts to revive these shows without Cohan have not done well—an energetic 1982 Broadway revival of *Little Johnny Jones* closed on its opening night. Although sometimes called revolutionary, these musicals abided by the same formula for musical comedy success that had been in effect since *Adonis* (1884): intriguing comic plot, extraordinary star, and a book packed with jokes and wisecracks. For a few years, Cohan adjusted the formula with a golden songwriting touch, turning out hit songs that have outlasted his era. None of the musicals Cohan wrote after 1906 are viewed as landmarks, and none would match the long runs enjoyed by his straight comedies, but his name became synonymous with musical theatre, and with Broadway itself. In part, this is because the motivating factor in Cohan's life was a passionate love for the theatre.

George outlived his beloved parents and sister Josie, but always ended his curtain calls with the same line he had used when they were together in vaudeville: "Ladies and gentlemen, my mother thanks you, my father thanks you, my sister thanks you, and, I assure you, I thank you!" Primarily remembered today because of the brilliant biographical film *Yankee Doodle Dandy* (Warner Brothers, 1942), Cohan's legacy was tremendous. By furthering the art of the conversational lyric, by making it acceptable for leading men to dance, and by encouraging the integration of song and dialogue in musical comedy, he set the groundwork for much that followed in the course of the twentieth century. And his name remained an important one through the 1930s, as upcoming chapters will verify.

Ziegfeld's Follies: *"A Pretty Girl Is Like a Melody"*

From his beginnings as a nightclub promoter in his native Chicago, Florenz Ziegfeld (1867–1932) had an eye for unusual talent and a keen instinct for publicity. He arrived on Broadway in 1896, producing the first in what would be a series of musicals starring his common-law wife, Anna Held (1873?–1918). A Parisian music hall star, Held depicted herself as the ultimate French ingénue, but she was originally a nice Jewish girl from Warsaw. With a thick Gallic accent and a naughty-but-innocent stage persona, she had enough personality to make up for her limited singing and acting talents. Ziegfeld added to Anna's fame with a series of calculated publicity stunts. When he noticed that Held's imported bath salts turned her tub water the color of milk, he proceeded to order truckloads of fresh milk from a New York dairy every day for a week. When the bill came due, Ziegfeld refused to pay, explaining that the milk was rancid, and Miss Held could only bathe in fresh milk. The idea of anyone bathing in milk ignited a nationwide journalistic frenzy, guaranteeing strong ticket sales for Held wherever she toured.

It was Held who first suggested that Ziegfeld produce a revue based on the French Folies Bergère model, spoofing the foibles and follies of society while showcasing a chorus of appealingly underdressed women. Up to now, Broadway revues had veered between the intimate comic olios of Weber and Fields and the circus-style visual spectacles staged at the 4,600-seat Hippodrome Theatre. Ziegfeld's revue would be something different. Theatre owner Abe Erlanger saw an opportunity to keep one of his less popular rooftop summer theatres busy, so he offered Ziegfeld a tight $13,000 production budget and a weekly salary as "production manager." Ziegfeld made the most of his limited resources by hiring the ever-dependable Harry B. Smith to pen the libretto, and Julian Mitchell to direct. He also persuaded Erlanger to give the New York Theatre's roof space a fresh coat of paint and a pretentious new name, the Jardin de Paris. There, *The Follies of the Day* (1907, 70 performances) premiered on June 8, billed as "Just One of Those Things in Thirteen Acts."

Contrary to what some have suggested, the 1907 *Follies* was not the first Broadway revue. *The Passing Show* (1894, 121 performances) claims that distinction, and the minstrel olios that had been around since the 1840s were a clear spiritual ancestor. What made Ziegfeld's revue extraordinary was his use of the female chorus. Unable to afford star salaries, Ziegfeld made his chorines the unofficial stars of the show, initially billing them as "The Anna Held Girls." Unlike the brash burlesque girls in tights, Ziegfeld's chorus dressed and (at least on stage) behaved like young ladies, providing a classy, unifying element. Amid sketches depicting such celebrities as Teddy Roosevelt and Victor Herbert, the chorines appeared in a variety of revealing but tasteful costumes. Ziegfeld even sent the girls down the aisles banging drums, to give customers a closer look. Under the circumstances, no one noticed the forgettable score, which had been churned out by various underpaid hacks. As business picked up, top vaudeville star Nora Bayes joined the cast. The summer run was followed by a few weeks at the Liberty Theatre and then a brief road tour, doing well enough to merit an even more successful second edition the following year (1908, 120 performances). Bayes was on hand to sing her vaudeville favorite "Shine on Harvest Moon," not written for the *Follies* but the biggest hit heard in early editions of the series.

By the time these revues were officially retitled *The Ziegfeld Follies* in 1911, a clear Ziegfeld style had begun to emerge, involving girls, spectacle, and clean comedy. Ziegfeld now took full command as well as full credit, concentrating his dollars on hiring a few select star performers while maintaining the overall glamour of the production. When preparing a new edition, he compiled an overabundance of songs and sketches, most provided by hacks, and would allow the reaction of the tryout audience to determine what material would stay or go.

In the course of a run, Ziegfeld's star performers could be replaced with minimal impact. The ladies of the ensemble, now known as "The Ziegfeld Girls," kept ticket sales brisk, appearing in inventive production numbers inspired by current events. Over the years to come, they rode the good ship *S. S. Vaudeville*, appeared as curvaceous New Jersey mosquitoes flying to Manhattan through the newly-opened Holland Tunnel, paraded as "the Merry Widows of the world," and even wore head-borne battleships that electrically lit up to suggest a naval flotilla at night. In some sequences, pure fantasy reigned as the ladies appeared decoratively draped in sequins, rhinestones, and pearls, often balancing massive matching headdresses. Many of the *Follies* chorines could sing and dance, but standard talent was not a necessity. In Ziegfeld's eyes, beauty was a talent. The popular fashion model Dolores was featured in several editions of the *Follies*, but never uttered a sound or danced a step. Showcased in glorious costumes, she either stood stockstill or gracefully walked across the stage. While the ongoing parade of feminine beauty pleased the men in the audience, Ziegfeld delighted female theatregoers with an endless stream of haute couture. Several early editions of the *Follies* included gowns by leading high society designer Lady Duff-Gorden.

A few of the Ziegfeld girls went on to independent fame—including future film star Barbara Stanwyck—but the real stars of the *Follies* were the comedians. When Ziegfeld hired Bert Williams for the 1910 edition, several white cast members threatened to walk out rather than work on the same stage with a negro. Ziegfeld pointed to the stage door, saying he could do the show without any of them, but not without Williams. On opening night, Williams appeared dressed as a threadbare hobo, singing a song that he had introduced in vaudeville, "Nobody":

> *When Winter comes with snow and sleet,*
> *And me with hunger and cold feet,*
> *Who says "Here's two bits, go and eat"? Nobody.*

Well, I ain't never done nothin' to nobody,
I ain't never got nothin' from nobody, no time,
And until I get something from somebody, sometime,
I don't intend to do nothin' for nobody, no time.

With a melody by Williams, this song was a battle cry for the ignored, not the stereotypical "coon" song. Although he still followed the minstrel tradition of wearing blackface makeup, he dispensed with the old minstrel stereotypes and portrayed an all-suffering everyman. People of all races and classes identified with Williams. He starred in eight editions of the *Follies*, and in an era of unbending racism became one of the most beloved performers on the American stage. But the persistence of bigotry could get him down. After Williams died of overwork at age forty-seven, longtime friend and colleague W. C. Fields said, "He was the funniest man I ever saw, and the saddest man I ever knew."

In that same 1910 *Follies*, the coon song "Lovey Joe" went to newcomer Fanny Brice (1891–1951), a Jewish girl born on Manhattan's Lower East Side. Erlanger was opposed to a white girl singing such a number in one of his venues, but the young veteran of burlesque made such a hit during out-of-town tryouts that Erlanger literally broke his straw hat applauding for her. The song and the singer both stayed in the show. Brice earned her place as both a chanteuse and a comedienne, eventually appearing in more editions of the *Follies* than any other featured performer. She was the first Jewish performer to rise to American stardom while waving her ethnicity like a banner in her comic songs and routines. She could also put across searing torch songs, making her a true singing comedienne. The roster of *Follies* comics in the years that followed reads like a who's who of American comedy in the early twentieth century: Will Rogers, W. C. Fields, Eddie Cantor, Leon Errol, Charles Winninger, and Ed Wynn all attained stardom in the *Follies*.

Hailed as the "Great Glorifier" of the American girl, Ziegfeld was also a dedicated private admirer of the female sex. Longtime companion Anna Held had to look the other way as Ziegfeld had his flings. Contrary to popular belief, he did not treat his chorus line as a harem. Most of the Ziegfeld girls lived decent lives, and he treated the overwhelming majority of them with avuncular affection, paying for their trousseaus or covering the down payments for their first homes. But those who were not worried about their reputations or who had notions of seducing Ziegfeld were another matter. His affair with teenage showgirl Lillian Lorraine (1892–1955) was so public that it humiliated Held. The lovely Lorraine was a hopeless alcoholic, her furious emotions often bouncing from one extreme to another. At one point, she spitefully married another man and told him that Ziegfeld had wronged her—whereupon her enraged husband tracked Ziegfeld down and gave him a horrific beating in a restaurant. The producer took no legal action. Not long afterward, Lorraine dumped her husband and went back to Ziegfeld. The game was on again, but not for long.

On New Year's Eve 1913, Ziegfeld and Lorraine attended a costume ball at the opulent Astor Hotel. Lorraine had one of her inebriated tantrums and stormed out. Anna Held was there dressed as the Empress Josephine and realized that this was the perfect moment to attempt a reconciliation. But before she could make her move, Ziegfeld was transfixed by the sight of actress Billie Burke (1885–1970) entering down a grand staircase. Seventeen years Ziegfeld's junior, this effervescent redhead had triumphed in a series of comedies produced by Ziegfeld's friend and occasional competitor Charles Frohman (1860–1915). Burke did not realize the identity of the tall, silver-haired man asking for a dance, and had no idea why a woman dressed as the Empress Josephine kept glaring as they whirled about the floor. In the months that followed, Frohman tried his damnedest to quash the budding romance, thinking that Ziegfeld was merely looking to steal Burke's contract, but Ziegfeld's charm and persistence won out: he married Burke in the spring of 1914. Frohman never forgave them, taking his resentment to the bottom of the Atlantic when he went down with the Lusitania the following year.

Flo Ziegfeld was a man of jarring eccentricities. He had such a morbid fear of death that he never visited sick friends or attended funerals. When Anna Held died of cancer in 1918, he pretended it wasn't happening. Throughout his adult life, he was a passionate collector of elephant knickknacks and statues, but only if the pachyderms stood trunk-up—when he received any with trunk-down, he smashed then to pieces, no matter how valuable. Ziegfeld didn't care for telephones.

He much preferred sending telegrams that ran for pages at a time, and had a special contact with Western Union allowing him to send three million words per year at a reduced, prepaid rate. Close colleagues and staff members working in his offices were more likely to get a telegram than a phone call. When traveling, it was not unusual for him to wrap his toothbrush, pajamas, and a change of underwear in a newspaper, fold it under his arm, and go. Even everyday concerns had to be resolved in an extravagant manner. On one occasion, a crass dinner guest complained that Ziegfeld's plates were substandard. Days later, wife Billie Burke found their home choked with packing crates containing a spectacular dinner service stamped with golden double eagles. Flo had purchased the dinnerware of the late Tsar Nicholas II, which his communist executioners had sold off for a mere $38,000.

As of 1913, the *Follies* moved into the New Amsterdam Theatre, the opulent 1,700-seat art nouveau flagship of Klaw and Erlanger's empire, a popular summer novelty turned into a hallowed Broadway institution. The runs became longer and the production values more ambitious. Audiences of the *Follies* were dressed in their formal best, the ladies in their most elegant gowns and the gentlemen in their "soup and fish" tailcoats with white ties. Some sitting in the balcony might get by in a suit and tie, but a Ziegfeld production was an event. Anyone who was anyone went not only to see, but to be seen by others. Eventually, Ziegfeld noticed that many of his customers were heading off to find aftershow entertainment at nightclubs, so he initiated a series of *Midnight Frolics* in the New Amsterdam's well-equipped rooftop theatre. After a full evening at the *Follies*, theatregoers could head upstairs to see many of the same performers in a more intimate but equally posh environment. Since customers had just spent hours applauding the *Follies*, Ziegfeld placed small wooden mallets on the tables and encouraged everyone to save their weary hands by knocking on the table to show approval.

In our next chapter, we see Ziegfeld reach beyond the *Follies* and *Frolics* to take part in the ongoing redefinition of Broadway musical comedy, but there is no question that his revues are the basis for his legend. People who have never seen a Broadway show know the name "Ziegfeld" as a synonym for show business glamour. In "glorifying the American girl," he raised theatrical production standards to new levels.

A Chinese Honeymoon: *A Forgotten Hit and*
The Shubert Brothers

Although Broadway was developing a healthy strain of homegrown musical theatre during the first decade of the twentieth century, a steady stream of London hits crossed the Atlantic to try their luck. These shows were among the most popular theatrical works up to that time, but a lack of lasting hit songs has effectively pushed these titles and the names of their creators out of our cultural memory. American-born composer Howard Talbot (1865–1928) composed eighteen musical comedies for the West End. Rarely mentioned today, in the early 1900s he was one of the most popular songwriters on earth. He collaborated with lyricist/librettist George Dance on *A Chinese Honeymoon* (1901, 1,075 performances). The plot involved Englishman Samuel Pineapple who honeymoons in the mythical Chinese city of Ying Yang. Pineapple's wife cordially kisses the emperor while Samuel does the same for a princess—not knowing that local custom decrees that any two people who kiss are automatically married. The rather *Mikado*-esque development is eventually resolved by the passing of a new law. As Princess Soo-Soo, seventeen year-old soprano Lily Elsie (1886–1962) made her London debut and became an immediate favorite. Written in four weeks, a low budget staging of *A Chinese Honeymoon* toured the British provinces with unexpected success before a more lavish version was mounted for London's West End. It became the first musical production in world history to run for more than a thousand consecutive performances.

In the meantime, three brothers were trying to make a name for themselves as New York theatre owners. Russian Jewish immigrants Sam Shubert (1876–1905), Lee Shubert (1873–1953), and Jacob Shubert (1878–1963) had risen from an impoverished childhood in Syracuse, New York, by getting into local theatre management, eventually owning a small chain of theatres that reached into Manhattan. One of their proudest acquisitions was The Casino Theatre, a Moorish fantasia that stood at Broadway and 39th Street and had been one of New York's most desirable musical venues since its construction in 1882. The Shuberts decided to mark their ownership of this high-profile theatre with a surefire hit, and that led them to import *A Chinese Honeymoon* (1902, 376 performances).

When the Casino suffered a major fire early in 1905, the Shuberts made the rebuilding an excuse to increase the seating capacity from 875 to 1,458. While work on the Casino was still underway, twenty-nine year old Sam died in a train wreck. Reigning theatre magnate Abe Erlanger reneged on several contracts with the Shuberts, refusing to honor "an agreement with a dead man." Swearing revenge, Lee and Jacob (better known as Jake or "J. J.") built a competing nationwide empire of legitimate theatres that would eventually eclipse Erlanger and make the Shuberts the most powerful businessmen in the theatre. The two brothers were so contentious that they often went for years without speaking to one another, communicating through attorneys and lawsuits. Whether dealing with themselves or others, they proved to be far more ruthless than Erlanger had ever been. Their monopolistic control eventually included almost every legitimate theatrical venue in the United States, giving the Shuberts tremendous influence over every aspect of the business, including musical theatre.

The Merry Widow: *Refusing to Say "I Love You"*

By the early 1900s, both Broadway and London's West End had stopped paying much attention to Vienna's theatrical output, but the capital of the Austria-Hungarian Empire was still home to a small but thriving musical theatre industry. A circuit of theatres presented a steady stream of native operettas, romantic works flavored with splashes of broad comedy. Except for a few hits by the late Johann Strauss II, these works were rarely performed outside of the empire and neighboring Germany. Catchy melodies and colorful settings could not make up for libretti that offered little wit and sentimental, cliché-ridden plots. The Viennese seemed so content with the sheer sameness of these operettas that producers distrusted any project that did not adhere to the standard "boy gets girl, boy loses girl, boy regains girl" formula.

That contentment is why the managers of the Theatre an der Wein were skeptical about *Die Lustige Witwe/The Merry Widow* (1905, 400+ performances), a new work involving a couple refusing to admit that they love each other. But there was a gap in the theatre's schedule, and no other new work was available. Composer Franz Lehar (1870–1948) had a few minor successes to his credit, and the libretto

by Victor Léon (1858–1940) and Leo Stein (1861–1921) was based on
L'Attaché d'Ambassade, an 1861 French comedy by Henri Mielhac,
one of Offenbach's favorite librettists. But the score was ambitious.
Lehar used the sort of cutting-edge orchestral coloring one expected
from serious composers like Debussy, Mahler, or Richard Strauss.
Could such sophisticated sounds work in a lighthearted theatre piece?
The composer believed in the show, and so did his two leading players, soprano Mizzi Günther and her frequent costar Louis Treumann.
When the producers decided to use leftover sets and costumes,
Günther volunteered to pay for lavish new gowns, and Treumann personally covered the cost for a custom made royal dress uniform. As
rehearsals progressed, the producers became increasingly pessimistic
about Lehar's innovative music. At one point, they even offered Lehar
five thousand crowns to shut down the production. The composer
refused, but such maneuvers must have added to everyone's preopen-
ing jitters.

The action of *Die Lustige Witwe* begins during a ball at the Paris
embassy of Pontevedro, a fictional Eastern European kingdom that
faces bankruptcy if its wealthiest citizen, lovely young widow Hannah Glawari (Günther), should marry a foreigner. Ambassador Zeta
orders the playboy diplomat Count Danilo (Treumann) to woo the
widow, knowing full well that Hannah and Danilo were once lovers—
and that their romance ended when the king would not permit his
royal nephew to marry a then-poor commoner. Hannah realized that
Danilo is unwilling to be classed with the fortune hunters that swarm
about her, so she taunts him. From the original English translation:

SONIA: Well now, in view of my estates, my houses, my horses, my
cows, my pigs ...

DANILO: Quite a menagerie!

SONIA: ... and my millions—I believe the noble old uncle would no
longer object to the noble young nephew bestowing his affections on
me if it had rested with him.

DANILO: (Going to her) And do you think that I?

SONIA: (Cross LEFT) All men are alike.

DANILO: All other men may be, but I'm not.

SONIA: When a man says to me, "I love you," I know he means my money.

DANILO: You class me with all other men?

SONIA: You are all alike!

DANILO: (Angrily) I, at any rate …

SONIA: Yes, they all say that.

DANILO: Do they? I, at any rate, shall never say to you, "I love you."

SONIA: (Going right up to him with upturned face) Never?

DANILO: (Rushing away from her) Never, never, never.

It is obvious that both characters are still crazy for each other, so the battle lines are drawn. To complicate matters, Ambassador Zeta's much younger wife Valencienne is carrying on a secret affair with handsome Parisian roué Camille de Rosillon. The following day, during a garden party at Hannah's mansion, Valencienne and Camille are almost caught kissing in a garden pavilion. Hannah takes the married woman's place and impetuously announces that she will marry Camille, sending Danilo off in a jealous rage. That evening, Hannah turns her home into a replica of the famous nightspot Maxim's for yet another party, at which she explains to Danilo that her engagement was a farce, and that under the terms of her husband's will, she loses her fortune if she remarries. Danilo then publicly proclaims his love for her, only to learn that Hannah's fortune automatically transfers to her new husband!

When *Die Lustige Witwe* opened on December 30, 1905, Vienna's critics were modest in their praise, and it seemed as if the producers were right. Then Lehar's infectious waltzes, mazurkas, and polkas made their way into Vienna's cafes and ballrooms, where their sensuous sound spoke more eloquently than any newspaper revue. Ticket sales built to sellout, and the production kept extending its run. The producers celebrated the 300th performance by finally investing in lavish new sets and costumes, and Lehar marked the 400th by adding a new overture. By that time, *Die Lustige Witwe* had also triumphed in Hamburg, Berlin, and Budapest. The first English-language version of *The Merry Widow* debuted in Great Britain (1907, 778 performances), where it was presented by George Edwardes in an English adaptation that made several major changes to the text: Pontevedro became Marsovia, Hannah Glawari became Sonia Sadoya, Count Danilo became a prince, and the final scene was moved into the actual Maxim's. This version was used when the show premiered at Broadway's New Amsterdam Theatre later that same year (1907, 416 performances). Lehar's masterpiece inspired a surprising selection of unauthorized *Merry Widow* merchandise, including cigars, hats, parasols, and a popular style of corset.

Frequently retranslated, recorded, and revived, it has been estimated that *The Merry Widow* was performed a half million times during its first sixty years. It has made its way into the repertory of the New York's illustrious Metropolitan Opera Company and is the only musical of the early 1900s that is regularly performed today—and not as a museum piece. In any language, *The Merry Widow* still provides wonderful entertainment. What has kept it so fresh, so vital? First credit must go to Lehar's music, which still rates as one of the most seductive, beguiling scores in any genre. Léon and Stein's libretto is just as seductive and beguiling, and has kept audiences laughing with characters that are three-dimensional and believable. Artistically speaking, Lehar's music and the Léon-Stein libretto are the most important match in *The Merry Widow*, because they are thoroughly integrated, and this coherence keeps the show engaging and enjoyable.

At first glance, *The Merry Widow* is a witty story about true love ultimately leading to marriage, but on closer inspection, this show offered audiences an enticing glimpse of how the upper half lived in fin de siècle Paris, with diplomatic intrigue, forbidden encounters, and the decadence of an infamous eatery where the cream of French society mixed with dancing girls of the demimonde. Lehar's sensual waltz became a respectable expression of sexual passion. When Danilo and Hannah swirl about to the strains of the main love theme, it is lust in three-quarter time, adding a new degree of sensuality to a form that reached back to Offenbach, Gilbert and Sullivan, and Johann Strauss. This alluring and somewhat daring mix was presented in such a stylish and melodic package that even the prudes approved.

Léon and Stein changed the way musical librettos would be shaped in the decades to come. Up until *The Merry Widow*, all the characters in musicals took part in one central storyline. A secondary couple was often on hand to provide comic relief, but could invariably be edited out of the libretto without affecting the main story's outcome. *The Merry Widow* was the first major musical to make its main storyline and subplot completely interdependent. The clandestine romance between Camille and Valencienne—and the jealous reaction of Valencienne's bumbling husband—plays a key role in resolving Hannah and Danilo's story. When properly used, such interwoven plots make librettos far more interesting, so it is not surprising that they became a standard feature in operettas and musical comedies.

Hannah and Danilo were the first in a long line of musical stage lovers who would captivate audiences by refusing to say "I love you." Such couples had long been a literary staple (for example, Beatrice and Benedick in Shakespeare's *Much Ado About Nothing*), but the comedic tension generated by such relationships has proven particularly sympathetic to musicalization. Simply put, it is fun to watch lovers playing "hard to get," and that fun seems to increase when the game is set to music. *Oklahoma!*, *Kiss Me Kate*, *My Fair Lady*, *Hello, Dolly!*, *Grease*, and many other musicals would echo *The Merry Widow*'s core theme of love denied in the name of pride.

The Merry Widow set off a demand for more Viennese waltz-fests in Britain and America. Dozens of such works were exported to London and New York in the years that followed. One of the most successful was Oscar Straus's *The Chocolate Soldier* (1909, 296 performances in New York; 1910, 500 performances in London) with its story of a young woman falling in love with a peace-loving enemy soldier. "My Hero" ("Come, come, I love you only, my heart is true") became one of the most popular songs of the era. It seemed that the only person who did not like the show was playwright George Bernard Shaw, who so despised this romanticized version of his anti-romantic comedy *Arms and the Man* that he would not allow any more musical adaptations of his plays during his lifetime. This is why Shaw's *Pygmalion* only became available for musicalization halfway into the new century, when it was adapted into *My Fair Lady*.

Vienna-born operettas continued to flood Broadway and London's West End, giving American and British producers a steady crop of pre-tested material. It would take two things to stem this musical tide: an American composer capable of synthesizing a new and sophisticated American sound, and a nightmarish war that was both unnecessary and unavoidable.

7

American Ascendance (1914–1919) — "In a Class Beyond Compare"

Harrigan, Braham, Cohan, and Herbert laid the groundwork, but it took two gunshots in Serbia to open the way
for the international ascendance of American musical comedy. When Archduke Ferdinand, the heir to the Austro-Hungarian
throne, was assassinated by a Serbian terrorist on June 28, 1914, a
system of alliances that had prevented war for forty years rolled into
action. Austria and Germany declared war against Serbia, giving
Russia the excuse to declare war as Serbia's defender, bringing matching declarations from Russia's allies, France and Great Britain. All of
these nations went to war with terrifying enthusiasm, each blindly
confident of victory within a matter of months.

Anti-German feeling in Britain was so vehement that its royal family was forced to change their surname from "Saxe-Coburg-Gotha"
to "Windsor," becoming the only dynasty in world history to name
itself after a building. (Germany's Kaiser Wilhelm II, who spoke flu-
ent English, said that he couldn't wait to see "the first production of
Shakespeare's *The Merry Wives of Saxe-Coburg-Gotha*.") In such an
environment, German and Austrian operettas were suddenly "ver-
boten" on London's West End. Although the United States remained
officially neutral for the first three years of the war, German attacks
on international shipping made most Americans openly supportive
of Britain and its allies, so waltz-schmaltz quickly lost its cachet on
Broadway. At the same time, the threat of war led to packed theatres
on both sides of the Atlantic as people sought distraction.

American musical comedy certainly offered tons of fun, but like the few American wines of that era, it was only considered fit for domestic consumption. As war broke out in Europe, one of New York's biggest homegrown hits was *Chin Chin* (1914, 295 performances), which featured David Montgomery and Fred Stone as Chin Hop Hi and Chin Hop Lo, magical servants of Aladdin's fabled lamp. They took on various disguises while saving the lamp and its owner from the machinations of an evil shopkeeper. The script was little more than a roadmap from one sight gag to another, with songs along the way. The score by Belgian-born composer Ivan Caryll (1860–1921) included no lasting hits, but the song "Good-bye Girls, I'm Through" did well enough for lyricist John Golden to give up songwriting and become a producer. Audiences applauded Stone's solo proclaiming that "ev'ry chink goes just as dippy as a coon from Mi-si-si-pi" for those "Ragtime Temple Bells." In a line that would have repercussions for another hit the following year, Stone's character at one point masqueraded as a ventriloquist who repeatedly said to his dummy, "Very good, Eddie"—a line that became part of everyday conversation among theatre-savvy New Yorkers. During the run, the producers interpolated the wartime hit "It's a Long, Long Way to Tipperary" into the show, even though the song had no possible relevance to a fairy tale set in ancient China. Montgomery and Stone's blend of topical jokes and physical clowning delighted all age groups, and the Broadway run was followed by a profitable tour. Despite its popularity, no one considered bringing this show to London. Outside of the United States, audiences would have found it incomprehensible.

Aside from the thousands dying in the European war, three deaths in the theatre community helped set the stage for a new era. As mentioned earlier, Charles Frohman, who produced dozens of musicals in both London and New York, went down with the Lusitania in 1915. That same year, British producer George Edwardes succumbed to a terminal illness, bringing an end to his long line of exportable musical comedy hits. Comedian David Montgomery died unexpectedly in 1917, leaving Fred Stone to carry on alone in stage vehicles tailored to his style. With these men gone and no more operettas coming from Vienna or Berlin, a crucial gap opened in musical theatre production, and by happy coincidence, a New York–born composer was on hand to create musicals worthy of export, providing a new voice and inspiring a new vision of what musical comedy could be. The composer himself was hardly new. In fact, he had been a familiar behind-the-scenes face on Broadway for a decade.

Jerome Kern: From Interpolation to Reinvention

Born in Manhattan and trained in Europe, Jerome Kern (1885–1945) was small in size but packed with enough energy and ambition to match his formidable musical talents. After getting his start as a Tin Pan Alley song plugger, Kern worked as a rehearsal pianist for various Broadway musicals. He played his compositions during breaks for anyone who would listen, and was on hand to offer his talents when American producers of British imports decided that they were not satisfied with an existing score. Since a number of English socialites rarely arrived at a theatre before intermission, West End musicals of the early 1900s tended to save their best material for the second act. These shows had to be revised for New York audiences, who arrived for the first curtain and left at intermission if the first act was not up to par. Beginning with *Mr. Wix of Wickham* (1904, 41 performances), Kern's interpolated songs breathed much needed energy into a procession of now-forgotten imports. He worked with whichever lyricists came to hand, only occasionally finding a wordsmith who could match his fresh melodic style. Most of Kern's interpolations received no credit, so he remained unknown to the public, but he developed a reputation for dependability among theatrical professionals. This reputation was not enough for the young composer, who yearned for a breakout hit song that would make him a household name.

The Girl from Utah (1914, 120 performances in New York) first opened in London in 1913, one of the last in a long line of "girl" musicals presented by George Edwardes. The plot, which involved an American girl who flees to London so she can avoid becoming the umpteenth wife of a wealthy Mormon, had comic potential, but producer Charles Frohman realized that the score was unremarkable. He hired Jerome Kern and veteran lyricist Herbert Reynolds to write five new numbers. Both men had written their share of anonymous interpolations, and this time demanded full program credit.

On August 14, 1914, headlines proclaimed the outbreak of hostilities in Africa, and the French launched the Battle of the Lorraine.

That night in New York's Knickerbocker Theatre, the distant mayhem was forgotten as Julia Sanderson and Donald Brian sang the Kern-Reynolds ballad "They Didn't Believe Me."

> *And when I told them how beautiful you are,*
> *They didn't believe me, they didn't believe me.*
> *Your lips, your eyes, your curly hair*
> *Are in a class beyond compare,*
> *You're the loveliest girl that one could see.*
> *And when I tell them (and I certainly am going to tell them),*
> *That I'm the man who's wife one day you'll be,*
> *They'll never believe me, they'll never believe me,*
> *That from this great big world you've chosen me.*

It is doubtful that anyone in the audience was aware that they were witnessing a historic moment. As far as any of them knew, it was just great entertainment. But "They Didn't Believe Me" brought forthright sentiment face to face with refined romance, and the resulting sound pointed to the Broadway musical's future. The lyric had the easy flow of everyday conversation, and the melody still sounds warm and fresh today. This song was far more than just a breakout hit; it was a new way of expressing human emotion in song. Musical theatre and the art of popular songwriting had been set on a new course.

The Princess Theatre Musicals

Kern went into creative overdrive, composing nineteen complete Broadway scores over the next five years. Of those, seven were for a series produced in (or at least intended for) Broadway's tiniest house, the 299-seat Princess. Producer Ray Comstock built this jewel box as a home for dramatic repertory. When that plan failed, agent Elizabeth Marbury suggested small, low-budget musicals as an alternative to the usual lavish Broadway fare. The producer and the agent joined forces, hired Kern, lyricist Schuyler Greene, and British librettist Guy Bolton (1884–1979), set a production budget of only $7,500 (about one-third the average price tag for a musical comedy at that time) and optioned the absurdly titled British operetta *Mr. Popple of Ippleton*. With a radically downsized cast, revised book, and an entirely new score, *Nobody Home* (1915, 135 performances) found enough of an audience to break even, but that was enough to convince Comstock's team that they were onto something. It was the first of the so-called Princess Theatre musicals, only four of which would actually play the Princess. The venue didn't matter nearly as much as the new style of writing and performance that it inspired.

The story of the Princess musicals might have ended right here, but luckily Kern overslept on May 1, 1915, and missed a chance to sail with Frohman on the final voyage of the Lusitania. Had Kern gone down with that ship six days later, the remainder of this book would have been radically different. Musical theatre would have continued to evolve without Kern, but not as we know it. He was poised to change the art form as no other composer of his day could.

Kern, Bolton, and Greene came up with an entirely original musical comedy involving two newlywed couples who get involved in some innocent misunderstandings while taking a honeymoon cruise on a Hudson River steam cruiser. Both the characters and setting of *Very Good Eddie* (1915, 341 performances) were familiar to New York theatregoers, as was the title, which was inspired by Fred Stone's much-quoted line in *Chin Chin*. The intimacy of the Princess allowed the cast to give far more realistic performances than they could in larger Broadway theatres. The relatively small cast of two dozen performers and an orchestra of only eleven pieces made audiences feel as if they had been to an exclusive party—the perfect approach at the Princess, which was only fourteen rows deep. All of the songs fit naturally into the plot and had remarkable charm, but only "Babes in the Wood" proved a lasting hit. Booking conflicts forced the show to move to the much larger Casino Theatre and then to the 39th Street Theatre before finally returning to the Princess. *Very Good Eddie* was more than a major hit—it became a trendsetter. In Gerald Bordman's landmark *American Musical Theatre: A Chronicle*, he states that this show "formed the mold out of which poured a half century of American Musical Comedy."

With the addition of British-born lyricist and colibrettist P. G. Wodehouse (1881–1975) in 1917, the core team for the Princess series was complete. Best known as a comic novelist (among other characters, he created the hapless Wooster and resourceful butler Jeeves), Wodehouse had a knack for writing naturalistic dialogue, and was the first Broadway lyricist to craft inventively rhymed conversational lyrics in the Gilbertian tradition. This was a particular challenge since Kern preferred to compose his melodies first and have lyricists fit in words afterward.

Although Wodehouse's first collaboration with Kern and Bolton, *Have a Heart* (1917, 76 performances) would not play the Princess, it is usually considered part of the Princess series. Ray Comstock insisted that the new creative team adapt the old Charles Hoyt comedy *A Milk White Flag* for the Princess, but the trio felt that a story about two sisters attending their father's funeral was not promising material for a musical. Comstock went ahead with the ill-advised project using other writers and lost a small fortune. Producer Henry Savage took on *Have a Heart*, the story of a young couple who go on a honeymoon to save their shaky marriage, only to meet up with the husband's old girlfriend. All is resolved by the machinations of a clever elevator boy. Savage booked this small-scale project into the sizeable Liberty Theatre, where it folded after two months. By that time, Kern and his collaborators were back with Comstock.

Oh Boy! (1917, 63 performances) was the longest running show in the Princess series. In it, a young husband innocently lets a beleaguered college girl hide in his home while his wife is away. A crisis ensues when the wife unexpectedly returns, but all is resolved by the final curtain. Fast paced and beguiling, and with a score that included "Till the Clouds Roll By," *Oh Boy!* marked the start of a new era when it transferred successfully to London. The West End producers changed the title to *Oh Joy!* (1919, 167 performances), moved the action to London, and interpolated a song by British writers. The longstanding procession of British hits coming to Broadway now turned into a two-way exchange, and American musical comedy began to reach an international audience on a regular basis. Several concert productions in recent years have verified that *Oh Boy!* is one of the oldest American musical comedies that is still thoroughly entertaining in its original form.

With *Oh Boy!* keeping the Princess packed, Comstock opened *Leave It to Jane* (1917, 167 performances) at the Longacre, which at 1,005 seats was still a relatively intimate Broadway house. Jane Witherspoon (Edith Hallor) is daughter of the president of Atwater College, where she is the resident "Miss Fix-It." When the school football team faces a losing season, Jane romances Billy Bolton (Robert Pitkin), the star quarterback from a rival team who agrees to play for Atwater under an assumed name. Just as Jane realizes that she has fallen in love with Billy, the All-American lug suspects that he has been duped. Jane needs no more than the Kern-Wodehouse love duet "What I'm Longing to Say" to set things right with Billy before he leads Atwater to a gridiron victory. *Leave It to Jane* had a comparatively brief run of just over five months, but this charming show redeemed itself four decades later when a 1959 off-Broadway revival racked up 928 performances.

Kern penned five full-length Broadway scores in 1917, and still found time to dash off the occasional interpolation. As German attacks on commercial shipping made America's entry into World War I inevitable, Klaw and Erlanger found themselves stuck with the rights to the Viennese operetta *Gypsy Princess*. In a desperate attempt to make the show "less German," they hired Bolton to write a new libretto, transforming the main character into a vaudeville dancer. Retitled *The Riviera Girl* (1917, 100 performances), it faded after twelve weeks, but the one added song by Kern and Wodehouse, "Bungalow in Quogue," took on a life of its own. Wodehouse's lyric poked gentle fun at the new craze for buying weekend homes on suburban Long Island:

> *Let's build a little bungalow in Quogue*
> *In Yaphank or in Hicksville or Patchogue.*
> *Where we can sniff the scented breeze,*
> *And pluck tomatoes from the trees,*
> *Where there is room to exercise the dog.*
> *How pleasant it will be through life to jog*
> *With Bill the bull and Hildebrand the hog:*
> *Each morn we'll waken from our doze,*
> *When Reginald, the rooster, crows,*
> *Down in our little bungalow in Quogue.*

Kern set this well-constructed, conversational lyric to a simple melody that used multiple sets of repeated notes—a simple but risky technique that charmed listeners. When *Very Good Eddie* was successfully revived on Broadway in 1975, "Bungalow in Quogue" was interpolated, with showstopping results.

In 1918, Kern got rather involved in building a new home in the Bronx, so his output slowed to four scores that year. Only one of those was for the Princess, and it was Kern's final contribution to the series. In *Oh Lady! Lady!* (1918, 219 performances), a young woman's wedding plans are endangered when her dressmaker turns out to be her fiancé's former girlfriend. The usual harmless misunderstandings are worked out when all the principal characters bump into each other at a party in Greenwich Village. A warm critical reception led to a decent run, but there were signs that audiences were losing interest. As Kern aimed his talents elsewhere, Bolton and Wodehouse teamed with longtime Shubert Brothers' staff composer Louis Hirsch (1887–1924) for *Oh, My Dear!* (1918, 189 performances), which fell short of a 200-performance run and effectively ended the Princess series. Comstock would reunite his "holy trio" a seventh and final time for *Sitting Pretty* (1924, 95 performances), but the years following World War I brought a radical change in public tastes, and the sweet, wistful charms of the Princess Theatre series were drowned out by musicals offering much bigger sounds, sights, and emotions.

A great deal has been written about the Princess series, and much of it is off the mark. Bolton, Wodehouse, and Kern were not the first writers to successfully integrate song and story—several ancient Greeks had beaten them to that claim, as had such men as Offenbach, Gilbert, and Sullivan. Cohan had put recognizable contemporary characters in familiar settings a decade before. And as to the Princess series being "American" musicals, both Bolton and Wodehouse were Englishmen. So what made the Princess series remarkable? A number of factors set these shows apart:

1. The intimacy of the Princess Theatre made a more natural performing style possible, foreshadowing the appeal of sound film.
2. This was the first series of musicals set primarily in New York City and its environs. Up to this point, most operettas were set in faraway times and/or places, and American musical comedies were usually set in smalltown U.S.A. From here on, the common setting for contemporary Broadway musicals would be New York, the city where the western world's popular culture was now being defined.
3. In the best of the Princess musicals, every element was organic, developing naturally from story and character. This type of

development allowed these shows to dispose of the star turns, interpolated songs, and forced comic characters found in most previous American musical comedies.

4. In an integrated musical, where storytelling is the prime goal, the libretto matters more. The songs serve as a continuation of the book and are only good insofar as they carry on the work of a good libretto. A wonderful song stuck in a dull script isn't worth much—and for the Princess series, the team of Bolton and Wodehouse didn't write yawners.

5. These were the first musicals to fully benefit from the creative genius of Jerome Kern. Bolton and Wodehouse's words mattered immensely, but it was the Kern melodies that made these shows so popular. The fact that the series faded away without Kern's involvement seems to verify that his music was the key factor. Many have tried to explain the indefinable quality that made his music unique. Perhaps Stephen Sondheim came the closest to the truth when he said that Kern's compositions exhibit a "hard-won simplicity."

6. This is the earliest body of American musical comedies so well written that they can still be performed in their original form with entertaining results. With few exceptions, the works of Cohan and Herbert are seen only in revised forms.

7. The Princess musicals directly inspired the new crop of songwriters that would spring up in the 1920s. Richard Rodgers, Lorenz Hart, the Gershwins, and others would openly admit that their creative ambitions took shape while enjoying the musicals of Bolton, Wodehouse, and Kern.

Kern once told an interviewer, "I'm trying to apply modern art to light music as Debussy and those men have done to more serious work." A serious artist with solid business sense, he balanced this admirable ambition with a healthy desire to write hit songs. We will see in the next chapter how Kern's dual focus led to his involvement in some of the greatest stage hits of the 1920s.

Irving Berlin: "I Want to Listen to Rag"

At the same time that Kern was winning recognition, another habitué of Tin Pan Alley was making the move to Broadway. Russian-Jewish immigrant Israel Baline had dropped out of school at age thirteen, and had swiftly risen from newspaper boy to singing waiter to songwriter. A misspelled credit on his first published song ("Lyric by I. Berlin") inspired a permanent name change, and Irving Berlin (1888–1989) soon co-owned his own publishing firm. In time, the lyricist tried his hand at composing. The fact that he had limited knowledge of the piano keyboard and did not read musical notation was no barrier. He worked out melodies on a piano using only the black keys, and then dictated the results to a musical secretary who laid out the tune in formal musical notation and played the results for Berlin's final approval. At first, Berlin specialized in ethnic comedy songs. He had major hopes for a rhythmic ditty about a ragtime orchestra, but its first public performances drew little response. Then in 1911, charismatic vaudeville vocalist Emma Carus introduced the song in Chicago.

Within days, "Alexander's Ragtime Band" became the fastest selling sheet music in the United States. The craze soon reached international proportions. With this song, America began to set the pace and rhythm of worldwide popular culture. Technically, Berlin's hit, with its judicious touches of syncopation, was not a rag at all—just a song *about* rag. But the public ignored such technicalities, and Berlin turned out more rag-styled hits. Berlin was hailed as "The King of Ragtime," a title that annoyed some African Americans, who resented a white composer co-opting their genre. After all, they had invented and refined ragtime in the late nineteenth century.

Berlin had already contributed individual songs to several revues when producer Charles Dillingham (1868–1934) offered him a chance to compose the entire score for *Watch Your Step* (1914, 175 performances), a show featuring America's most popular dance team, Vernon (1887–1918) and Irene Castle (1893–1969). Bringing a modern sense of intimacy and humor to the art of ballroom dancing, the Castles had introduced a slew of popular dances, including the Turkey Trot, the Grizzly Bear, the Bunny Hug, the Fox Trot, and the Maxixe. Although it functioned as a revue, there was a wisp of story involving a young man and woman competing to win an inheritance by each proving they have never been in love. While wandering about Manhattan they (of course) fall for each other. Berlin loaded the score with dance numbers for the Castles, including the "Syncopated Walk."

The best remembered song in the score was "Play a Simple Melody," which begins with a woman singing a slow, nostalgic ballad:

> *Won't you play a simple melody*
> *Like my mother sang for me?*
> *One with good old-fashioned harmony,*
> *Play a simple melody.*

A man then offers a bouncy reply:

> *Musical demon, set your honey a-dreamin'*
> *Won't you play me some rag?*
> *Just change that classical nag*
> *To some sweet beautiful drag.*
> *If you will play from a copy*
> *Of a tune that is choppy,*
> *You'll get all my applause,*
> *And that is simply because*
> *I want to listen to rag.*

These two seemingly mismatched numbers are then sung in simultaneous counterpoint. Even older theatregoers who initially distrusted the "new" ragtime craze found this melodic juxtaposition irresistible. In years to come, counterpoint showstoppers would become a Berlin specialty. While *Watch Your Step* marked a major beginning for Berlin, it proved to be the only time the Castles would star in a Broadway musical. A loyal Canadian, Vernon Castle joined the Royal Air Force soon after war broke out in Europe and was killed in 1918 while training a new pilot. Irene eventually returned to performing in vaudeville, and in later years helped to reconstruct period dance routines for the musical biopic *The Story of Vernon and Irene Castle* (RKO, 1937).

After a profitable run, Dillingham followed up *Watch Your Step* with another revue, *Stop! Look! Listen!* (1915, 105 performances). Berlin provided an up-to-date score, including the popular "I Love a Piano." French music hall star Gaby Deslys (1881–1920), a beguiling comedienne who overcame limited talents and looks to achieve brief stage stardom in the early 1900s, talk-sang Berlin's next-to-closing number, "Everything in America Is Ragtime."

Scandals, Vanities, and Such

Florenz Ziegfeld's *Follies* became a functional pop culture legend during these years. Ziegfeld's focus was on casting, staging, and décor. To him, songs and skits didn't matter nearly as much as who performed them and how they were presented. In 1915, Ziegfeld added designer Joseph Urban (1872–1933) to his production team. This ingenious artist, whose work embodied the art deco style at its most glorious, put an eye-popping personal stamp on almost all future Ziegfeld productions, including every edition of the *Follies* through 1931. Urban created the lavish settings and elegant costumes, the lines of showgirls parading down endless staircases in bangles, beads, and neck-numbing headdresses that we now think of as trademarks of the *Follies*. And directing it all was Ned Wayburn (1874–1942), who divided chorus girls according to height and invented the trademark "Ziegfeld Walk," which balanced the forward thrust of each hip with an equivalent thrust from the opposite shoulder, making it possible for girls to descend stairs while balancing huge headpieces.

If you have ever wondered how musicals can fail despite the presence of experienced talent, consider the most talent-packed flop of all time. *Miss 1917* (1917, 72 performances) was coproduced by Ziegfeld and Charles Dillingham and directed by Wayburn, with music by Victor Herbert and Jerome Kern, and a slight script coauthored by Bolton and Wodehouse. Urban designed the sets, and eight high-priced designers provided hundreds of costumes. The cast included Irene Castle, Lew Fields, Marion Davies, Ann Pennington, and operetta diva Vivienne Segal. For good measure, the rehearsal pianist was the then-unknown George Gershwin. All in all, these were the sort of talents one would expect to see connected with a hit. But this production was so overstuffed with talent that each performance cost more than the box office could possibly take in. Dismissed by the critics as a big and beautiful bore, it mercifully sank into a sea of debt after nine weeks.

Ziegfeld was famous for spending lavishly on his shows, but not when it came to songwriters. He usually insisted that songs had to be in hand within three weeks or less and fit the all-important costume and set designs. The first decade of *Follies* scores included only a few hit songs, several of which had already been heard in vaudeville. In 1919, Ziegfeld finally reconsidered his priorities and asked Irving Berlin to contribute several numbers. Berlin gave tenor John Steele a song that became the unofficial anthem of the *Follies*, "A Pretty Girl Is Like a Melody." Berlin also wrote the hilarious "You'd Be Surprised" for Eddie Cantor (1892–1964), a wide-eyed, hyperkinetic comedian who had managed a Berlin-like ascent from the impoverished Lower East Side to early success in vaudeville and now stardom in the *Follies*. Ziegfeld also presented a tribute to minstrelsy with Cantor as Mr. Tambo and Bert Williams as Mr. Bones. To give Williams a star turn, Berlin came up with an amusing comment on the anti-drinking movement, "You Cannot Make Your Shimmy Shake on Tea."

Despite the laughter, America had already amended its constitution to make the sale of liquor illegal. Instead of discouraging the use of alcohol, Prohibition glamorized it, making it suddenly fashionable for respectable people to break the law. Unable to compete with establishments that served illegal liquor, Ziegfeld was forced to end his *Midnight Frolics* series. It was a tough blow, coming at a time when Ziegfeld faced a growing platoon of competitors.

After all, what was there to a Ziegfeld-style revue but sketches, songs, show girls … anyone with a bankroll could throw something like that together. At least that's what Lee and Jacob Shubert thought. Intrigued by the notion of a year-round theatre that would allow audiences to enjoy the casual atmosphere of a rooftop summer garden all year long, the Shuberts purchased the old horse exchange building just north of Times Square and renovated it into an auditorium with a steel-beamed ceiling and well-stocked bars on all levels. They decided that the new Winter Garden would house revues, just the sort of fare that one expected at a rooftop theatre. Since the Shuberts had a full-time staff of writers, composers, and designers on hand, it was easy to piece together enough material for a revue—as to quality, that was in the eye of the beholder.

The Shuberts opened the Winter Garden with *La Belle Paree* (1911, 104 performances), a collection of vaudeville acts set in a tissue-thin plot involving a wealthy widow whooping it up in Paris. Plot or not, most witnesses agreed that it was a revue. The first performance dragged on for more than four hours, and many in the audience had already left by the time a brash male singer stepped out of the pack to offer a knockout solo. Fortunately, the Shuberts had the young man under a long-term contract, so they shuffled the running order. The next night Al Jolson came on early and stole the show, becoming a fixture, both at the Winter Garden and in show business history. Our next chapter offers a detailed profile of Jolson and his career.

Encouraged by the success of *La Belle Paree*, the Shuberts decided to launch an annual series of Winter Garden revues, presenting *The Passing Show* on an irregular basis from 1912 until 1924—whenever a Jolson production was not making use of the house. Staged on a tight budget, these productions put the emphasis on displaying girls who were clothed as minimally as the law would allow. When Jacob Shubert decided that even less (clothing) might make more (money), he initiated a separate series called *Artists and Models*. The very title suggested images of women posing in the nude, and that's just what this series offered. During rehearsals, Shubert blithely tore material off the girls' costumes until enough flesh was showing to suit his taste. At times, ladies of the ensemble were left wearing nothing more than wristbands or a necklace—in effect, full nudity. These displays drew so much condemnation in the press that curious audiences packed the theatre for three long-running annual editions between 1923 and 1925.

Songwriter Earl Carroll (1893–1948) went even further in his *Vanities* and *Sketchbooks*, two popular series of revues produced between 1923 and 1940. He often presented his chorines stark naked, flaunting the law and earning mountains of publicity. Carroll also had a taste for the kind of low humor that was not permitted in a Ziegfeld show. He showcased brash vaudeville comedians like Joe Cook and Milton Berle, and the bawdy belter Sophie Tucker. Carroll's racy private life and outrageous publicity stunts kept him in the headlines and landed him in jail on several occasions, but that only earned him admiration in an era when many developed an increasing disdain for the law.

The most successful contender for Ziegfeld's crown was once a member of his team. George White (1890–1968) had appeared as a featured dancer in two editions of the *Follies* before frankly suggesting to Ziegfeld that the series could use better songs and dance routines. The Great Showman responded by firing the young hoofer, who set about producing the *Scandals* (1919–1939). Instead of aiming below Ziegfeld's standards, White dared to aim higher, with classy sets and costumes, as well as better music and choreography. The first edition did so well that Ziegfeld offered White two thousand dollars a week to return to the *Follies*. White countered by offering Ziegfeld and Billie Burke three thousand a week to appear in the next *Scandals*! The war was on. White would never eclipse Ziegfeld's legend, but he certainly made the old master uneasy, particularly when several editions of the *Scandals* outran concurrent editions of the *Follies*.

White lured away some of Ziegfeld's top performers, including dancer Ann Pennington and W. C. Fields. Early editions of the *Scandals* had songs by George Gershwin. From 1926 onward, the series featured songs by the team Bud DeSylva (1895–1950), Ray Henderson (1896–1970), and Lew Brown (1893–1958) who penned "The Birth of the Blues," "Lucky Day," and the backside-shaking dance hit "Black Bottom." White brought in the famed artist Erté to provide costumes for the 1922 edition, bedecking showgirls every bit as attractive as those in the *Follies*. The Shuberts and Ziegfeld also hired Erté for their revues, but he returned to White in 1923 and 1925, contributing fanciful costume designs that are still prized by collectors. Just as Ziegfeld boasted of "Glorifying the American Girl," White stood by his motto, "Talent Is What the Public Wants."

Not all of Ziegfeld's competition came from Broadway. John Murray Anderson directed the first *Greenwich Village Follies* at a small downtown theatre in 1919. A master of stagecraft, Anderson made the most of a minimal budget by stressing satirical comedy and creative simplicity, using inexpensive materials like painted burlap to create eye-catching visual backdrops. The content both evoked and satirized the bohemian spirit of Greenwich Village. Vaudeville's most outrageous female impersonator, Bert Savoy, was on hand to win laughs with his campy blend of glamorous gowns and gossipy banter. Billing itself as "a Revusical Comedy of New York's Latin Quarter," the *Greenwich Village Follies* played to sold-out houses for several weeks before moving to the Shubert Theatre. All told, the series had eight successful editions, becoming bigger and more elaborate each year. Anderson moved on to other projects after 1924, directing everything from musical comedies to seven editions of the Ringling Brothers–Barnum & Bailey Circus.

World War I: "Goodbye Broadway, Hello France"

When the Imperial German government announced that it would begin unrestricted submarine warfare in an attempt to end British control of the high seas, the United States abandoned its long-held policy of neutrality and entered Word War I in April of 1917. America's vast economic resources and manpower effectively guaranteed eventual victory for the Allies, but it would take nineteen more months of bloody fighting to make good on that guarantee. The professional theatrical community made an ongoing contribution to the war effort. Many served in uniform; many more served by using their talents. On the home front, George M. Cohan wrote the stirring anthem "Over There," while stars entertained the troops and raised millions of dollars performing in war bond drives. Jolson delighted fans by introducing a tongue-twisting wartime hit:

> *Sister Susie's sewing shirts for soldiers.*
> *Such skill at sewing shirts our shy young sister Susie shows!*
> *Some soldiers send epistles,*
> *Say they'd sooner sleep in thistles*
> *Than the saucy soft short shirts for soldiers Sister Susie sews!*

Serious plays about the war would not appear until years after the fighting, but revues featured a broad range of war-themed songs and skits. The 1917 edition of the *Follies* offered Victor Herbert's new song "Can't You Hear Your Country Calling?" and a "March of the Continentals" paying tribute to the Allies. It also included a series of patriotic tableaux depicting Paul Revere, George Washington, and President Woodrow Wilson surrounded by bare breasted Ziegfeld girls on hand to personify "Liberty." The Shuberts, who almost never saw a self-serving opportunity that they didn't like, stripped their 1917 *Passing Show* chorus girls in the name of encouraging patriotism. During its run, that revue added a new finale dedicated to departing troops, "Goodbye Broadway, Hello France."

Like many other eligible American men, Irving Berlin found himself drafted into the army. Since his days as a singing waiter, Berlin's habit had been to work through the night and sleep through the morning, so waking to the sound of sunrise reveille at Camp Upton in Yaphank, Long Island, was even harder for him than most doughboys. Salvation came when the camp commander asked if Private Berlin could put together a show to raise thirty-five thousand dollars for the construction of a visitor's center. Relieved of all regular duties, the newly promoted Sergeant Berlin could write and sleep whenever he wanted, and was assigned a staff, cast, and crew of more than three hundred other theatrical professionals who had wound up in uniform.

With this all-Army team, *Yip Yip Yaphank* (1917, 32 performances) soon moved from Camp Upton to Broadway's 2,300-seat Century Theatre. Thrilling choral numbers and antic comic skits included a number of soldiers appearing in full drag. The hits of the show were a mock minstrel number entitled "Mandy" (which would later wind up in Ziegfeld's 1919 *Follies*) and Berlin himself warbling the sentiment of every person who has ever worn a uniform:

> *Oh, how I hate to get up in the morning!*
> *Oh, how I'd love to remain in bed!*
> *For the hardest blow of all*
> *Is to hear the bugler call:*
> *"You've got to get up, you've got to get up,*
> *You've got to get up this morning!"*
> *Someday I'm going to murder the bugler;*
> *Someday they're going to find him dead—*
> *I'll amputate his reveille,*
> *And step upon it heavily,*
> *And spend the rest of my life in bed.*

Berlin delivered this lyric with a distinctive Lower East Side accent ("Someday I'm goin' ta moidah da bewg-lah"), which only added to the public's delight. Ticket sales extended what was originally supposed to be a weeklong run into a sold-out month. On *Yip Yip Yaphank*'s final night, the audience was caught off guard when the cast finished the closing number by marching down the aisle to troop transports. To all appearances, they were headed for the front. In reality, they were taken back to the safety of Camp Upton. It was September 1918, and the fighting was dying down. The armistice came two months later, and Berlin returned to civilian life without ever reaching the front. As it turned out, Camp Upton never got around to building the promised visitor's center, and Berlin never found out what happened to the funds his show raised. He had been spared reveille, and as far as he was concerned, that made the whole effort of *Yip Yip Yaphank* worthwhile.

Wartime England: "Any Time's Kissing Time"

The growing wave of American musicals reaching London's West End during these years left some in the British theatrical community feeling uneasy, but most audiences seemed quite satisfied with the new sounds coming over from Broadway. While many native-grown British shows were produced during the war years, only two achieved lasting popularity. Both involved fictional gangs of criminals in far-off locales, and both offered light-hearted distraction to audiences with far too much on their minds. With German zeppelins bombing London by night, a little lighthearted escapism was deeply appreciated. Although both of these shows had exceptionally long London runs, neither would find a substantial audience outside of England.

Australian-born actor Oscar Asche had made his name touring in Shakespearean repertory and playing Haaj the Beggar in the popular melodrama *Kismet* before he concocted a lavish version of the *Arabian Nights* tale "Ali Baba and the Forty Thieves." *Chu Chin Chow* (1916, 2,235 performances in London) offered such storybook wonders as the treasure trove that only opened to the magic words "open sesame," a spectacular Arabian wedding, and a climactic scene where a cunning servant girl pours deadly doses of boiling oil over forty bandits hiding in jars. Asche starred as bandit chieftain Abu Hasan, while Courtice Pounds played the lazy Ali Baba. The first musical production in world history to run for more than six years, *Chu Chin Chow*'s most notable numbers were the incongruously British "Any Time's Kissing Time" and the chant-like "Cobbler's Song," both of which became concert standards in England. A 1917 Broadway mounting coproduced by Ray Comstock ran 208 performances, but otherwise this pageant remained a British phenomenon. A 1934 film version starring Anna May Wong as the bandit-boiling servant is so tedious that most contemporary viewers wonder what the fuss was about.

After the death of George Edwardes in 1915, his beloved Daly's Theatre faced financial ruin. In desperation, his estate commissioned *The Maid of the Mountains* (1917, 1,352 performances in London), a traditional operetta with a better than average libretto by British comic playwright Frederick Lonsdale. Teresa, the longtime hostage of a band of brigands who loves their chieftain, betrays him when she suspects him of loving another, and then ultimately frees him

from prison and accompanies him to freedom. Soprano Jose Collins
(1887–1958) had the greatest triumph of her long stage career in the
title role, and introduced "Love Will Find a Way" and "A Paradise for
Two." The show played to capacity audiences throughout its run of
almost four years, closing only because Collins was bored. She was so
closely identified with the show that the producer insisted there was
no point in trying to run it without her. However, road productions
toured Britain successfully, and there would be several major West
End revivals. A 1918 New York production faded after just thirty-
seven performances.

Plague and Contention

As World War I entered its final months, American show business
faced an unexpected crisis as a deadly worldwide influenza pandemic
reached the United States. It is unclear where and when this particular
strain of the virus first appeared, but an early outbreak in Spain led
to it being called the "Spanish Flu." Although the first cases in the
United States appeared in military camps during the spring of 1918,
the main outbreak hit the general population that autumn as some
twenty-five million United States citizens contracted the disease.
Doctors could do little more than watch as raging fever and nose-
bleeds swiftly developed into pneumonia, the lungs flooding with
blood and pus. People who appeared perfectly healthy one day would
be dead the next. Those who survived the virus were so weakened
that they sometimes fell prey to other deadly infections afterward. In
some communities, it reached the point where there were not enough
gravediggers left alive to bury the dead.

In most East Coast cities, the flu peaked in September and October
of 1918. The Federal government, with its resources focused on the
war, actively ignored the crisis, refusing to curb the domestic troop
movements that were clearly helping to spread the killer virus. Newspapers obediently downplayed the emergency, and the lack of clear
information only added to the public's sense of panic. Local governments did what they could. Church services were cancelled, schools
shut down, and war bond rallies suspended. Many communities
banned public meetings of all kinds, and theatres were either urged
or ordered to close. Business-conscious New York City allowed its

theatres to stay open, but many people refused to risk their lives for the sake of an evening's entertainment. With the streets and theatres near empty, determined producers held on, but after a few weeks vaudeville and the legitimate theatre faced the very real prospect of financial ruin.

Then the flu virus mutated, and death tolls plummeted. Celebrations of Germany's surrender in November 1918 drew people back into the streets, and word that hard-to-get tickets were available soon filled the theatres again. More than 675,000 Americans had died, and medical experts now believe that estimates of twenty-one million deaths worldwide reflected only a fifth of the true total. Over the next two years, sporadic but deadly localized flu outbreaks continued; for example, eleven thousand New Yorkers died of it in early 1920. As if by some silent agreement, journalists and historians reduced this national calamity to a rarely mentioned wartime footnote, and cultural amnesia set in. The world had other things to worry about.

Broadway faced a long-delayed war of its own. Back in 1913, a group of 112 actors had formed the Actors Equity Association in an effort to give themselves some protection against abusive producers. At that time, actors received no pay for rehearsals, were expected to cover the cost of their own costumes, and often found themselves stranded without pay when road tours closed unexpectedly. It was also common for performers to win rave reviews on opening night and then be threatened with replacement if they did not accept substantial salary cuts. Producers often put on extra holiday performances and pocketed all the proceeds, giving actors no additional pay. As Equity grew in size to more than twenty-five hundred members, producers formed the Producer's Managing Association (PMA) and announced that they would never recognize the new union. During the war, any sort of labor action could have been seen as unpatriotic, so Equity bided its time while the PMA pretended the union did not exist.

Soon after the fighting in Europe ceased, Equity president Francis Wilson demanded that the PMA accept a new standardized contract for all actors. Months of acrimony followed, and a strike was finally called. On August 7, 1919, the casts of twelve Broadway shows walked out. Five days later, when Ziegfeld announced that he had joined the PMA, Eddie Cantor and the *Follies* chorus joined the walkout. The strike spread to the road, and surprised producers dug in for a siege.

An unlikely figure took a leading role in the battle against Actors' Equity—the actor's actor, George M. Cohan. He felt that actors were artists, not laborers. As a producer, Cohan had always treated actors decently. He believed that if other managers were unscrupulous, actors could seek work elsewhere, just as he had in his years of struggle. Cohan resented Equity's demand that only union members be hired for Broadway productions, responding that he had the right to hire anyone he pleased without asking a union's approval. His contempt for the idea of actor's unionizing blinded him to the very real need for such an action. Cohan was not alone, and formed an alternative group that called itself the Actor's Fidelity League. Equity members nicknamed it "Fido," like a dog ready to do its master's bidding.

A battle for public sympathy was fought in the press, inspiring strong rhetoric on both sides. Cohan announced that if Equity were ever recognized, he would withdraw from the theatre and become an elevator operator. Longtime friend Eddie Cantor pointed out that in order to operate an elevator in New York City, Cohan would first have to join a union. The situation grew ugly as Equity's leadership was threatened with permanent blacklisting and Cohan's home in Great Neck was sprayed with gunfire. By September of 1919, the stagehands' and musicians' unions joined in the strike, effectively bringing the professional theatre to a nationwide standstill. More than thirty-seven Broadway productions had been shut down, and sixteen more were unable to open. In a last-ditch maneuver, Cohan called for a standard contract that would grant all the strikers' demands *except* recognition of Equity. Nobody went for it. With millions of dollars lost, the producers caved in on September 6, recognizing Equity and accepting a standard contract. It would take years to bring producers into full compliance, but from here on in actors had some leverage, and producers had a new and persistent union to gripe about.

The big loser in the strike of 1919 was George M. Cohan. Many of his fellow actors viewed his behavior as a betrayal. William Harrigan, son of the same Ned Harrigan that Cohan had immortalized in song, sent this telegram:

BOTH OUR DEAD FATHERS WERE GREAT MEN. MINE IS SLEEPING PEACEFULLY IN HIS GRAVE. I'LL BET YOUR FATHER HAS TURNED OVER IN HIS BECAUSE OF YOUR TREATMENT OF ACTORS.

Cohan ended his longtime producing partnership with Sam Harris, perhaps to spare his beloved friend any collateral damage. Cohan remained a major force as a producer, director, and performer, but he spent the rest of his life feeling angered and hurt by the lingering resentment of his fellow actors. He remained an implacable enemy of Equity, refusing to perform under the required union contract. Equity could have forced the issue, but chose to ignore it—Cohan's friends and fans were still legion. However, more than half a century later, attempts to honor Cohan's memory would draw official complaints from Equity executives.

America wasn't interested in bad feelings. Repelled by the horrors of war, the United States refused to take part in the new League of Nations. Politicians pursued isolationist policies, vowing that America would never again let its sons die in "foreign wars." A new mood pervaded every aspect of American life, embodied in a new native-born music called "jazz." After some initial reluctance, Broadway songwriters embraced this new sound, igniting a period of cultural dominance so extraordinary that many now refer to it as *the* golden age of musical theatre.

8

Al Jolson—"The World's Greatest Entertainer"

How do we know that Al Jolson (1883–1950) was "the world's greatest entertainer"? Well, his critics and fans confirmed it, and the Shubert Brothers (who were never profligate in their praise for anyone) were the first ones to give him that billing. But no one ever believed it more completely than Jolson did himself. He was without question the greatest musical star to come out of the golden age of big Broadway revues. His career deserves a special examination because it successfully bridged minstrelsy, vaudeville, Broadway, Hollywood, recordings, and radio.

In the late eighteenth century, the Russian government forced almost all Jewish citizens to move into the western portion of the empire, a region stretching from Lithuania down to the Ukraine that came to be known as the Pale of Settlement. Within this region, Jews were further restricted to shtetls, small all-Jewish communities that were often attached to larger towns. By necessity, these shtetls were self-sustaining, with their own separate educational and medical facilities. In these villages, Jews had no guarantee of safety. At any time, their Russian Orthodox neighbors could descend on them in a violent anti-Semitic *pogrom*, indiscriminately destroying property and murdering Jewish men, women, and children with the full approval of Tsarist authorities. During the late nineteenth and early twentieth centuries, millions of Jews would emigrate from the Pale to the United States, including many who would play major roles in the development of twentieth century show business—performers, producers, songwriters, and film moguls.

It was in a tiny one-street Lithuanian shtetl called Seredzius that Asa Yoelson was born. Although he would later claim that his birth date was May 26, 1886, no formal records survive, so he may have fudged both the day and the year. He was the youngest of four surviving children (another had died in infancy) born to Rabbi Moishe Yoelson and his wife Naomi Cantor Yoelson. When Asa was four, the rabbi went to the United States of America to find a new home for his family. Four years later, he was hired by the Talmud Torah Congregation in Washington, D.C., and he sent for Naomi and the children. Within a matter of months, Naomi died of an unidentified illness, and Rabbi Yoelson faced the task of raising a family that he hardly knew. His daughters were docile, but Asa and his older brother Hirsch were another matter. The duo became troublemakers and fell in love with popular American culture, sneaking into theatres to catch vaudeville and burlesque shows.

Attempts to train the boys as cantors proved futile. Determined to enter show business, they changed their first names to Al and Harry, and Americanized their last name to "Jolson"—ostensibly so it would fit more easily on business cards and marquees. The boys took turns running away from home, and after unsuccessful solo efforts, formed a joint vaudeville comedy act in 1903. "The Hebrew and the Cadet" made little headway until a mutual friend suggested the reticent Al try performing in blackface. Covering the face with burnt cork did far more than make white performers appear like negros—it also gave performers a protective layer of anonymity. Perhaps the French novelist Colette put it best when, in quite another context, she stated that, "Nothing is so emboldening as a mask." Al Jolson found that a mask of blackface gave his stage performances a new level of confidence. Instead of just bolstering the act, he suddenly dominated it, truly coming into his own as a performer. Soon afterward, Al struck out on his own as a singer and comedian. He and his brother would forever afterward struggle with a love-hate relationship. A clear vocal and physical resemblance made comparisons inevitable, and Harry was never able to escape being referred to as "Al Jolson's brother"—a classification that he despised.

Al Jolson was one of the first performers to appear in San Francisco after the cataclysmic earthquake of 1906. The theatre he had been booked into was no longer standing, but the management had set up a tent in an adjoining lot so performances could continue. With the clamor of construction rolling in from all sides, none of the performers could be heard—except Jolson. He ran into the midst of the audience, leapt onto a chair, and sang at the top of his rather substantial lungs. His energy and dash electrified the audience. Jolson became the toast of the city and was promoted to headliner status. After two years of solo stardom in vaudeville, Jolson took a major cut in salary to become second comedian in Lew Dockstader's acclaimed minstrel troupe, one of the last of its kind. When the company reached New York City, critics and audiences made such a fuss over Jolson that the ruthless Shubert Brothers threatened Dockstader with substandard bookings until he gave them control of Jolson's contract.

Broadway & "Gus"

From his debut in the Shubert Brothers' Winter Garden production of *La Belle Paree* (1911, 104 performances), Jolson provided a potent blend of powerhouse vocals and impromptu asides that made him a favorite with Broadway audiences. No one sold a song as Jolson did, improvising melodies, altering or repeating phrases, and delivering it all at a high volume that resonated in even the most cavernous theatres. Clinging to minstrel tradition, he appeared in blackface, throwing in an occasional hint of a southern accent but otherwise avoiding stereotypical racial mannerisms. Jolson began introducing new gags and songs, so fans kept coming back to see what he would do. A musical that had been intended as an all-star cavalcade gradually became Jolson's personal vehicle.

Realizing that a volatile talent like Jolson had to be handled carefully, the Shuberts gave him gradually larger roles in a series of revue-like musicals. He offered dynamic renditions of songs like "Waitin' for the Robert E. Lee" and "Row, Row, Row." Beginning with *The Whirl of Society* (1912, 136 performances), Jolson played Gus, an African American underdog who outsmarted his enemies while exchanging wisecracks with the audience. He would continue to portray Gus in most of his stage musicals through the 1920s.

When costar Gaby Deslys dropped out of *The Honeymoon Express* (1913, 156 performances), Jolson finally got top billing—a position he would retain for the remainder of his stage career. In this show he introduced one of his most lasting hits, "You Made Me Love You." From this point on, Jolson's shows abandoned the revue format, becoming full-fledged star vehicles. Jolson's musicals were among the hottest tickets of his time, and yet none of them could be revived today. The librettos were little more than stretches of amusing dialogue designed to get the characters from one song to the next, a format custom-tailored to encourage Jolson's vaudeville-honed gift for improvisatory banter. On his one night off each week, Jolson appeared in Sunday night concerts at the Winter Garden, doing a fifteen-minute set that often stretched to forty minutes or more.

In the delightful memoir *All My Friends* (Putnam, 1989), George Burns explains how Jolson would stop a musical midscene and in Gus's pseudosouthern drawl say: "You know how dis ends. The horse, he wins the race, and the boy gets de girl. Now, you wanna see that, or you wanna hear Jolson sing?" He then sent the cast home and offered a prolonged selection of his hit songs. Mind you, this only happened when the audience was enthusiastic. If Jolson sensed a lack of response, he walked through scenes and dropped verses, getting the show over as soon as possible.

However "big" Al Jolson got, there was one person who could always take him down a peg. In December of 1915, Al ended a year-long tour of *Dancing Around* (1914, 145 performances) in his old hometown, Washington, D.C. When President Woodrow Wilson announced he would attend a Friday night performance, Al sent a dozen front row seats to his father. When the big night came, Al made his entrance to tumultuous applause from the President and couldn't help noticing his family's seats were empty. Days later, he visited Rabbi Yoelson and asked why the tickets went unused. His father reminded him that the performance was on *Shabbos* eve, when an orthodox Jew would be in temple. Al said that his father could have made an exception; after all, *Al* was singing for the *president*. Papa Yoelson quietly responded, "*I* was singing for *God*."

Robinson Crusoe Jr. (1916, 139 performances) is a good example of the kind of stage vehicles the Shuberts built around Jolson at this time. Gus Jackson (Jolson) is the black chauffer of millionaire playboy Dick Hunter (Frank Carter). Hunter falls asleep and dreams that he is novelist Daniel Defoe's famed creation Robinson Crusoe, with Gus as his man Friday. Kidnapped by pirates, Crusoe and Friday finish act one by walking the plank, and then inexplicably start act two in the "Silver City" of Ragmachottschie. Just when things look hopeless (for the audience?), the millionaire wakes up, and decides to celebrate escaping his bad dream by throwing a ball. The program credits read "Music by Sigmund Romberg and James Hanley," but most of Jolson's big solos were interpolations, including "Yaka Hula Hickey Dula" and the somewhat more thematic comedy number "Where Did Robinson Crusoe Go with Friday on Saturday Night?"

After approximately six months on Broadway, Jolson would tour most of his productions for a year or more. To keep himself and any return customers interested, Jolson was on a constant lookout for new songs to interpolate. Soon, publishers would do anything to interest him in their songs, knowing he could make almost any tune sound like a hit. During the prolonged national tour of his 1918 hit *Sinbad*, Jolson attended a party where he heard a young pianist play a driving, catchy tune. When he asked about it, pianist George Gershwin explained that he and lyricist Irving Caesar had written the song for an unsuccessful revue. In January 1920, Jolson interpolated "Swanee" into *Sinbad*, and the song became a top-selling sensation. Of course, even Jolson couldn't make the most of every number. When his rendition of "If You Knew Susie" made little impact, he passed it off to friend and competitor Eddie Cantor, who turned it into an eye-rolling, hand-patting trademark hit. Cantor claimed that in later years, Jolson often chided, "If I knew how big that song would be, I never would have given it to you."

Powerful as Jolson's voice was, what set him apart was his delivery. He turned songs into emotional orgasms, approaching numbers with the same spirit of improvisation that he brought to dialogue, repeating words, altering melodic lines, and doing it all in a brash, in-your-face manner. Jolson didn't just sing; he catapulted songs from the core of his being. When he was on stage, he viewed the audience as his personal possession, to be cajoled, kidded, and caressed as he saw fit. Even people who sat far from the stage claimed that Jolson made them feel as if he was performing for them one-on-one, a neat trick in a 1,500-seat theatre. To reinforce this process, the Shuberts installed a special runway that extended from the stage directly into the middle of the Winter Garden's orchestra seats, letting Jolson literally sing in the midst of his fans.

Behind the scenes, the Shubert brothers were known to subject Jolson to the same kind of strong-arm tactics they used with everyone else in the business, but he often got the upper hand on his bosses. At one point, the Shuberts upped the ante by putting Harry Jolson under contract, threatening to put him on in Al's place. Al settled with the Shuberts on his own terms, and nothing came of the threat, leaving Harry with yet another reason to hate his brother.

In short order, Jolson was hailed as Broadway's top male musical star. He spent most of the decade appearing in three consecutive hits:

- *Sinbad* (1918, 164 performances) had Gus as a porter who inexplicably lands in a wild variety of historic settings. Jolson interpolated "Rock-a-bye Your Baby with a Dixie Melody," "Swanee," and "My Mammy" into the otherwise disposable score. The Shuberts kept him touring in this one until mid-1921.
- *Bombo* (1921, 219 performances) turned Gus into a deckhand for Christopher Columbus. Jolson kept audiences cheering by adding "Toot, Toot, Tootsie," "April Showers," and "California Here I Come" to the show.
- *Big Boy* (1924, 180 performances) had Gus as a jockey, featuring live horses racing on treadmills. Jolson interpolated "Keep Smiling at Trouble" and reprised the best of his past hits. With occasional interruptions, Jolson traveled in *Big Boy* for more than three years.

Jolson's shows during this period were arguably the ultimate Broadway star vehicles. Most 1920s musicals tried to cram as much talent onto the stage as possible, but the Shuberts understood that the only important talent in a Jolson show was Jolson. No one else was allowed a big number or even a major laugh—from start to finish, these shows were all about Al. Even though no one could compete with Jolson, he made damn sure that no one had the chance. Promising talents that might compete for audience approval would have their songs cut, or were fired outright. Those beyond his power at the very least faced Jolson's personal wrath. When a young song and dance team went over particularly well at one of the Sunday night Winter Garden concerts, they came offstage to find Al growling, "Don't ever let *that* happen again." He then stepped on stage with a beaming smile, anxious to win back "his" audience. As a result, Jolson's greatest challenge was living up to his billing. A confident demigod on stage, he could be a self-doubting demon behind the scenes. Audiences had no idea that the World's Greatest Entertainer suffered from such stage fright on opening nights that he had buckets placed on either side of the stage so he could vomit without seriously interrupting the show.

By the mid-1920s, the endless round of performing and touring began to take its toll on Jolson. His disagreements with the Shuberts grew more frequent, as did the occasions when illness forced him to suspend performances. Now in his forties, Al thought nothing of suspending performances—invoking laryngitis or a chronic lung ailment—and then heading to Florida for a few days of sunshine, which he called "good ol' Doctor Sol." While some of these illnesses were probably faked, an increasing number of them were all too real. Road tours and Broadway runs were compromised, with each illness costing the Shuberts a fortune in returned tickets. Although performing was essential to Jolson's existence, he needed to find a less exhausting way to reach his adoring fans. New technology came along at the same time as a project that practically demanded Jolson's talents.

Movies Learn to Sing

In 1926, playwright Samson Raphaelson wrote a drama with music about a Jewish vocalist who must choose between a show business career and following in his father's footsteps as an orthodox cantor. *The Jazz Singer* intrigued Jolson, who did not mind that the plot was blatantly inspired by details of his early life. It became a major Broadway hit for young vaudeville comedian George Jessel (1891–1981), who was then signed by Warner Brothers to star in a silent screen version.

Silent films meant little to Jolson, who knew he needed sound in order to "go over" with audiences. In 1926, he starred in an experimental short sound film for Warner Brothers using Vitaphone, a process that synchronized screen images with separate sound disks. Although clumsy, this process allowed for reasonably audible sound reproduction in large movie theatres. Al appeared in blackface, offering a monologue and renditions of "April Showers," "Rock-a-bye Your Baby with a Dixie Melody," and "When the Red, Red Robin Comes

Bob, Bob, Bobbin' Along." It debuted as part of a program of sound shorts, easily outshining the rest of the program, which included a filmed comedy routine by Jessel. Audiences responded so warmly to these experiments with sound that the Warners decided to use Vitaphone for several songs in *The Jazz Singer*. Since Jessel's contract only covered the use of his image, he justifiably wanted a bonus for the use of his voice. The budget-conscious Warners decided that if they had to pay a star salary, they might as well get a top-notch star. They dropped Jessel and signed Jolson for $75,000—more than double Jessel's price, but paid on an installment plan.

It was the wisest move Warner Brothers ever made. During the first sound sequence in the film, Jolson is seen in a San Francisco nightclub singing "Dirty Hands, Dirty Face." When the audience of actors applauded, Jolson automatically ad-libbed,

> Wait a minute, wait a minute. You ain't heard nothin' yet. Wait a minute, I tell ya! You ain't heard nothin'. You wanna hear "Toot, Toot, Tootsie"? All right, hold on, hold on. (To the bandleader) Lou, listen, play "Toot, Toot, Tootsie," three choruses, ya understand? In the third chorus, I whistle. Now give it to 'em hard and heavy, go right ahead!

He then delivers the promised song with the ear-piercing whistle and frenetic hip wiggles that were his stage trademarks. Some sources suggest Jolson's patter was all planned in advance, while others describe a horrified panic in the sound booth when he started improvising. Either way, the resulting footage was wonderfully exciting, and the Warners quickly inserted another dialogue sequence for Jolson, where he interrupts a jazzy rendition of Irving Berlin's "Blue Skies" for some disarming Oedipal banter with his mother, played by Eugénie Besserer. Later on in the film, Jolson sang the traditional prayer "Kol Nidre" during a synagogue service as his dying father (played by Warner Oland, who would soon find fame as Charlie Chan) is seen smiling with relief. In a final scene filmed on location in Broadway's Winter Garden, Jolson offers a syrupy rendition of "Mammy" to his mother, who smiles tearfully in the front row.

Sam Warner died of a brain infection just one day before *The Jazz Singer* premiered in New York on October 6, 1927, which may explain why the surviving Warner brothers seemed too stunned to appreciate the film's full impact. Most critics dismissed it as a melodramatic mess, but Jolson's performance got a tumultuous reception, with the opening night audience chanting his name until he ran up on stage to take a live bow. Richard Watts of the *Herald Tribune* wrote, "This is not essentially a motion picture, but rather a chance to capture for comparative immortality the sight and sound of a great performer." That performer turned a cinematic novelty into an epochal event. When *The Jazz Singer* debuted, there were only seven theatres in the world equipped to show it with sound, but at a $422,000 investment, it grossed over two and a half million. Public demand forced reluctant theatre owners all across the United States to invest in costly sound equipment, and that led to an immediate demand for more sound pictures. Viewed today, *The Jazz Singer* is a so-so silent film that only comes to life when Jolson sings, but it was enough to establish sound film as the only option for Hollywood's future—and Al Jolson was this new genre's first musical star.

Jolson's talent was surpassed only by his ego. He made it clear to colleagues that he didn't really see anyone as a peer. Jolson's vaudeville career had ended before the Palace Theatre opened, so he was one of the few legendary names not to play that house. According to Eddie Cantor, when fellow performers once playfully ribbed Jolson about this, he responded:

> I can tell you the exact date I'll play the Palace—the day Eddie Cantor, Groucho Marx, and Jack Benny are on the bill. I'm gonna buy out the house, tear up all the tickets but one, and sit there yelling, "Come on, slaves, entertain the king."

In his private life, Jolson treated a series of wives to bizarre psychological abuse, urging them to drop everything and rush to his side cross country and then treating them with total disinterest and sending them back home—only to repeat the pattern soon afterward. When his much younger third wife Ruby Keeler (1909–1993) landed a starring role in Ziegfeld's *Show Girl* (1928), Jolson stole early performances from her by singing "Liza" from a seat in the audience—many thought this a warm husbandly gesture, but Keeler later confirmed it was nothing of the kind. Soon afterward, he demanded that she walk out on the show and join him in Hollywood. Having vowed to love, honor, and obey, Keeler did as she was told, and a furious Ziegfeld was forced to close the show at a loss.

Odds are that Jolson eventually regretted dragging Keeler out to Hollywood. The thrill of sound and the gooey ballad "Sonny Boy" made Jolson's *The Singing Fool* (1929) one of the highest grossing pictures up to that time, raking in some $5.8 million. For a shining moment, he was the biggest star in motion pictures. But his outsized acting and industrial-strength sentiment soon fell out of fashion, and an early glut of badly made Hollywood musicals turned the public against the genre. This opened the way for the street-smart, kaleidoscopic spectacles of choreographer Busby Berkeley. Within one year, *42nd Street* (1933), *Gold Diggers of 1933* (1933), and *Footlight Parade* (1933) made the unpretentious Ruby Keeler a top box office star—at the same time that her husband's star was falling. Al seethed and did not hesitate to vent his frustrations by verbally abusing Ruby. The Warners costarred the Jolsons in *Go Into Your Dance* (1935), but Al realized his days as a film headliner were over, as was his increasingly acrimonious marriage. He and Ruby divorced in 1940.

Jolson continued to play supporting roles in major films and made frequent appearances on radio, always itching for a chance to step back into the main spotlight. He returned to Broadway in *The Wonder Bar* (1931, 76 performances) and *Hold on to Your Hats* (1940, 158 performances), but both shows forced him to stick to a script and proved to be commercial disappointments. He never withdrew from the public eye, but it began to look as if the public was losing interest.

World War II gave Jolson a chance to get back in front of receptive audiences. He visited boot camps and military hospitals all across the United States and had a special portable piano built so he and an accompanist could tour right up to the front lines. When servicemen begged him to call their anxious relatives back home, he would do so at his own expense. Selfless as all this seemed, he made sure the public knew about his efforts—and about several bouts with malaria contracted during a Pacific tour. Jolson's knack for unabashed sentiment went over well with wartime audiences. During a radio appearance with Milton Berle, Jolson soliloquized:

> It's only today that I'm really playing what you'd call the big time. Let me tell you, of all the wonderful audiences I've played to in my whole

life, the one's that have given me the greatest thrill were thousands of miles away from Broadway on the battle swept deserts of Africa, in the hell and mud of Italy, and in the jungles of the South Pacific. You see Milton, those kids out there fighting and dying have the same ambition; to have peace and tolerance and democracy for the whole world. So as soon as I get a little better—I'm not so strong—I wanna go back out there and sing for those kids. They promised me they'd fix it so I could sing in Hirohito's palace, if there's anything left of it, and sing this song. And by the song I mean, (sings) *Mammy, my little mammy* ... (Studio audience bursts into cheers).

In the midst of this activity, Jolson met and married Erle Galbraith, a twenty-one-year-old X-ray technician who was forty years his junior. Maybe time had mellowed Al's personality, or perhaps Erle was the first woman with the inner strength to stand up to his nonsense, but the yo-yo abuse of his past marriages did not reoccur. The couple eventually adopted two children, and it appears that they had a happy and peaceful relationship.

By the war's end, Jolson was viewed with renewed professional respect, and Columbia Pictures mogul Harry Cohn offered to make a film biography of Jolson's life. Twentieth Century Fox had raked in a fortune turning George M. Cohan's life into the fanciful *Yankee Doodle Dandy* (1942), so why not a similar treatment for Jolson? As with Cohan, many unpleasant details would be left out of the story— Jolson's mother would live, his first two marriages never happen, and even though Ruby Keeler was replaced by a fictional character, she demanded and got $25,000 from the studio for the use of her unnamed identity. This did not annoy Jolson nearly as much as having to record the musical soundtrack for another actor. He put up a good front for publicity purposes, telling the press that he admired how the relatively unknown Larry Parks lip-synched to his vocals, but he was not a happy dubber.

The Jolson Story (1946) featured two dozen of Al's biggest hits, and added a new one—"The Anniversary Song" ("Oh, how we danced on the night we were wed . . ."). Schmaltzy but stylish, the film grossed millions and put Jolson back in the front ranks of show business celebrities. Between increased record sales, a new radio series, and a percentage of the film's profits, he was making a fresh fortune. It was during the filming of the big-budget sequel *Jolson Sings Again* (1949) that Al's antagonism toward Larry Parks revealed itself in a sound stage tirade. Jolson was so vituperative that he was barred from the lot. The film was another great success. Offers poured in for work in film, radio, and even the new medium of television, but America had stepped into the Korean War, and Al put everything on hold to go perform for the troops. Despite a head cold that would have silenced most performers, he gave forty-two concerts in seven days. Days after returning to the United States, a still-exhausted Jolson was in a San Francisco hotel room playing cards with friends when he complained of indigestion. When doctors were called in, he jokingly belittled his symptoms until he felt for his own pulse. He quietly moaned, "Oh, I'm going," and collapsed.

With an unparalleled career that saw him reach the top in every entertainment medium of his lifetime, Al Jolson had some right to claiming a crown. As it was, he usually settled for the title of "the world's greatest entertainer."

9

The Jazz Age (1920–1929) — "I Want to Be Happy"

On September 10, 1920, the news flashed round the world: vivacious Ziegfeld *Follies* girl Olive Thomas had been found in a Paris hotel room, dead at age twenty-six. Her husband Jack Pickford—brother of silent film diva Mary Pickford and a minor movie star in his own right—claimed that Olive had accidentally ingested a bottle of mercury bichloride, a crystal solution used primarily as a topical treatment for syphilitic sores.

From the start, officials had trouble accepting this story, especially when an inconclusive autopsy revealed no signs of mercury in Thomas's body. Smelling a scandal, the press dug in and found that Thomas had been one of Florenz Ziegfeld's mistresses. Realizing that the Great Glorifier would never leave his wife and daughter, Thomas had walked out on him in 1916 and married notorious playboy Pickford, whose addictions to alcohol, drugs, and gambling led to a rocky marital life. Reports circulated that the couple had spent their final days in Paris, alternating between wild parties and even wilder arguments. Had Olive committed suicide, or had she been murdered? In New York just twelve days after Thomas's death, her close friend and fellow *Follies* chorine Anna Daly took a fatal overdose of barbiturates, leaving behind a cryptic, hysterical note: "He doesn't love me anymore and I can't stand it and Olive is dead." Although the "he" in that note was never positively identified, many believed it was none other than Ziegfeld. The American public could accept a man having mistresses, but driving two of them to suicide was another matter.

Ziegfeld avoided the public spotlight for a time and concentrated his energies on mending relations with his outraged wife, Billie Burke.

A torrent of lurid scandals filled newspapers throughout the 1920s, a decade of widespread social and artistic upheaval. The nightmare of World War I encouraged a new sense of isolationism, and a series of Republican presidents resolutely kept America as uninvolved in international affairs as possible. The stock market flourished, which did wonders for the general economy. The new Eighteenth Amendment prohibited the manufacture, importation, transportation, and sale of alcoholic beverages, and thirsty Americans suddenly found it chic to break the law. Some filled their bathtubs with raw alcohol, mixed in various flavorings, and served the results at private parties. Millions frequented "speakeasies," clandestine bars set up in garages and basements where anyone could gain entry by whispering a generic password such as "Joe sent us." The "imported" liquor was often homebrew, but few questioned the well-armed gangsters who supplied the hooch and managed the establishments. Whether the setting was public or private, booze was usually served up with generous helpings of the latest musical craze, jazz.

Jazz was so unprecedented that it still defies definition. It combined the syncopated rhythms of ragtime and the emotional wail of country blues, adding an element of improvisation. Jazz could be written on the page, but it was mostly defined by the unique touches singers and musicians brought to each performance. Born in the bordellos of New Orleans and nurtured in such cities as Chicago, Memphis, and Kansas City, jazz was an African-American invention. And like many other such cultural inventions, it would over time be co-opted by whites. Listeners didn't care what color the musicians were so long as the jazz was hot. When author F. Scott Fitzgerald dubbed the 1920s "The Jazz Age," he was speaking for a discontented generation that found in this music an expression of their passion, their sorrows, their anger, and their sheer energy. Embittered by the senseless carnage of "the war to end all wars," they were out to have one hell of a good time, and jazz was the sound they partied, mated, and wept to. By the end of the decade, the rise of jazz embodied the new American domination of popular culture worldwide. As a later lyric would put it, the sound of "Le Jazz Hot" went round the world "from Steamboat Springs to La Paz."

Although many classically trained musicians viewed jazz with suspicion, a new generation of Broadway composers accepted it as part of their compositional vocabulary. Some of the old guard stood their ground for a while, and a few had extraordinary success writing operettas that seemed to stand in blissful defiance of the new sound, but if Broadway was to remain the primary source for popular songs, it had to keep pace with this massive change in public taste.

And what a pace Broadway set during the 1920s! On average, more than fifty new musicals came to the Main Stem each season. During one incredible six-day period in 1925, four major musical hits opened on Broadway in unbroken succession:

- September 16: *No, No, Nanette*—the most lasting musical comedy smash of the decade
- September 18: *The Vagabond King*—a shamelessly romantic operetta
- September 21: *Sunny*—a musical comedy with songs by Jerome Kern and starring Marilyn Miller
- September 22: *Dearest Enemy*—the first musical comedy by Rodgers and Hart

Each of these four shows drew worldwide attention and introduced songs that became international standards. Through most of the decade, film was silent, commercial radio was in its infancy, and vaudeville provided the legitimate theatre with a steady stream of new talent. Broadway was indisputably the world's main source of entertainment, particularly of new hit songs.

Oh, what a difference a decade would make!

Cinderella Stories

Almost every culture has its own variation of the Cinderella myth, the story of a poor but deserving girl who winds up marrying a handsome prince. This theme was particularly popular with Americans, who relished the idea of seemingly insurmountable class barriers collapsing in the face of love. Broadway's first major postwar musical hit was *Irene* (1919, 675 performances), the story of a Manhattan shop girl who becomes a high-fashion model and wins the hand of a handsome

Long Island millionaire. The twist is that the millionaire must win over Irene's poor Irish immigrant mother, who is suspicious of wealth. The score by composer Harry Tierney and lyricist Joseph McCarthy had no hint of jazz, offering instead a reassuring blend of prewar rhythms, including the sentimental hit waltz "Alice Blue Gown," in which Irene recalls a favorite dress from her childhood. *Irene* broke *A Trip to Chinatown's* twenty-eight-year-old record and became the longest running Broadway musical. American ingénue Edith Day (1896–1971) became an immediate star in the title role. When *Irene* went to London, she went with it and stayed on to become one of the reigning stars of the British musical stage.

The following year, George M. Cohan optioned *The House That Jack Built*, a musical about an architect who plans to build moveable homes that he calls "love nests." Jack stops pursuing a lustful divorcée when he realizes that his true love is his mother's sweet and simple secretary Mary. After a few misunderstandings are cleared up, Jack strikes oil, and Mary is set for a wealthy life of happily ever after. Cohan liked the tuneful score by composer Louis Hirsch and librettists Frank Mandel and Otto Harbach (1873–1963), particularly the breezy song "Love Nest." In one of his classic "Cohanizations," Cohan changed the title to *Mary* (1920, 219 performances), adjusted the song placements, and added a series of rousing dance routines that proved to be a key factor in the show's success. He extended the pre-Broadway tryout for several months, and even sent off an additional road company before bringing the original cast to Broadway. With "Love Nest" already a major hit (a columnist in *Life* complained that it had become "the national anthem"), *Mary* overcame so-so reviews and had a healthy Broadway run.

This trend of rags-to-riches Cinderella musical comedies reached an early zenith when Florenz Ziegfeld created a vehicle for Marilyn Miller (1898–1936), a diminutive blonde dancer who had risen from vaudeville to appearances in several Broadway revues, including two editions of the *Follies*. Ziegfeld had romantic designs on Miller, and sources disagree as to how close they became. It is clear that he was quite annoyed when Miller married *Follies* vocalist Frank Carter. When Carter died soon afterward in a car accident, Ziegfeld sent the heartbroken Miller on a European vacation, hoping to have a new show ready for her upon her return. It was at this point that the deaths of Olive Thomas and Anna Daly buried Ziegfeld in a torrent of foul press coverage. One way to counter all that leering publicity was to produce a big, wholesome hit, and what could be more wholesome than a Cinderella story?

Ziegfeld approached the old Princess team of Kern, Bolton, and Wodehouse, who promptly offered him a story idea they had set aside some years before. It involved a poor dishwasher who dances her way to wealth and fame. When other commitments forced Wodehouse to bow out of the project, lyricist Clifford Grey (1887–1941) stepped in. Bolton adjusted his book, letting the dishwasher win the love of yet another handsome Long Island millionaire while simultaneously attaining stardom in (what else?) the Ziegfeld *Follies. Sally* (1920, 570 performances) also included rubber-limbed comedian Leon Errol as Connie, the deposed Duke of Czechogovina, who is reduced to working as a waiter in the same restaurant as the title waif. Connie gets invited to a party at the millionaire's home and brings Sally along masquerading as a famous dancer. She proceeds to kick and twirl her way into everyone's hearts, getting the *Follies* gig and her man.

Sally's Kern-Grey score had several outstanding songs, including "The Wild Rose" and the far more enduring "Look for the Silver Lining." Joseph Urban provided some spectacular sets and costumes, but the main attraction was Miller. Those who saw Miller onstage insist that her few films and recordings do not begin to capture the incandescence of her live performances. Other stage legends have had the same problem, including Al Jolson, Ethel Merman, and Carol Channing. Watching these beloved talents in their film appearances, viewers often shake their heads and wonder why they were acclaimed as stage sensations. In person, such performers emit a spark of spontaneous combustion that no camera has been able to capture. This was particularly so with Miller—that is, until she danced.

Miller starred in the 1929 screen version of *Sally*, one of the earliest full-length talking films. Her acting amounts to little more than reciting lines, and her singing borders on the amateurish, but when she kicks up her heels, the screen comes to life—particularly in the few surviving minutes of color footage in "Wild Rose." Combining ballet, ballroom, and jazz steps, Miller suddenly radiates vital charm, giving us some sense of what made her live performances so popular. At a time when librettos gave characters little dimension, *Sally* was not much on the page, but Miller made the show compelling—with more than a little help from Ziegfeld's showmanship. Ziegfeld was so convinced that *Sally*'s appeal relied on Miller that he would only tour the show with her in the lead. Altogether, she played the exhausting role for three years, bringing in an estimated five million dollars at the box office. However, the show thrived without its original star in London, where American émigré Dorothy Dickson kept the show kicking for 387 performances.

Back in New York, Lee and J. J. Shubert verified the popularity of contemporary "Cinderella" musicals by putting together something called *Sally, Irene, and Mary* (1922, 313 performances). Chided by the critics for being every bit as derivative as its title suggests, this show still had a profitable run. The creators of the original namesake musicals all considered legal action, but opted to dismiss this imitation as a heavy-handed form of artistic flattery that ultimately did their hits no harm.

We'll never know for sure whether Ziegfeld and Marilyn Miller ever had a genuine affair. He seems to have resumed his pursuit of her during *Sally*'s run, only to be subjected to frequent diva tirades. Knowing that nothing bothered the Great Glorifier as much as bad publicity, Miller told the press that she had to lock Ziegfeld out of her dressing room. She also claimed that he would marry her in a minute if Billie Burke didn't "wave her kid at him like George M. Cohan waves the American flag." In a final reckless gesture, Miller resorted to marrying Jack Pickford, the man Ziegfeld blamed for Olive Thomas's death.

Ziegfeld got the hint and focused on repairing his marriage while Miller went off to work for producer Charles Dillingham. In *Sunny* (1925, 517 performances), she starred as a British bareback rider who loves an American millionaire. Bidding him bon voyage on an ocean liner, she winds up as an unintentional stowaway and to avoid arrest is forced to marry her beloved's best friend. They reach the States, and all is straightened out after a gratuitous but colorful foxhunt sequence—thrown in because Miller looked fetching in a riding habit. Jerome Kern's score included the wistful "Who?" with lyrics cowritten by Otto Harbach and newcomer Oscar Hammerstein (1895–1960). A 1926 London version starring British favorite Binnie Hale (1899–1984) ran for 363 performances.

Sunny's New York running costs were so high that Dillingham hardly made any profit. The pragmatic Miller decided to bury all hatchets and sign a new contract with Ziegfeld, who then showcased her in a musical inspired by Queen Marie of Rumania's highly publicized goodwill tour of the United States. In *Rosalie* (1928, 327 performances), Miller played the title character, a princess of fictional Romanza who falls in love with a West Point cadet. In the end, her royal father (Frank Morgan) abdicates so his daughter can marry her uniformed commoner. Creaky as this plot was, audiences welcomed anything starring Miller, and the show ran for just under a year. In Alexander Woollcott's review for the *World*, he offered a rapturous and often quoted description of Miller's entrance at the New Amsterdam Theatre:

> There comes a time once in every two or three years when the vast stage of that playhouse begins to show signs of a deep and familiar agitation. Down in the orchestra pit the violins chitter with excitement and the brasses blare. The spotlight turns white with expectation. Fifty beautiful girls in simple peasant costumes of satin and chiffon rush pell-mell onto the stage, all squealing simple peasant outcries of "Here she comes!" Fifty hussars in fatigue uniforms of ivory white and tomato bisque march on in columns of four and kneel to express an emotion too strong for words. The lights swing to the gateway at the back and settle there. The house holds its breath, and on walks Marilyn Miller.

Rosalie's score was an unusual mix of operetta and jazz with melodies by both Sigmund and George Gershwin, the latter collaborating with his brother Ira to contribute "How Long Has This Been Going On?"

Irving Berlin: "Say It with Music"

Irving Berlin continued to contribute to the Ziegfeld *Follies*, but now had a revue of his own to compose for. He had teamed up with producer Sam Harris to build the handsome Music Box Theatre on West 45th Street, and having spent nearly a million dollars on the building, they didn't shrink from blowing a record-setting $187,613 on the first *Music Box Revue* (1921, 440 performances). In a wry bow to its competition, the first edition had burglars breaking into the theatre while singing "We'll Take the Plot to Ziegfeld," and threatening that if he doesn't want it, they'll "take it to Dillingham!" The production was staged by relative newcomer Hassard Short (1877–1956), whose all-encompassing eye for coordinated stage activity and evocative lighting soon won him a reputation as one of the top directors in the business. His staging of "Dining Out" presented showgirls dressed as the courses of a banquet. Berlin, who made a cameo appearance, wrote an attractive score, including "Say It with Music." The Brox Sisters introduced the syncopated "Everybody Step," the sort of dance number that became a regular feature in 1920s musicals. Thanks to an unusually high top ticket price of five dollars, the year-long run pulled in a profit of more than half a million dollars. There were four annual *Music Box Revues* between 1921 and 1924, each enjoying progressively shorter runs. The final two editions included operatic diva Grace Moore, who introduced the Berlin hits "What'll I Do" and "All Alone."

Berlin saw a phalanx of fresh legends-to-be join him at the front rank of American songwriters during the 1920s. Most of these newcomers worked in teams, but one other American created words and music singlehandedly. In a field that now belonged almost exclusively to Jewish Americans, he was the only prominent Protestant.

Cole Porter: "You've Got That Thing"

His grandfather made a fortune in the California Gold Rush and invested in timberlands, which, once stripped of their trees, proved to be pocked with generous deposits of coal and oil, so Cole Porter (1891–1964) was born to substantial wealth. He was raised in the small town of Peru, Indiana, where his doting mother published his first song when he was only eleven. As president of the Yale University glee club and a member of the famed Wiffenpoofs, he composed several fight songs still in use at the school today, including "Boola, Boola," "Bingo Eli Yale," and "Bull Dog." While in college he also augmented music with two other passions that would prove lifelong: clothing and men. Although all levels of society condemned homosexuality in the early twentieth century, gays and lesbians with a proper sense of discretion could play the game of compliance in public and do whatever they pleased in private. This was particularly true for the rich, and so it was for Cole.

After Yale, a quick stint in Harvard Law School ended when the dean frankly encouraged him to pursue songwriting. Porter's *See America First* (1916, 16 performances) showed that he was capable of composing tuneful songs in the Kern-Wodehouse style. When that production died a quick death, a disappointed Porter headed off to France and served as an ambulance driver for the Foreign Legion. He switched to the American forces when they joined the war a year later.

It is unclear if Cole saw much action, but he apparently spent a lot of time in Paris, where he met and married divorced socialite Linda Lee Thomas. Linda's previous marriage to an abusive drunk left her so emotionally and physically battered that the prospect of a witty, sophisticated husband who would make no sexual demands must have seemed ideal. As Linda's fortune was nearly twice that of Cole's, the Porters lived in high style, with an apartment in Paris, a series of palazzos in Venice, a country mansion in Massachusetts, and a residential suite in Manhattan's ultra exclusive Waldorf-Astoria Hotel. Cole had several homosexual affairs in the course of their marriage, but usually limited his encounters to male prostitutes and the occasional sailor. Such "tricks" were not likely to talk and would not be believed if they did.

During a 1926 dinner at the Porter's Venetian palazzo, Cole confided to fellow composer Richard Rodgers that he had stumbled upon a formula for hit songs: "I'll write Jewish tunes." Rodgers took this to be a joke, but on reflection realized that this Episcopalian millionaire from Indiana wrote some of his most enduring hits using minor key melodies that were "unmistakably eastern Mediterranean." In the bridges of later hits like "Begin the Beguine" and "My Heart Belongs to Daddy," we hear cantorial melodic lines that would be at home in any synagogue.

Cole and Linda Porter were not bigots and detested snobbery in any form. When Jewish Irving Berlin dared to elope with Roman Catholic socialite Ellin Mackay, her enraged father (a divorced but self-righteous Catholic) saw to it that the young couple was cut off by most of the social register. The Porters went out of their way to invite the Berlins to dinners and parties, forcing an end to the ban. Irving never forgot this kindness, and when producer Ray Goetz wanted a new musical for his wife Irene Bordoni, Berlin sent him to Porter. *Paris* (1928, 195 performances) featured Cole's first memorable hit song, "Let's Do It." At a time when most love songs were decidedly innocent, here was one with a jazzy rhythm and a lyric heralding the amorous adventures of birds, bees, and educated fleas. The meaning was scandalous, but the words were squeaky clean, and the public embraced the song.

The following year, Porter provided a hit-packed score for *Fifty Million Frenchmen* (1929, 254 performances), which had a featherweight plot involving a rich American in Paris who tries to win a fifty thousand dollar bet by wooing a girl without mentioning or spending a penny of his family's money. William Gaxton (1893–1963) played the lead, introducing "You Do Something to Me," with the wooden but cynical stage persona that was already making him a top rank musical comedy leading man. Jack Thompson and Betty Compton (the mistress of New York's corrupt Mayor Jimmy Walker) sang "You've Got That Thing," in which a man reassures his girl that she has what it takes to make him "order an extra bed with an extra spring." Such sophisticated sexual content delighted the general public, and the show enjoyed a profitable run. With two successes in as many years, Cole Porter had definitely arrived.

Richard Rodgers and Lorenz Hart: "An Isle of Joy"

On March 31, 1917, fourteen year-old Richard Rodgers (1902–1979) was taken by his older brother William to the Saturday matinee of Columbia University's annual varsity show. The jumbled collection of skits and songs was nearly stolen by journalism student Lorenz Hart (1895–1943), who donned full drag for a hilarious impersonation of silent film star Mary Pickford. After the show, the stagestruck Rodgers was too shy to approach Hart, but was introduced to the show's lyricist, law student Oscar Hammerstein II. Rodgers later wrote that "no deathless words were exchanged"—it would be a quarter century before the names Rodgers and Hammerstein would become professionally entwined. But that day in 1917, Dick resolved that he would eventually attend Columbia so he could compose future varsity shows.

With that goal in mind, a mutual friend arranged some two years later for Rodgers to meet Larry Hart, who had graduated from Columbia but still contributed material to varsity productions.

Both Rodgers and Hart were nice Jewish boys raised in comfort on Manhattan's Upper West Side, and both shared a passion for the adventurous songwriting of Kern and Wodehouse. Beyond that, they were total opposites. Rodgers came from a contentious family where explosive arguments were followed by weeks of glacial silence. The one place where emotion could be safely expressed in the Rodgers's household was at the piano. From early childhood, Dick could play tunes by ear upon first hearing, winning the adulation of his quarrelsome, theatre-loving relatives. By the time he teamed with Larry, Dick Rodgers was attractive, well ordered, emotionally insulated, and thoroughly devoted to popular music.

Hart stood not quite five feet in height and had been raised in an emotionally freewheeling environment, where his effusive charm and penchant for writing light verse were encouraged. Disorganized, impulsive, and utterly irresponsible, he was also a heavy drinker, often useless by midday and loaded by sundown. He was constantly on the move, either pacing about a room endlessly rubbing his hands together, or heading off without warning to the next party. Larry was also a deeply closeted homosexual, too racked by guilt to handle the sort of compromises that Cole Porter managed. This issue would pose no immediate problems in Rodgers and Hart's collaboration, but over time it would take a crippling emotional toll on the insecure lyricist.

Rodgers soon learned that he had to practically pin Hart down to get him to work, and when he did work, the results were impressive. A friend introduced them to Lew Fields, the longtime comedy partner of Joe Weber and now a solo success as an actor and producer. He interpolated their song "Any Old Place with You" into his Broadway production *A Lonely Romeo* right after the 1918 Equity strike. So Rodgers had his first Broadway credit at age seventeen, Hart at the ripe old age of twenty-four. Unfortunately, as Fields's daughter Dorothy would one day write, "If you start at the top, you're certain to drop." Over the next seven years, the new team wrote just one Broadway score, half of which the producer replaced with the work of others. Outside of that, Rodgers and Hart were relegated to turning out songs for amateur productions. Rodgers was ready to chuck his theatrical career and accept an offer to sell children's underwear. Then an invitation came from the Theatre Guild, acclaimed for its productions of distinguished dramas. The Guild was building a new theatre, and its young apprentices—including future notables Sterling Holloway, Romney Brent, Edith Meiser, Lee Strasberg, and Sanford Meisner— were putting on a benefit revue to raise money for the new theatre's decorative tapestries. Hart had no desire to write a revue, but Rodgers persuaded him that it was worth a try.

When *The Garrick Gaieties* (1925, 311 performances) played its two planned performances on May 17, 1925, the production proved a tremendous audience pleaser, with skits and songs spoofing current Broadway hits, the behavior of audiences, and even the Guild itself. The highlight was "Manhattan," a lighthearted musical salute to that unlikely "isle of joy." Added matinées sold out despite an early summer heat wave, so the Guild closed its production of *The Guardsman* starring Alfred Lunt and Lynn Fontanne, and *The Garrick Gaieties* wound up having a healthy open-ended run. According to Rodgers, years later he and Hart attended a performance in the Guild's new space (now called the August Wilson Theatre), and Hart said, "See those tapestries? We're responsible for them." Rodgers replied, "No, Larry. They're responsible for us."

Rodgers and Hart became the hottest talents on Broadway, turning out thirteen Broadway scores over the next five years, plus one original for London's West End. Dick and Larry saw deadlines as a challenge and thrived under the pressure. Nine of these efforts involved book writer Herb Fields (1897–1958), Lew's son. Herb proved a ready hand at turning out librettos that—at their best—gave a fresh spin to the standard period musical comedy formulas. *Dearest Enemy* (1925, 286 performances) was based on the true story of a New York hostess who detained the British high command long enough to give Washington's troops time to retreat from Manhattan in 1776. Herb created a fictional romance between British Captain Copeland (Charles Purcell) and female revolutionary Betsy Burke (Helen Ford), who meet while she is taking a nude swim. She makes her first onstage appearance wearing only a barrel, and when the Captain claims that at first glace he thought she was a boy, feisty Betsy replies, "Well you should have taken a second look!" Director John Murray Anderson was on hand to give the overall production a smooth flow and a polished period appearance. The success of the ballad "Here in My Arms" helped the show overcome sluggish ticket sales and become a profitable hit.

The Girl Friend (1926, 301 performances) was a typical star vehicle featuring vaudeville team Sam White and Eva Puck as an athlete and coach out to win a six-day bicycle race. The score featured a jaunty title song ("She's knockout, she's regal, her beauty's illegal"), and the hit ballad "Blue Room" exhibited the sort of unexpected melodic invention that became a Rodgers hallmark. The partners opened the second *Garrick Gaieties* (1926, 174 performances) with the ensemble admitting "We Can't Be as Good as Last Year," but the song "Mountain Greenery" proved a huge favorite with its evocation of a country home so welcoming that "beans could get no keener reception in a beanery."

Peggy-Ann (1926, 333 performances) had an unusual Herb Fields libretto about a young woman confronting her life's problems in a series of dreams. As this show went into production, producer Florenz Ziegfeld bullied the songwriters into immediately providing a score for *Betsy* (1926, 39 performances), the story of a girl from Manhattan's Lower East Side who must find a husband to appease her overbearing Jewish mother. We can only wonder why Ziegfeld was surprised when Rodgers and Hart wound up paying more attention to their other show. On *Betsy*'s opening night, Ziegfeld shocked the songwriters with an unannounced interpolation by Irving Berlin: "Blue Skies." The song earned encores, but *Betsy* was such a clunker that it faded away after barely a month. Although *Peggy-Ann* did far better, its lack of hit songs has left it little more than a historical footnote.

The following year brought *A Connecticut Yankee* (1928, 418 performances), an updated adaptation of Mark Twain's classic comic novel. In this version, socialite Alice (Constance Carpenter) catches fiancé Martin (William Gaxton) flirting with another woman on the eve of their wedding. She conks him on the head with a champagne bottle, and he inexplicably awakens in King Arthur's Camelot. Martin soon finds himself managing the kingdom, introducing such modern innovations as the billboard, telephone, and radio. The knights of Camelot utter such polyglot lines as, "Methinks yon damsel is a lovely broad." Rodgers conducted the premiere performance, and later wrote that when Gaxton began singing "Thou Swell," the audience reaction was "so strong that it was like an actual blow." The score also included the popular ballad "My Heart Stood Still," inspired when a girl sharing a taxicab with the songwriters reacted to a near-collision by exclaiming, "Oh, my heart stood still!" Running a full year, *A Connecticut Yankee* was Rodgers and Hart's biggest hit to date.

Present Arms (1928, 155 performances) was the story of a U.S. Marine private masquerading as a captain to impress the daughter of an English peer. Former drill instructor Busby Berkeley (1895–1976) not only won attention by staging the kind of precision dance formations that would later mark his films, but also got to introduce "You Took Advantage of Me" with ingénue Joyce Barbour. The rest of Rodgers and Hart's 1920s musicals are only remembered for their songs. For example, *Spring Is Here* (1929, 104 performances) was an unremarkable love story that ran for just over three months, but the rapturous "With a Song in My Heart" became a standard. As the decade ended, Rodgers and Hart were the most prolific top-level team in their field. At a time when most tunesmiths switched partners on a frequent basis, these two were the first Broadway songwriting team to work together exclusively for twenty-five years. Much of their best work lies in the chapters ahead.

The West End in the 1920s: Coward and Company

As the 1920s progressed, it seemed as if London's West End was awash in American imports like *Irene*, *Sally*, and *Sunny*. The number of new British musicals worthy of export slowed to a trickle, but two determined producers kept that trickle steady and too potent to ignore by jointly introducing the work of several star performers and one multi-talented genius–Noel Coward (1899–1973).

Paris-born Andre Charlot (1882–1956) was one of the most prolific West End producers of the twentieth century. With more than forty-five productions to his name, he is best remembered for creating a series of intimate 1920s revues that relied on elegant simplicity rather than spectacle, showcasing outstanding British talent. Charlot's discoveries included dancing ingénues Binnie Hale and Jessie Matthews (1907–1981), zany comedienne Beatrice Lillie (1898–1989), song and dance man Jack Buchanan (1891–1957), and the iridescent Gertrude Lawrence (1898–1952). But such talents required great material in order to shine.

A gifted playwright-lyricist-composer stepped forward to provide them with songs and skits. Noël Coward had been a professional performer since childhood and now came into his own as a writer. He contributed songs to Charlot's revue *London Calling* (1923, 316 performances in London), including the memorable "Parisian Pierrot" for longtime friend Gertrude Lawrence. His fame skyrocketed when he wrote, codirected, and starred in *The Vortex* (1924), a harsh drama about drug addiction and sexual misconduct in an upper class family. The play proved to be a smash on both sides of the Atlantic. That same season, Coward provided songs for two of Charlot's West End revues, as well as a compilation that brought Lawrence, Bea Lillie, and Jack Buchanan to Broadway (1924, 298 performances in New York). After years of struggle, Coward was suddenly a hot property.

Producer Charles B. Cochran (1872–1951) was often—to his annoyance—referred to as "the British Ziegfeld." His revues may not have had as distinctive a personal style as Charlot's, but they were often no less successful. Coward provided a full score for Cochran's *On with the Dance* (1925, 229 performances in London), which included the cautionary "Poor Little Rich Girl" ("cocktails and laughter, but what comes after, nobody knows"). Cochran also produced Coward's hit revue *This Year of Grace* (1928, 316 performances in London), which featured Sonnie Hale and Jessie Matthews singing "A Room with a View." Songs like "Dance Little Lady" made it clear that a distinctly British composer could handle jazz. In the Broadway edition of the same revue (1928, 157 performances), Bea Lillie dressed as an office boy and perched on a stool to introduce "World Weary."

Defying expectations, Coward then resurrected the lost world of hoop-skirted, continental operetta in *Bitter Sweet* (1929, 697 performances in London), the tale of a British heiress who runs off to Vienna with her music teacher, only to see him murdered by a jealous aristocrat. American Peggy Wood starred, and the score included "I'll See You Again" (also known as "The Bitter Sweet Waltz"), "If Love Were All," and the daring gay quartette "Green Carnation." Filled with the glamour of prewar Mitteleuropa, this lavish Cochran production struck a chord with London audiences and became a long-running success. When the show reached Broadway later that same season (1929, 159 performances), British soprano Evelyn Laye (1900–1996) starred and Florenz Ziegfeld produced, but ticket sales shriveled in the wake of a crippling stock market crash. Undaunted, Coward would remain the brightest light in British theatre for years to come.

George and Ira Gershwin: "Fascinating Rhythm"

In 1910, Morris and Rose Gershovitz brought a piano into their New York apartment expecting that their bookish, eldest son Israel would learn to play it, but their troublesome second son Jacob soon monopolized the keyboard. Within four years, Jacob went from his first lesson to earning a respectable fifteen dollars a week demonstrating songs on Tin Pan Alley. The world would later know Jacob as George Gershwin (1898–1937) and his brother Israel as Ira (1896–1983), the only fraternal team in the top rank of American songwriters. Because Ira always deferred to his more glamorous and outgoing younger brother, George got the lion's share of attention.

In the early twentieth century, vaudevillians in search of new material made their way to Manhattan's music publishers, who made sheet music available to them free of charge and kept pianists on hand to demonstrate samples. In 1915, George Gershwin was just such a "song plugger" at Remick's, where he played through numbers for seventeen-year-old Fred Astaire (1899–1987), who had been dancing in vaudeville since childhood with his sister Adele (1898–1981). The two young men discussed their dreams of making it to Broadway, and George said, "Wouldn't it be great if I could write a musical show and you could be in it?"

George first made it to Broadway as a rehearsal pianist, getting a first-hand look at the process of making musicals. A natural extrovert, George was a shameless promoter of his own music. As long-time friend Oscar Levant would later quip, "An evening spent with George Gershwin is a Gershwin evening." We've already seen how George's habit of hogging the piano at parties had led to Jolson making the neglected "Swanee" into a hit. At this stage of his career, he worked with various lyricists, turning out his first complete score for the musical comedy *La, La, Lucille* (1919, 104 performances), which died a premature death due to the Actor's Equity Strike. Beginning the following year, Gershwin contributed songs to five consecutive editions of George White's *Scandals*, including "I'll Build a Stairway to Paradise" and "Somebody Loves Me." These early hit tunes show George using the staccato rhythms and blue notes of jazz. While other Broadway composers hesitated, he plunged into the new sound.

In 1924, bandleader Paul Whiteman invited George to submit material for a concert entitled "An Experiment in Jazz." The audience at New York's Aeolian Hall went wild over Gershwin's "Rhapsody in Blue," and dismissive reviews could not prevent this piece from becoming an immediate sensation. With an opening note that sends a clarinet swooping across two and a half octaves, the "Rhapsody" served as a declaration that jazz and George Gershwin were now part of the musical mainstream. From this point onward, most serious music critics attacked his classical compositions, but the more they grumbled, the more the public cheered.

La, La, Lucille producer Alex Aarons (1891–1943) now teamed up with former chorus performer Vinton Freedley (1891–1969) to finance *Lady, Be Good* (1924, 330 performances), the first Gershwin musical with lyrics by Ira, and the first written as a vehicle for Fred and Adele Astaire. The libretto by Fred Thompson and Guy Bolton was airheaded nonsense involving a brother-sister song and dance team that falls on hard times until the girl gets involved in a scheme that requires passing herself off as a Spanish heiress. George and Ira translated jazz into the showtune tradition, both in the buoyant title song and in the jubilant dance ensemble "Fascinating Rhythm." As a rule, George wrote melodies first, playing them through several times until Ira got an idea for a lyric. On first hearing this pounding, insistent melody, Ira asked, "For God's sake, George, what kind of lyric do you write to a rhythm like that?" Ira thought for a moment before noting, "It's a fascinating rhythm...." The Astaires repeated their triumph when they took *Lady, Be Good* to the West End two years later (1926, 326 performances).

When Aarons and Freedley wanted a Broadway vehicle for Gertrude Lawrence, they hired the Gershwins and the old Princess team of Bolton and Wodehouse to come up with *Oh, Kay!* (1926, 257 performances). Lawrence played Lady Kay, the sister of an English nobleman who uses his yacht to smuggle illegal booze for Prohibition-parched Americans. The nobleman appropriates the basement of a Long Island mansion as a base of operations, which works well until the mansion's unknowing owner Jimmy Winter pays a visit. Although Jimmy is engaged to be married, he is smitten by Kay, who poses as a housemaid. With the help of gangster Shorty McGee (Victor Moore), who poses as a butler, Kay and Jimmy outwit both his fiancée and a government agent who stumbles into the chaos. Moore won big laughs when he quipped, "The difference between a bootlegger and a federal inspector is that one of them wears a badge." The score included the jazzy "Fidgety Feet," the pseudo spiritual "Clap Yo' Hands," and the breezy "Do, Do, Do" ("what you done, done, done before"). One day before rehearsals began, George started absentmindedly playing a fast dance number at a slower tempo. Ira pointed out that the tune sounded better as a ballad, and "Someone to Watch Over Me" was born. Instead of singing it straight at the audience, Lawrence crooned to a Raggedy Ann doll about the unknown someone she was "longing to see." The song became a standard, and the show a major hit.

Alex Aarons and Vinton Freedley built their own Broadway theatre in 1927, combining the first syllables of their given names to dub it the Alvin; now known as the Neil Simon, it remains one of New York's most coveted musical theatre venues. For its premiere production, the producers mounted yet another Gershwin musical starring the Astaires, *Funny Face* (1927, 250 performances). Fred played guardian to Adele, who spent the show romancing a Lindbergh-esque aviator while trying to save her pearls from theft by inept thugs. The hit-packed score included the title song, "My One and Only," "He Loves and She Loves," and the slangy "S'Wonderful" ("s'marvelous you should care for me"). "The Babbitt and the Bromide," a tongue-twisting conversation between two blowhards, gave the Astaires a perfect opportunity to do their signature "runaround" step. With hands poised as if on invisible bicycle handlebars, Adele ran about in a circle several times before Fred joined in for their big exit. This simple maneuver wowed audiences on both sides of the Atlantic. *Funny Face* had an even warmer reception in Britain (1928, 263 performances in London), and decades later provided the basis for the long-running Tommy Tune production *My One and Only* (1983).

After contributing part of the score to the aforementioned 1928 hit *Rosalie*, the Gershwins worked on two disappointing projects, *Treasure Girl* (1928, 68 performances) and the aforementioned Ziegfeld production *Show Girl* (1929, 111 performances). Despite these stumbles, the Gershwins were poised to help redefine musical comedy in the decade ahead. In the midst of the 1920s, few would have believed that musical comedy would ever need to be redefined.

Musical Comedy Triumphant: "Can't You See How Happy We Could Be?"

Star vehicles have long been part of the theatre, but few were as unabashed as *Stepping Stones* (1923, 241 performances). Producer Charles Dillingham lined up Jerome Kern and the prolific but rarely remembered lyricist Anne Caldwell (1867–1936) to showcase the real-life "stepping" Stones. In a curious redo of the Red Riding Hood story, acrobatic *Wizard of Oz* veteran Fred Stone played Peter Plug, a plumber trying to save Rougette Hood (seventeen-year-old daughter Dorothy Stone) from a forced marriage to Otto de Wolfe (Oscar "Rags" Ragland). Fred's wife Allene Stone was also on hand to play Rougette's widowed mother. The senior Stone inserted whatever physical gags he felt might amuse, making his entrance by parachute and finishing the first act with tricks on a horizontal bar. His big solo showpiece was a tongue-twisting musical list of more than two dozen varieties of "Pie." Otherwise, he generously designed the show to revolve around his little girl. Kern and Caldwell dutifully provided the father-daughter duet "Wonderful Dad," as well as a "Raggedy Ann and Andy" number that the Stones turned into a loose-limbed dance specialty. Audiences and critics embraced the show with enthusiasm, but it was so reliant upon the specific talents of the Stones that it had no life after the original production. As with previous Stone vehicles, there was a tour, but no suggestion of sending the show to Britain.

The most perennially popular musical comedy of the 1920s had a particularly rocky pre-Broadway tryout. The complicated plot of *No, No, Nanette* (1925, 321 performances) involved Jimmy Smith, a bible publisher who innocently finances the careers of three young ladies. When Smith's adopted teenage daughter Nanette rebels and runs off to Atlantic City, the resulting fuss inadvertently reveals papa's seeming indiscretions. After a few weeks on the road, producer H. H. Frazee decided his show needed a radical overhaul, so he took over as director and called on composer Vincent Youmans (1898–1946) and lyricists Irving Caesar and Otto Harbach to replace five songs. The new numbers included "Tea for Two" and "I Want to Be Happy." Chicago audiences reacted with such enthusiasm that *No, No, Nanette* stayed for an open-ended run. In the year that followed, Frazee replaced most of the leading cast members, saw several of the Youmans-Caesar songs become major hits, and even authorized a West End production (1925, 665 performances). By the time *No, No, Nanette* reached Broadway, its success was practically preordained, which may explain why New York's critics reacted with a resentful chorus of grumbles and shrugs. As the well-meaning Smith, comedian Charles Winninger (1884–1969) finished his rendition of "I Want to Be Happy" with a giddy backflip. The Youmans score moves smoothly between sweet sentiment ("Peach on the Beach"), torch songs ("The Where Has My Hubby Gone Blues"), and Charleston-style dance tunes ("You Can Dance with Any Girl at All"). Film versions in 1930 and 1940 did well despite using few of the original songs, and a revamped stage version would find even greater success in 1971.

Youmans was unhappy with the way his *Nanette* score was handled, so in order to have a greater degree of creative control, he went so far as to coproduce his next show, *Hit the Deck* (1927, 352 performances). Clifford Grey and newcomer Leo Robin (1900–1984) provided the lyrics, and Herb Fields provided his first libretto for someone other than Rodgers and Hart. A Newport heiress falls in love with a sailor and follows him around the world in an attempt to win his affections, only to learn he is reluctant to marry a wealthy woman. She wins his hand by bequeathing her fortune to their theoretical first-born. The score boasted the love duet "Sometimes I'm Happy" and the rousing ensemble number "Hallelujah." Both songs had been originally written for previous projects—at a time when composers often worked on several shows in a given season, such recycling was quite common. Aside from the almost yearlong Broadway run, *Hit the Deck* had several national touring companies and successful film versions in 1933 and 1955.

The songwriting team of lyricist B. G. "Buddy" DeSylva (1895–1950), composer Ray Henderson (1896–1970), and lyricist Lew Brown (1893–1958) got their collaboration off to a good start with "It All Depends on You," which Al Jolson interpolated into *Big Boy*. Their complete scores for the 1925 and 1926 editions of George White's *Scandals* included "The Birth of the Blues" and "Lucky Day." For their first full-length book musical, DeSylva, Henderson, and Brown landed a story about a small college desperate to win the big football game—something *Leave It to Jane* had handled a decade earlier. But

Good News (1927, 557 performances) became a cultural phenomenon in its own right by immortalizing the hedonistic college lifestyle of the 1920s. In the opening chorus, students at fictional Tait College explain that they learn "how to sin, not how to think." Football team captain Tom Marlowe (John Price Jones) won't be able to play unless poor but bookish Constance Lane (Mary Lawlor) can tutor him into passing astronomy. Tom passes, Tait wins the game, and a series of romantic misunderstandings are cleared up in time for Tom and Constance to link up in the final scene. Jones and Lawlor sang "The Best Things in Life Are Free," which lists pleasures money cannot buy, including flowers in spring and robins that sing. Zelma O'Neal introduced "The Varsity Drag," a "down on your heels, up on your toes" celebration of youth that joined the Charleston and Black Bottom as Broadway-born 1920s dance sensations. The producers went so far as to have the pit orchestra enter down the aisles of the 46th Street Theatre, attired in Tait College letter sweaters and giving a football cheer.

Promoted to star status by Ziegfeld in the *Follies*, diminutive comedian Eddie Cantor continued to make appearances in that series while starring in two of Ziegfeld's book musical hits. *Kid Boots* (1923, 479 performances) had Cantor as a golf club caddie who uses crooked balls to keep clients coming back for more lessons—he also sells bootleg booze on the side. When the score needed a likely hit, Irving Berlin sent over song plugger Harry Akst to audition some of Berlin's newest compositions. Cantor didn't care for any of the submissions, but perked up when the exasperated Akst played a composition of his own—"Dinah," with lyrics by Sam Lewis and Joe Young. Berlin was understandably irked, but in a shrewd move, agreed to publish the song, which became a standard. After the year-plus Broadway run, Cantor spent fifteen exhausting months taking *Kid Boots* on tour.

Cantor always played a streetwise nebbish in his musicals, putting on blackface (which had been one of his trademarks in vaudeville) for selective songs. In *Whoopee* (1928, 407 performances), he became Henry Williams, a quivering hypochondriac who helps a reluctant bride escape a forced wedding in the Wild West. The score by composer Walter Donaldson and lyricist Gus Kahn made no attempt to integrate the sizzling torch song "Love Me or Leave Me"; Ruth Etting (1907–1978) just strolled out, sang it, and stopped the show. At least Cantor's character was en route to a wedding when he introduced

"Makin' Whoopee," in which a judge warns a philandering husband to "keep her, you'll find it's cheaper." The song became Cantor's life-long signature tune. After more than a year on Broadway, Cantor toured in *Whoopee* before starring in a full-length sound version for Goldwyn Pictures in 1930. Choreographer Busby Berkeley restaged his Broadway dances, using overhead cameras to capture the kaleido-scopic routines—a technique that he would soon use to revolutionize cinematography in musical films.

It should be noted that Broadway clowns of the 1920s who attained stardom in sound films are still remembered—including Cantor, Ed Wynn, Will Rogers, Bert Lahr, W. C. Fields, and Jolson. Equally pop-ular stage comics who did not make it on the big screen—such as Joe Cook or the team of Joe Clark and William McCullough—are now only recalled by hard-core historians. Somewhere in between is Bea Lillie, who preserved a few memorable bits on film but is now little more than a fading camp icon.

Black Musicals: "Love Will Find a Way"

In February of 1922, Bert Williams was touring for the Shuberts. A dedicated workaholic, the star ignored ominous symptoms until he collapsed on stage in Detroit and was rushed back to New York. He died days later at age forty-eight, leaving colleagues shocked and heartbroken. By this time, a new generation of African-American talent was making a fresh assault on Broadway. Although the white-dominated culture was ready to applaud this effort, it later proved equally ready to forget that the black musicals of the 1920s had ever taken place.

Shuffle Along (1921, 504 performances) was the first major Broad-way production in more than a decade written and performed exclu-sively by African Americans. Essentially a revue, it is often classified as a book musical, thanks to a minimal plot. Comedians Flournoy Miller and Aubrey Lyles expanded their vaudeville routine "The Mayor of Dixie" into a full-length script involving an election in all-black "Jim Town." Lyricist Noble Sissle (1889–1975) and composer Eubie Blake (1883–1983) had also appeared in vaudeville, writing and performing songs that ignored the old racial stereotypes. In *Shuffle Along*, they offered "I'm Just Wild About Harry" and "Love Will Find a Way," hit numbers with no hint of "coon song" mentality, and no connection to the plot. However, *Shuffle Along* was still burdened by hateful conventions. Most of the black skinned cast still felt it necessary to blacken their faces, and variations of the swindling Zip Coon character were still on hand, albeit using different names. *Shuffle Along* opened at the 63rd Street Theatre, several blocks north of the accepted theatre district, but was such a sensation that the police were forced to change the street into a one-way thoroughfare to ease the extra traffic. Several extraordinary talents got their first major attention in this production, including Adelaide Hall, Josephine Baker, Florence Mills (1895–1927), and Paul Robeson (1898–1976). The longest running all-black production up to that time, *Shuffle Along* inspired numerous imitators, none of which eclipsed its reputation. Noble and Sissle would contribute to several mainstream white stage revues, but their future productions never matched *Shuffle Along*'s success.

Shuffle Along's librettists Miller and Lyles made another stab at Broadway in *Runnin' Wild* (1923, 228 performances), which revisited the same Jim Town characters and is remembered primarily because of one song: "The Charleston," written by African-American songwriters James P. Johnson and Cecil Mack and introduced by the talented black songstress Elisabeth Welch (1904–2003). With its high-kicking, syncopated rhythm, "The Charleston" became the definitive dance craze of the 1920s.

Beginning in 1926, white producer Lew Leslie put together a series of *Blackbirds* revues featuring all-black casts performing material written mostly by whites. Florence Mills was joined by black vaudeville singer Ethel Waters (1896–1977) and tap dancing legend Bill "Bojangles" Robinson (1878–1949). Painful images were still in use, with one *Blackbirds* backdrop depicting a huge smiling "pickaninny" eating watermelon while sitting on a plantation fence. The longest running edition was *Blackbirds of 1928* (1928, 519 performances), which boasted "I Can't Give You Anything but Love" and "Doin' the New Low Down" by the white composing team of Jimmy McHugh (1901–1965) and lyricist Dorothy Fields (1905–1974). Daughter of the great Lew Fields, Dorothy was just coming into her own as a lyric writer, and over the next five decades would become the most successful woman in a field dominated by men. Leslie presented further editions of *Blackbirds*, but the public soon seemed to lose interest. With the end of the 1920s, the renaissance of black musical theatre quickly subsided, and the genre would not reappear with any frequency until another half a century had passed.

American Operetta: New Seeds of Integration

Despite the rise of jazz and the bloody advent of World War I, American audiences were not altogether ready to quit operetta cold turkey. They had become accustomed to generous doses of romance sung in three-quarter time. The American theatre developed a home-grown breed of romantic operettas. The two composers behind the best of these works were born in the borders of Austria-Hungary, but were both proud, naturalized citizens of the United States of America. These men gave the old genre a refreshing splash of New World energy, and both collaborated with a lyricist-librettist who did more than any other individual to reshape musical theatre in the mid-twentieth century. First, we'll discuss the composers; then meet the incipient innovator.

Hungarian-born composer Sigmund Romberg (1887–1951) had been studying engineering in Vienna when an ushering job at the Theatre An Der Wein fired his passion for theatrical music. He worked his way to New York, were he spent several years conducting a restaurant orchestra before the Shuberts took him on as a staff composer. A prolific human synthesizer, he could turn out melodies in most any style–some admittedly more original than others. Throughout his career, Romberg would borrow a harmonic line or a melodic phrase, and not always intentionally. The Shuberts' used his dependable music in everything from revues to Al Jolson's book musicals. None of Romberg's early songs were big hits, but they kept many a profitable production chugging tunefully along.

All that changed when the Shuberts optioned the 1913 Viennese hit *Ein Tag im Paradies*. For Broadway, it became *The Blue Paradise* (1915), and the less memorable numbers in Edmund Eysler's score were replaced with new ones by Romberg. Perhaps it was the sentimental plot about a wealthy man learning that it is unwise to revisit one's youth that inspired Romberg to write a waltz of remembrance, "Auf Wiedersehen." He certainly could not have been inspired by the incomprehensible Herbert Reynolds lyric ("Love is never knowing no word like goodbye"). Newcomer Vivienne Segal (1897–1992) introduced the song in an appealing soprano voice that made her a star, a status she would retain for the next four decades. "Auf Wiedersehen" became a major hit and Romberg was suddenly in demand. The Shuberts were able to keep him on staff only by promising to find him more projects in the same vein. While their agents searched, Romberg kept slaving away, contributing to as many as six forgettable Shubert scores per season.

The German operetta *Wie einst im Mai* (1913) had that rarest of gems, a novel plot. Although Ottilie loves her father's poor apprentice Fritz, she is forced to marry her seemingly well-off cousin, who soon dies and leaves her penniless. In later years, Ottilie asks the now successful Fritz to protect her single daughter from the machinations of his married son. A generation later, Ottilie's granddaughter and Fritz's grandson fall in love, fulfilling the romantic destiny of their ancestors. The Shuberts called in *Naughty Marietta* librettist Rida Johnson Young, who retained the main outline of the plot, reset the action in nineteenth century New York, turned "Fritz" into "Richard," and added a new twist involving the grandchildren rediscovering a deed and ring that their grandparents buried in a garden. Renamed *Maytime* (1917, 492 performances), it became Broadway's biggest wartime hit. Peggy Wood (1892–1978) introduced Romberg and Young's "The Road to Paradise" with costar Charles Purcell, as well as "Will You Remember," with its familiar refrain ("Sweetheart, sweetheart, sweetheart"). *Maytime* would tour for years to come, and for a brief time the Shuberts had two companies running on Broadway simultaneously.

Romberg went back to hack work until the Shuberts bought the rights to *Das Dreimäderlhaus* (*The House of Three Maidens*), a Viennese operetta inspired by the life and melodies of classical composer Franz Schubert. In love with one of three sisters but too shy to express his feelings, Schubert writes a love song and has a friend sing it—the girl thinks the singer is expressing his own emotions, so she runs off with the vocalist, leaving the composer alone. Adapting this charming fiction into *Blossom Time* (1921, 592 performances), Romberg used tunes from Schubert's marches and lieder, and turned a theme from the well-known Unfinished Symphony into the score's big hit, "Song of Love." This was still Schubert's music, but with plenty of

Built by William Niblo in 1828, Niblo's Garden was one of New York's most fashionable theatres in the mid-nineteenth century. Destroyed in an 1846 fire, it was rebuilt three years later, and this second Niblo's was home to *The Black Crook* (1866). This period newspaper engraving shows what the ornate 3,000-seat auditorium looked like in mid-performance. Note the presence of respectably dressed women in the audience—not something to be taken for granted at that time. (Author's collection)

Robin Hood (1890) was one of the most popular American comic operas, a genre that peaked after the widespread popularity of Gilbert and Sullivan. This 1919 Broadway revival was lavishly costumed and generously populated, but note the state-of-the-art sets—all inexpensive painted flats. A far cry from the costly stage effects of the early twenty-first century! (Author's collection)

Girls in tights were a longtime attraction in the extravaganzas, burlesques, and early musical comedies of the 1800s. This is Fay Templeton, most likely in costume for Edward Rice's *Excelsior Jr.* (1895). Although *Yankee Doodle Dandy* (1942) has kept Templeton's name alive, she was nothing like the statuesque soprano depicted in that film. Short, feisty, and throaty-voiced, the real Templeton was one of Broadway's most beloved comediennes from the 1880s onward. She was married three times, and her final union in 1906, to industrialist William Patterson, made her one of the wealthiest women in America. After her husband's death, Templeton made a final trip to Broadway as Aunt Minnie in *Roberta* (1933), introducing the sentimental Jerome Kern–Otto Harbach ballad "Yesterdays." (Author's collection)

Lillian Russell's hourglass figure, bright blue eyes, golden hair, lovely face, and clear (if colorless) soprano made her one of Broadway and vaudeville's first great female singing stars. She surprised critics and fans when she made the switch from operetta to musical comedy, costarring with Joe Weber and Lew Fields in a series of zany burlesques, beginning with *Whirl-i-gig* (1899), in which she introduced "Come Down Ma' Evenin' Star," the touching ballad that became her signature tune. In later years Russell's celebrated hourglass figure swelled to hefty proportions, with her weight topping 160 pounds. She delighted some fans (and scandalized others) when she spoke out in favor of women's suffrage. Russell bid farewell to Broadway in the Weber and Fields hit *Hokey Pokey* (1912), but continued to tour in vaudeville until shortly before her death a decade later. She is buried in a solid silver casket in Pittsburgh's Allegheny Cemetery. (Author's collection)

The souvenir program for Broadway's *Florodora* (1901) shows the famed original sextet singing "Tell Me Pretty Maiden" with their top-hatted admirers. All six young ladies reputedly married millionaires; they certainly raised a first-class fuss with their prim appearance, a far cry from those brazen ladies in tights. (Author's collection)

George M. Cohan and his first wife, Ethel Levy, met and fell in love during their vaudeville days and then costarred on Broadway in several of George's early musicals. Here they are seen strutting their stuff in *Little Johnny Jones* (1904). Cohan's predilection for extramarital activities did not sit well with Levy, who divorced him in 1907. Although they had a daughter, the Catholic Church granted an annulment—proving fame to be more powerful than dogma. Cohan soon married chorus girl Agnes Nolan. Levy remained a top star in vaudeville, and continued appearing on Broadway into the 1940s. (Author's collection)

Danilo (Donald Brian) waltzes with Sonia (Ethel Jackson) in the first New York production of *The Merry Widow* (1907). When Lew Fields staged a full-length spoof of the show, producer Henry Savage cheerfully allowed him to use the set and costume designs, as well as the original orchestrations—knowing full well that a Fields parody would only boost ticket sales for the real thing. Both productions made handsome profits. (Author's collection)

In *The Whirl of Society* (1912), Al Jolson played his perennial character Gus, a black servant who must constantly outwit the world to save himself and his bosses. Here he is an American butler contending with Lawrence D'Orsay as the Archduke Frederich. Like all of Jolson's early hits, this show played New York's Winter Garden. (Author's collection)

The finale of *Oh, Boy!* (1917) finds newlyweds George (Tom Powers) and Lou Ellen (Marie Carroll) clearing up an innocent misunderstanding. The realistic Long Island country club setting and the intimate cast were hallmarks of the Princess Theatre musicals. *Oh, Boy!*'s big hit song was "Till the Clouds Roll By," introduced by Powers and Anna Wheaton—who was the "innocent misunderstanding." (Author's collection)

A publicity flyer for *Lady, Be Good* (1924), with comedian Walter Catlett and the brother-sister dance team of Adele and Fred Astaire. All were veteran vaudevillians and Broadway stars, and although Catlett never attained the legendary status of the Astaires, he is still remembered thanks to dozens of film appearances—most notably as the giddy voice of the evil fox J. Worthington Foulfellow, introducing "Hi-Diddle-Dee-Dee" in Walt Disney's animated classic *Pinocchio* (1940). (Author's collection)

Marilyn Miller was Broadway's top female musical star in the 1920s. This photo by Alfred Cheney Johnston shows Miller en point in her biggest hit, *Sally* (1920). No great shakes as a singer or actress, it was her dancing that made her a lasting favorite. The picture of elegant beauty on stage, this vaudeville veteran could become a razor-tongued hellcat when dealing with the offstage advances of her randy producer, Florenz Ziegfeld. (Author's collection)

The showgirls of the great revues were often showcased in the most outlandish getups. Here we see dancer Tilly Losch in producer Charles B. Cochran's London production *Wake Up and Dream* (1929), which had a score by Cole Porter and costumes by Oliver Messel and other designers. A success in London, it had the misfortune to reach Broadway in the wake of the stock market crash and soon closed. We can only imagine what it was like for Losch and others to dance in such garish headgear. (Author's collection)

Scenes and Characters from *"The Desert Song"*

Casino Theatre   New York

A postcard from the original Broadway production of *The Desert Song* (1926) captures several scenes: at lower left, Benny (Eddie Buzzell) tries to coax a mule into action; lower center finds the bitter native girl Azuri (Pearl Regay) in a fiery dance of revenge; lower right we see Margot (Vivienne Segal) struggling in the arms of that hunky terrorist, the Red Shadow (Robert Halliday). Above is the penultimate scene, where the Governor's son informs the neatly lined-up ensemble that he has killed the Red Shadow. In the mid-twentieth century, it was common for producers to make such postcards available to audiences free of charge, and even mail them postpaid—a low-cost form of publicity for any show. (Author's collection)

Ethel Merman as she appeared in *Red, Hot and Blue* (1936). This photo may come as something of a surprise to those who only know her in later years. This former stenographer made good use of her secretarial skills, handling all her own correspondence and maintaining a detailed set of scrapbooks chronicling her entire career—with typewritten captions for each item. (Author's collection, photo by White Studio)

THE PLAYBILL
FOR THE ST. JAMES THEATRE

The original stars of *Oklahoma!* (1943), from left to right: Lee Dixon as Will Parker, Celeste Holm as Ado Annie, Alfred Drake as Curly, Joan Roberts as Laurey, Joseph Buloff (kneeling) as Ali Hakim, an unidentified chorus member, and Betty Garde as Aunt Eller. The "Surrey with a Fringe on Top" made its only appearance as seen here in the finale. The 2002 revival replaced the surrey with an early model horseless carriage, just one of many ill-advised changes made for that production. (Reprinted by permission of *Playbill*, cover from author's collection)

Mako (center) serves as reciter/narrator for *Pacific Overtures* (1976), leading the ensemble in Sondheim's ode to Japan's once isolated existence, "The Advantages of Floating in the Middle of the Sea." In keeping with Kabuki tradition, the female roles in this opening scene are all played by males. (Photo by Van Williams, from the personal collection of Bruce Levy)

Harry Groener and the ladies of the *Crazy for You* (1992) ensemble performing "I Can't Be Bothered Now," which choreographer Susan Stroman staged as a tribute to the platinum-haired showgirls of the Ziegfeld era. Note the marquee announcing THE ZANGLER FOLLIES. (Author's collection, photo by Joan Marcus)

Nathan Leopold (Stephen Dolginoff) stands behind his murderous friend
Richard Loeb (Shonn Wiley) in the York Theatre's production of *Thrill Me*
(2006). A musical about real-life thrill killers may seem unlikely, but it has
found a worldwide audience—and it was born and nurtured at a nonprofit
off-Broadway theatre company, the kind of place where musical theatre's
future is being determined. (Photo by James Morgan, used by permission
of the York Theatre)

Romberg thrown in. The book and lyrics were by Dorothy Donnelly (1880–1928), a prominent dramatic actress who here began a new career writing for the musical stage. She would provide the words for six more musicals, four of them in collaboration with Romberg.

Romberg and Donnelly's biggest success was *The Student Prince in Heidelberg* (1924, 608 performances). While attending the university in Heidelberg, Prince Karl Franz (Howard Marsh) learns about the joys of life outside his family's stuffy royal court. He encounters beer, friendship, and a forbidden romance with the beautiful waitress Kathy (Ilse Marvenga). When Karl Franz's royal grandfather suddenly dies, the prince reluctantly chooses duty over love. (Although he does not know it, the princess he is being forced to marry is making the same sort of choice.) A year later, King Karl Franz revisits Heidelberg and bids a forgiving Kathy farewell. The score features the sweeping love songs "Serenade" and "Deep in My Heart, Dear," as well as a three-quarter-time "Drinking Song," which delighted Prohibition-era audiences with its militant cries of "Drink! Drink! Drink!" Here is American operetta at its most mature, rejecting unlikely plot twists and devoting every note and word to the service of the central story. Usually referred to as *The Student Prince*, this show proved a long-term goldmine for J. J. Shubert, who kept it on continual tour for the next two decades. Every so often, he had a newly mounted low budget production play for two weeks in New York, and then sent it on the road, advertising it as "Direct from Broadway."

The other leading composer of late American operetta was Rudolf Friml (1879–1972). Born and trained in Prague, he was composing light classical pieces when fate intervened. Victor Herbert refused to compose another score for temperamental *Naughty Marietta* star Emma Trentini, and desperate producer Arthur Hammerstein (1873–1955) was referred to Friml. With lyrics by Otto Harbach (1873–1963), Friml's *The Firefly* (1912) was a major success, as was Trentini's big solo "Giannina Mia." For the next dozen years, Friml provided music for a string of forgettable operettas, frequently in collaboration with Harbach. In 1924, Harbach approached Friml with a new idea and a new writing partner.

Oscar Hammerstein II (1895–1969) was heir to a genuine show business dynasty. His namesake grandfather was a mythic impresario who had financed costly opera productions through profitable forays into vaudeville and Broadway, producing *Naughty Marietta* along the way. Oscar II's father William ran grandpa's Victoria Theatre, using innovative programming to make it America's premiere vaudeville house until the Palace was built in 1912. William tried to steer his son away from the family business and into a legal career. Oscar II went to Columbia University on the pretext of studying law, and instead poured most of his energies into writing and appearing in the annual varsity musicals. After William's death, his brother Arthur gave "Ockie" his first opportunities to write for the stage, teaming him with Harbach, who proved the perfect teacher.

Harbach taught Oscar that every song and line of dialogue in a musical should be motivated by plot and characterization, which was not standard procedure in the early 1920s. The new duo had a few "almosts" before coauthoring the musical comedy hit *Wildflower* (1923, 477 performances), but their main focus was on operetta, a genre that aimed for integration. When they began work with Friml, Arthur Hammerstein brought in composer Herbert Stothart for additional support and suggested that a story set in Canada might have fresh audience appeal.

In *Rose-Marie* (1924, 557 performances), Harbach and Hammerstein built the plot around a murder that takes place in full view of the audience. Wealthy, Canadian fur trapper Ed Hawley wants to marry hotel vocalist Rose-Marie La Flemme (Metropolitan Opera soprano Mary Ellis), but she only has eyes for handsome miner Jim Kenyon—with whom she shares a secret musical signal, "The Indian Love Call" ("when I'm calling you-oo-oo, oo-oo"). When Hawley's half-Indian former mistress Wanda kills a drunken lover, Hawley arranges for the evidence to incriminate Kenyon, who goes into hiding. The Canadian Mounted Police under Sergeant Malone arrive to investigate, and a desperate Rose-Marie agrees to marry Hawley if he will clear Kenyon of all charges. Kenyon's mining buddy Hard-Boiled Herman (a Jewish miner?) tricks Wanda into confessing the truth, and helps her realize that Hawley is using her. Wanda interrupts the big wedding and reveals all, destroying Hawley and leaving Jim and Rose-Marie to sing their "oo-oo-oos" in blissful peace. As Kenyon, dashing British baritone Dennis King (1897–1971) began his reign as one of Broadway's most popular leading men.

Rose-Marie's score included a stirring march for "The Mounties," Rose-Marie's celebration of the "Pretty Things" wealth might buy her, and the inevitable love waltz, "Door of My Dreams." The showstopping dance number "Totem Tom-Tom" depicted Native Americans fondly recalling how their grandparents used to dance after drinking "fire water gin-gin." That song and Hard-Boiled Herman's Yiddish comedy "shtick" make *Rose-Marie* unrevivable today. It played a whopping 851 performances in London, and five road companies crisscrossed the United States. Hammerstein's share in all this made him a wealthy man at age twenty-nine, and established him as an important new talent.

One of Oscar Hammerstein II's favorite stories bears repeating here. He traveled to Great Britain to help cast the West End production of *Rose-Marie*, and during rehearsals, a rather prim English soprano who clearly had no previous knowledge of the score sight read the "Indian Love Call" in this manner: "When I'm calling you, double-o, double-o."

Friml next collaborated with playwright Brian Hooker, producer Russell Janney, and actor/lyricist W. H. Post to turn J. H. McCarthy's popular romance *If I Were King* into *The Vagabond King* (1925, 511 performances). In fifteenth-century Paris, King Louis XI indulges a whim and makes the condemned criminal Francois Villon (Dennis King) serve as king for a day, during which time he must win the love of the beautiful courtier Lady Katherine or forfeit his clever head. Villion forgets about his peasant lover Huguette, wins Katherine's affections, and boldly leads the rabble of Paris to put down a rebellion led by the treacherous Duke of Burgundy. In the thrilling "Song of the Vagabonds," Villion urges his fellow street riffraff to break the chains of oppression, "and to *hell* with Burgundy!" During the battle, Huguette is killed while saving Villon's life. The rebellion is smashed, and Villion receives a royal pardon and marries Katherine. Stilted dialogue makes this show a hard sell in our time, but the score is still appealing. King had the most memorable role of his career as Villon, introducing the "Song of the Vagabonds" and the ballad "Only a Rose." "Huguette's Waltz" gave that doomed character a charming dance opportunity, and as Lady Katherine, soprano Carolyn Thompson sang an endearing call for romance entitled "Some Day."

With operetta moving in such interesting creative directions, Harbach corralled Oscar Hammerstein II into collaborating with Jerome Kern on a musical comedy tailored for Marilyn Miller, the aforementioned

Sunny. Hey, a job was a job, and the meeting of Hammerstein and Kern proved momentous. From the first, it was clear that they were kindred spirits, each relishing the professionalism and dedication of the other, and each committed to the ideal of better integration between story and song. Kern still wrote the music first, so the burden of making integration happen fell to Harbach and Hammerstein. Producer Charles Dillingham wasn't concerned about integration; he just needed a big fat hit for Miller. Hammerstein got some idea of what the project would be like when he and his collaborators auditioned their material for the dancing star. After hearing the story and songs, she had only one question: "When do I do my tap specialty?" Also in the cast was Cliff Edwards (1895–1971). Now remembered as the voice of Walt Disney's Jiminy Cricket, he was known to vaudeville audiences as "Ukulele Ike." His contract specified that his ukulele specialty had to go on between ten and ten-fifteen, no matter what the plot was up to. Accommodating such star turns was not to Oscar's taste, so despite *Sunny*'s success, he resumed his focus on operetta.

Sigmund Romberg had finally ended his exclusive relationship with the Shuberts and was available for independent projects. He teamed up with Hammerstein and Harbach for *The Desert Song* (1926, 471 performances), which borrowed key elements from the silent movie hit *The Adventures of Zorro*, adding just enough of Rudolph Valentino's *The Sheik* to prove that alchemy can be a viable substitute for originality. They ripped their setting out of the headlines: colonial Morocco, where Riff freedom fighters were terrorizing the French foreign legion. The story centers on Pierre Birabeau (Robert Halliday), son of the French governor, who is so appalled by the way his countrymen oppress the Moroccans that he frequently dons a masked cowl and leads the Riffs as the daring Red Shadow. At home, he feigns a fey, foppish personality to avoid suspicion. This does not win any points with the girl he loves, Margo Bonvalet (Vivienne Segal), who yearns for bold romance and plans to marry the stolid Captain Paul Fonteyn (Glen Dale). In desperation, Paul slips into his Red Shadow drag to woo and kidnap Margot. As soon as his masked persona wins Margot's heart, he is challenged to a duel—by the governor. Unwilling to harm his clueless father, the Red Shadow surrenders and rides off into the desert unarmed, facing certain death. Soon afterward, Paul appears at the French headquarters carrying an empty masked cowl and claiming that he has killed the feared terrorist. His father has learned the truth and privately vows to work with his son. Paul dons the mask one final time to reassure Margot that the man she loves is alive and hers. A humorous subplot involving inept reporter Bennie Kidd amounted to little more than an excuse to insert some vaudeville-style comedy bits.

The show tried out in Boston as *Lady Fair*, a title Hammerstein didn't care for. On the train ride back to New York, he sketched out a lyric about "blue heaven" and "sand kissing a moonlit sky." "The Desert Song" proved to be both a hit number and a great new title for the show. The score's other big hit was the Red Shadow's moving "One Alone" ("to be my own; I alone to know her caresses"). *The Desert Song*'s shameless romance and unusually lush score kept it a staple in the musical theatre repertory for the next fifty years. To those who enjoy operetta, it remains one of the most beloved works in the genre.

Romberg teamed up one more time with Dorothy Donnelly for the Civil War operetta *My Maryland* (1927, 312 performances). This now-neglected musical version of the Barbara Fritchie legend ("'Shoot if you must this old grey head, but spare your country's flag,' she said") with its stirring title march was a big moneymaker for the Shuberts. It marked the end of Donnelly's brief career as a librettist when she died a few months after the show opened, at age forty-eight. Although heartbroken at the loss of a friend and colleague, Romberg was hard at work on several new projects.

The aforementioned *Rosalie* forced Romberg to miss the pre-Broadway preparations for an operetta he collaborated on with Oscar Hammerstein II—who was himself occupied with a little thing called *Show Boat* (more on that anon). By the time they saw their new operetta's Philadelphia tryout, the show was in serious need of revision. The production closed down "for rewrites," an announcement that usually meant a project was dead, but not this time. Romberg and Hammerstein performed major surgery over the next seven months, replacing most of the score while producers Frank Mandel and Laurence Schwab personally rewrote the script. It was worth the effort. *The New Moon* (1928, 509 performances) was the semi-fictional story of Robert Mission (Richard Halliday), a French noble-man hiding from the authorities in colonial New Orleans. Arrested for treason, he is freed by a band of supporters and sets up a new nation on a deserted Caribbean island. The swashbuckling is offset by Robert's rocky romance with the royal governor's daughter, Marianne (Evelyn Herbert), but all ends happily when a ship arrives announcing that France has deposed its king and become a republic. A 1929 London production, it ran only four months, but was one of the first stage productions to record most of the score using the stage cast and orchestrations. MGM produced two big-screen versions, the second in 1940 starring Jeanette MacDonald and Nelson Eddy.

As if determined to establish himself as the producer of all genres, Ziegfeld made his only foray into operetta by spearheading Friml's adaptation of *The Three Musketeers* (1928, 319 performances), the novel by Alexandre Dumas, père. It focused on the rise of D'Artagnan and the efforts to save the queen's diamond studs—here converted to a diamond heart, which would be easier for an audience to see on stage. The lyrics were handled by Clifford Grey and the libretto was left to William Anthony McGuire (who also directed), two hacks that Ziegfeld often hired at a reduced cost. Their lackluster contributions were alleviated by several outstanding Friml melodies—including a stirring "March of the Musketeers" and the beguiling ballad "Ma Belle"—and winning performances by Dennis King as D'Artagnan and Vivienne Segal as Constance. Attempts to revive this show have fallen flat because the tuneful score cannot make up for a stilted, one-dimensional dramatization.

After *The Three Musketeers*, the boom years of American operetta came to a sudden end. Romberg and Friml continued composing, but their new operettas met with unshakable indifference. The rise of jazz and the harsh realities of the Great Depression reduced the once substantial Broadway audience for these works. At the same time, many of Romberg and Friml's stage hits found a new worldwide audience through feature film adaptations, including a very popular MGM series starring Eddy and MacDonald. While keeping the most important melodies intact, these screen adaptations used little or none of the original stage plots and revised many of the lyrics. The bittersweet undertones so desperately needed to offset the sweeping melodic sentiment of these works were almost completely erased. Toward the end of the twentieth century, several opera troupes and record companies rediscovered the best of these operettas, to the delight of devoted fans.

But these efforts were not enough to dispel the general misconception that 1920s operettas were syrupy nonsense: an ironic legacy for the first genre to let integrated musical theatre grow and mature.

Insanity Reigns: The Marx Brothers

In 1924, the Shuberts filled a sudden vacancy at the Casino Theatre by bringing in the low-budget touring production *I'll Say She Is* (1924, 313 performances). The show was no great shakes, but it introduced Broadway to the Marx Brothers: Julius, Adolph, Leonard, and Herbert—better known as the wisecracking Groucho (1890–1977), the mute Harpo (1888–1964), the inexplicably Italian Chico (1886–1961), and the straight man Zeppo (1901–1979). Graduates of vaudeville, these Jewish-American brothers acted—both onstage and sometimes off—more like escapees from an insane asylum, offering comedy that placed modern life in a merciless, chaotic frame. Embraced by the intellectuals of the famed Algonquin Round Table, they quickly developed an enthusiastic public, and *I'll Say She Is* enjoyed a profitable run.

To create the Marx Brothers' next vehicle, producer Sam Harris called in top-notch talents. George S. Kaufman (1889–1961), a former journalist who had established himself as a leading comic playwright, served as librettist for *The Cocoanuts* (1925, 377 performances), which spoofed the sort of shady land deals that were then all the rage in Florida. Kaufman worked closely with the Marx Brothers, incorporating their madcap improvisations into the script. Hit-master Irving Berlin provided a surprisingly uninteresting score, but any song worth hearing would have been lost in the Marxian madness. *The Cocoanuts* brought another key member to the Marx team: musical comedienne Margaret Dumont (1889–1965), whose imposing patrician appearance made her the perfect comic foil for the zany, pretense-smashing brothers.

For *Animal Crackers* (1928, 191 performances), Kaufman and colibrettist Morrie Ryskind (1895–1985) turned Groucho into African explorer Captain Spaulding, who is on hand when the theft of a valuable painting opens the way to mayhem in the Long Island mansion of Mrs. Rittenhouse, played by Dumont. At one point, Chico naively suggests that everyone in the house should be asked if they stole the painting. Groucho points out the thief may not be in the house, so Chico responds that they can then ask next door. When Groucho asks "What if there is no house next door?" Chico triumphantly concludes, "Then we'll build a house." The score by Tin Pan Alley veterans Bert Kalmar (1884–1947) and Harry Ruby (1895–1974) included a number that became Groucho's personal theme song, "Hooray for Captain Spaulding."

Paramount Pictures cast the Marx Brothers in screen versions of *The Cocoanuts* (1929) and *Animal Crackers* (1930). Kaufman, who openly abhorred the ways of Hollywood, took no part in the making of these films. According to legend, at one of the brothers' stage performances, Kaufman had silenced a friend to say, "Wait! I think I just heard one of my own lines." But a perusal of the librettos verifies that most of what sound like Marx improvisations were actually Kaufman's lines. The playwright remained on good terms with the brothers, and would write screenplays for them in the future. It is a shame that they never returned to Broadway, and that their musicals are quite unrevivable without their unique talents. Even the best impersonators are still no more than echoes of Groucho and company. At least *The Cocoanuts* and *Animal Crackers* were filmed almost exactly as they were performed onstage, giving us some clue as to what made the Marx Brothers a theatrical sensation.

The Threepenny Opera: "The Shark Has Razor Teeth"

Thanks to an early surrender, Germany survived the loss of World War I with little in the way of physical damage, but the emotional effect of this defeat was devastating. From the moment the Kaiser was deposed, the new Weimar Republic was plagued with political unrest and the crushing burden of war reparations. The economy fluctuated, and political extremists literally battled in the streets. In the late 1920s, prosperity became widespread and the chaos eased, giving Germany a few years of relative stability. But avant-garde writers and artists continued to attack an establishment they viewed as hypocritical and corrupt.

Berlin had regained its position as a center for the performing arts. With dozens of cabarets and more than eighty legitimate theatres, there was ample room for traditional as well as experimental works.

When the owner of the Theatre am Schiffbauerdamm asked composer Kurt Weill (1900–1950) and playwright Berthold Brecht (1898–1956) to come up with a new piece, they offered to adapt John Gay's *The Beggar's Opera*. They kept the plot and characters, but updated the action to a cartoonish version of Victorian London. In *Die Dreigroschenoper (The Threepenny Opera)* Brecht and Weill wanted to spotlight the hypocrisy and corruption found in every age and locality. As a Marxist, Brecht took particular aim at the less respectable elements of the middle class. In his libretto, the murderous thief Macheath (a.k.a. "Mack the Knife") affects the dress and manners of a proper businessman. He has long avoided arrest because chief of police Tiger Brown was a wartime comrade. Macheath marries young Polly Peachum, enraging her seemingly respectable parents who run a school for phony street beggars. Mrs. Peachum bribes Macheath's longtime lover, a prostitute named Jenny, to turn the killer in. Macheath has also been the sometime lover of Tiger Brown's daughter Lucy, who helps Macheath to escape from prison. The Peachum's then use their corrupt influence to get him rearrested and condemned to death. Just as Macheath is being led to the gallows, Queen Victoria celebrates her coronation day by granting him a full pardon and a peerage.

Weill used a mix of atonality, jazz, folk songs, and operatic forms. He opened the show with a *moritat*, a traditional type of German folk song involving a death. In the haunting "Ballad of Mack the Knife," a street singer recounts Macheath's recent crimes, noting that while a shark has sharp teeth in its mouth, Mack has only a dagger that he keeps in a less obvious place. Polly celebrates her wedding by singing "Die Seeräuber-Jenny" ("Pirate Jenny"), a tavern-style ballad about an abused scullery maid who turns out to be a pirate queen, commanding the deaths of those who once ordered her about. Macheath and Tiger Brown recall their army days in the bombastic "Kanonen-Song" ("The Cannon Song"). The "Zuhälterballade" ("The Pimp's Ballad") is a tango in which Macheath and Jenny recall the "good old days" when they shared the same whorehouse bed while he sold her services to others.

Die Dreigroschenoper opened on August 31, 1928, and the same middle class that Brecht and Weill aggressively jabbed at unexpectedly embraced the show. Despite its Victorian setting, this musical became a lasting icon of jazz-age Berlin. Few realized how quickly that age

would end. The great Depression spurred the rise of Hitler and the
Nazis, who forced both Brecht and Weill into exile, along with many
other artists and intellectuals. The first English language versions of
The Threepenny Opera did not fare well in the harsh 1930s; a handsome Broadway production (1933, 12 performances) met with critical
jeers and closed in a matter of days. Weill eventually made his way to
the United States, and later chapters will cover the brief but impressive tally of musicals that he composed for Broadway. It would not
be until the prosperous 1950s that America and Great Britain would
finally "discover" *The Threepenny Opera*, appreciating it as an off-
beat satirical gem.

Show Boat: Premature Revolution

In the autumn of 1926, Jerome Kern was only partway through reading
a new novel when he rang up Oscar Hammerstein II, proclaiming that
he had their next project. It had an epic romantic story and "a million-
dollar title": *Show Boat* (1927, 572 performances). Hammerstein had
already read the book and was enthusiastic about the idea. But would
renowned author Edna Ferber allow a musical adaptation? Without
waiting for an answer, Kern and Hammerstein tried an experiment.
Each one independently plotted out a musical treatment, and their
outlines were almost identical. In a move that was very unusual at that
time, they began writing before obtaining either the rights or a producer's commitment. As work progressed and the two men realized
they were creating something extraordinary, it became imperative to
line up those missing elements.

Since longtime friend Alexander Woollcott was closely associated
with Ferber (both were charter members of the Algonquin Hotel's
now-legendary Round Table of pundits), Kern asked for an introduction. Soon afterward, Kern and Woollcott bumped into each other at
the opening of Kern's *Criss Cross* (1926, 210 performances), another
vehicle for dancing comedian Fred Stone. Kern asked again about
an introduction to Ferber, and Woollcott slyly said that something
might be arranged. No sooner had Kern expressed his thanks than
Woollcott turned to a woman standing a few feet away and called
out, "Oh, Ferber! This is Kern." The novelist was initially skeptical
that her epic story could work as a musical comedy, but Kern made it

clear that he and Hammerstein had something very different in mind. This would be a show that blended the integration of operetta with the unabashed spirit of musical comedy. A rights option was signed a month later, and days after that the songwriters were auditioning for Ziegfeld, who promptly wrote to a friend, "This show is the opportunity of my life."

Despite his initial enthusiasm, Ziegfeld had several other projects in hand. He opened his new Ziegfeld Theatre at the corner of 6th Avenue and 54th Street with *Rio Rita* (1927, 494 performances), a hybrid musical comedy–operetta about a Texas Ranger who hunts a bank robber in exotic Mexico and finds love with the fiery title character. Like most of Ziegfeld's book musicals, this one had visual punch but no consistency of content—and most of the score was on the weak side. The main attraction was the vaudeville comedy team of baby-faced Bert Wheeler (1895–1968) and bespectacled Robert Woolsey (1888–1938), who played two American tourists unwittingly caught up in the action. Wheeler and Woolsey also starred in a 1929 sound film version, and aside from the comic shenanigans, the film preserves few hints of what made the show a success. With *Rio Rita* packing the Ziegfeld, Flo had no urgent need of *Show Boat* and kept the Kern-Hammerstein project on the back burner for the better part of a year. Ziegfeld may have had second thoughts. Considering what a departure this show would be from anything the Great Glorifier had done to date, it would have been almost impossible for him *not* to wonder what he was getting into.

As adapted by Hammerstein, *Show Boat* begins in the early 1890s on The Cotton Blossom, a floating theatre that brings melodramas and olios to Mississippi River towns under the management of Captain Andy Hawks (Charles Winninger). His daughter Magnolia (Norma Terris) dreams of a stage career and flirts with the handsome but penniless river gambler Gaylord Ravenal (Howard Marsh), who urges her to "Make Believe" that they are in love. The ship's negro stevedore Joe comments that the girl would do well to ask "Ol' Man River" what he thinks, since "he knows all 'bout dem boys." Helen Morgan (1900–1941) played Julie La Verne, the ship's leading lady who is forced to admit that her mother was black—which makes her marriage to leading man Steve biracial and therefore illegal in many southern states. To avoid a scandal, Julie and Steve leave the Cotton Blossom. Much to Captain Andy's relief—and the annoyance of his persnickety wife Parthy (Edna May Oliver)—Magnolia and the rakish Gaylord take over the leads with tremendous success. After romancing each other on and off stage, Magnolia and Gaylord marry.

Thanks to a fresh turn in Gaylord's gambling luck, he takes Magnolia and their newborn daughter Kim to live the high life in Chicago. When his luck turns cold, a despondent Gaylord abandons his family. In desperation, Magnolia auditions for work in a nightclub, not knowing that the established singer there is her onetime friend Julie, who is somewhat the worse for years of heartbreak and drink. Overhearing the audition, Julie walks out on the club, forcing them to hire the untried Magnolia, who debuts on New Year's Eve before a rowdy audience. Captain Andy, who just happens to be in the crowd, calms her nerves and coaxes the customers into accepting her. The final scenes move the action right up to 1927, with an aging Captain Andy inviting established Broadway star Magnolia back to visit the Cotton Blossom. There she finds Gaylord, and the reunited lovers see their daughter Kim enjoying the full glory of young adulthood as Joe leads the ensemble in a final reprise of "Ol' Man River."

Ziegfeld urged the authors to treat the show as a musical comedy, but it was far more, its score covering many musical and theatrical styles:

- Negro folk song ("Can't Help Lovin' That Man")
- Spiritual ("Ol' Man River")
- Operetta ("Make Believe," "You Are Love")
- Musical comedy ("Life on the Wicked Stage")
- Tin Pan Alley ("Goodbye My Lady Love," "After the Ball")

The vintage hits "Goodbye, My Lady Love" and "After the Ball" were interpolated to provide genuine period flavor. Kern was delighted to find a use for "Bill," a torch song he had written with lyricist P. G. Wodehouse for the 1918 Princess musical *Oh, Lady! Lady!* Cut from that show, it almost made it into half a dozen others, but was always excised. Hammerstein tweaked the lyric to fit the tragic Julie, and it became a standard, thanks in large part to a heartbreaking rendition by Helen Morgan. The diminutive alcoholic soprano had earned fame singing in speakeasies, where she sang sitting on top of pianos in order to be seen. By repeating this trademark gesture when she performed "Bill" onstage, Morgan created an iconic moment. Paul Robeson was originally scheduled to play Joe, but months of production delays forced him to accept other commitments, so "Ol' Man River" was actually introduced by Jules Bledsoe. However, Robeson eventually played the role in the 1928 London production, the 1932 Broadway revival, and the 1936 screen version. For the rest of his public life, Robeson's concerts and speaking engagements were not complete until he appeased audiences with "Ol' Man River."

Ziegfeld's original instinct that this show was *the* opportunity of his life proved accurate. As much as people identify him with the *Follies*, the only Ziegfeld creation still in regular use is *Show Boat*. No two productions have been exactly alike. Kern and Hammerstein kept tinkering with the score and libretto, making a bewildering array of additions and deletions as long as either lived. In the ensuing years, a long line of directors and producers has made further changes. In 1988, when conductor John McGlinn recorded every note that had ever been used in the score, the resulting set included three hours and forty minutes of music. *Show Boat* is so compelling that every succeeding era has felt a need to reconceive it. The history of all other 1920s musicals is pretty much done; *Show Boat*'s story is still being written.

Many critics recognized that *Show Boat* was something new and made it clear that more comparable would find a warm welcome. Kern and Hammerstein soon obliged with *Sweet Adeline* (1929, 234 performances), a nostalgic celebration of the 1890s. Helen Morgan played Addie Schmidt, a nice girl from Hoboken who sees the man she loves go off to fight the Spanish-American War. She consoles herself by going into show business and becoming a Broadway star. Although *Sweet Adeline*'s content was not nearly as serious as *Show Boat*'s, it reflected the same careful integration of song and story. Morgan sang "Why Was I Born?" in what critic Burns Mantle described as a "brave little voice." Opening on September 3, 1929, the show was acclaimed as a successor to *Show Boat* and did sellout business. Many Broadway writers and producers must have wondered if a revolution was in progress.

The Crash

Bad timing can sabotage even the most well-intentioned revolution. On Thursday, October 24, 1929, stock prices on Wall Street took an alarming plunge. Leading financiers joined forces to avert an all-out crash, but despite their efforts, panic set in on Tuesday, October 29, 1929. The market lost $30 billion in value, a figure ten times the size of the federal budget.

The Crash of 1929 was a devastating man-made disaster with profound consequences. Countless small investors who had bought stocks "on margin"—for pennies on the dollar—now owed their full value, and were wiped out. More conservative souls who had kept their money in savings accounts lost every penny when banks declared themselves insolvent. There were waves of business closures and firings, and those out of work found that new jobs were almost nonexistent. Since social security and unemployment insurance did not exist, the loss of a job often translated into the loss of a home. Many who still had jobs saw their wages slashed. At first, people had no way of grasping the size of the catastrophe, and assured themselves that all slumps are temporary. During the first weeks after the crash, Broadway's box office sales remained healthy. But as the slump wore on and deepened, attitudes changed. People scraping together ten cents for a loaf of bread could only dream of spending three dollars to see a Broadway musical.

Producer Arthur Hammerstein kept *Sweet Adeline* going in hopes that the economic climate would improve but wound up closing at a loss. Within a year, he was a ruined man, forced to sell off his theatre and the rights to all his theatrical properties. His nephew Oscar and Jerome Kern joined a legion of Broadway songwriters heading out to Hollywood where the rise of talking films created a new high-paying market for their talents. Broadway musicals? Anyone with sense could have told you that they were a doomed species.

10

Depression Era Miracles (1930–1940) — "Trouble's Just a Bubble"

By 1932, more than twelve million adults in the United States could not find work, and those still working had an average annual family income of $1,600 or less. Of the five hundred-plus millionaires who had filed tax returns two years before, only twenty still qualified. President Herbert Hoover assured the nation that good times were "just around the corner." He wasn't the only one who failed to understand how profoundly things had changed.

Florenz Ziegfeld did what he had always done, spending whatever it took to put on a show. *Simple Simon* (1930, 135 performances) starred comedian Ed Wynn (1886–1966), whose colorful costumes, lisping delivery, and genially insane humor had made him a great favorite. Audiences were particularly fond of Wynn's zany "inventions"— like a reconstructed typewriter that allowed him to eat corn on the cob without getting his hands dirty. In *Simple Simon*, the comedian played a newsstand owner who dreams he is in the fairy-tale world of Mother Goose. The score by Richard Rodgers and Larry Hart featured "Ten Cents a Dance," which Ruth Etting crooned while sitting atop Wynn's latest invention, a piano that rolled about on bicycle wheels while the he canoodled at the keyboard. Critics loved Wynn but hated the show, which folded in less than four months. Ziegfeld "forgot" to pay his songwriters until Rodgers threatened action by the Dramatists Guild.

Ziegfeld next teamed Marilyn Miller with Fred and Adele Astaire in *Smiles* (1930, 63 performances), certain that this stellar trio would sell tickets. The libretto, which used the timeworn premise of a Salvation Army girl getting mixed up with high society, was so creaky that no one noticed the Vincent Youmans score, and the production closed in seven weeks. Ziegfeld then put on his most costly *Follies* (1931, 165 performances) ever, spending more than $250,000—a far cry from the $13,000 he spent on the first edition back in 1907. Despite a decent run, the ponderous price tag made it impossible for Ziegfeld to turn a profit.

In a desperate gesture, Ziegfeld used mobster funding to bring back *Show Boat* (1932, 181 performances) with most of the original leads, now joined by Paul Robeson. But there were not enough ticket buyers, and the production lost money. In a coarse departure from his usual style, he presented Bert Lahr and Hollywood has-been Lupe Velez in *Hot-Cha* (1932, 119 performances), a musical comedy so crude that it was subtitled "Laid in Mexico." Even semi-smut was not enough to sell tickets. With bill collectors hounding him, Ziegfeld was forced to access his office via a back alley fire escape. His health began to fail, and he submerged a lifelong fear of illness and death in a series of embarrassing infidelities. During a radio appearance, Flo sounded so frail that Billie Burke finally intervened and brought him out to California to recuperate. It was there that America's most famous showman died on July 22, 1932, unable to understand that his Broadway, his world, had disappeared.

Another show business legend came to an end that November when New York's Palace Theatre played its last continuous vaudeville bill and switched over to showing motion pictures. As the depression deepened, vaudeville houses had been closing down all over the country. Americans either went to the movies or stayed at home and listened to their favorite stars on the radio. The once-dictatorial vaudeville magnate E. F. Albee found to his profound shock that he had lost control of his empire to new business partner Joseph Kennedy, who turned the Keith-Orpheum Circuit into Radio Keith Orpheum's new chain of movie theatres. When the Palace gave up the old two-a-day, even those who had been in denial realized that vaudeville was dead. It did not soften the blow when the Palace's first feature film turned out to be *The Kid from Spain*, a musical starring vaudeville's own Eddie Cantor. If vaudeville was wiped out, could the legitimate theatre be far behind?

As things turned out, the Shubert brothers were next in line. Attorneys and accountants urged Lee and J. J. to sell off their theatres, but in a rare face-to-face meeting, the contentious brothers spoke with one mind—they were not about to let their life's work disappear. They poured hundreds of thousands of dollars into their company to keep it afloat and then succumbed as so many others had to the ongoing financial miasma of the Depression. The courts finally ordered the Shuberts to liquefy their assets, but unlike most ruined businessmen, Lee Shubert had a plan, and a little something tucked away for a rainy day. When the bankruptcy auction took place, there was only one bidder. A theatrical empire once valued at $25 million was purchased for a mere $400,000 by Select Theatre Incorporated—a new company owned by Lee Shubert, who used this transaction to take full control and leave his hated brother a powerless cofigurehead. But while nothing short of death would end their feud, the Shuberts had seen to it that their theatres would stay in business. For one shining hour, Lee Shubert was a white knight, a bona fide hero. Within a few more business deals, his halo faded, and he was back to being one of the most hated men in show business.

The 1930s turned out to be a fascinating decade for the musical theatre. Although fewer new works were produced, the best of those that made it to Broadway or the West End provided exceptional entertainment, sometimes nostalgic, sometimes inventive. Revues got smaller but funnier, musical comedies became sharper and better crafted, and operetta gave up any pretense of intellectual content, offering more romantic spectacle than ever. Typical runs were shorter, but there were still enough ticket buyers to keep musical theatre alive. Innovation was rare, but definitely not extinct.

Post-Ziegfeld Revues: "Noisy Cafés and Whispering Breadlines"

Revues featuring feathered and beaded showgirls were an endangered species. In 1931, despite the crippling effects of the Great Depression, Earl Carroll built a 3,000-seat art deco showplace. Billed as "the largest legitimate theatre in the world," it opened with the ninth edition of his *Vanities* (1931, 278 performances). Despite the usual plethora of nude women, the theatre proved so costly to run that Carroll was forced into foreclosure. Ziegfeld took over the venue, an expensive gesture that only sped Ziegfeld's own slide into bankruptcy. After a brief stint as a nightclub, the building was converted to retail space. George White managed to produce three editions of his *Scandals*, but quality productions and strong scores could not prevent the series from petering out by the decade's end.

Lee Shubert offered the debt-laden Billie Burke Ziegfeld a handsome sum for the rights to stage a new Follies using her late husband's name, and she wasn't about to refuse. The resulting *Ziegfeld Follies* (1934, 182 performances) was produced for $125,000—less than half of what the Great Glorifier had spent on his last edition. But it was mounted with surprising taste and thanks to the box office appeal of comedienne Fanny Brice (who introduced her "Baby Snooks" character) and shrewd business management, this edition made money. Two years later, another Shubert-produced *Follies* (1936, 227 performances) did even better, teaming Brice with former burlesque comic Bob Hope (1903–2003) and African-American dancer Josephine Baker, who had proven a sensation in Paris. After years of competing with Ziegfeld, it must have given Lee Shubert great satisfaction to succeed with the *Follies* brand name. Shubert staffer Harry B. Kaufman received no official credit, but was considered by many in the business to be the brains behind these *Follies*.

The most memorable Broadway revues of the 1930s departed from the long dominant Ziegfeld style. Banks of chorus girls were reduced to a mere handful, dollars were spent with caution, and the quality of the material took precedence. *The Little Show* (1929, 321 performances) grew out of informal Sunday afternoon concerts given by Broadway unknowns. A team of producers led by Dwight Deere Wiman (1895–1951) put this mix into a sophisticated but inexpensive package. An heir to the John Deere tractor fortune, Wiman would prove a major figure in redefining musicals during the 1930s. Former attorney Arthur Schwartz (1900–1984) provided most of the music, with lyrics by MGM's longtime publicity director Howard Dietz (1896–1983). "I Guess I'll Have to Change My Plan" proved an audience favorite, but the most talked about number in *The Little Show* was the torch song "Moanin' Low," which had music by the show's pianist, Ralph Rainger. Libby Holman (1906–1971) delivered the song in a sultry key before Clifton Webb (1891–1966) joined her for a dance that ended with him strangling her. Webb had made his mark as a dancer, and enjoyed a brief vogue in Broadway revues before becoming a popular character actor in films. There were two more editions of *The Little Show*, but neither recaptured the surprise popularity of the original.

Former actor Hassard Short turned to directing musicals in the 1920s, including the first three of Irving Berlin's *Music Box Revues* (1921–1923). Short took a long-overdue cue from the London revues of Charlot and Cochran, helming productions that stressed visual elegance and comic content. This approach made it possible to please audiences while keeping within tight production budgets. Short worked frequently with producer Max Gordon (1892–1978), who had gotten his start in the previous decade presenting plays. Short's *Three's a Crowd* (1930, 272 performances) proved to be a moneymaker during the darkest days of the Depression. Schwartz and Dietz wrote a top-drawer score. Libby Holman sang "Something to Remember You By" and "Body and Soul," and the latter was also danced to by Clifton Webb and exotic Tamara Geva. For this production, Short eliminated traditional footlights, replacing them with floodlights suspended from the front mezzanine, a practice that soon became standard in professional stage productions.

Short went even further with *The Band Wagon* (1931, 260 performances), using two massive turntables to execute quick scene changes in full view of the audience. Fred and Adele Astaire led the cast, which included dancer Tilly Losch, as well as future film stars Frank Morgan and Helen Broderick. Schwartz and Dietz's score included the sensuous "Dancing in the Dark" and the oom-pah waltz "I Love Lousia." All of the skits were credited to Dietz and playwright George S. Kaufman. Soon after the run of this show, Adele Astaire left show business for good and married Britain's Lord Cavendish. Many wondered if Fred could have any sort of performing career without her.

Some critics suggested that no revue could top *The Band Wagon*, so Hassard Short and veteran producer Sam Harris decided to take up the challenge. Despite some very funny dialogue courtesy of comic playwright Moss Hart (1904–1961), *Face the Music* (1932, 165 performances) had the trappings of a book musical but played like a revue, with song and dance specialties set to a score by Irving Berlin. The opening scene depicted impoverished high society "Lunching at the Automat," where two young lovers decide that "trouble's just a bubble," so "Let's Have Another Cup o' Coffee" ("and let's have another piece o' pie"). The minimal plot involved corrupt cops investing in a surefire Broadway flop, then trying to turn it into a nudie show in hopes of making a fortune. Movie actress Mary Boland starred as the wife of the police commander, and made her entrance for the finale riding on top of a life-sized papier-mâché elephant. Berlin's score included "Soft Lights and Sweet Music," and "Manhattan Madness," a frenetic tribute to the city's "noisy cafes and whispering breadlines."

Although *Face the Music* only made a slim profit, that was sufficient reason for Harris to bring the same creative team together again for *As Thousands Cheer* (1933, 400 performances). Berlin and Moss Hart came up with the idea of bringing a newspaper to life, the perfect format for a wide-ranging commentary on current celebrities and events. The sets and backdrops were designed to look like newspaper columns, and each skit or song was introduced by an appropriate headline. "FRANKLIN D. ROOSEVELT INAUGURATED TOMORROW" showed the Hoover's moving out of the White House, with the First Lady (Helen Broderick) asking her unpopular husband, "What did you want to be President for? You had a good job!" "JOAN CRAWFORD TO DIVORCE DOUGLAS FAIRBANKS JR." had Hollywood's young glamour couple (played by Clifton Webb and Marilyn Miller) furious that publicity for their breakup has been eclipsed by the announcement that Mary Pickford and Doug Sr. are separating.

During rehearsals, director Short asked Ethel Waters if she minded following Miller and Webb's surefire song and dance duet "How's Chances." She replied, "There's nothing I like better than working on a *hot* stage!" Sure enough, the stage of the Music Box got even hotter when a headline proclaiming record temperatures led to Waters singing about a "Heat Wave" started by a young lady "letting her seat wave." Later on, an article about an unidentified negro being lynched by a southern mob introduced Waters in rags, wondering how to call her children to "Supper Time" when "that man o' mine ain't comin' home no more." Such social relevance was a novelty on the musical stage, and audiences proved receptive. The visual coup of the evening was the first act finale. Sunday newspapers of the time had sepia-toned photographic magazines known as rotogravures, which Short invoked by recreating the "Easter Parade" of 1883 using a set and costumes in varying shades of brown and tan.

Marilyn Miller had feared that she was passé, but *As Thousands Cheer* proved she could hold her own on a stage filled with equally bright stars. Few would have believed that this show marked her final appearance on Broadway. Since childhood she had suffered from severe sinus infections and migraines, often ignoring blinding pain to get through performances. Miller continually sought out new therapies. Aggressive but inept medical treatment made matters worse, and she soon became a semi-recluse. In 1936, a quack physician prescribed insulin treatments, which did nothing for her pain and proved fatal. Millions of fans were shocked when Marilyn Miller, long terrified of growing older, died at age thirty-seven.

Lee Shubert tried his hand at producing an intimate revue with the "musical holiday" *At Home Abroad* (1935, 198 performances). The score by Schwartz and Dietz provided no hits but gave Ethel Waters and dancer Eleanor Powell (1912–1982) ample opportunities to display their talents. This production is mostly remembered for the creative direction and stage designs of newcomer Vincente Minnelli (1913–1986), and the zany performance of comedienne Beatrice Lillie. For the rest of Lillie's career, she would repeat the *At Home Abroad* skit in which she portrayed an upper-crust matron trying to order "a dozen double damask dinner napkins" in a department store, and fans still treasure her demented recording of Schwartz and Dietz's razor-toothed spoof of Parisian tributes, "Paree" ("your Right Bank, your Left Bank are close to my heart, oh *je t'adore* Paree").

Former vaudevillians Ole Olsen and Chic Johnson devised a very different sort of low budget revue where comic chaos was the order of the day. *Hellzapoppin* (1938, 1,404 performances) opened with a newsreel of Hitler haranguing a crowd ... in Yiddish? From there on in, it was catch-as-catch-can, with a man in a monkey suit chasing a girl through the auditorium, dancing in the aisles, and a flower shop delivery man wandering the theatre with a potted plant that grew larger with each appearance. The gags changed from week to week, delighting many repeat customers. There was a score that no one paid any real attention to, so *Hellzapoppin* became Broadway's longest running musical production of the 1930s.

Pins and Needles (1937, 1,108 performances) began life as an amateur entertainment staged by members of the International Ladies Garment Workers Union. It didn't hurt that their union hall happened to be the old Princess Theatre, and that aspiring songwriter Harold Rome (1908–1996) provided the score. The material had a leftist political slant, but the main aim was to inspire laughter with numbers like "Sing Me a Song of Social Significance" and "Nobody Makes a Pass at Me," and skits that poked fun at local and international issues. The production kept adding performances, and finally moved to the much larger Windsor Theatre for a two-and-a-half-year run. New material was added over time, including "It's Better with a Union Man." *Pins and Needles* was the only amateur musical production to ever find success on Broadway. The beloved Princess Theatre spent its final years as an artsy movie venue, and was demolished in 1955.

Operetta

Sigmund Romberg racked up four disasters in this decade, along with one moderate success—*May Wine* (1935, 213 performances), which involved a Viennese psychiatrist who is driven to near madness by suspicions that his innocent wife is cheating on him. With fine lyrics by Oscar Hammerstein II and a well-integrated libretto, this production had a fair run, but none of its songs became hits.

Max Gordon presented Jerome Kern's operetta *The Cat and the Fiddle* (1931, 395 performances), which librettist Otto Harbach set in modern day Brussels. The story: love blooms between a surly Romanian composer (Georges Metaxa) and an exuberant American songwriter (Bettina Hall) until a pushy producer interpolates some of her songs into his newest operetta. Kern created an almost continual flow of music, underscoring major stretches of dialogue. During rehearsals, he became annoyed by Hall's upper-crust accent, which included trilling the letter "r" in a British manner. When Hall asked how she should get from one part of the stage to another, Kern quipped, "Just roll over on your Rs." Critics praised the careful integration of elements, and the public embraced "The Night Was Made for Love" and "She Didn't Say 'Yes'" ("she didn't say 'No'"). A West End production starring Peggy Wood (1932, 219 performances in London) also did well.

Emboldened by the success of *The Cat and the Fiddle*, Kern reteamed with Oscar Hammerstein II for *Music in the Air* (1932, 342 performances). The plot involved an aging Bavarian musician (Al

Shean) writing "I've Told Ev'ry Little Star." His lyricist is the hand-some schoolteacher Karl (Walter Slezak), who takes fiancée Sieglinde (Katherine Carrington) on a hike to Munich. The song catches the fancy of operetta star Frieda (Natalie Hall) and her lover, librettist Bruno (Tullio Carminati). Karl and Sieglinde get caught up in the tempestuous relationship between the show biz professionals, and disaster looms when Bruno has the inexperienced Sieglinde take over Frieda's role in a new production. Sieglinde fails, and the disillusioned young lovers hike back home. This unusual blend of naiveté and lederhosen proved a charmer. Kern took the main theme of "I've Told Ev'ry Little Star" from the call of a Cape Cod sparrow that he later described as "a complete phrase, and a perfectly rounded melodic treatment."

Kern and lyricist Otto Harbach veered toward musical comedy with *Roberta* (1933, 295 performances), the story of an all-American fullback who inherits his Aunt Roberta's Parisian dress shop and falls in love with her chief designer. He drops his American girl-friend, makes the shop a bigger success than ever, and learns that his new beloved is a Russian princess. Classically trained baritone Ray Middleton (1907–1984) had a non-singing role as the fullback, with beloved comedienne Fay Templeton making a final stage appearance as his dying aunt. Now a hefty 250 pounds and in failing health, she performed most of her role while seated, including the poignant "Yesterdays." Bob Hope was on hand as Middleton's wisecracking sidekick, and sang "You're Devastating." Ukrainian actress Tamara Drasin (who performed under her first name only) introduced the sultry "Smoke Gets in Your Eyes." The critics dismissed Harbach's book as a bore, but "Smoke Gets in Your Eyes" became such a popular hit that it kept the show running for the better part of the year. For the 1935 film version, Kern and lyricist Dorothy Fields added "Lovely to Look At" and "I Won't Dance"—the latter a showcase for Fred Astaire, who danced to "Smoke Gets In Your Eyes" with Ginger Rogers.

What if the richest man in the world built a theatre and had nothing to put in it? Aging tycoon John D. Rockefeller was in just such a position with The Center Theatre, a 3,822-seat auditorium in Manhattan's newly built Rockefeller Center complex. The aging oil tycoon wanted something that would make use of the theatre's massive, well-equipped stage and still make a profit at the box office.

Hassard Short had just returned from directing *Waltzes from Vienna* (1931, 607 performances), a lavish West End staging of a Viennese pastiche that used spectacular sets and some freely adapted Strauss family music to dramatize the real-life feud between Johann Sr. and his namesake eldest son. Who could finance such a project in New York? Short went to his frequent producer Max Gordon, who then went to Rockefeller, who agreed to cover all production costs. To give the piece some added bite, Gordon commissioned Moss Hart to revise the British redo of the Viennese libretto. Despite Hart's inevitable bursts of humor, *The Great Waltz* (1934, 297 performances in New York) libretto still oozed schmaltz, but Short's sense of visual spectacle overrode all objections by taking audiences back to a fantasy vision of Imperial Vienna. For the finale, Short staged the biggest transformation scene since the days of *The Black Crook*. As the actor playing Johann Jr. conducted "The Beautiful Blue Danube," he and the costumed orchestra of fifty-three were noiselessly lifted from the pit to the rear of the stage. Ten gilded columns rolled in on either side, eight massive crystal chandeliers dropped in from above, and thirty couples waltzed to the melody as twenty-four chorus girls in military uniforms ringed the dance floor. With more than two hundred in the cast and ninety-one in the crew, *The Great Waltz* was the largest Broadway production of its time, and the huge house was able to make a profit at a mere $3.30 top ticket price. Despite its popularity, this mammoth version of *The Great Waltz* never toured. In fact, only its name lived on. An acclaimed 1938 MGM film kept the title but used a different plot and score; still more *Great Waltz* productions toured in the 1940s using various new librettos. A 1970 London production credited thirteen different writers and used none of the Hart script.

German producer Erik Charell made it big with his Berlin hit *Im Weissen Rossl* (1930), a genial tale of confusing romantic shenanigans at an Alpine Inn. Relying on the appeal of a lavish production and beguiling melodies by various composers, he brought it to the West End as *The White Horse Inn* (1931, 650 performances), where an even larger production played to packed houses. For the Broadway staging (1936, 223 performances), Charell converted the interior of the Center Theatre into a mountain village, with life-size house fronts and a panoramic Alpine mural covering the walls of the lobby and auditorium. On stage, there was a 1,000-gallon rainstorm, a rotating merry-go-round, a small zoo's worth of wild animals, a steamboat, and an actor playing Austrian Emperor Franz Joseph thrown in for the heck of it. Warner Brothers was the primary backer, but costs ran so high that Rockefeller had to step in with additional funding. Popular leading man William Gaxton and operatic soprano Kitty Carlisle were almost lost in the hubbub, but *The White Horse Inn* became a popular attraction, entertaining some 700,000 people during its New York run.

John D. Rockefeller died in 1937, after which a series of failures played the Center Theatre. There were great hopes when Charell announced plans for *Swingin' the Dream* (1939, 13 performances), a jazz adaptation of Shakespeare's *A Midsummer-Night's Dream* that had bandleader Benny Goodman and his sextet, sets based on Walt Disney cartoons, and a cast headed by Louis Armstrong as Bully Bottom and Butterfly McQueen as Puck. The score interpolated numerous jazz standards, but the libretto by Charell and cultural critic Gilbert Seldes drew scathing reviews and the production folded in two weeks. In 1940, the Center Theatre installed an ice rink on stage and housed a series of popular skating spectaculars produced by Sonja Henie. In the early 1950s, the theatre became a television studio for NBC, and was demolished in 1954 to make way for a parking garage.

British Blockbusters: "Crest of the Wave"

Noël Coward was not the most successful creator of West End musicals in the 1930s. That distinction belonged to Ivor Novello (1893–1951), a handsome Welshman who had been a major celebrity when Coward was still struggling for recognition. Songwriting since his teens, Novello composed the hit World War I anthem "Keep the Home Fires Burning" at age twenty-two. His striking profile led to success as a silent screen star, and he later demonstrated genuine stage presence in several West End dramas. Novello did not begin writing full musicals until the mid-1930s, when the management of the Theatre Royal Drury Lane asked if he could write something to fill their historic 2,273-seat venue.

Glamorous Night (1935, 243 performances in London), had lyrics by actor Christopher Hassall (1912–1963) whose florid verbiage matched the lush melodies of this unapologetic operetta. Novello cast himself as a British inventor of television who meets and falls in love with a gypsy princess (American soprano Mary Ellis). After they escape a sinking ocean liner (which went down in full view of the audience) and celebrate a gypsy wedding, the princess is forced to give up her foreign beloved so that she can become queen. The broken-hearted hero returns to England, where he watches a broadcast of the distant coronation on his invention. The score included "Fold Your Wings," "Shine Through My Dreams," and the surprising "Far Away in Shanty Town" for African-American chanteuse Elisabeth Welch, who had become a fixture of the London theatre scene.

Despite capacity audiences, *Glamorous Night* was forced to close because the Drury Lane had committed to producing a holiday pantomime. After that surefire Christmas production failed, the theatre's humbled board invited Novello to stage a new piece on his own terms. *Careless Rapture* (1936, 295 performances in London)—which wags dubbed "Careless Rupture"—proved another winner. Novello played a man in love with his brother's fiancée, a ravishing musical comedy star portrayed by Dorothy Dickson. "Why Is There Ever Good-bye" was one of the more memorable numbers. In *Crest of the Wave* (London, 1937), the author played both the hero and the villain. *The Dancing Years* (1939, 187 performances in London) was the story of a fictional German-Jewish operetta composer (Novello) who cannot marry the soprano he loves (Mary Ellis) due to a misunderstanding. He is saved from a Nazi concentration camp when the soprano—now married to a prince—uses her connections to free him. Forced to close by the first bombings of World War II, *The Dancing Years* went on tour and then settled into London's Adelphi Theatre for a further 969 performances. The score included "I Can Give You the Starlight" and "Waltz of My Heart."

Novello's success was all the more impressive considering that this one-time boy chorister could barely sing a note as an adult. He did his matinee idol bit in the dialogue scenes and left all the vocals to his costars. Strange as this arrangement may seem, Novello's legion of devoted fans had no difficulty accepting it. Few of those fans knew that Novello was gay. He and longtime companion Robert Andrews led scandal-free lives, so their relationship caused no gossip. But those in the theatrical community certainly knew the truth, leading some to nickname his long-running hit "The Dancing Queers." Novello's work is mostly unknown in the United States, where producers and publishers were convinced his material was "too British." They may have been right, but his best melodies are magnificent.

American producers took the same dismissive attitude toward the longest running West End musical of the 1930s, *Me and My Girl* (1937, 1,646 performances). It featured comedian Lupino Lane (1892–1959) as Bill Snibson, a brash London cockney who inherits an earl's title and fortune. Novelty composer Noel Gay's lively score included the jaunty "Lambeth Walk," a knee-and-elbow-slapping cakewalk that ended each refrain with a cocked thumb raised to a defiant lower class cry of "Oy!" King George VI and Queen Elizabeth delighted their subjects by clapping and singing along during a command performance. The song became so popular that the Nazis moronically condemned it as "Jewish" music. In 1939, a performance of *Me and My Girl* was broadcast live on BBC television, but so few Brits owned sets at the time that it did not harm ticket sales. Audiences continued to pack the Victoria Palace Theatre through the early part of World War II. Lane spent most of his remaining years starring in a series of tours, sequels, and revivals, but American producers dismissed the show as "too British." In 1985, London welcomed a heavily revised version starring Shakespearean actor Robert Lindsay, who received an Olivier Award for his performance. The show finally traveled to New York the following year, where Lindsay picked up a Tony for Best Actor in a Musical and the "too British" *Me and My Girl* racked up 1,420 Broadway performances.

Noël Coward remained a creative dynamo, writing, composing, and appearing in a myriad of plays and films. He wrote notable songs for several non-musicals. Gertrude Lawrence introduced Coward's "Someday I'll Find You" in the comedy *Private Lives* (1930), and his epic upstairs-downstairs Drury Lane drama *Cavalcade* (1931) included the "Twentieth Century Blues." His operetta *Conversation Piece* (1934, 177 performances in London) featured French soprano Yvonne Printemps as the ward of a Parisian nobleman (played by Coward) who hopes to arrange a profitable British marriage for her, not realizing that she is already in love with him. Speaking hardly a word of English, Printemps had to learn the role phonetically, including "I'll Follow My Secret Heart." A New York production later that same year closed after just fifty-five performances.

Coward came up with a unique challenge for Gertrude Lawrence and himself–nine one-act plays (including four musicals), to be played in trios during three successive performances. Called *Tonight at 8:30* (1936, 157 performances in London), this repertory proved a solid success during limited runs in England and on Broadway (1936, 118 performances). "The Red Peppers" was an affectionate one-act look at a quarrelsome husband and wife team performing in a British music hall, with the two stars in sailors uniforms for the comical "Has Anybody Seen Our Ship?" and then in tuxedos and top hats for "Men About Town." "We Were Dancing" was the title tune of another one-act in which the stars played a jaded couple looking back on the irrational passion of their first meeting.

Coward's *Operette* (1938, 132 performances in London) featured Fritzi Massary as an aging Viennese opera star who warns young Peggy Wood not to marry a nobleman. Despite the wit of "The Stately Homes of England" and the endearing "Where Are the Songs We Sung," this attempt at nostalgia had the misfortune to open just as Hitler annexed Austria. Suddenly, Vienna was not something to sing about. When war came, Coward was determined to do his bit. Aside from turning out plays and films, he performed for troops all over the globe, and took part in some intelligence activities that remain classified.

The Gershwins: "Who Cares If the Sky Cares to Fall in the Sea?"

After revving up to speed in the previous decade, brothers George and Ira Gershwin became defining talents in 1930s musical theatre. No other team matched the sheer range of their efforts.

Back in 1927, the Gershwins had collaborated with George S. Kaufman on *Strike Up the Band* (1927), in which an American cheese manufacturer convinces the government to raise tariffs on imported cheese and declare war on Switzerland. He even offers to pay for the war if it is named after him. But times were too good for American audiences to embrace such a cutting satire, which Kaufman once defined as "something which closes on Satire-day night." Despite a promising score, the show shut down in Philadelphia. Perhaps the deepening of the Depression made Kaufman's jabs at government and big business easier to accept, or perhaps it was the somewhat gentler humor of Morrie Ryskind, who revised the book, turning the war with Switzerland into a harmless dream. The new *Strike Up the Band* (1930, 191 performances) also featured the comedy team of Bobby Clark and Paul McCullough, as well as the Gershwin gems "Soon," "I've Got a Crush on You," and the stirring title song. Shortly after the opening, when producer Edgar Selwyn told Kaufman and Ryskind that a hard-hitting musical satire could never fill a Broadway house, they took it as a challenge, and began plotting a new piece with the Gershwins.

While that plan simmered, the Gershwins went to work on *Girl Crazy* (1930, 272 performances) for their longtime producers Alex Aarons and Vinton Freedley. The libretto by Guy Bolton and John McGowan involved a "girl crazy" Manhattan playboy (Allen Kearns) who is banished by his millionaire father to an Arizona town with an all-cowboy population. It turns out there are two girls in town: the single but tough-as-nails postmistress Molly (Ginger Rogers) and a married saloon singer named Kate. The latter role went to Ethel Merman (1909–1984), a twenty-one-year-old singing stenographer from Astoria, Queens, whom Freedley discovered at the Brooklyn Paramount. Sent to the Gershwin penthouse for an audition, Merman later admitted, "Not only was I in awe of the great George Gershwin; I was in awe of the apartment building." After playing through her solo numbers, George asked if Ethel wanted any changes. Stunned, she replied that the songs would be just fine as they were—a statement many would later misinterpret as brash.

On opening night of *Girl Crazy*, Rogers introduced "Embraceable You" and "But Not for Me," and did well. But Merman walked off with the show singing the jazz anthem "I Got Rhythm." After the first verse, Merman belted a high C note and held it for sixteen bars while the orchestra played the melody. As she wrote with surprising modesty years later in her autobiography *Merman*, "The audience went a little crazy." No doubt it helped that the orchestra included future jazz legends Jimmy Dorsey, Benny Goodman, Gene Krupa, and Jack Teagarden, all conducted by the composer himself.

Film buffs please note: When Ginger Rogers needed a choreographer to cook up a dance routine for *Girl Crazy*, Gershwin called in his old buddy Fred Astaire. The two dancers dated briefly, and the resulting chemistry paid off a few years later when a brief head-to-head dance in *Flying Down to Rio* (RKO, 1932) launched them into screen stardom.

The hard-hitting satire that Kaufman and Ryskind prepared with the Gershwins went through various permutations before coming to life as *Of Thee I Sing* (1931, 441 performances). The target was presidential politics. In order to elect candidate John P. Wintergreen (William Gaxton) and his forgettable running mate Alexander P. Throttlebottom (Victor Moore), an unnamed political party opts for a "love" platform. A beauty contest is held in Atlantic City, with Wintergreen set to marry the winner if he is elected President. Just as southern belle Diana Devereaux (Grace Brinkley) claims the prize, Wintergreen says that he is already in love with his secretary Mary Turner (Lois Moran) because "she can bake corn muffins." After campaigning and proposing to Mary all across the country, Wintergreen wins the election, and there is a combination inauguration/wedding. A southern senator and the French ambassador demand justice for the jilted Devereaux, but the otherwise amoral Wintergreen stands by the wife he loves. With an impeachment vote underway, Mary announces that she is pregnant—and no one is about to impeach an expectant father. Months later, the Supreme Court rules (in a strict party-line vote) that it's a boy—twice. A nurse explains that Mary had twins, a boy and a girl. Throttlebottom solves the Devereaux crisis by marrying the curvaceous vixen, invoking his constitutional obligation to take on unfulfilled presidential duties.

The score displayed George Gershwin's patented blend of jazz and Broadway, with Ira building humorous musical scenes and finales in something like the style of Gilbert and Sullivan. Standout musical moments include the nonsensical "Wintergreen for President," "Love Is Sweeping the Country," the majestic title campaign song, and the breezy "Who Cares?" *Of Thee I Sing* offered a constant stream of ingenious touches, such as the French Ambassador entering to a familiar theme from "An American in Paris," and a musical Senate roll call that can't be bothered to include states that don't rhyme. There were strikingly handsome sets by Jo Mielziner (1901–1976), a former stage manager whose handsome, innovative designs would grace thirty-five Broadway musicals and dozens of plays in years to come. Gaxton and Moore established themselves as a team, but their propensity for ad-libbing raised the ire of Kaufman, who is said to have sent Gaxton a telegram in mid-performance: "Am in back of house. Wish you were here." *Of Thee I Sing* became the first Broadway musical to have its book and lyrics published, the first musical of the 1930s to top four hundred performances, and the first American musical to win the Pulitzer Prize for Drama. Only the librettists and lyricist were named as honorees, leaving George Gershwin conspicuously overlooked. The Pulitzer committee did not honor the composer until 1998.

Even the Gershwins could hit a rough patch. *Pardon My English* (1933, 46 performances) did so badly that producer Alex Aarons left the theatre for good, and Vinton Freedley fled the country to avoid his creditors. George and Ira then reteamed with Kaufman and Ryskind to write a sequel to *Of Thee I* Sing. In *Let 'Em Eat Cake* (1933, 90 performances), ex-president Wintergreen takes back power in a neofascist coup. Gone within three months, the show's only lasting legacy was the song "Mine." *Let 'Em Eat Cake* was the first Broadway book musical sequel, a subgenre that as of this writing has reaped nothing but failure.

For some years, George Gershwin had been interested in composing a full-length grand opera incorporating stylistic elements of jazz, Broadway, and classical music. After considering various subjects, he chose *Porgy*, a novel by DuBose Heyward that depicted the lives of poor negroes living in a waterfront tenement in Charleston, South Carolina. The story of the crippled beggar Porgy and his morally unsteady girlfriend Bess certainly had the makings of opera, but the novelist's wife Dorothy had just adapted the story as a drama for the Theatre Guild, and the success of their 1928 production staged by Russian-born director Rouben Mamoulian (1889–1987) delayed all other plans. After years of conflicting commitments, Heyward and the Gershwins finished *Porgy and Bess* (1935, 124 performances), which was also produced by the Theatre Guild. Gershwin even went so far as to orchestrate the score himself, a rarity among Broadway composers. Mamoulian brought the same innovative directorial hand to this daring work, creating memorable stage pictures. Now recognized as a masterpiece, *Porgy and Bess* initially inspired critical confusion—no one knew what to make of a Broadway opera. True, poet Gertrude Stein and composer Virgil Thompson had already attempted such a creature with their *Four Saints in Three Acts* (1934, 48 performances), but Stein's lyrics were pretentious gobbledygook, and Thompson's music was in a traditional classical mold. Heyward and the Gershwins came up with something far meatier: a powerful story filled with vivid characters and emotions, and the sort of varied, accessible score that could only have been devised for Broadway. The Gershwins called it a "folk opera," which is what the American musical theatre had been driving toward for some time.

The overture flowed directly into a lone woman (Abbie Mitchell) cuddling a baby while singing the lullaby "Summertime" ("and the livin' is easy"). Soon afterward, another ensemble character (Edward Matthews) sang the more cynical warning "A Woman is a Sometime Thing." Porgy (Todd Duncan) proclaimed "I Got Plenty o' Nothin'," and expressed his love for Bess (Anne Brown) in "Bess, You Is My Woman Now." That love is shaken by Bess's old passion for the murderous Crown (Warren Coleman), whom Porgy kills in self-defense. The hustler Sportin' Life (John W. Bubbles) shows his contempt for Bible-toting morals in "It Ain't Necessarily So," and offers Bess cocaine to lure her away in "There's a Boat Dat's Leavin' Soon for New York." At the final curtain, Porgy aims his goat cart northward, determined to win Bess back in "I'm on My Way."

Editors of the major New York newspapers were uncertain how to categorize *Porgy and Bess*, so most sent their opera *and* theatre critics to review the show. Neither group was altogether satisfied. The music critics jeered at a Tin Pan Alley tunesmith for having the nerve to dabble in opera, and Broadway commentators wondered why the brothers who wrote scores for *Girl Crazy* and *Of Thee I Sing* now offered something so solemn. A few African-American journalists took issue with white men writing something that depicted blacks as beggars, criminals, drug addicts, and whores. Cool reviews and an uncertain public kept the run to a little over four months, by no means an outright failure, but not nearly enough to cover the high production costs. Today, we look back and find it hard to understand what all the contention was about—*Porgy and Bess* is a masterful Broadway musical that also happens to be an opera. By any name, it's a solid piece of entertainment.

Somewhat disheartened by the reception for *Porgy and Bess*, George and Ira headed out to Hollywood, where it was always summertime and the living was far easier. While creating film scores for the likes of Fred Astaire, George began suffering strange symptoms;

dizziness, disorientation, and sensing the smell of burnt rubber. Doctors eventually identified an inoperable inner brain tumor. George Gershwin died at age thirty-seven. He did not live to see audiences rediscover *Porgy and Bess* and hail it as an American classic. Aside from numerous regional and international productions, there were acclaimed Broadway revivals, and in 1985 it became the first Broadway composition to enter the repertory of the Metropolitan Opera. Some triumphs are so great that it takes fifty years for them to set in. Ira went on to write with other composers, and proved a tireless promoter of his brother's legacy.

Cole Porter: "I'm Ridin' High"

Cole Porter came from the sort of "old money" that rarely dabbled in the stock market, so he was unaffected by the Wall Street crash. From a unique inside viewpoint, Porter wrote songs depicting the privileged world of the rich, but he also had a flair for expressing how the seamier side lived. His score for *The New Yorkers* (1930) included "Love for Sale," which depicted a white prostitute bemoaning her lot ("Old love, new love, ev'ry love but true love") while sitting in a midtown restaurant. The mainstream press howled until the number was restaged to depict a black prostitute sitting in Harlem's Cotton Club. Censors still banned the song from radio airwaves.

We mentioned earlier that Fred Astaire's career prospects were doubtful after his sister Adele married. His first solo project had to be a winner that would give him a new solo identity, and Astaire found exactly that in Porter's next show, *Gay Divorce* (1932). The plot involved a young noblewoman (Claire Luce) who mistakes a famous novelist (Astaire) for the professional correspondent "assisting" in her divorce. By the time the misunderstanding is cleared up, the two leads are ready to dance happily ever after. Porter tailored Astaire's songs to make the most of a limited vocal range, knowing his star's dancing would do the rest. Everyone expected "After You, Who" would be the hit, but it was the sensual "Night and Day" that helped *Gay Divorce* overcome uneven reviews and become a moneymaker. This show marked the end of Astaire's stage career. Studio moguls had misgivings about his looks, but RKO put him under contract. When the screen version of *Gay Divorce* was made in 1934 costarring

Astaire and Ginger Rogers, censors insisted that the title be changed; a divorce could not be happy! Since it was all right to say someone getting a divorce was carefree, the film was finally called *The Gay Divorcée*. "Night and Day" was the only song from the stage score that made it to the screen. Much of the seductive stage choreography for that number was also intact.

Porter's next Broadway hit was a collection of accidents. Bankrupt producer Vinton Freedley spent several months sailing around the Pacific in a borrowed yacht, trying to concoct a Depression-proof hit that would restore his fortunes. He came up with the idea of a musical involving an ocean liner that sinks and leaves its passengers and crew marooned on a desert island—a supersized ancestor to the TV sitcom *Gilligan's Island*. With an all-star cast and a score by the Gershwins, it would be a cinch to find backers. Freedley snuck back into New York City, and lined up *Of Thee I Sing* stars William Gaxton and Victor Moore, as well as his *Girl Crazy* discovery Ethel Merman, assuring each one top billing. Show biz veterans, they soon compared notes and realized that Freedley was manipulating them, but all three took it in stride. The Gershwins were in the midst of writing *Porgy and Bess*, so Freedley sailed to Europe and found Cole Porter paddling a flatboat along the Rhine by day and lounging in a private yacht by night. The composer was enthusiastic about the project, so Freedley next lined up star librettists Guy Bolton and P. G. Wodehouse. One catch—Bolton was in England, Wodehouse was in France, and tax issues made it impossible for either to travel. Freedley arranged for them to collaborate by long distance telephone, a novel idea at the time. In a few months, Freedley had investors lined up and *Bon Voyage* was ready to go into rehearsal for a fall opening.

Then disaster struck—literally. On September 8, 1934, the liner *Morro Castle* caught fire off the coast of New Jersey, taking 137 lives. Suddenly, a musical comedy about an accident at sea was not a funny idea. With Bolton and Wodehouse still stuck in Europe, Freedley turned to his director, playwright Howard Lindsay (1888–1968), who insisted that in order to rewrite the libretto while staging the show, he would need a collaborator. According to legend, a supposedly psychic friend of Cole Porter's told him that writer Russell Crouse (1893–1966) was the man they were looking for. It was late summer, a time when New Yorkers of means hightailed it to cooler climes. After a fruitless search for Crouse, legend has it that Freedley and Lindsay leaned out of the windows of the Alvin Theatre hoping for a breath of air. Across West 52nd Street, they saw someone leaning out of one of the Theatre Guild's windows: Crouse. Rehearsals resumed for the newly christened *Anything Goes* (1934, 420 performances), with the new librettists literally making up dialogue on the spot. Expert stenographer Merman took down the new lines in shorthand, typed them out each evening and passed them out to the cast. At the dress rehearsal in Boston, the cast was onstage waiting to rehearse the final scene when Lindsay and Crouse emerged from the men's room with the last bits of dialogue scribbled on sheets of toilet paper.

In the final plot, evangelist-turned-nightclub singer Reno Sweeney (Merman) is in love with handsome businessman Billy Crocker (Gaxton), who finds himself pining for socialite Hope Harcourt (Bettina Hall). They all wind up on a transatlantic ocean liner, with Billy a stowaway. Also on board is Public Enemy Number 13, mobster Moon-Face Mooney (Moore), who is masquerading as a Christian missionary. Billy dons various disguises in his pursuit of Hope, and becomes the toast of the ship when he is mistakenly identified as Moon-Face. After identities are cleared up, Reno lands a British nobleman, Billy winds up with Hope, and Moon-Face learns that the FBI now considers him too harmless to arrest.

The score to *Anything Goes* is one of Porter's best. Merman introduced "I Get a Kick Out of You," its intricate internal rhymes offsetting any sense of the singer's heartbreak at loving someone who obviously does not return her affections. She also triumphed with the belter's pseudo-spiritual "Blow, Gabriel, Blow," and the topical title song. Gaxton introduced "All Through the Night" and joined forces with Merman for "You're the Top," a scintillating list of rhyming superlatives: Mahatma Gandhi and Napoleon Brandy, a symphony by Strauss and Mickey Mouse, a dress from Saks's and last year's taxes. Inspired by an after-dinner word game, "You're the Top" became the prototype for the comic list songs Porter would specialize in for the rest of his career. Porter genuinely admired Merman's no-nonsense personality and was in awe of her vocal ability, saying "I'd rather write songs for Ethel Merman than anyone else in the world. She sounds like a brass band going by." Of her thirteen Broadway musicals, five would have Porter scores.

Playwright Moss Hart (1904–1961) attained fame collaborating with George S. Kaufman, and independently contributed librettos to various book musicals and revues. Having grown up in poverty, he reveled in the kind of affluent life that his writing made possible. When Hart bought a country home and spent more than six figures to reshape the surrounding landscape, Kaufman quipped, "It's what God would have done if he had the money." Cole Porter suggested that he and Hart write a musical while taking a world cruise on the *Franconia*. The result was *Jubilee* (1935, 169 performances), which involved a fictitious royal family masquerading as commoners to find out how the other half lives. This show is almost forgotten, but its score is not. Along with "Just One of Those Things" and "A Picture of Me Without You," it includes Porter's exotic "Begin the Beguine," a smoldering melody inspired by a native war dance that the composer witnessed when the cruise visited Indonesia. The song did not peak in popularity until bandleader Artie Shaw recorded a hit swing version in 1938. Although *Jubilee* was never filmed, the swing "Begin the Beguine" made it to the big screen as an unforgettable tap duet for Fred Astaire and Eleanor Powell in *Broadway Melody of 1940*.

Porter's *Red, Hot, and Blue* (1936, 183 performances) was intended as a reunion of the *Anything Goes* cast and crew, but Gaxton and Moore were not available. Perhaps they read Lindsay and Crouse's confused mish-mosh of a libretto. As it turned out, Moore was replaced by Jimmy Durante (1893–1980) who played an ex-convict working with a jaded heiress (Ethel Merman) and wisecracking sidekick (Bob Hope) as they run a nationwide search for a woman with a waffle iron mark on her posterior—seriously, that's the plot. Before the show went into production, agents for Durante and Merman went to war over that most sacred theatrical status symbol, top billing. Both stars claimed they didn't really care whose name came first, but once it became an issue, the pride of their agents was at stake. Porter solved the dilemma by suggesting that their names be crisscrossed in the Playbill and on all advertising, giving each equal prominence. Merman introduced Porter's swinging title song, the ecstatic "Ridin' High," and the popular torcher "Down in the Depths on the Ninetieth Floor." Since the latter's lyric specified that the singer was in a "pet pailletted gown," Merman insisted that producer Vinton Freedley blow a few thousand dollars and provide one. While Merman proved a deft comedienne in her book scenes with Durante, her funniest musical moment came in a duet with Hope. Porter later claimed that the title was inspired by another bit of after-dinner badinage: his observation that a meal had been "delightful" led his wife Linda to say it was "delicious," and longtime friend Monty Wooley gurgled, "It's De-Lovely." The lyric traces the course of a romance through courtship and marriage, with "the crowd in that church" and "the proud parson propped on his perch." One night, Hope improvised some physical business during the song, and the stage manager warned him never to try it again. Once Merman's performance was perfected, it was set in stone—duets included. Hope got the message and remained on friendly terms with Merman.

In 1937, Porter was horseback riding on Long Island when something startled his mount. The animal fell, rose, and then fell again, crushing both of Cole's legs. While waiting for help, he later claimed that he took his mind off the blinding pain by completing the lighthearted lyric to "At Long Last Love." Bone marrow infection set in, but when doctors advised immediate amputation, Cole refused. Too vain to face life as a paraplegic, over the next twenty years he underwent dozens of operations. During good spells, he hobbled about on a cane, but he often had to be bodily lifted into and out of cars, chairs, and hospital beds. Most of the public had no clue that the urbane Cole Porter suffered almost constant agony. Work was his only distraction, so he continued to turn out two to three projects a year for the stage and screen.

Mary Martin (1913–1990), an unknown singing actress from Weatherford, Texas, made her Broadway debut in Cole's next opus, *Leave it to Me* (1938, 291 performances). The plot told of befuddled American ambassador Alonso "Stinky" Goodhue (Victor Moore) and his brash wife (vaudeville veteran Sophie Tucker) trying to get recalled from the Soviet Union with the help of a slick newspaper reporter (William Gaxton). Martin played Dolly Winslow, an incidental man-hungry character who darn near stole the show by appearing in a Siberian railway station dressed in nothing more than high heels, a hat, and an abbreviated fur coat. She perched on top of some luggage and explained to a chorus of six parka-clad hunks that she might dream of joining their team, but "My Heart Belongs to Daddy" (and as a similar character in *Gentlemen Prefer Blondes* would explain a decade later, "the one you call your daddy *ain't* your pa"). Martin's jazzy, mock-innocent performance of this number made her an instant celebrity. Tucker, who delighted audiences with the cynical "Most Gentlemen Don't Like Love" ("they just like to kick it around"), gave the newcomer a tip on how to put over a naughty lyric: "On the last line, *never* look at the audience; look straight up to heaven, fold your hands, and sing."

Porter's next project was *DuBarry Was a Lady* (1939, 408 performances), which began when songwriter-turned-producer Buddy DeSylva and librettist Herb Fields came up with a great comic premise: neurotic nightclub washroom attendant Louie (Bert Lahr) is in love with singing star May (Ethel Merman). Louie accidentally consumes a drugged cocktail that he had intended for the singer's boyfriend, and dreams that he is King Louis XV of France, while May is the lovely but reluctant royal mistress, Madame DuBarry. Porter's score gave the stars two showstopping duets: a laundry-list tribute to "Friendship," and the bawdy "But In the Morning, No," which was so sexually suggestive—with references to political "third parties" and accounting "double entries"—that it was banned from radio airwaves. Then-unknown dancers Betty Grable and Charles Walters shared "Well, Did You Evah?" While rehearsing a scene in which Lahr chased Merman around the royal bed, Ethel was so much faster that she actually bypassed her costar. The effect was so hilarious that they made it part of the show. A 1943 film version dropped most of the score, along with most of the laughs. Attempts to revive this show without its original stars have fallen flat, in large part because few actors know how to play this kind of material today. *DuBarry Was a Lady* opened in the same year that Lahr appeared as the Cowardly Lion in MGM's screen version of *The Wizard of Oz*. When a friend congratulated the insecure worrywart on his multiple successes, he grumbled, "Yeah, but what about next year?" Porter had no such worries. After all, he was being hailed as the king of musical comedy.

Kurt Weill: "A Long, Long While from May to December"

The Threepenny Opera had failed in New York, but that did not dissuade composer Kurt Weill from emigrating to the United States. He knew that the most likely place to pursue his theatrical ambitions was on Broadway. His first effort there was an intriguing score for the Group Theatre's bitter indictment of war, *Johnny Johnston* (1936, 68 performances), which critics dismissed as being preachy. Weill wanted his music to make a socially relevant statement, but he also wanted it to make money. With this in mind, he teamed with Pulitzer Prize–winning dramatist Maxwell Anderson (1888–1959) to write a musical comedy that dealt with the deadly worldwide struggle between democracy and totalitarianism. The trick was to wrap this heavy message in an entertaining package.

Knickerbocker Holiday (1938, 168 performances) starred Hollywood favorite Walter Huston as Pieter Stuyvesant, the dictatorial peg-legged Dutch governor of New Amsterdam—the first colonial name of New York City. Stuyvesant finds himself at odds with strapping colonist Brom Brock (played by future producer Richard Kollmar), who has "a really fantastic and inexcusable aversion to taking orders, coupled with a complete abhorrence for governmental corruption, and an utter incapacity to do anything about it." In short, he is one of that troublesome new breed, Americans. Brock wins his beloved Tina's heart with one of Weill's most underrated melodies, "It Never Was You." Unfortunately for Brock, Stuyvesant is also determined to marry Tina, and he subtly terrifies the girl into submission with the deceptively lyrical "September Song," saying that as his "days dwindle down to a precious few," he *will* spend them with her. The corrupt town council is initially unable to resist the governor's ruthless, dictatorial policies, but finally heeds Brock's call for defiance. Stuyvesant eventually relents, partly out of deference to posterity, and partly because he too has never cared for following orders—a genial end to a show that, in effect, condemned democracy's seeming inability to resist the spread of fascism. A healthy run and the success of "It Never Was You" and "September Song" made it clear that Weill had arrived and would be an important voice on Broadway.

Earlier that same year, Weill's longtime disciple and champion, the multitalented Marc Blitzstein (1905–1964) singlehandedly wrote *The Cradle Will Rock* (1938, 108 performances), a politically charged allegory that had Steeltown factory owner Mr. Mister battling with union organizer Larry Foreman, played by character actor Howard Da Silva (1909–1986). The government-run Federal Theatre Project (FTP) agreed to produce the show, but with union issues rocking the real steel industry, *Cradle* was judged too controversial. On the planned opening night of June 16, 1937, the FTP locked the theatre. After making desperate inquiries, production supervisor John Houseman and director Orson Welles led the cast and the audience over to the empty Venice Theatre (formerly the Jolson) at 7th Avenue and 59th Street. Since Actor's Equity would not authorize the change of venue, the cast was not allowed to appear onstage. Instead, they played the show from seats in the audience, with the composer accompanying them on an onstage piano. The material was rather preachy and obvious, but the unique staging survived nineteen performances and then reopened at the Windsor Theatre the following January for 108 conventional performances. *The Cradle Will Rock* has been revived on several occasions, and inspired a 1999 docudrama, but Blitzstein's strident, bitter tone makes for poor entertainment, even for audiences who agree with its point of view.

Rodgers and Hart

After starting out the decade with the aforementioned failure of *Simple Simon* and the poorly received *America's Sweetheart* (1931, 135 performances), Richard Rodgers and Larry Hart took a prolonged hiatus from Broadway. They had enjoyed a success in England with *Ever Green* (1930, 254 performances in London), which featured Jessie Matthews (1907–1981) as a young woman who wins publicity by claiming to be a sixty-year-old triumph of cosmetology. But high-paying offers from Hollywood proved impossible to resist, so Rodgers and Hart headed west. After three lucrative but frustrating years in the movie business, during which their efforts were either underappreciated or altogether ignored, the songwriting duo bid farewell to the film studios and returned to Broadway. While many old-guard producers had either died or had been forced out of the business, ambitious young hopefuls were rising to take their place, and several were only too glad to present musicals by Rodgers and Hart.

Former stenographer and songwriter Billy Rose (1895–1966) had graduated to managing nightclubs and producing for the stage. He approached Rodgers and Hart with the idea for *Jumbo* (1935, 233 performances), a variation on *Romeo and Juliet*; this time, the young lovers belong to families that own competing circuses. No Broadway stage could hold such a story, so Rose renovated the massive Hippo-drome Theatre to look like the interior of a circus tent. He then hired a mammoth cast, leased a legion of circus animals, and had John Murray Anderson coordinate the gargantuan physical production. Playwright and acclaimed dramatic director George Abbott (1887–1995) took on his first-ever musical assignment by directing the book scenes. Jimmy Durante played a bankrupt circus owner who at one point tries to sneak a live elephant out of the theatre, only to be confronted by a sheriff demanding to know where he is taking the elephant. Durante replied with wide-eyed innocence, "What elephant?"

After costly production delays, Rose refused to allow radio air-play of *Jumbo*'s songs until it was too late to boost ticket sales, so even though the show had a respectable run, it never recouped its costs, which rumor set at $340,000. But the eventual success of "My Romance" and "The Most Beautiful Girl in the World" reestablished Rodgers and Hart as a Broadway songwriting team. The Hippodrome was demolished in 1939, and eventually replaced by a parking garage that bears the old theatre's name.

Before *Jumbo* went into production, Rodgers and Hart had been talking with producer Dwight Deere Wiman about a musical in which Fred Astaire would play a former vaudeville hoofer who becomes a music scholar and winds up dancing with a European ballet troupe. When Astaire turned down the project, *On Your Toes* (1936, 315 per-formances) became a vehicle for lanky eccentric dancer Ray Bolger (1904–1987). Since the show would require formal ballets, Wiman hired the most acclaimed classical choreographer of the mid-twentieth century, Russian-born George Balanchine (1904–1983), who proved to be a willing and adventurous collaborator. He created two ballets that had some connection to the plot—"Princess Zenobia" spoofed traditional ballet, while the jazzy "Slaughter on 10th Avenue" gave Bolger an opportunity to avoid being shot by vengeful gangsters. Rodgers provided completely original scores for both ballets, resist-ing the temptation to recycle melodies used in the songs. Balanchine's success opened the eyes of serious choreographers to the possibilities of the musical theatre. Librettist George Abbott stepped in as direc-tor when the Boston tryout proved disastrous. His commanding air and sense of stagecraft pulled the production together. The rubber-limbed Bolger scored a great success, introducing "There's a Small

Hotel" and "It's Got to Be Love," and shared the gleeful title tune with costar Doris Carson, who also sang the melancholy "Glad to Be Unhappy." Monty Wooley made his acting debut as a ballet impresario and joined Louella Gear to sing the merciless "Too Good for the Average Man." A British production (1937, 123 performances in London) was not quite as well received, and the 1939 film version inexplicably disposed of the songs, but *On Your Toes* would be periodically rediscovered in years to come.

Rodgers and Hart decided to try a musical with no stars, writing the libretto themselves. *Babes in Arms* (1937, 289 performances) involved the teenage children of unemployed vaudevillians putting on a show in a barn to avoid being sent off to a work farm. The production stressed youthful creativity; costumes for an Egyptian sequence consisted of towels, bath mats, and scrub mops, all worn with two-toned tap shoes. The cast included twenty-three-year-old newcomer Alfred Drake (1914–1992), a handsome Brooklyn-born baritone whose rousing rendition of the title song set him on a course to Broadway stardom. Former child screen star Mitzi Green introduced "The Lady Is a Tramp" and the much-loved "My Funny Valentine." She shared the *déjà vu* love song "Where or When" with Ray Heatherton. The score also included "Johnny One Note" and "I Wish I Were in Love Again." Sensational African-American tap dancers Fayard Nicholas (1914–2006) and his brother Harold (1921–2000) made their only appearance in a Broadway book musical. They were soon snatched up by Hollywood, where their color proved an insuperable barrier to the level of stardom their talent deserved.

Both Rodgers and Hart were excited by the prospect of collaborating with George S. Kaufman and Moss Hart (no relation to Larry) on *I'd Rather Be Right* (1937, 290 performances), a genial musical satire of President Franklin Roosevelt and his administration. But the songwriters were dismayed when song and dance man George M. Cohan was cast as the wheelchair-bound FDR. During their Hollywood sojourn, they had worked on Cohan's only musical film, *The Phantom President* (Paramount, 1933), and found him embittered and resentful. Producer Sam Harris, Cohan's longtime friend and producing partner, insisted that Cohan had just triumphed in Eugene O'Neill's comedy *Ah, Wilderness* (1933) and was anxious to make his renaissance complete by starring in a musical hit. As it turned out, Cohan was more difficult than before, clearly annoyed to be performing words and music written by men who had been toddlers back when he was at his peak. Cohan's attitude and Kaufman's open declaration that a libretto was intrinsically far more important than songs, spelled an unhappy experience for Rodgers and Hart. The rarely heard "Have You Met Miss Jones" was the closest thing to a hit in the lackluster score, but audiences were so delighted to have Cohan back that the show had a healthy run and a profitable tour. It proved to be Cohan's last taste of theatrical glory. After appearing in several quick failures, he was forced off the stage by cancer and died in 1942 at age sixty-four.

Rodgers and Hart promptly went back to work for the genial Dwight Deere Wiman, who persuaded MGM to release rights to *I Married an Angel* (1938, 338 performances), an unfilmed project the songwriters had submitted during their Hollywood sojourn. The plot involved a Hungarian count (Dennis King) whose prayer for a pure wife is answered when he marries an actual angel (Vera Zorina) from heaven. With Hart's alcoholism beginning to affect his ability to work, it took uncredited revisions by thirty-year-old director Joshua Logan (1908–1988) to get the book into working shape. As the count's mother, Vivienne Segal coached the angel in the ways of human deception in order to save the marriage. King introduced the rapturous title song, while Zorina and Segal shared "At the Roxy Music Hall," an irrelevant but amusing send-up of the new and lavishly appointed Radio City Music Hall, where "the seats caress your carcass with their plushes."

Rodgers and Hart continued working together, with Rodgers cast in the role of taskmaster to the often truant Hart. A resentful Larry went so far as to nickname Dick "teacher," but despite growing tensions, they still turned out extraordinary songs. Amazed that no one had ever tried to formally adapt one of Shakespeare's works as a musical comedy, they selected *The Comedy of Errors*, with its story of two sets of twins from the ancient Greek city of Syracuse. Separated at birth, they all meet years later in Ephesus, where mistaken identities abound. The title of *The Boys from Syracuse* (1938, 235 performances) was an inside joke: theatre owners Lee and J. J. Shubert had grown up in Syracuse, New York, and "the boys from Syracuse" was one of their cleaner nicknames in the business. George Abbott served as producer, director, and sole book writer. As one of the twins, Eddie Albert (1908–2005) made his musical debut singing "Dear Old Syracuse" and the breezy "This Can't Be Love." He shared the second with soprano Muriel Angelus who shared the witty harmonic trio "Sing for Your Supper" ("and you'll get breakfast") with Wynn Murray and Mary Westcott. Angelus also introduced "Falling in Love with Love" ("is falling for make-believe"), a prime example of Rodgers and Hart's tendency to blend romantic melody with lyrical irony.

The team's fourth collaboration with producer-director Abbott, *Too Many Girls* (1939, 249 performances), used a plot that borrowed elements from *Good News* and *Girl Crazy*: a millionaire sends his well-chased daughter to a remote college in New Mexico, hiring several members of the football team to act as her bodyguards. To no one's surprise, the handsomest of the boys falls in love with her. "I Didn't Know What Time It Was" proved to be a hit, and cabaret singers have long favored "Give It Back to the Indians," a comic complaint that New York City was no longer worth keeping. This production was plagued by Larry Hart's prolonged drinking binges, which led to missed appointments and recurring bouts with pneumonia. As you will see in our next chapter, it would soon become more than Rogers could handle.

Very Warm for May: *"The Angel Glow That Lights a Star"*

Very Warm for May (1939, 59 performances) had all the earmarks of a hit, so when it ran for less than two months, everyone involved with the production was disappointed. Many blamed producer Max Gordon, who demanded extensive rewrites that supposedly diminished the final product. Although a failure, this musical comedy about young actors making good at a summer stock theatre was a landmark for many of the talents involved. It certainly marked a beginning for several young hopefuls in the cast, including future greats Vera Ellen, June Allyson, Max Showalter, Hiram Sherman, and Eve Arden. Codirector Vincente Minnelli was about to be snatched away from the theatre by MGM, where he would have a brilliant film career.

It marked an ending for Donald Brian, Broadway's original Danilo in *The Merry Widow*, who made his final stage appearance in a featured role. It was also an ending for Max Gordon, who would continue producing hit plays but would never again present a successful musical. Since critics praised the score of *Very Warm for May*, fifty-four-year-old composer Jerome Kern took the quick closing in stride, unaware that the demands of Hollywood and increasingly poor health would make this his last Broadway bow. Some pundits felt that this show marked an ending for lyricist-librettist Oscar Hammerstein II, who had been bedeviled by flops for six years. People in the business were dismissing him as a has-been, and he wasn't altogether sure they were wrong.

But *Very Warm for May* held two seeds that would bloom into future success for Hammerstein. One was a bit of dialogue in which a warmhearted dowager advised a lovestruck teenager that a girl should be like a blossom and keep her honey for just one man—a line Oscar would put to better use a dozen years later in *The King and I*. Even more noteworthy was the song "All the Things You Are." For generations to come, songwriters and scholars would praise this ballad for its breathtaking blend of harmony and poetry. In particular, it caught the attention of composer Richard Rodgers, who was beginning to understand that his partnership with Larry Hart was coming to an end. Hammerstein had been a friend since they worked together on varsity shows at Columbia University. If Oscar had not had a hit in a few seasons, so what? As Rodgers wrote years later in his autobiography *Musical Stages*, "I was convinced that any man who could write … the lyric to Jerome Kern's 'All the Things You Are' was far from being through, and that his talent was being misused rather than used up." It was just a thought, but as a future musical would put it, worlds are turned on such thoughts.

11

A New Beginning (1940–1950) – "They Couldn't Pick a Better Time"

The big opening chorus number had been a staple in musical theatre since Offenbach's time, with a huge chorus (preferably of females) there to grab the audience's attention. So the opening night regulars were caught off guard when a new Broadway musical began with a lone woman on stage in the middle of a busy morning. Moments later, a man came on to sing the opening number as a solo, with no ensemble in sight. The effect was fresh and charming, as was the heroine's dream ballet, where she got to choose between two suitors. No wonder *Louisiana Purchase* (1940, 444 performances) was a hit.

If you thought I was describing another show, that's understandable. Misinformed sources have suggested that *Oklahoma!* invented such features as a two-person opening scene, a dream ballet, and (most laughably) the integration of song, dance, and dialogue. There is no question that *Oklahoma!* was a landmark work. In fact, any serious discussion of musical theatre in the 1940s breaks down into everything that came before *Oklahoma!* and everything that came after. But many of the seemingly "new" things in it had been brewing on Broadway for some time. For example, *Pal Joey* (1941) used a two-character opening, *Lady in the Dark* (1941) staged most of its musical numbers as dream sequences, and dream ballets had been around since the nineteenth century. *Oklahoma!* was not an anomaly, but rather the culmination of an ongoing effort on the part of a few determined artists to make the Broadway musical grow up.

In the early 1940s, most people in the business saw little reason to take musical theatre so seriously. With war reigniting in Europe and Asia, the only thing audiences supposedly expected from a stage musical was a solid good time. *Louisiana Purchase* began life when songwriter-turned-producer Buddy DeSylva came up with the basic story idea, which Morrie Ryskind fleshed out in the libretto. A straightlaced U.S. senator with presidential ambitions (Victor Moore) investigates a corrupt New Orleans politician (William Gaxton), who happens to be falling in love with a beautiful refugee from Nazi-dominated Europe (Vera Zorina). With a plausible comic premise and a stellar cast, all that was needed was a top-rank songwriter. Irving Berlin's score included no hits, but it gave tuneful pleasure between the gag-packed scenes.

There was a lot of traffic in a musical comedy, and Edward MacGregor (1878–1957) had been directing winners since 1918, with a résumé that included *Good News* and *DuBarry Was a Lady*. He came from a generation of stage directors who served primarily as traffic cops. Leaving themes to the writers and interpretation to the actors, these directors told actors where to stand and maintained a safe flow of action on stage. MacGregor kept *Louisiana Purchase* moving at a merry pace, and was not averse to exotic touches. For example, he had Zorina choose between Gaxton and Moore in a comic dream ballet choreographed by George Balanchine (who was Zorina's husband at the time). The two-person opening scene was a self-spoof, the lone woman being a stenographer who took dictation from an attorney warning the creative team that *Louisiana Purchase* would earn them a hail of lawsuits. Audiences loved the show, which ultimately attracted no lawsuits, ran for more than a year, and was filmed by Paramount in 1941.

MacGregor was also at the helm for DeSylva's production of *Panama Hattie* (1940, 501 performances), the first Broadway book musical to top five-hundred performances since the 1920s. It was also the first time Ethel Merman received solo star billing, a status she retained for the rest of her stage career. A non-dancing belter with surefire comic instincts, she was so unlike any star that came before her that it had taken a decade for writers to catch on and take full advantage of her abilities. DeSylva and Herb Fields coauthored a libretto that cast Merman as brassy Hattie Maloney, a nightclub owner in the Panama Canal Zone who tries to win the approval of her blueblood fiancé's eight-year-old daughter Geraldine (Joan Carroll), and in the process thwarts a nefarious plot to blow up the canal. Cole

Porter's score included "My Mother Would Love You" and "Make It Another Old Fashioned, Please," which ended with Merman's plea to "Make it a straight rrrrrrrrye!" The real challenge was Merman and Carroll's duet "Let's Be Buddies." Child labor laws made it illegal for an eight-year-old to sing and dance on Broadway at the time, so Porter used an easygoing rhythm that the two could just walk to and wrote Carroll's lines as spoken counterpoint—creating a much-needed hit without irking the powers that be.

The busy MacGregor next directed Vinton Freedley's production of *Let's Face It* (1941, 547 performances), which had a Porter score and a book by Herb and Dorothy Fields about three Southampton housewives (Vivian Vance, Edith Meiser, and Eve Arden) who get even with their philandering husbands by setting out to seduce three inductees from the local army base. In his first starring role, Brooklyn-born comedian Danny Kaye (1913–1987) scored major points as one of the soldiers. Kaye's wife Sylvia Fine provided him with several comic specialties including "Melody in Four F," a tongue twisting look at army life for the newly conscripted. "You Irritate Me So" was sung by Eddie Hilliard and former vaudevillian Nanette Fabray (1922–). Although MacGregor remained active for years to come, *Let's Face It* was his last hit. He was still a good traffic cop, but the kind of musicals being produced soon required very different talents.

Six weeks after *Let's Face It* opened, the Japanese attack on Pearl Harbor hurled the United States into World War II. All aspects of the entertainment industry quickly fell into line, including the theatre. If you are looking for an example of how the musical comedies of the early 1940s incorporated wartime themes—and just how lightheaded these shows could be—it's hard to beat Porter's next show, *Something for the Boys* (1943, 422 performances). Herb and Dorothy Fields took their plot from two real-life news items: one about someone picking up radio transmissions through a Carborundum tooth filling, and another about three cousins who had never met sharing an inheritance. For the sake of the libretto, the inheritance became a four-hundred-acre Texas ranch adjacent to an Army Air Corps base. One of the inheritors is defense worker Blossom Hart (Ethel Merman) who falls for Sergeant Rocky Fulton (Bill Johnson), one of her favorite big-band leaders in peacetime. When Blossom turns the ranch house into a residence for the flyer's wives, a jealous rival for Rocky's affections tells the army that the place is a bordello! All misunderstandings fade when a plane's radio fails and Blossom guides it to safety by picking up landing instructions through the Carborundum in her teeth. Frankly, no one gave a gnat's backside about the plot. The dialogue was packed with snappy slang, such as this assessment of Blossom's legs when the leads first meet:

> ROCKY: Man, look at those drumsticks.
>
> BLOSSOM: How would you like a kick in the teeth from one of those drumsticks?
>
> ROCKY: And this is the womanhood I'm fighting to protect?
>
> BLOSSOM: And this is the womanhood *I'm* fighting to protect!

Porter's songs are packed with the same sort of argot, plus plenty of swing. Merman sang the rousing title tune, proclaiming she was always doing something for the boys, "and they're doing something for me!" The swinging love song "Hey, Good Lookin'" suggested that Merman was "the missing link" between operatic soprano Lily Pons and Hollywood sex goddess Mae West. For the eleven o'clock number, Blossom and her cousin Chiquita (Paula Laurence) put on an act for the troops, portraying two cartoonish Native American women pining for their common husband ("our co-papa") who is back home "By the Mississinewah." The song had no connection to the plot, but audiences demanded encores, and Merman won extra laughs by swinging the long braids of her wig during the number. At one performance, Laurence stole this bit. The stage manager gave a stern warning to desist, and when Laurence repeated the theft days later, the producer fired her. Some have suggested this incident showed Merman as an egotist, but stars have never been expected to tolerate the unprofessional appropriation of their comic ideas.

Another "business as usual" musical comedy called *Banjo Eyes* (1941, 126 performances) brought Eddie Cantor back to Broadway after a dozen years of stardom in film and radio. Fans who walked in thinking that the show's title referred to the wide-eyed star were tickled to learn that "Banjo Eyes" was actually a horse. Cantor played a mild-mannered author of greeting card verses who gets reliable horseracing tips in his dreams—from the horses themselves, played by men in animal suits.

Gamblers find out about Cantor's unusual gift, and he must find a way to escape their clutches and return to the wife (June Clyde) he loves. When the star demanded a showstopper, composer Vernon Duke (1903–1969) and lyricist Harold Adamson obliged with "We're Having a Baby," a mildly risqué duet for Cantor and Clyde. Audiences reveled in watching Cantor play his usual milquetoast character, and cheered nightly for a second act medley of his old standards. Four months into the run the fifty-year-old "apostle of pep" was felled by emergency hemorrhoid surgery, and refused to return, forcing a potential hit to close at a loss. Cantor's longtime pal Al Jolson had also pleaded ill health when he pulled out of *Hold on to Your Hats* (1940, 158 performances) the year before. Neither of these monumental talents would return to Broadway again.

Two classic Viennese operettas enjoyed hit revivals. A feisty little organization called the New Opera Company (NOC) presented *Rosalinda* (1942, 521 performances), an adaptation of *Die Fledermaus* that boasted choreography by Balanchine. It proved such a smash that the NOC and Balanchine then brought back *The Merry Widow* (1943, 321 performances) starring the husband and wife team of Martha Eggerth and Jan Kiepura. The scores and plots were intact but the translations were new, restoring both works to active theatrical usage. After several less successful productions, the New Opera Company went out of business.

Glimmers of Change

While most Broadway musicals just wanted to have fun—or failing that, make enough noise to at least *seem* as if they were having fun— signs of change appeared once or twice each season in the early 1940s, trying valiantly to marry the joy of musical comedy to the integration of operetta.

Banjo Eyes composer Vernon Duke was actually Russian-born Vladimir Dukelsky, who came to the United States hoping to emulate his heroes, George Gershwin and Irving Berlin. He got his start in theatre composing for revues, most notably the Shubert-produced *Ziegfeld Follies of 1936*. His first book musical was *Cabin in the Sky* (1940, 156 performances), with libretto by playwright Lynn Root, lyrics by John LaTouche (1917–), and the entire production staged by Balanchine. It was an African-American fable about Lucifer Jr. (Rex Ingram) and the Lawd's General (Todd Duncan) battling for the soul of Little Joe (Dooley Wilson), a well-meaning black man who loves his devoted wife Petunia (Ethel Waters) but is also attracted to the sizzling Georgia Brown (Katherine Dunham). Petunia's tearful plea at the Pearly Gates finally earns Joe entry into heaven. Waters introduced "Taking a Chance on Love," and future dance legend Dunham sang "Honey in the Honeycomb." *Cabin in the Sky*'s five-month run was respectable, but not long enough for the show to start any trends. MGM's 1943 film version interpolated the Harold Arlen–E. Y. Harburg ballad "Happiness Is Just a Thing Called Joe," which has been used in most concert stagings and revivals.

Innovation had always been a given in Kurt Weill's compositions, which may explain why a chance to collaborate with him and librettist Moss Hart drew Ira Gershwin back to Broadway for the first time since his brother George's death. *Lady in the Dark* (1941, 467 performances) was the story of Liza Elliott (Gertrude Lawrence), a successful magazine editor going through psychoanalysis as she chooses between her career and the three men in her life: her already-married lover Kendall (Bert Lytell), a handsome but empty-headed movie star (Victor Mature), and a smart-mouthed assistant editor (Macdonald Carey). The music was limited to Liza's dreams, the only place where she could face her feelings. Three dreams became extended musical scenes. Danny Kaye came perilously close to stealing the show, playing a wildly effeminate magazine photographer. He appeared as a judge in one dream to sing "Tchaikowsky," a rapid-fire list of unpronounceable Russian composers—its absolute irrelevance to the plot a fitting feature in a dream. Immediately after it, Lawrence promptly reconquered the audience with her tour de force rendition of "The Saga of Jenny," which told of a poor creature who had the annoying habit of making up her mind. In a surprising echo of *Naughty Marietta*, Liza realizes she loves her wisecracking assistant when he completes her dream melody, "My Ship." Billed as "a play with music," *Lady in the Dark* was so packed with talent that audiences embraced it through two Broadway runs and a successful tour. Producer Sam Harris died during the run at age sixty-nine, a triumphant ending to a career that stretched back to the 1904 landmark *Little Johnny Jones*.

Richard Rodgers and Lorenz Hart started out the new decade with *Higher and Higher* (1940, 84 performances), a trifle about servants trying to pass off one of their own as an heiress. Director Joshua Logan later admitted that he knew that this show was doomed when opening night was stolen by a trained seal. Novelist John O'Hara then suggested that the songwriters consider a musical based on his short stories about an amoral nightclub dancer—not the sort of thing one expected in musical comedy, but Rodgers and Hart took up the challenge. O'Hara and producer-director George Abbott penned the libretto for *Pal Joey* (1940, 374 performances). The title character woos a naïve twenty-something while sleeping with a millionaire's wife— who has set him up in his own club. By the final curtain, both women dump Joey, who walks off having learned nothing from his losses.

Rodgers and Hart did not write musicalized scenes, but instead relied on the standard song and dialogue structure of conventional musical comedy. Gene Kelly (1912–1996), who played Joey's seediness with such obvious star power that he was soon off to Hollywood, introduced "I Could Write a Book." Operetta diva Vivienne Segal dazzled as the worldly, well-heeled Vera, who openly admitted to being "Bewitched, Bothered, and Bewildered" by her passion for this obvious user. Perhaps it was a mistake to open such a harsh show on Christmas Day. Critics did not know what to make of a singing, dancing antihero. Brooks Atkinson of the *New York Times* made the oft-quoted complaint that it was hard to "draw sweet water from such a foul well."

Seen today, *Pal Joey* has a gruff, gutsy charm, and its humor holds up well—particularly Hart's razor sharp lyrics. When Joey and Vera sing about trysting "In Our Little Den of Iniquity," they never have to worry about the maid who is "so refined," but they have taken no chances because "of course, she's deaf and dumb and blind!" The original production had a very profitable run. "Bewitched, Bothered, and Bewildered" did not hit the pop charts until the late 1940s, but it led to a 1948 studio cast recording of the full score, which in turn inspired a 1952 revival that ran 540 performances—and inspired Atkinson to reassess the show as a gem. *Pal Joey* has been periodically rediscovered in restagings and concert versions ever since.

Having taken musical comedy about as far as it could go, Rodgers and Hart next turned out the polished but less daring *By Jupiter* (1942, 421 performances). The songwriters again took credit for the libretto, which had ancient Greeks going to war with the mythical Amazon warrior women. Ray Bolger starred as Sapiens, the effeminate male bride of Hippolyta (Benay Venuta), the macho Amazon Queen. The dialogue was filled with comic sexual reversals ("You swear like a longshorewoman!"), as was the mock war anthem "The Boy I Left Behind Me." The euphoric "Wait Till You See Her," the introspective "Nobody's Heart Belongs to Me," and the battling duet "Ev'rything I've Got" all fit the plot and characters, but are so generalized that they could fit into any number of musical comedies. However, the public was delighted, and *By Jupiter* became Rodgers and Hart's longest running original production. The sold-out run could have gone on far longer if Bolger had not insisted on going off to entertain the troops.

Rodgers and Hammerstein: The Birth of *Oklahoma!*

After collaborating on twenty-eight musicals, Rodgers and Hart were still creating fresh, audience pleasing shows, but their partnership was at the breaking point. Hart was obsessed with his dwarfish height and unsightly appearance, and crippled by guilt because of his homosexuality. As Larry drowned his tortured feelings in one-night stands and prolonged drinking sprees, working with him became virtually impossible. Rodgers later claimed that he had to complete some of the lyrics for *By Jupiter.*

Then the Theatre Guild, which had given Rodgers and Hart their big break with the *Garrick Gaieties*, asked the songwriters to adapt Lynn Riggs's unsuccessful cowboy drama *Green Grow the Lilacs* as a musical. Rodgers approached Hart, who refused, saying Hollywood had turned singing cowboys into a cliché. Rodgers announced that he was prepared to write the show with Oscar Hammerstein II. Hart endorsed the idea, and headed off for a binge in Mexico. Such is the story as Rodgers told it. Since his death, his daughters and some colleagues have revealed that the composer drank heavily throughout his adult life. So the official version of Rodgers and Hart's breakup amounts to one gifted alcoholic's self-justifying dismissal of another. Unfortunately, Hart never recorded his version of this momentous discussion.

Both Rodgers and Hammerstein had been accustomed to the Tin Pan Alley songwriting tradition of the music being written first, with lyrics then tailored to the music. They now opted for the Gilbert and

Sullivan model of writing the words first, which they hoped would encourage a more thorough integration of song and story. They spent several days talking through the plot of *Green Grow the Lilacs*, determining where the action and emotions called for expression in song, and discussing what the content and style of each number should be. Hammerstein then went off separately to write the libretto and craft the lyrics, some of which took days or even weeks to perfect. By the time he sent Rodgers a completed lyric, the composer had already developed musical ideas based on their conversations, and often had the completed melody on paper within an hour or less.

Because the once prosperous Theatre Guild had fallen on hard times, Rodgers and Hammerstein faced the arduous process of auditioning for a parade of potential investors. As compensation, the songwriters demanded and got an unusual degree of creative control over the project, initially titled *Away We Go*. Seeing dance as an essential element in this show, they chose ballet choreographer Agnes DeMille (1905–1993), who had minimal theatrical credentials but a progressive attitude toward dance as a storytelling tool. They also pushed for the hiring of director Rouben Mamoulian, known for his innovative approach to stage and screen musicals. Guild executives wanted to cast a major name like Shirley Temple as box office insurance, but Rodgers and Hammerstein vetoed this idea, insisting instead on an ensemble of relatively unknown performers. In accordance with the practice of that time, the dancing and singing ensembles were chosen separately, with DeMille in charge of casting the dancers. When selecting the rest of the cast, the authors preferred strong singers who could act over actors who could more or less sing.

Away We Go started its pre-Broadway tryout in New Haven, and the usual cadre of spiteful theatre professionals took the commuter train up from New York—Alan Jay Lerner called such people "the dear shits." Although the consensus was that the show was promising, several people would eventually claim credit for originating a damning assessment quoted in Walter Winchell's gossip column: "No gags, no girls, no chance!" Prominent producer Max Gordon was so pessimistic that he sold off his investment in the show—a decision that he would regret in years to come. Extensive revisions began as the tryout moved on to Boston, where one of the chorus singers suggested that a second act dance number might be more effective as a harmonized chorale. Rodgers agreed. On a Sunday, the full cast crowded into the lobby of the Colonial Theatre to learn the new arrangement. The number was staged immediately and added to the show the next day, to electrifying effect. For the first time, the curtain calls drew a standing ovation, which was a rare tribute in 1943. The revised song not only gave the show a much needed emotional boost, but a new exclamatory title too—*Oklahoma!* (1943, 2,212 performances).

Set in the early twentieth century when Oklahoma was still called Indian Territory, the story involved farm girl Laurey (Joan Roberts) deciding who should take her to a local dance—the handsome cowboy Curly (Alfred Drake) whom she hates to admit she loves, or her fearsome but intriguing farmhand Jud Fry (Howard Da Silva). After a drug-induced dream, Laurey chooses Jud, but runs off after he makes a crude pass. That same night, after the dance, she accepts Curly's proposal of marriage. On their wedding day, Jud appears and attacks the couple in a murderous rage that ends with his landing fatally on his own knife. In a subsidiary plot, neighborhood good-time girl Ado Annie, played by Celeste Holm (1919–), must give up her horizontal pursuits with men like rapacious salesman Ali Hakim (Joseph Buloff) if she is to keep the affections of cowhand Will Parker (Lee Dixon).

The score is a string of highlights. The curtain rises on Laurey's Aunt Eller all alone on stage churning butter as Curly comes on from the wings singing about bright golden haze on the meadow and cattle standing like statues in "Oh, What a Beautiful Morning." He tempts the hard-to-get Laurey with images of going to the big box social dance that night in "The Surrey with a Fringe on Top," and they then slyly warn each other to avoid public displays of affection or else "People Will Say We're in Love." Ado Annie expresses her dilemma in a phrase—"I Cain't Say No." The chorus gets to shine in "The Farmer and the Cowman" ("should be friends") and the jubilant title song celebrating Oklahoma's imminent statehood. DeMille's greatest moment came in the act-one finale's celebrated dream ballet. There were empty seats when *Oklahoma!* opened at the St. James Theatre on March 31, 1943. Unanimous rave reviews and ecstatic word of mouth kept those seats filled for the next five years. *Oklahoma!* became the longest running Broadway musical up to that time, bringing backers a 2,500% return on their investment. Touring companies crisscrossed the United States through the 1950s, and a British staging

(1947, 1,548 performances in London) was the first of many successful international productions.

Oklahoma! came along at precisely the right moment, when a war-torn world was particularly susceptible to its reassuring images of home and young love, and songs that spoke to millions of hearts. Before *Oklahoma!*, composers and lyricists were songwriters—after *Oklahoma!*, they were dramatists, using every word and note in the score to develop character and advance the action. As Mark Steyn explains in *Broadway Babies Say Goodnight,* in lyrics by Lorenz Hart or Cole Porter, you hear the lyricist—with Hammerstein, you hear the characters. And those characters now had to be three-dimensional, far more sympathetic than the cartoonish two-dimensional figures that had dominated the musical stage since the 1800s.

Throughout the show, every word, number, and dance step was an organic part of the storytelling process. Instead of interrupting the dialogue, each song and dance continued it. For the first time, everything flowed in an unbroken narrative line from overture to curtain call. As Rodgers later said, "The orchestrations sounded the way the costumes look." *Oklahoma!* was most certainly not the first integrated musical, but it was the first *organic musical play*, in which every element serves as a crucial, meaningful piece of the whole. Musicals following this new form would continue to be billed as "musical comedies" in years to come, but that was a misnomer. While laughs still counted, they took a backseat to dramatic coherence. Plot-irrelevant gags and star specialties were suddenly dinosaurs.

Oklahoma! ushered in another innovation: the original cast recording. Before this, stage stars had occasionally recorded numbers with studio musicians and arrangements that bore little resemblance to what was heard in the theatre. There had been a few partial cast recordings made in England, and the original New York cast of *The Cradle Will Rock* had preserved several numbers. But *Oklahoma!*'s popularity was such that Decca Records producer Jack Kapp decided to have the entire original cast and orchestra record all the songs exactly as heard in a theatrical performance—with some adjustments made to fit time limitations. The recording was released on a set of six 10-inch 78 r.p.m. shellac disks packaged in a cardboard covered album of paper sleeves. It became an immediate best-seller, with many of its songs topping the pop charts. When long-playing records were introduced in the late 1940s, the phrase "album" stuck. As sheet music sales declined, record sales became a major source of auxiliary income for theatrical songwriters. From this point onward, hundreds of musicals were preserved on original cast recordings, including all the major New York and London hits, as well as many less successful shows and quite a few outright flops. It is no accident that the 1940s provided the first substantial battery of lasting hits in the musical stage repertory. Millions of people who never got to see these shows could hear them on cast recordings, including generations yet unborn. We can only speculate about the way *No, No, Nanette* or *Let's Face It* originally sounded onstage—thanks to cast recordings, we can hear the original sound of *Oklahoma!* and most of the noteworthy musicals that followed it.

Larry Hart attended the opening night of *Oklahoma!*, and although he warmly assured Rodgers that "This show of yours will run forever," it must have grieved Hart to see his longtime partner achieve such a triumph with another collaborator. Since Hammerstein was anxious to complete *Carmen Jones* (1943, 502 performances), his African-American update of Bizet's grand opera, Rodgers was free to pursue another project with Hart. Rather than take on the burden of an entirely new show, they settled on updating their 1927 hit *A Connecticut Yankee* (1943, 135 performances), resetting the contemporary scenes in wartime and adjusting the topical humor throughout the libretto. Larry attacked the project with more gusto than he had shown in years, concocting "To Keep My Love Alive," a comic soprano showstopper with bass notes for Vivienne Segal, who as the bloodthirsty Morgan Le Fay cataloged the many husbands that she had "bumped off" in the name of self-preservation. As soon as the production went into rehearsal, Hart had nothing to do and his uncontrolled drinking resumed. On opening night, he suddenly appeared at the back of the theatre, singing along and audibly replying to dialogue. Forcibly ejected, he spent the night on his brother's sofa before disappearing again. He was found days later sitting in a Manhattan gutter, drunk, coatless, and soaked to the skin by an icy November rain. Pneumonia set in, and after a few days in the hospital, he died at age forty-eight. According to a nurse, Hart's last words before lapsing into a final coma were, "What have I lived for?"

Rodgers launched wholeheartedly into a multilevel partnership with Hammerstein. Aside from their writing, they published their own songs and became active producers of works by themselves and others. The Theatre Guild, flush from the success of *Oklahoma*, was sole producer for Rodgers and Hammerstein's next musical, *Carousel* (1945, 890 performances), an adaptation of Ferenc Molnár's *Liliom* reset in seaside New England during the 1870s. The score is another succession of treasures. Dispensing with the usual overture, the opening waltz was staged as an eight-minute pantomime, wordlessly introducing the major characters. Naïve factory weaver Julie Jordan (Jan Clayton) falls in love with carousel barker Billy Bigelow, a role originated by strapping baritone John Raitt (1917–2005). Julie's a dreamer and Billy's irresponsible—a dangerous mismatch. They try to deny their immediate mutual attraction in "If I Loved You," the centerpiece of the so-called "bench scene," one of the most romantic and beguiling musical sequences ever written for the popular stage. Here we see Rodgers and Hammerstein hitting their full stride in a prolonged and seamless interplay of song and dialogue.

Billy and Julie marry and have a dysfunctional, abusive relationship. In a secondary plot, Julie's friend Carrie (Jean Darling) marries righteous fisherman Enoch Snow (Eric Mattson). The ensemble celebrates summer in "June is Bustin' Out All Over." When Julie becomes pregnant, Billy goes into a seven-minute "Soliloquy," contemplating what his unborn child will be. Not wanting the child to be raised in poverty as he was, Billy decides to take part in a robbery, during which he dies by falling on his own knife. It was one thing to kill off the villain at the climax of *Oklahoma!*, but by killing off *Carousel*'s hero, Hammerstein introduced Broadway to its first musical tragedy. The first act ended with Julie's Aunt Nettie (Wagnerian soprano Christine Johnson) reassuring her widowed niece that "You'll Never Walk Alone."

Act two takes place fifteen years later, when Billy's spirit gets permission from the heavenly Starkeeper (Russell Collins) to return from heaven for one day to help his wife and outcast teenage daughter Louise (Bambi Lynn), who expresses her loneliness in a DeMille ballet. When Billy appears, his well-intentioned words frighten Louise, so he hits her—just as he used to hit her mother. But Billy gets to see Louise find new hope during her high school graduation ceremony, and before returning to eternity, he whispers a final farewell in his wife's ear: "I loved you, Julie. Know that I loved you!" Rouben Mamoulian's clear direction cemented a show that proved to be a personal favorite for both

Rodgers and Hammerstein. The 1950 London production of *Carousel* ran for 566 performances, and the show enjoyed successful revivals on both sides of the Atlantic through the end of the twentieth century.

Rodgers and Hammerstein pushed the envelope a bit too far with *Allegro* (1947, 315 performances), the story of an idealistic small town doctor who goes to the big city and is almost destroyed by ambition. The score was so thoroughly integrated with the book that it was difficult to identify specific songs, with the notable exception of "The Gentleman is a Dope," sung by Lisa Kirk (1926–1990) as the doctor's frustrated nurse. Hammerstein made many bold decisions in this show, using a chorus to comment on the action, and having DeMille both direct and choreograph. Because *Allegro* was built around a staging concept, some consider it the first concept musical, but since it is essentially the story of one man and lacks the assortment of fascinating characters that populate concept musicals, that label does not really fit. Although *Allegro* ran the better part of a year and made a small profit, it had no international productions or film version and swiftly faded from the theatrical repertory. Rodgers and Hammerstein had revolutionized the musical theatre, and were learning that the hardest part of any revolution is sustaining it.

First Followers: "You Appear and I Hear Song Sublime"

The Rodgers and Hammerstein partnership coincided with a time when America was enjoying renewed prosperity and an optimistic national spirit. The United States had served as the world's arsenal through the final years of World War II, and after victory became the world's breadbasket and financial patron, profitably helping allies and former enemy nations to rebuild. Jobs were plentiful, and Americans exhibited a growing appetite for quality entertainment on stage and screen. In the wake of *Oklahoma!*, critics and audiences gradually made it clear that "business as usual" musicals were no longer enough. At first, some tried to maintain the old status quo. Consider these three 1944 hits:

- Cole Porter's *Mexican Hayride* (1944, 481 performances) had no hit songs, but its tale of an American fugitive who heads south of the border and gets mixed up with a lady bullfighter provided a profitable vehicle for brash comic Bobby Clark.

- The longest running production of 1944 was *Hats Off to Ice* (1944, 889 performances), one of Sonja Henie's skating revues at the Center Theatre.
- Right behind it was *Follow the Girls* (1944, 882 performances), an old-style musical comedy using low, burlesque-style humor. The plot involved a hefty 4-F civilian (Jackie Gleason) competing with a hunky naval officer for the love of a stripper (Gertrude Niesen). Wartime audiences appreciated the bawdy fun, including a comedy number in which a wedding gown–clad Niesen quoted a wartime mother of newborn twins crying, "I Want to Get Married." But change was in the air, and after a year-plus London run, this very profitable show faded from memory.

That same season brought a wave of new shows that made a conscious attempt to follow Rodgers and Hammerstein's new integrated model, in particular by using dance as a narrative device:

- *Bloomer Girl* (1944, 654 performances) cast Celeste Holm as Evelina, a northern abolitionist suffragette in love with a southern slave owner during the 1860s. This slice of Americana had a fine score by composer Harold Arlen (1905–1986) and lyricist E. Y. Harburg. DeMille's choreography included a widely praised "Civil War Ballet." This was Arlen's only major stage hit; the bulk of his songwriting was done for screen musicals.
- *The Song of Norway* (1944, 860 performances) was a romantic operetta about classical Norwegian composer Edvard Grieg, who winds up choosing between a sophisticated opera diva and his simple childhood sweetheart—the latter, of course, wins out. Grieg's melodies were adapted into songs by former MGM songwriters Robert Wright (1914–2005) and George Forrest (1915–1999), including the hit ballad "Strange Music." Creatively staged by George Balanchine, it surprised many by running for more than two years.
- *On the Town* (1944, 462 performances) was directed by George Abbott, but was primarily created by extraordinary newcomers. Its inspiration was *Fancy Free*, a ballet with music by symphonic conductor Leonard Bernstein (1918–1990) and choreography by

dancer Jerome Robbins (1918–1998). With book and lyrics by cabaret comics Betty Comden (1915–2006) and Adolph Green (1915–2002), this show used song and dance to depict the romantic adventures of three navy gobs on a twenty-four-hour shore leave in New York City. The score included "New York, New York" ("a hell of a town"), "A Lonely Town," and "I Can Cook Too." Repeated attempts to revive this show in New York have failed to find an audience.

- *Up in Central Park* (1945, 504 performances) was a love story set in Boss Tweed's New York, with sets and staging that recreated the look of Currier and Ives prints. Composer Sigmund Romberg's first foray into musical comedy had lyrics by Dorothy Fields, and included "Close as Pages in a Book." This was the first hit for choreographer Helen Tamaris (1903–1966), a modern dance pioneer who would stage dances for thirteen Broadway musicals, specializing in movement tailored to fit historic or exotic settings.
- *St. Louis Woman* (1946, 113 performances) was an unsatisfying blend of folk fable and musical comedy involving a jockey (Harold Nicholas) who kills a romantic rival, only to see his life ruined by the rival's deathbed curse. The score by Harold Arlen and lyricist Johnny Mercer included "Anyplace I Hang My Hat is Home" and "Come Rain or Come Shine." Jazz vocalist Pearl Bailey (1918–1990) rocked the house with steamy performances of "Legalize My Name" and "A Woman's Prerogative."

Acclaimed in their time, none of these fine musicals has ever been successfully revived on Broadway, and all have fallen out of the standard musical theatre repertory. Why? Each was integrated, with fine scores and impressive choreography; all were preserved in some kind of cast recording; and all except *Bloomer Girl* made it to the big screen. Perhaps they failed not because of what they had, but what they lacked. The new organic musical was more than just a matter of form. From early on, journalists referred to "The RH Factor," referring to Rodgers and Hammerstein's knack for irresistible, character-driven storytelling that made everyday situations timeless and compelling. The minor travails of three sailors in *On the Town* had meaning for wartime audiences in 1944, but the story seems inconsequential to generations out of touch with that era. On the other hand, thanks to

Rodgers and Hammerstein, the squabbling romance of a farm girl and a cowboy in circa 1900 still matters immensely, as does the unhappy 1870s marriage of a factory weaver and a carnival barker. Cynics often carp about Hammerstein's "folksiness," but his common touch is the very thing that makes his best musicals relevant to succeeding generations. Rodgers used music to capture and even deepen the emotion of any given scene. Songwriters now had to be dramatists, and as of the mid-1940s, Rodgers and Hammerstein were still without peers in that regard.

Revues: "I Left My Heart at the Stage Door Canteen"

When America entered World War II, Irving Berlin wasted no time in pulling together *This Is the Army* (1942, 113 performances), a revue built along the same lines as his Word War I production, *Yip, Yip Yaphank*. Once again, the cast consisted entirely of enlisted men, many (but not all) with professional performing credentials. They spent most of the show in full uniform, slipping into female drag as needed for a series of highly entertaining skits and songs reflecting the lives of contemporary servicemen. A chorus of 150 introduced the title march, and "I Left My Heart at the Stage Door Canteen" immortalized a popular servicemen-only theatre district nightclub run by the American Theatre Wing, the same organization that would later establish the Tony Awards. As a nostalgic treat, Berlin himself appeared to reprise "Oh, How I Hate to Get Up in the Morning." *This Is the Army* followed its sold-out New York run with a prolonged world tour, stopping in Hollywood long enough to make a screen version. By the war's end, Berlin's revue had raised more than nine million dollars for the Army Emergency Relief fund.

Broadway audiences marked the end of the war by embracing *Call Me Mister* (1946, 734 performances), a revue that sang and kidded about soldiers returning to civilian life. The cast and creative crew had all either served in uniform or toured the front in U.S.O. shows. Harold Rome's score included the thrilling round "Going Home Train," and Betty Garrett sang a merciless send-up of the craze for back-wrenching Latin American dances, "South America, Take It Away."

The last hit revue of the decade was *Lend an Ear* (1948, 460 performances). Born in Pittsburgh, this show gestated in Los Angeles before it was shepherded to New York by Gower Champion (1920–1980), a nightclub dancer taking his first shot at directing. It was written and performed by newcomers, most notably sketch writer Joseph Stein (1912–) and the tall and gangly comedienne Carol Channing (1921–), both of whom would enjoy long careers on Broadway. The highlight of the evening was the first-act finale, "The Gladiola Girl," a spoof of 1920s musicals that gave audiences a laugh-filled opportunity to see just how much the book musical had changed in the few years since *Oklahoma!*. The sort of talent that powered Broadway revues was being siphoned off by radio and film, and would soon make an irrevocable move into the new medium of television.

Reestablished Masters: "Doin' What Comes Naturally"

Some feared that the new school of musical play spelled the end of musical comedy, which had been looking pretty tired. But as it turned out, the organic approach brought musical comedy a new lease on life.

As producers, Rogers and Hammerstein approached Jerome Kern with a tempting offer: come back to New York to supervise a revival of *Show Boat*, and while you're at it, collaborate with Dorothy and Herb Fields on a musical comedy about Wild West sharpshooter Annie Oakley. With his Hollywood career stalled by years of poor health, Kern accepted. While browsing a bookstall on a Manhattan street corner, he suffered a massive stroke. In the hospital, Hammerstein quietly sang "I've Told Ev'ry Little Star" into his old friend's ear, and knew by the lack of response that one of America's greatest composers was lost. Kern died at age sixty, but many who lived and worked far longer would be unable to match the profound effect he had upon the musical theatre.

The libretto for the Oakley musical was ready, and investors were lined up. Since Rodgers and Hammerstein were in the midst of writing *Allegro*, they asked Irving Berlin if he would be interested in handling the score. Unsure that he could write for the new integrated type of musical, Berlin asked for a weekend to consider. The following Monday, he presented the bawdy "Doin' What Comes Natur'lly" and the moving "They Say It's Wonderful"—star numbers organically grounded in plot and character. Berlin insisted that since his songs for *Annie Get Your Gun* (1946, 1,147 performances) all grew out of the libretto, the Fields should receive an equal percentage of the gross, which was not standard procedure. Director Josh Logan had a hand in shaping the final script, though how much of a hand is open to debate. He bucked a trend by minimizing the use of dance, a decision that served this show well.

Completed in less than three months, *Annie Get Your Gun* proved that musical comedy could be tailored in the organic style. Merman triumphed as Ozarks hick Annie Oakley, whose sharp shooting skills lead to stardom in Buffalo Bill's Wild West Show. There she develops a passionate love-hate relationship with fellow marksman Frank Butler (Ray Middleton), and realizes "You Can't Get a Man With a Gun." Their ongoing combat comes to a head in the contentious duet "Anything You Can Do I Can Do Better." In a bow to prevailing 1940s attitudes about gender roles, Annie chooses to lose a big shooting match in order to win proud Frank's affection. Berlin effectively balanced his instincts as a hit-master with the demands of being a musical dramatist, so that every song in the score was integral to the story—and a handful became independent hits. "There's No Business Like Show Business," which Buffalo Bill and his cronies use to entice Annie into the world of performing, became a lasting anthem for the American theatre. Merman belted the song with pride for the rest of her career. *Annie Get Your Gun*'s success was not tied to Merman's presence. The 1947 London production starring Dolores Gray ran for 1,304 performances, and Mary Martin received one of the newly instituted Antoinette Perry Awards—now known as the Tonys—for starring in the national tour.

Berlin next collaborated with Pulitzer Prize–winning playwright Robert Sherwood on *Miss Liberty* (1949, 308 performances), which starred Eddie Albert as an American reporter making an 1885 search for the French girl who modeled for the newly erected Statue of Liberty. "Let's Take an Old-Fashioned Walk" became a hit, and Berlin's setting of the Emma Lazarus poem "Give Me Your Tired, Your Poor" became a standard on patriotic occasions. Although light on plot content and not nearly as popular as *Annie Get Your Gun*, this underrated crowd-pleaser verified Irving Berlin's credentials as a musical dramatist.

Cole Porter was just as uncertain about working in this new form of musical theatre. After composing the unsuccessful revue *Seven Lively Arts* (1945, 183 performances) and the poorly conceived Orson

Welles musical *Around the World* (1946, 75 performances), Porter had reason to wonder if his theatrical career was over. Then writers Sam and Bella Spewack approached him with an idea for a plot: a divorced couple stars in a musical version of Shakespeare's *Taming of the Shrew*, their arguments behind the scenes echoing their colorful battles onstage. *Kiss Me Kate* (1948, 1,077 performances) starred Alfred Drake and Patricia Morrison (1915–) as the argumentative leads, jointly introducing the mock operetta waltz "Wunderbar" and the ballad "So in Love." Drake got the ribald list song "Where Is the Life That Late I Led?" and Morrison soloed the belligerent "I Hate Men." Lisa Kirk played an ingénue who asked her boyfriend "Why Can't You Behave?" but dismissed her own sexual side trips by assuring him she was "Always True to You (In My Fashion)." For the eleven o'clock number, two gangsters caught up in the backstage brouhaha literally stopped the show with the vaudeville-style turn "Brush Up Your Shakespeare." With witty and sometimes coarse references to many of the Bard's most famous works, the song was so good that no one cared that it was gratuitous. The production was staged by Noël Coward's ex-lover John C. Wilson (1899–1961), whose directorial skills were limited at best. Porter had the satisfaction of reestablishing himself with the longest running hit of his career, and *Kiss Me Kate* received the first-ever Tony Award for Best Musical.

Kurt Weill had always seen himself as a composer-dramatist, so he was right at home in the post-*Oklahoma!* period. He collaborated with poet Ogden Nash on *One Touch of Venus* (1943, 567 performances), which echoed the historic hits *Die Schöne Galathee* and *Adonis* by having a statue of Venus come to life in modern day New York. The difference is that this character, played by Mary Martin, is actually the ancient goddess of love. Agnes DeMille's choreography included a street ballet where Venus impetuously altered the love lives of people passing on a sidewalk. Eventually, Venus decides mortals are boring and turns back into stone. But in a parting gesture, the goddess arranges for the heartbroken barber (Kenny Baker) who loved her to meet a live lookalike. The fully integrated score included "I'm a Stranger Here Myself," "Speak Low," and "That's Him."

The rest of the decade brought Weill a series of frustrations. For *Street Scene* (1947, 148 performances), Elmer Rice adapted his own Pulitzer Prize–winning play about the lives of people living in a block of apartments, and Weill provided an ambitious symphony of haunting music. Billed as a "dramatic musical," *Street Scene* was really a grand opera, always a hard sell with Broadway audiences. It closed before recouping its costs. Weill fared somewhat better collaborating with lyricist-librettist Alan Jay Lerner (1918–1986) on *Love Life* (1948, 252 performances), a "vaudeville" that allegorically viewed American history through a marriage that somehow lasts from 1791 to 1948. Ray Middleton and Nanette Fabray won praise as the ageless couple. The score included a cavalcade of musical styles, and although "Here I'll Stay" and "Green-Up Time" are admired by Weill aficionados, the show and its score are mostly forgotten. Lerner's libretto delved into marriage with some bitterness, contrasting unattractively with Weill's music. Brooks Atkinson described *Love Life* as "cute, complex and joyless—a general gripe masquerading as entertainment."

Weill reunited with his *Knickerbocker Holiday* collaborator Maxwell Anderson for *Lost in the Stars* (1949, 281 performances), an operatic "musical tragedy" about a black minister (Todd Duncan) whose criminal son faces execution in South Africa during the age of apartheid. During the run, Weill died of a heart attack at age fifty. Although he never matched the widespread popularity of some contemporaries, his ambitious music provides living testimony to his inventive gifts, and his efforts to expand the horizons of musical theatre have earned him a lasting place in the pantheon of great stage composers.

New Talents: "All the Music of Life"

A younger generation of writers and composers was anxious to follow the organically integrated path, proving they had caught on to what Rodgers and Hammerstein had accomplished. The days of comfortable musical theatre formulas were over—now, the more unusual the material, the better. And the organic musical proved to be quite versatile, incorporating a wide range of theatrical styles and conventions

How about an organic musical satire? That's what lyricist-librettist E. Y. "Yip" Harburg came up with in the romantic satirical fantasy *Finian's Rainbow* (1947, 725 performances), the story of Irish immigrant Finian McLonergan (Albert Sharpe) stealing the leprechauns' legendary crock of gold and burying it near Fort Knox in the hopes that it will grow in such "rich" soil. Finian and his daughter Sharon

(Ella Logan) find themselves among a multiethnic group of poor sharecroppers. As Sharon falls in love with local troubadour Woody (Donald Richards), a leprechaun named Og appears to retrieve the stolen gold. Distracted from his mission by his first taste of mortal lust, Og mischievously turns a bigoted U.S. senator into a negro. In the end, the gold evaporates, proving the only real treasures are loving relationships and the ability to dream. Fred Saidy coauthored the libretto, and Harburg teamed with composer Burton Lane (1912–1997) to sprinkle this story with enchanting songs. Ms. Logan offered full-throated renditions of "How Are Things in Glocca Morra?" and "Look to the Rainbow," sharing the steamy "Old Devil Moon" with Richards. As Og, David Wayne (1914–1995) sang "Something Sort of Grandish" and "When I'm Not Near the Girl I Love" ("I love the girl I'm near!"), becoming the first performer in a musical to win a Tony award. Shifting racial attitudes have made some people uneasy about *Finian's Rainbow*, so it is rarely done—and what a loss that is!

Could an organic musical have the shameless romantic spirit of old-time operetta? Lyricist/librettist Alan Jay Lerner and composer Frederick Loewe (1904–1988) had collaborated on several projects with mixed results, but hit pay dirt with *Brigadoon* (1947, 581 performances), the story of two men who stumble into a village that magically reappears in the Scottish highlands for only one day every hundred years. Tommy (David Brooks) falls in love with local girl Fiona (Marion Bell), and must decide by day's end between returning to the modern world or forever becoming part of hers. With a distant setting and big-voiced score ("Almost Like Being in Love," "Come to Me, Bend to Me"), *Brigadoon* had the look and sound of operetta, but it also had the coherence and contemporary energy of an organic musical play. Agnes DeMille created some of her most acclaimed choreography here, including a daredevil sword dance and a barefooted, stage-pounding dance of mourning. Despite a disappointing film version, the show remains a standard, frequently revived by amateurs and professional companies.

Even farce had its place in the new genre. When musician Cy Feuer (1911–2006) and radio executive Ernest H. Martin (1919–1995) decided to become Broadway producers, they got their start with *Where's Charley* (1948, 792 performances), an adaptation of the British classic *Charley's Aunt*. Director George Abbott wrote the libretto, but it was Feuer who had the idea that Charley should masquerade as his own aunt, creating a tour de force role for Ray Bolger. Songwriter Frank Loesser (1910–1969), who had built a solid reputation on Tin Pan Alley and in Hollywood with such hit songs as "Praise the Lord and Pass the Ammunition" and "Baby, It's Cold Outside," proved an able musical dramatist.

Mixed reviews almost killed the show, which was saved by a serendipitous accident. One night early in the run, Bolger forgot the lyrics to his eleven o'clock solo, "Once in Love with Amy." Feuer's eight-year-old son happened to be in the audience, and helped out by singing along. The audience was delighted, and the wily Bolger got everyone to join in. This sing-along became a permanent part of the show, catapulting *Where's Charley* to hit status and putting Feuer, Martin, and Loesser in line for major accomplishments in years to come. A 1958 London production starring Norman Wisdom ran 404 performances, but subsequent attempts to revive this show without Bolger have done poorly.

Composer Jule Styne (1905–1994) was another graduate of Tin Pan Alley and Hollywood who proved an immediate master of organic musical comedy. With lyrics by Sammy Cahn and both book and direction by George Abbott, *High Button Shoes* (1947, 727 performances) starred former burlesque comic Phil Silvers (1911–1985) as a con artist who swindles a 1913 New Jersey family, leads them on a merry chase through Atlantic City, and gets mixed up in a big college football game. Nanette Fabray graduated from featured roles to star status as the mother of the cheated family, singing both "Papa, Won't You Dance with Me" and "I Still Get Jealous" with Jack McCauley. Jerome Robbins unleashed seaside chaos in a memorably funny "Mack Sennett Ballet" featuring Keystone Cops, bathing beauties, and a marauding gorilla, proving that theatrical ballet could be comical. Widely performed for the better part of a decade, this nostalgic musical has fallen into disuse primarily because the role of the con artist requires a broad comic technique few performers command today.

Tall and gangly Carol Channing might have seemed an unlikely choice to play novelist Anita Loos's 1920s flapper heroine Lorelei Lee, but her outsized performance in that role helped to make *Gentlemen Prefer Blondes* (1949, 740 performances) Broadway's last major musical comedy hit of the decade. In a pursuit of men and jewels that takes Lorelei from New York to Paris via transatlantic liner, she innocently explains that she's just "A Little Girl from Little Rock," but later advises that although men may be attractive, "Diamond's Are a Girl's Best Friend." John C. Wilson directed (his only other hit besides *Kiss Me Kate*), and Agnes DeMille choreographed. A film version starring Marilyn Monroe has its admirers, but it took Channing starring in a somewhat revised stage version to give this material new life a generation later.

London in the 1940s

The British musical theatre continued to thrive, but only within Britain's borders. In a complete reversal of the way things had been half a century before, a constant stream of American musicals now appeared in London, while the West End found itself unable to export a hit to Broadway. With a few exceptions, it would take several decades for the artistic pendulum to swing back again.

The Drury Lane Theatre celebrated the end of World War II with *Pacific 1860* (1946, 29 performances), a gala production written and directed by Noël Coward and starring Mary Martin. When a dispute arose over costume designs, Martin's protective husband Richard Halliday leapt fiercely to her defense, and Coward returned fire. A full-blown feud left the major contributors to this production not speaking to one another. The show was a disappointment all around, part musical comedy, part operetta, and altogether rather dull. *Oklahoma!* soon took over the Drury Lane and stayed for four years. Coward remained a major songwriter, playwright, and performer, but was so grounded in old-style musical comedy that he never wrote a hit post-*Oklahoma!* musical.

On the other hand, Ivor Novello enjoyed unbroken success with the same kind of romantic spectaculars that he had perfected during the Great Depression. No wonder Coward, with a mixture of envy and affection, said, "the two loveliest things in the British theatre are Ivor's profile and my mind." Since voice lessons had done nothing for Novello's nonexistent singing, he continued to play the romantic leads and left the vocals to his costars. His melodies had a sound that was somewhere between Coward and Lehar, and brought him a tremendous following in Britain. After spending most of World War II appearing in *The Dancing Years*, Novello wrote and starred in *Perchance to Dream* (1945, 1,022 performances in London), the story of three generations of dysfunctional romance in a noble family living in a grand country manor house. "We'll Gather Lilacs" and "Love Is My Reason for Living" proved to be major hits, but as in the past, the songs were adornments, adding nothing to plot or characterization.

Novello made an effort to give his songs greater relevance in *King's Rhapsody* (1949, 839 performances in London), the story of a petulant king who cannot choose between his longtime mistress and the devoted royal bride who bears his child. When his churlish behavior turns his subjects against him, the king is forced to flee, leaving his wife to raise the next monarch. As the princess, Vanessa Lee introduced "Someday My Heart Will Awake." With this hit in progress, Novello wrote the book and score for *Gay's the Word* (1951, 504 performances), a musical comedy vehicle for West End favorite Cicely Courtneidge. Humorous numbers were reasonably integrated into the action, including the star's big solo "Vitality," and a spoof of Novello's own operettas called "Guards on Parade." Less than a month after this second hit opened, Novello returned home from a performance of *King's Rhapsody* and suffered a fatal heart attack at age fifty-eight.

South Pacific: "Fools Give You Reasons, Wise Men Never Try"

Carousel and *Allegro* had both been—to varying degrees—profitable, but some wondered if Richard Rodgers and Oscar Hammerstein II could ever come up with another cultural phenomenon like *Oklahoma!*. Joshua Logan approached them with the idea of basing a musical on a short story in James Michener's best-seller *Tales of the South Pacific*. While the songwriters saw possibilities in the doomed romance between an American officer and a Polynesian girl, they saw more potential in the story of a navy nurse whose love for a French-born plantation owner is jeopardized when she discovers that he has biracial children from a previous marriage. Logan coauthored the libretto with Hammerstein and staged the entire production. This time around, there was no choreographer, and no sign of a ballet.

South Pacific (1949, 1,925 performances) relied on a unique setting, fascinating characters, a brilliantly evocative score, and several stellar performances. Mary Martin portrayed Ensign Nellie Forbush, who is in love with planter Emile de Becque, played by former Metropolitan Opera basso Ezio Pinza (1892–1957). Martin and Pinza radiated sex appeal during the introspective "Twin Soliloquies," which ended with them silently sipping cognac as the orchestra built to a crescendo. Pinza then sang "Some Enchanted Evening," an obvious hit that was absolutely rooted in plot and character. Having found Nellie in the midst of war, he intends to "never let her go." He also sang the more challenging soliloquy "This Nearly Was Mine." Martin was so captivating when she sang "Cockeyed Optimist" and "I'm in Love with a Wonderful Guy" that her Arkansas-born character's ingrained bigotry became all the more surprising and upsetting. She enacted the lyrics of "I'm Gonna Wash That Man Right Out of My Hair" onstage eight times a week, using a jerry-rigged shower, fast-lathering shampoo, and a drip-dry bodice custom-made by designer Mainbocher.

As the lovestruck officer, William Tabbert sang "Younger Than Springtime," a joyous love song that ends with a devastating three-vowel combination ("I with you") that has beleaguered singers ever since. Tabbert also introduced "You've Got to Be Carefully Taught," a damning assessment of prejudice that has drawn frequent criticism from bigots over the years. As the scheming native Bloody Mary, African-American jazz artist Juanita Hall sang "Happy Talk" and the seductive "Bali Ha'i." It took Hammerstein weeks to create the lyric to "Bali Ha'i," but Rodgers polished off the complex melody in less than five minutes. Years later in his autobiography, Rodgers explained that the melody came quickly because he and Oscar had been discussing the song for weeks. His statement, "If you know your trade, the actual writing should never take long," suggests that this creative genius never understood how unique his gift was.

South Pacific took Broadway by storm, enjoyed an excellent run at the Drury Lane (1951, 802 performances), and toured the United States for years. It became the second musical to win the Pulitzer Prize for Drama (this time with the composer included in the honor), and in 1950 became the second show to receive the Tony Award for Best Musical. Perhaps it is the artistically uneven film version that has led many over time to label *South Pacific* as "dated," but a Carnegie

Hall concert version in 2005 proved this material still packs tremendous emotional power.

The success of *South Pacific* indirectly triggered a radical change in the way the American theatre did business. For many years, the Shuberts had made a handsome profit by secretly charging a premium to ticket brokers for blocks of seats to hit shows—the more the demand, the higher the premium. Seats to *South Pacific* were in such demand that they were being sold at anywhere from five to ten times the legal box office price of eight dollars. The public grumbled but paid. Legend has it that when leading politicians were forced to pay the same price, they smelled a rat. Whatever the reason, in the late 1940s, various levels of government launched investigations of Broadway business practices. The Shuberts had enough influence to quash the state and local efforts, but the federal inquiry proved damning. By controlling the ownership, management, bookings, and ticket sales for most of the legitimate theatres in the country, the Shuberts were in effect operating an illegal trust. In the 1950s, the Shuberts were forced to sell off many of their theatres and give up direct control of bookings and ticket sales. Lee died in 1953, leaving J. J. to share control of the beleaguered empire with his son John. Although the Shuberts were still powerful, their stranglehold on the American commercial theatre was broken. Few mourned.

The Great Depression and World War II were fading into memory, and an era of general prosperity loomed. With a worldwide audience, the American musical theatre saw its "golden age" go into sixteen years of creative overdrive.

12

Broadway Takes Stage (1950–1963)—"The Street Where You Live"

Home entertainment devices have long been status symbols for Americans. At one time it was the piano, then the phonograph, then the radio—having one was a sign of success. At the start of the 1950s, along came television, a box with a tiny glass screen that brought black and white images of news and entertainment into one's living room. It took a lot of enticement to get people to cough up $250 or more for one of the early models. Television networks adopted favorite programs from radio, and corporate sponsors staged all-star "spectaculars" that had a heck of a time looking spectacular on a twelve-inch screen. The secret was to pack that screen with lively talent and make television something more than just radio with pictures. Since early television broadcasts were live events, performers with theatrical credentials were in demand.

On June 15, 1953, the Ford Motor Company marked its fiftieth anniversary with a television revue costarring Mary Martin and Ethel Merman. The climax of the show had the two stars trading solos before belting their way through joint medleys staged with the utmost simplicity by Jerome Robbins. It was estimated that more than 60 million people watched the joint NBC-CBS broadcast live from New York's Center Theatre. That meant it was seen on almost every American television in existence at the time. Decca quickly released a live recording of the Merman-Martin act, which sold 100,000 copies in its first two days.

Broadway had been a primary source of entertainment since World War I, but the mid-twentieth century marked a high point. The latest

Broadway hits were hot news worldwide. Popular music took its cues from Broadway. Stage musicals sent songs to the top of the charts so regularly that when people heard a great new tune, they didn't ask who wrote it; they asked what show it came from. Tin Pan Alley's publishers relocated from an array of offices on West 28th Street to the Brill Building just north of Times Square, to be closer to the action. For composers, writers, and performers, success on Broadway was the quickest shortcut to success in film and television. Hollywood stopped developing original musicals by 1956 and limited itself to adapting Broadway hits for the big screen. On London's West End, the overwhelming majority of big musicals were Yankee imports. More than ever before, Broadway was "the main stem" of show business, especially where musicals were concerned.

Berlin and Porter: Final Hits

In the years since Howard Lindsay and Russell Crouse first teamed up for *Anything Goes*, they had become one of Broadway's top playwrighting teams, with the record-setting comedy *Life with Father* (1939) and the Pulitzer Prize–winning *State of the Union* (1945) to their credit. When President Harry Truman appointed wealthy Democratic Party contributor Perle Mesta ambassador to Luxembourg, it arched many political eyebrows and set Lindsay and Crouse to thinking—what a great musical comedy scenario that would make for Ethel Merman, particularly if they could persuade Irving Berlin to write the score. As Merman and Berlin were fresh from their triumph with *Annie Get Your Gun* and both ardent Republicans, they leapt at the chance to be part of a show that poked genial fun at Truman's administration.

Call Me Madam (1950, 644 performances) had songs by Irving Berlin, George Abbott directing, and Jerome Robbins to stage the dance numbers. Movie actor Paul Lukas played the suave foreign diplomat Merman fell for, and clean-cut newcomer Russell Nype proved an audience favorite as her clean-cut embassy assistant. As Sally Adams, Merman delivered one of the best comic performances of her career, relishing the character's earthy directness as she answered calls from the Truman White House with a booming, "Hiya, Harry!" Berlin let Merman boast that she was "The Hostess with the Mostes' on the Ball," and confidently tell Lukas that "The Best Thing for You Would Be Me." When tryouts in Boston revealed a slow spot in the second act, Abbott suggested that Berlin write one of his signature counterpoint duets for Merman and Nype. Overnight, Irving composed "You're Just in Love," which had to be encored at every performance. Lindsay and Crouse kept making little changes in the script until a few days before the transfer to New York, when Merman said, "Boys, as of right now, I am Miss Birdseye of 1950. I am frozen. Not a comma!" The score included "They Like Ike," a tribute to likely presidential candidate Dwight Eisenhower. On the show's opening night, Eisenhower was on hand, and the tumultuous response to this song supposedly encouraged him to run. *Call Me Madam* certainly ran, and Merman repeated her performance two years later in a delightful big screen version that had to leave out "They Like Ike"—seeing as "Ike" was President by that time, it might have sounded a bit awkward. While *Call Me Madam*'s topical references make the libretto sound dated today (including a laundry list of now-forgotten political names like Stahl, Stassen, and Vandenburg), the score is a joy, and there is ample timeless humor in the dialogue. The main reason revivals are rare is that damn few can provide a powerhouse star presence to equal Merman's.

Berlin concentrated on film projects over the next few years, returning to Broadway when Lindsay and Crouse invited him to collaborate on *Mr. President* (1962, 265 performances), the story of a fictional Chief Executive and his family leaving the White House and returning to private life. Nanette Fabray dazzled as the First Lady, and Anita Gillette won praise as the president's teenage daughter, singing "The Secret Service Makes Me Nervous." But the show had little substance, and the once-formidable director Josh Logan was no longer in a position to make much of a difference. For years he had suffered severe manic-depressive episodes, doing his most inspired directorial work during manic phases. Now fully medicated, Logan lived and directed on an even keel, and none of his future stage projects would match his former successes. After *Mr. President*'s disappointing run, Berlin accepted that times had changed and retired from composing. He made one exception, creating the counterpoint duet "Old Fashioned Wedding" for Ethel Merman's 1966 revival of *Annie Get Your Gun*. When the new number got encored nightly, Berlin had the satisfaction of ending his career on a high. He gradually withdrew from public life but continued to carefully manage his shows and songs until his death at age 101. At the time of his passing in 1989, newspapers reprinted Jerome Kern's oft quoted assessment, "Irving Berlin has no place in American music; he *is* American music."

Cole Porter found *Kiss Me Kate* a hard act to follow. No one could fault his brilliant score for *Out of This World* (1950, 157 performances), an update of the Amphitryon legend, but the production team put too much energy into lavish sets and costumes and not enough into fixing a disjointed libretto. Porter next joined forces with producers Cy Feuer and Ernest Martin, who hired their *Guys and Dolls* librettist Abe Burrows (1910–1985) to write and direct *Can-Can* (1953, 892 performances). French music hall chanteuse Lilo starred as Pistache, a nightclub owner in 1893 Paris who tries to present the sexy title dance despite the opposition of a prudish judge. Lilo's big moment came during a rooftop scene, singing "I Love Paris" as Jo Meilziner's backdrop offered a sweeping view of the city. Lilo also sang the bouncy "C'est Magnifique," and the raucous title number, a classic Porter list song insisting that if the Louvre custodian, the Guard Republican, plus Van Gogh and Matisse and Cézanne can, "Baby, you can can-can too!" Some backstage sources suggest that Lilo was none too thrilled when the reviews were stolen by Gwen Verdon (1926–2000), who as the comely dancer Claudine made her Broadway debut with a quirky blend of fresh-faced innocence and raw sex appeal. Michael Kidd showed Verdon off to excellent effect in several dance sequences, including a thrilling quadrille and an Apache dance. Verdon and Kidd both received Tonys, and the show proved a solid moneymaker. A handsome 1981 New York revival failed thanks to uneven casting and clueless direction, but a 1988 touring version starring Chita Rivera (who had danced in the original 1953 chorus), and a 2004 Encores staging with Patti LuPone proved that in capable hands, *Can-Can* remains a delight.

The death of Porter's wife Linda in 1954 left him emotionally and physically drained, as did the ongoing efforts to save his injured legs. He hoped to bounce back by composing the score for Feuer and Martin's *Silk Stockings* (1955, 478 performances), a musical version of Greta Garbo's MGM comedy *Ninotchka*. The show wound up having a healthy run, and the song "All of You" achieved some popularity, but German actress Hildegard Neff was no Garbo. The pre-Broadway try out proved to be such a brutal experience that neither Porter nor director George S. Kaufman ever worked on a new Broadway musical again. Porter wrote a few songs for film projects, but soon after completing the score for a TV version of *Aladdin* (1958 CBS), he faced the long dreaded amputation of a leg. He never composed another note and lived in semi-seclusion, battling severe depression until his death in 1964. Of Porter's twenty-five Broadway musicals, only *Anything Goes* and *Kiss Me Kate* are still regularly performed. However, dozens of his songs remain favorites in the "great American songbook," audible embodiments of his lost era of passionate elegance.

Rodgers and Hammerstein: "Something Wonderful"

Dick Rodgers and Oscar Hammerstein II had become household names, their partnership providing an internationally recognized standard that all other theatrical songwriters were compared to. In the 1950s, their new musicals were treated as major cultural events. Frequently serving as their own producers, the duo enjoyed a high degree of creative freedom and continued to take creative risks, up to a point. After the failure of *Allegro*, the duo realized that the theatre-going public was open to innovation, but only within limits.

Although Rodgers and Hammerstein usually came up with their own ideas for projects, *The King and I* (1951, 1, 246 performances) began life when Gertrude Lawrence suggested that the songwriters adapt Margaret Langdon's semifictional *Anna and the King of Siam*, a best-seller based on the experiences of British widow Anna Leonowens, who had served as tutor of Siam's royal family in the 1860s. The clash of eastern and western cultures had already provided the basis for a popular film starring Irene Dunne and Rex Harrison. Lawrence was the obvious choice to play Anna, but it took months to find an appropriate King Mongkut. Both Harrison and Alfred Drake turned down the role, and legend has it that Noël Coward also declined. It was Mary Martin who eventually suggested Yul Brynner (1911?–1985), a Russian-born actor who could veer believably between boyish enthusiasm and animalistic ferocity. During rehearsals, Lawrence and Brynner began playing their scenes with an unspoken subtext of romantic attraction. Hammerstein soon caught on, and according to Brynner gave his wholehearted approval. The resulting interplay between the two leads gave *The King and I* a far greater dramatic impact, turning a duel between cultures into a love story where the protagonists never dare to verbalize their feelings.

The subsidiary story of the king's unhappy young Burmese wife Tuptim (Doretta Morrow) and her forbidden lover Lun Tha (Larry Douglas) plays a key role in bringing the central plot to its climax. At a banquet Anna arranges to impress foreign diplomats; Tuptim presents the "Small House of Uncle Thomas Ballet," dramatizing Harriet Beecher Stowe's anti-slavery novel. Sensing the king's anger over this daring call for freedom, Tuptim flees the palace. While congratulating Anna on the overall success of the evening, the king falls into a conversation comparing eastern and western ideas of love. The result is "Shall We Dance." The king offers an "old Siamese rhyme" that says a woman is like a flower with honey for just one man—a sentiment Oscar resurrected from his 1939 flop, *Very Warm for May*. As Anna teaches the king a simple polka step, it becomes the excuse for him to put his hand on her waist—a seemingly trivial gesture that carries a sexual knockout punch. They then whirl about the floor with all the passion that they cannot articulate, but their celebration ends when Tuptim is dragged in for questioning. All hint of intimacy between Anna and the king evaporates as she shames him into holding back his vengeance. Unable to face the contradiction between his instincts and his intellectual aspirations, the king runs from the room—even as word arrives that Tuptim's lover has been found dead. The final scene brings a reconciliation between Anna and the dying king, as the Crown Prince begins initiating the changes that his father cannot accept.

This was great storytelling, placing multidimensional characters in a believable tale that overflowed with comedy and tragedy, all set to exquisite music and expressed in words that were at once accessible and poetic. Almost every number qualifies as a highlight: Anna reassuring her son in "Whistle a Happy Tune," recalling her own youthful romance in "Hello, Young Lovers" and sharing the maternal "Getting to Know You" with the king's army of children. Robbins put those same tykes to splendid use in "March of the Siamese Children" by giving each child an entrance that defined his or her character. Tuptim and Lun Tha share the operetta-sized duets "We Kiss in a Shadow" and "I Have Dreamed," and the king's first wife Lady Thiang (Dorothy Sarnoff) explains that her husband is always liable to do "Something Wonderful." Some prominent critics paraded their ignorance (or was it tone deafness?) by initially complaining that the score was not up to par. However, a worldwide audience was fully prepped by Rodgers and Hammerstein's previous works and embraced *The King and I* as an instant classic.

The show received the Tony Award for Best Musical, with honors also going to Brynner and Lawrence. It was a final triumph for the fifty-four-year-old actress, who was diagnosed with leukemia eighteen months into the run. Dying days later, Lawrence was buried in Anna's pink satin ball gown. Although Brynner played other roles, he made a life's work out of the king, winning an Academy Award for the 1956 film version and starring in a series of revivals. But this masterwork was never dependent on Brynner for its popularity, as the consistent success of subsequent productions has verified.

There was much to like in *Me and Juliet* (1953, 358 performances), an original backstage romance that Hammerstein framed as a love letter to the theatre. But the story and songs lacked the appeal of Rodgers and Hammerstein's best efforts, and the songwriters made the mistake of selecting George Abbott as director. Any show by Rodgers and Hammerstein required shadings that simply were not in Abbott's dramatic palette. In *Me and Juliet*, Hammerstein has a character drink because he is unhappy. Instead of seeing this gesture as a poignant moment, Abbott automatically saw drinking as an excuse for comedy. This inherent difference in approach led to weaknesses in this show's dramaturgical development. In the end, the reviews praised Jo Meilziner's creative set design for moving its focus from backstage to on stage and even up into the overhead rigging without a break. When critics walk out humming the sets, something is very wrong. A heavy advance sale guaranteed a profitable run, after which the show and its underrated score were forgotten.

The authors had high hopes for *Pipe Dream* (1955, 246 performances), but their adaptation sanitized the fun out of novelist John Steinbeck's raffish *Sweet Thursday* characters—a whorehouse madam played by Metropolitan Opera favorite Helen Traubel wound up coming across as a sort of motherly landlady. Dick and Oscar took a break from stage projects to supervise film versions of *Oklahoma!*

and *Carousel*, and to create a television musical version of *Cinderella* (CBS, 1957). They returned to Broadway with *Flower Drum Song* (1958, 600 performances), a genial musical comedy about an immigrant girl (Miyoshi Umeki) finding love in San Francisco's Chinese-American community. Direction by Gene Kelly and a melodic score that included "I Enjoy Being a Girl" and the ravishing "Love Look Away" were not enough to prevent grumbles that this was not the sort of innovation expected from Rodgers and Hammerstein.

Those grumbles rose to a truculent chorus for the debut of *The Sound of Music* (1959, 1,443 performances). This massive hit was inspired by the real life story of the Von Trapp Family Singers who left their native Austria after the Nazi *Anschluss* in 1938. At age forty-six, Mary Martin might have seemed unlikely casting as the nineteen-year-old Maria Rainer, who leaves a convent to serve as governess to the seven children of the dictatorial widower, Captain Georg Von Trapp (Theodore Bikel). But Martin's charm and her extraordinary rapport with children wiped aside all protests, and Rodgers and Hammerstein wrote an extremely appealing score. Martin introduced the title tune, taught the children a basic musical scale in "Do Re Mi," and joined them in the mock-yodel "The Lonely Goatherd." As the Mother Abbess of Maria's abbey, contralto Patricia Neway joined Martin to sing "My Favorite Things" and soloed the majestic "Climb Ev'ry Mountain." Bikel accompanied himself on guitar while singing "Edelweiss," which was written with such deft simplicity that many listeners mistook it for a genuine Austrian folk song. Since the libretto by Howard Lindsay and Russell Crouse included Alpine settings and costumes, small-minded critics dismissed the show as a sticky-sweet return to the days of operetta. Those critics are all dead and forgotten, and *The Sound of Music* remains one of the world's most beloved musicals. The 1961 London production became the longest running American import up to that time at 2,385 performances, and the 1964 film version set new box office records worldwide, remaining in theatrical release for several years.

Just before the original stage production of *The Sound of Music* went into rehearsal, Oscar Hammerstein II complained to his doctor about suffering late-night indigestion. Tests revealed inoperable stomach cancer. Only his closest friends and family were informed, and he was able to finish work on the show before retreating from the public eye. A few days before the opening, Oscar gave what proved to be his final lyric to friend and leading lady Mary Martin. It was the introductory verse to a second-act reprise of "Sixteen Going on Seventeen." It ended with a phrase that seemed to reflect the whole spirit of Hammerstein's creative life: "Love in your heart wasn't put there to stay; love isn't love till you give it away." Ten months into *The Sound of Music*'s run, the gentle giant who had done more than any individual to reshape the modern musical theatre died at age sixty-four. He had redefined the roles of librettist and lyricist, and given the art of musical theatre newfound possibilities. Practically everything of value that the American musical has achieved since Hammerstein's death has been built to some extent on his achievements. If the American theatrical community really cared one dot about its legacy, it would have long since seen to it that a statue of Oscar Hammerstein was erected just across from George M. Cohan's memorial in Times Square. No one deserves such an honor more than Oscar—not even the great Cohan.

Guys and Dolls: Loesser Is More

Journalist Damon Runyon loved romanticizing the slang-slinging riffraff of Times Square in his writing. Producers Feuer and Martin originated the idea of a musical loosely based on several of Runyon's colorful short stories. After misfires by other librettists, the script for *Guys and Dolls* (1950, 1,200 performances) was completed by Abe Burrows, who was making his first foray into musical theatre after a long career writing comedy for commercial radio. Unbound by traditional thinking and guided by director George S. Kaufman, Burrows constructed a story with four co-equal leads. Nathan Detroit (Sam Levene) runs a popular dice game, much to the dismay of the nightclub showgirl Adelaide (Vivian Blaine) who has been his fiancée for an astounding fourteen years. When Nathan suddenly needs to raise a thousand dollars to rent out space, he bets that handsome gambler Sky Masterson (Robert Alda) will not be able to get a date with the beautiful but righteous missionary Sarah Brown (Isabel Bigley). The date happens, love blooms, and events tear the two couples apart, but since this is a musical comedy, true love wins out in the end.

The score by Frank Loesser is one of the best ever written for the musical stage. Every number is a gem and an organic continuation of the script. After an opening ballet (originally staged by Michael Kidd) introduces the denizens of "Runyonland," three gamblers compare their racing bets in the contrapuntal "Fugue for Tinhorns," and Nathan's business is chorally introduced as "The Oldest Established Permanent Floating Crap Game in New York." The hilarious mock ballad "Adelaide's Lament" has the showgirl reading a medical textbook explaining the psychosomatic symptoms that she suffers because of her endless engagement, and her nightclub routine "Take Back Your Mink" reflects the proper aspirations palpitating beneath her sexy exterior. Sky and Miss Sarah admit their mutual attraction in "I've Never Been in Love Before," which Sky prefaces with the brief but jewel-like bit of *lieder* "My Time of Day." He also heads the male ensemble "Luck Be a Lady," which became an excuse for Kidd to stage a sizzling, macho dance number in the depths of a city sewer. An inebriated Sarah cuts loose in "If I Were a Bell." As gambler Nicely-Nicely Johnson, portly comic actor Stubby Kaye (1918–1997) stopped the show with the rollicking mock spiritual "Sit Down, You're Rocking the Boat."

In Feuer's autobiography *I Got the Show Right Here* (Simon & Schuster, 2003), he tells how Loesser wanted a second-act reprise of "I'll Know When My Love Comes Along." Once a common practice with songs that seemed likely hits, such reprises served no dramatic purpose and were falling out of fashion. When all arguments against this reprise failed to dissuade the songwriter, Kaufman said, "I'll tell you what; we'll agree to a reprise of a first-act song in act two if you'll agree to let us reprise some of the first-act jokes." Loesser got the point. Times had changed, and every element (including every reprise) now had to organically serve the storytelling process. Such attention to detail paid off. Alda, Bigely, and the show won Tonys. There was a 555-performance run in London, and a film version that succeeded despite the casting of non-singing star Marlon Brando as Sky. Revived successfully on both sides of the Atlantic for more than half a century, *Guys and Dolls* remains the model musical comedy.

Loesser surprised many when he single-handedly wrote the book and score for a completely different musical. *The Most Happy Fella* (1956, 676 performances) is an operatic version of Sidney Howard's play *They Knew What They Wanted*. Metropolitan Opera basso Robert Weede made his Broadway debut as Tony, an aging Napa

Valley vintner who falls in love with a young San Francisco waitress he calls Rosabella (Jo Sullivan). In the course of building a relationship, both of them make selfish mistakes that both must learn to forgive. Loesser's versatile score blended all-out arias like "My Heart is So Full of You" with pop songs like the chart-topping "Standing on the Corner" ("watching all the girls go by"). A favorite with critics and cherished by devout fans, this wonderful show has failed to find a widespread audience despite several first-class revivals, but it marks Loesser as a gifted innovator. The Tin Pan Alley veteran became a guru of musical theatre composition, and when he wasn't working on his own hits, he mentored the careers of others. He encouraged one longtime friend to turn memories of an Iowa childhood into one of Broadway's most beloved musical hits.

Meredith Willson: "Seventy-Six Trombones Led the Big Parade"

A onetime member of John Phillip Sousa's legendary concert band, Meredith Willson (1902–1984) became one of the most sought after musicians on network radio. He spent years writing the book, music, and lyrics for *The Music Man* (1957, 1,375 performances), the fictional story of 1912 con man Harold Hill convincing a small Iowa town that he can turn their boys into a marching band, even though he cannot read a note of music. Hill falls in love with local librarian Marian Paroo, played by Barbara Cook (1927–). By some miracle Hill's band actually plays—sort of. After years of rejections, rewrites, and constant encouragement from Frank Loesser, the show opened to astounding acclaim, with Robert Preston (1918–1987) winning raves as Hill. Preston took charismatic command of the stage in the revival meeting–style "Trouble," and brought a nonexistent band to tangible life in "Seventy-Six Trombones." The crystal-voiced Cook introduced the soaring ballad "My White Knight," shared the sentimental "Till There Was You" with Preston, and sang a showstopping "Lida Rose" with a barbershop quartet called The Buffalo Bills. Choreographer Onna White (1922–2005) created dance routines that seemed like believable, spontaneous extensions of everyday movement, the perfect compliment for Willson's score, which found music in such mundane sounds as the clackety-clack of a speeding train, neighborly greetings on Main Street, or the jabbering gossip of housewives. At Tony time, *The Music Man* beat out *West Side Story* for Best Musical, with honors for Preston and Cook. Preston got to repeat his performance in the delightful 1962 film version, costarring with Shirley Jones. Willson replaced "My White Knight" in the film score, fueling suspicions that Loesser had assisted in writing at least part of that number. The show has aged amazingly well, and after half a century remains a staple on professional and amateur stages.

Willson's *The Unsinkable Molly Brown* (1960, 532 performances) starred whisky-voiced Tammy Grimes (1934–) as the real-life Missouri tomboy who married a millionaire and found fame by taking command of a lifeboat filled with fellow *Titanic* survivors. Highlights included Molly's dauntless march "I Ain't Down Yet," and the lyrical "I'll Never Say No to You" introduced by statuesque baritone Harve Presnell (1933–) playing Johnny Brown. Debbie Reynolds costarred with Presnell in a successful 1964 film version. *Here's Love* (1963, 334 performances), Willson's musical adaptation of the classic holiday film *Miracle on 34th Street*, lost money despite a decent Broadway run, and none of his future projects made it past the tryout stage. Although he spent his final years away from the public spotlight, his *Music Man* kept Willson's name a familiar one to anyone even mildly interested in the musical theatre.

Mister Abbott

In the 1950s, as the integration of musicals became a given, creative control logically moved from producers and songwriters over to the directors, who by definition were most responsible for bringing all the elements of a production together. It made equal sense that the first director to dominate this redefined field would be George Abbott. With four full decades of experience in the professional theatre, he commanded such respect that even longtime colleagues made a habit of referring to him as "Mister Abbott." He never requested this title: people simply used it as a matter of course, and being a practical man, he let it stand. Once earned, automatic respect is a powerful and useful tool.

In the twenty-seven years between *Jumbo* (1935) and *A Funny Thing Happened on the Way to the Forum* (1962), Abbott directed twenty-six Broadway musicals, of which twenty-two were money-makers. He also wrote all or part of the librettos for many of these shows, energizing them with what came to be known as "the Abbott touch." A brilliant dramaturgical organizer with a genius for clarifying content and disposing of inessentials, he perfected the art of streamlining a script, learning how to focus a scene and shape comic moments. Prolific as Abbott was, his expertise had limits. So what if a showstopper was not entirely generic to the plot? If it helped put the show over, it stayed. He was a recognized genius at casting, able to place exactly the right talent in key roles. He also appreciated the increasing importance of dance, at least to a degree, and proved it by collaborating successfully with some of the best choreographers of his time. When it came to making a lighthearted musical comedy tick, Abbott had no equal. However, on the few occasions when he directed musicals with serious content, the results were almost always disappointing. He certainly comprehended what the organic musical was about, but had no time for things like nuance of mood, preferring musicals that offered a straightforward blend of music and comedy—period.

After his success with *Call Me Madam*, and a last-minute attempt to save the ailing *Out of This World*, Abbott took on a musical based on Betty Smith's novel *A Tree Grows in Brooklyn* (1951, 267 performances), the story of a young girl coming of age in a family torn by poverty and her father's alcoholism. It had a warm and evocative score by composer Arthur Schwartz and lyricist Dorothy Fields, but Abbott (who coauthored the libretto with Smith) decided to downplay the tragic spirit of the story and pay added attention to the little girl's Aunt Cissy, a buoyant woman who has lived with a succession of common-law husbands and relishes life. As Cissy, Abbott cast Shirley Booth (1898–1992), fresh from her Tony-winning performance in *Come Back, Little Sheba*. The croak-voiced Booth was one of the most gifted actresses of her time, and whether kicking up her heels in "Look Who's Dancin'" or recalling a lover's charms in "He Had Refinement," she delivered the goods. But centering this story on Cissy was like focusing *Oklahoma!* on Ado Annie; the result was a musical that had many fine moments but left the main story on the sidelines. The best numbers in the score, including the mother's plea "Make the Man Love Me," and the father's rapturous promise "I'll Buy You a Star," indicate that in more appropriate directorial hands, this material could have become one of the highlights of the golden age, not just an also-ran.

Abbott was on more familiar ground with *Wonderful Town* (1953, 559 performances), Joseph Fields and Jerome Chodorov's adaptation of their comic play *My Sister Eileen*, with music by Leonard Bernstein and lyrics by Betty Comden and Adolph Green. Here the stress was on intelligent fun with a genial dose of farce. After twenty years in Hollywood, Rosalind Russell (1907–1976) returned to the stage as Ruth Sherwood, an aspiring journalist who comes to New York City with her sister Eileen (Edith Adams). They live in a basement apartment in bohemian Greenwich Village and through various adventures find romance in the big city. The initially terrified sisters wonder why they ever left "Ohio," and Eileen eventually admits that she's "A Little Bit in Love." Ruth offers up "A Hundred Easy Ways" ("to lose a man"), and her attempt to interview a flock of Brazilian sailors ends in a riotous "Conga" before she discovers the one man who can tell her "It's Love!" Broadway dancer Donald Saddler (1918–) made his debut as a choreographer, and Jerome Robbins was called in for an uncredited last minute tune-up. The show won seven Tonys, including Best Musical and awards for Russell and Saddler. Because MGM had already done a screen musical based on the same story, *Wonderful Town* never made it to the big screen. Otherwise, its post-Broadway life would probably have been greater than the occasional tours and revivals that followed.

We've already covered the disappointing *Me and Juliet*. Abbott did far better with his next three shows, collaborating with two choreographers who would go on to define a new category: the director-choreographer. Those shows (*The Pajama Game, Damn Yankees,* etc.) and men are discussed in the next section of this chapter.

As the 1950s ended, Abbott helmed the musical farce *Once Upon a Mattress* (1959, 244 performances), which debunked the classic fairy tale "The Princess and the Pea." It started life Off-Broadway at the Phoenix Theatre, where Carol Burnett's (1933–) outrageous performance as the princess who cannot sleep because a pea is lodged beneath twenty mattresses brought so many rave reviews that the show moved to the Great White Way. Jane White played the conniving Queen Aggravane, and comic Jack Gilford (1908–1990) did his share of scene stealing as a king cursed into silence. Mary Rodgers (eldest daughter of guess who) provided a tuneful score, with lyrics by Marshall Barer, who also cowrote the witty book. *Mattress* never made it to the big screen, but received three successful TV productions. The first two versions in 1964 and 1974 preserved Burnett's bedtime battle with the mountain of mattresses. In 2005, she switched over to playing the Queen, with equally delightful results. Sarah Jessica Parker did her best to breathe life into an ill-conceived 1996 Broadway revival, but without the right casting or directorial approach, this lighthearted comedy fell flat.

Fiorello (1959, 795 performances) is the wild card in Abbott's resume, the sort of sophisticated musical play that usually stumbled under "the Abbott touch." But in coauthoring the libretto with first-timer Jerome Weidman (1913–1998), Abbott respected the bittersweet aspects of the story, a semifictionalized account of the early political career of New York City's beloved Depression Era mayor Fiorello LaGuardia. In this and later projects, composer Jerry Bock (1928–) and lyricist Sheldon Harnick (1924–) established themselves as experts at musically capturing the spirit of lost eras. Tom Bosley won praise creating the title role, but veteran Howard Da Silva stole the show playing a Republican Party hack who assists in LaGuardia's rise to power. Da Silva was featured in two comic showstoppers: the Bowery-style waltz "Politics and Poker," and a spoof of Major James Walker's corrupt cronies telling a judge that their ill-gotten gains came from pennies saved in a "Little Tin Box." In a year that saw Rodgers and Hammerstein's *The Sound of Music* win most of the Tony Awards, a rare tie vote left that show sharing the Best Musical honors with *Fiorello*. Abbott picked up his fourth Tony for directing a musical, a tough thing to do in the days when one award covered both musicals and plays. *Fiorello*'s creators also had the rare distinction of winning the Pulitzer Prize for Drama. One of the best musicals of its time, it was never filmed and has gradually fallen out of the theatrical repertory. With the right casting, *Fiorello* may yet reenter the spotlight. Its authors did not rest on their laurels, In the decade that followed, they would do even finer work.

Director-Choreographers: Robbins, Fosse, and Kidd

Technically speaking, Julian Mitchell was Broadway's first director-choreographer, handling *Babes in Toyland* and several early editions of the Ziegfeld *Follies*. More recently, Agnes DeMille had performed both functions for *Allegro*, but with uneven results. It was up to others to perfect this new dual job.

Classically trained dancer Jerome Robbins had taken the unusual move of studying acting because of his belief that every step in dance should be motivated by character. As a director, he often ruled by sheer force, and was not above openly humiliating performers in front of each other. This earned him the nickname "Attila the Hitler." Many would come to respect his talent, but few would ever like him. Dislike became widespread contempt after he testified before the House Un-American Activities Committee in 1953, ruining the reputations of colleagues in order to avoid being blacklisted himself. His genius as a director was so acute that some people whose careers were harmed by that sham investigation (no real threats to America were ever uncovered by it) later agreed to work with Robbins. He became the most wanted "show doctor" in the business, and was called in to give uncredited assistance to many a troubled Broadway-bound musical. Abbott might do if the show in question was an old-style musical comedy, but organically integrated musicals needed Robbins.

The Los Angeles Civic Light Opera commissioned a musical version of the perennial favorite *Peter Pan* (1954, 152 performances) starring Mary Martin in the title role and Australian actor Cyril Ritchard (1897–1977) as a comically *swish*-buckling Captain Hook. Martin's husband and coproducer Richard Halliday recalled how well Robbins had handled the pressures of the 1953 Martin-Merman TV special, and hired him to serve as the new musical's director and choreographer. Robbins pulled together a troubled production with solid stagecraft and dictatorial authority. The initial score by the inexperienced team of composer Moose Charlap and lyricist Carolyn Leigh (1926–1981) had some fine songs, including "I've Gotta Crow," the Lost Boys anthem "I Won't Grow Up," and Peter's first-act finale "I'm Flying," which developed into a thrilling musical scene. Deciding this show required far more music, Robbins called in Betty Comden, Adolph Green, and composer Jule Styne to augment the score. This trio gave Ritchard the gleeful "Hook's Waltz," and while some of the poetic sentiments in their "Never Never Land" might seem inappropriate coming from young Peter, the song proved to be a sure-fire crowd pleaser. Martin and Ritchard shared the mock-operatic "Mysterious Lady," which gave the leading lady an excuse to show off her rarely heard coloratura. Robbins limited dance to appropriate points in the action and choreographed the flying sequences with flair, making thrilling use of limited, manually controlled technology.

Both Martin and Ritchard won Tonys, and despite strong ticket sales, *Peter Pan* closed after just five months because NBC paid a then-hefty half a million dollars to broadcast a live television version— about twice the costs of the stage production. Massive ratings led to a second live telecast the following year, and legions of fans kept up such a fuss that most of the cast reunited in 1960 for a videotaped full-color remake. That tape was rebroadcast intermittently through 1973, and after years of legal delays became a best-seller on home video. The most complete visual record of a 1950s Broadway musical, it is still a joy to watch. Although Martin played many roles in her stage career, she would be most fondly remembered as Peter Pan. Her stage version has been revived with extraordinary success, in the 1970s by Sandy Duncan, and in the 1990s by Cathy Rigby.

The same season as *Peter Pan*, Robbins and George Abbott codirected *The Pajama Game* (1954, 1,063 performances), a musical comedy based on the novel *7½ Cents* by Richard Bissel, who coauthored the libretto with Abbott. A midwestern factory superintendent (John Raitt) and a union leader (Janis Paige) try to keep a romance alive despite tensions between management and labor over a wage increase of seven and a half cents per hour. The producers were former stage manager Robert Griffith and Abbott's former assistant, Harold Prince (1928–). The score was by protégés of Frank Loesser, first-timers Richard Adler (1921–) and Jerry Ross (1926–1955), who mutually created music and lyrics. Their score had a fresh sound, and although each song was organically rooted in the libretto, they managed to include two chart-topping hits—the Latin-flavored "Hernando's Hideaway," and the pensive "Hey There," which Raitt sang as a duet with his own voice recorded on a dictaphone. Robbins left the choreography in the hands of Bob Fosse (1927–1987), a former nightclub dancer who won Broadway's attention by taking over the lead in a 1952 revival of *Pal Joey*. Fosse shared Robbins's ideas about dance as a form of dramatic expression, creating dances that teetered between antic comedy and sophisticated sexuality, as in the percussive "Steam Heat" number featuring the gamine Carol Haney (1924–1964). During the run, Haney suffered a broken leg and understudy Shirley

MacLaine went on and caught the eye of a Hollywood producer who happened to be in the audience. He put her under immediate contract to Paramount Pictures, putting her on a singular express trip from chorus line to screen stardom that has sparked the hopes of understudies ever since.

Adler, Ross, Fosse, and Abbott reteamed for *Damn Yankees* (1955–1,019), based on Douglass Wallop's best-selling fantasy novel about Joe Hardy, a middle-aged fan of baseball's perennial bad-luck team, the Washington Senators. Hardy sells his soul to the devil in exchange for youth, skill, and a chance to lead the team to a championship over the seemingly invincible New York Yankees. Going by the name Applegate (Ray Walston), the Devil tries to tempt Joe with demonic seductress Lola (Gwen Verdon), who winds up Joe's accomplice in outwitting damnation. Verdon proved a knockout in her first starring role, and Fosse played her innocent-sexy image to the hilt by staging "Whatever Lola Wants" as a raunchy strip tease. Members of the baseball team sang the popular "(You Gotta Have) Heart," and kicked up a macho storm in the comic hoedown "Shoeless Joe from Hannibal Mo." Fosse, Verdon, and Walston received Tonys, and the show was named Best Musical. Within months of the opening, Jerry Ross was dead of leukemia at age twenty-nine, ending a promising songwriting partnership. Adler remained active as a writer and a producer, but never recaptured the kind of success he knew with his late partner. *Damn Yankees* was filmed in 1958, faithfully preserving the lead performances and choreography, and letting Fosse share "Who's Got the Pain" with Verdon. The plot lost some of its resonance in 1960, when the Senators' baseball franchise left Washington and became the Minnesota Twins.

Robbins and Fosse reteamed to stage *Bells Are Ringing* (1956, 924 performances), a giddy musical comedy written by Betty Comden and Adolph Green as a vehicle for their former cabaret costar, Judy Holliday (1921–1965), with music by Jule Styne. Holliday starred as Ella Peterson, an answering service operator who gets personally involved in her clients' lives, particularly that of hunky playwright Jeff Moss, who was played by Sydney Chaplin (1926–). Son of the silent screen's most legendary star, Chaplin enjoyed a brief but stellar career as a leading man in several Broadway musicals composed by Styne. The plot creaked, but the outstanding score included two major hits: the jazzy duet "Just in Time" and the rueful "The Party's Over." This show marked the high point of Holliday's career, bringing her a Tony Award for Best Actress in a Musical. She costarred with Dean Martin in the surprisingly bland 1960 film version. Struck down by cancer five years later at age forty-two, this unique comedienne never had a comparable musical showcase.

Michael Kidd served as choreographer for *Guys and Dolls* and *Can-Can* before graduating to director-choreographer. His dynamic foot-stomping style worked well in *Li'l Abner* (1956, 693 performances), an affectionate adaptation of Andy Capp's long-running comic strip about the backwoods inhabitants of Dogpatch, U.S.A. Stubby Kaye turned the role of Marryin' Sam into a career highlight, leading the satirical "The Country's in the Very Best of Hands" and a tribute to that fictional model of Civil War ineptitude, General "Jubilation T. Cornpone." Kaye repeated his performance in the 1959 film version, which preserved most of Kidd's dances, including the "Sadie Hawkins Day Ballet." Kidd also helmed *Destry Rides Again* (1959, 472 performances), an entertaining vehicle for television star Andy Griffith who played a Wild West sheriff who falls for saloon entertainer Dolores Gray. Kidd's whip-cracking dances wowed the critics, but many felt that his direction left something to be desired.

Kidd also directed the Lucille Ball vehicle *Wildcat* (1960, 171 performances), which is best remembered for the star's croak-voiced rendition of "Hey, Look Me Over," a spirited march by jazz musician Cy Coleman (1929–2004) and lyricist Carolyn Leigh. Rough reviews did not deter audiences from loving Lucy, but after five months she pled illness and shut down the show. As the sole investor, she absorbed all of the resulting loss. Kidd's staging was one of the better features of the ill-advised *Subways Are for Sleeping* (1961, 205 performances), which could not win much attention with its moronic plot (cheap New Yorkers living in subway trains and museums?) and so-so score. However, theatre professionals still talk about producer David Merrick's (1911–2000), daring advertising ploy. Expecting poor reviews, he tracked down a group of people with the same names as New York's seven major newspaper critics, and got them to sign off on rave quotes like "Best musical of the century!" The *Herald Tribune* was the only paper willing to run the ad, which ignited reams of press coverage. Some people bought tickets out of curiosity, but nothing could keep Merrick's *Subways* running for more than an unprofitable six months.

In the meantime, Robbins staged *West Side Story* (1957, 732 performances), a contemporized version of Shakespeare that placed a Polish-American Romeo and a Puerto Rican Juliet in the middle of a New York City street gang war. Robbins made the most extensive use yet of dance as a storytelling tool in a Broadway musical. The show opened with a wordless choreographed prologue that established the bitter feud between the Puerto Rican Sharks and the Caucasian Jets. While a "Dance at the Gym" becomes a sizzling competition between the rival gangs, Jet cofounder Tony first sees Maria, sister of Shark leader Bernardo. Everything around Tony and Maria fades away, and after a gentle dance, they kiss—setting off a violent reaction by both gangs that pulls the lovers (and the audience) back into reality. When the gangs eventually battle in a choreographed "Rumble," Tony unwillingly kills Maria's brother and sets off a cycle of revenge that leads to his own death. Leonard Bernstein created extraordinary music for the dance scenes, and collaborated on an ambitious, sophisticated score with lyricist Stephen Sondheim (1930–), a twenty-seven-year-old protégé of Oscar Hammerstein II. Playwright Arthur Laurents (1918–) provided a libretto that gave full leeway to the dance elements. As Tony, handsome tenor Larry Kert (1930–1991) introduced "Maria" and shared "Tonight" with lissome soprano Carol Lawrence (1932–), who as Maria sang "I Feel Pretty." Playing Bernardo's fiery girlfriend Anita, dancer Chita Rivera (1933–) led the Shark girls in an electrifying mock tribute to "America," and shared the powerful "A Boy Like That—I Have a Love" with Lawrence. With this performance, Rivera began a long reign as one of Broadway's most beloved and enduring musical stars.

Like *Good News, Babes in Arms,* and *On the Town* had before—and just as *Hair, A Chorus Line, Rent,* and *Spring Awakening* would in years to come—*West Side Story* became the youth musical of its generation, speaking to the teens and twenty-somethings of the 1950s in their own terms and eliciting a passionate response. Although it won Tony awards for choreography and set design, its run was no record-setter. An exceptionally well-made 1961 film version preserved much of the Robbins choreography and a surprising amount of the show's excitement. In ensuing years, the rise of violent, heavily armed street gangs has made the switchblades of the Sharks and Jets seem almost quaint by comparison. Even so, *West Side Story* will forever stand as a landmark moment in the history of theatrical dance. For years to come, all serious Broadway choreography was compared to the work Robbins did in this show.

Gwen Verdon won another Tony starring in *New Girl in Town* (1957, 431 performances), a musical adaptation of Eugene O'Neill's *Anna Christie*. When director George Abbott overruled some of choreographer Bob Fosse's plans for that show, Fosse resolved to serve as both director and choreographer on all his future stage projects. This plan worked out well for *Redhead* (1959, 452 performances), which featured Verdon as a girl whose romance with an actor (Richard Kiley) attracts the attentions of a mysterious fiend in Victorian London. The score by composer Albert Hague and lyricist Dorothy Fields spawned no hits, not even Verdon and Kiley's ingratiating duet "Look Who's in Love." Fosse, Verdon, and the show received Tonys, but *Redhead* was so dependent on its original star and staging that it faded into obscurity after a brief post-Broadway tour. *Redhead's* most lasting legacy was that Fosse married Verdon during the New York run.

Gypsy (1959, 702 performances) may have seemed an unlikely choice for Robbins to stage. Inspired by the memoirs of the burlesque strip-tease star Gypsy Rose Lee, this musical comedy told the sometimes harsh story of Rose Hovick, the monstrous real-life stage mother who forced Lee and her sister June Havoc into vaudeville. Librettist Arthur Laurents pulled no punches, and with music by Jule Styne and lyrics by Stephen Sondheim, the score reflected every poignant, tawdry turn of a dysfunctional family rising, falling, and then rising again in Depression-era show business. Producer David Merrick realized that this material would be a hard sell, so he envisioned it as a vehicle for Ethel Merman, the one performer who the public might accept as the dominating Rose. Director-choreographer Robbins kept the use of dance to a minimum, allowing it to occur naturally—as part of stage acts, during a back alley rehearsal scene, etc. He helped Merman mold what many felt was the greatest performance of her career, climaxing in "Rose's Turn," which had Rose unleashing waves of rage at her children's ingratitude, finally proclaiming that what she does from now on will be "For me!" Sondheim originally wanted to cut off applause for what amounted to a nervous breakdown, but Oscar Hammerstein II advised that audiences desperately wanted to respond to Merman's powerhouse performance of the song. It became a showstopper, with a slightly demented Rose continuing to bow after the applause faded.

The Styne-Sondheim score also gave Merman "Everything's Coming Up Roses," Rose's upbeat but chilling refusal to give up show business at any cost. The two daughters share a dream of what life would be like "If Mamma Was Married," and Rose keeps up her cohorts' spirits in "Together Wherever We Go." The multipurpose "Let Me Entertain You" serves first as a vaudeville routine for the two girls, but then winds up as Gypsy's jazzy strip music in burlesque. Working with orchestrators Sid Ramin and Robert Ginzler, Jule Styne fashioned the most exciting overture ever heard in modern musical theatre, as sure a showstopper as any song in the show. Robbins was at his best staging "You Gotta Have a Gimmick," which had three hardened strippers coaching the young Gypsy in what it takes to succeed. While choreography was not a dominant feature of the original production, it should be noted that subsequent revivals that kept the Robbins dances have flourished, while those that did not have fared poorly. The 1962 film version has some fine moments, but Rosalind Russell's dubbed singing has never satisfied purists, who found far more to like in Bette Midler's spirited and handsomely produced 1993 television production.

After Loesser's ambitious musical fantasy *Greenwillow* (1960, 97 performances) failed, he reunited with Feuer, Martin, and Burrows for *How to Succeed in Business Without Really Trying* (1961, 1,418 performances), a musical comedy inspired by an identically titled satirical how-to book. Burrows directed, and although Hugh Lambert was credited as choreographer, he staged only one number. Feuer and Martin brought in Bob Fosse to provide most of the musical staging, including a slinky ode to the sacred office "Coffee Break," and the still-timely admonition "A Secretary Is Not a Toy." The disarming Robert Morse (1931–) won raves as the ambitious and ruthless J. Pierpont Finch, who uses the how-to book as his guide up the corporate ladder. Former pop crooner Rudy Vallee found fresh fame as a bumbling CEO, and comedian Charles Nelson Reilly (1931–2007) scored laughs as Vallee's brown-nosing nephew. Morse sang the inspirational "I

Believe in You" to himself, ignoring a threatening counterpoint sung by other executives while they all groomed for a board meeting—the sound of their electric shavers provided by kazoos. Morse shared the showstopping college fight song "Grand Old Ivy" with Vallee, and sang the mock-operatic "Rosemary" to the secretary in love with him (Bonnie Scott). Everyone joined in the gospel-style "Brotherhood of Man," in which Finch persuades the owner of the company that "mediocrity is not a mortal sin." *How to Succeed* won the Tony for Best Musical, and received the Pulitzer for Drama. Morse and Vallee repeated their roles in an excellent film version, which also preserved Fosse's dances. Loesser's future projects did not make it to Broadway. A longtime chain smoker, he died of lung cancer in 1969. Aside from the genius of his own work, Loesser's dedicated mentoring of Adler, Ross, Willson, and other songwriters did much to enrich the musical theatre.

One additional Loesser story: a friend arranged for him to meet with an aspiring songwriter from New Jersey. Loesser explained the art of song construction to the eager beginner by drawing a picture of a train and adding a colorful caboose—insisting that a really great showtune should always save a socko idea or statement for its closing moments. It was a lesson that young Jerry Herman took to heart, inspiring many of the great songs he would write in decades to come.

Fosse next served as director-choreographer for *Little Me* (1962, 257 performances), the farcical story of Belle Poitrine, a busty girl from the wrong side of the tracks who rises to fame and fortune through sheer determination ... and seven profitable marriages. Cy Coleman and Carolyn Leigh's score included "Real Live Girl" and "I've Got Your Number." This was the first musical to boast a libretto by Neil Simon (1927–), who was just beginning his reign as Broadway's top comic playwright. The show lasted for several months, thanks in large part to the presence of TV comedy legend Sid Caesar, who singlehandedly played all of the men in Belle's life.

That same season, George Abbott found himself in trouble during out of town tryouts for *A Funny Thing Happened on the Way to the Forum* (1962, 964 performances). This farce inspired by the works of Plautus was the first production with a score entirely by Stephen Sondheim. Former burlesque comedian Zero Mostel (1915–1977) gave a deliciously over the top performance as Pseudolus, a slave in ancient

Rome scheming to unite his young master Hero (Brian Davies) with a beautiful courtesan in exchange for the one thing Pseudolus dreams of: his freedom. In the classic burlesque tradition, every solution seems to create a new problem. The script by Burt Shevelove (1915–1982) and veteran TV writer Larry Gelbart (1928–) gave ample comic opportunities to Mostel and his colleagues, who included Jack Gilford as the aptly named house slave Hysterium and David Burns as the clueless homeowner. Audiences cheered when the male leads celebrated masculine lust in "Everybody Ought to Have a Maid," or when Mostel reassured a dubious Gilford that he was "Lovely" in drag. So there was nothing wrong with Sondheim's tuneful, varied score. Or was there? When Jerome Robbins was called in for consultations, he soon realized that the whimsical opening number "Love is in the Air" made listeners expect the sort of romantic comedy Abbott had served up back in the 1930s. It took audiences half an act to catch on that this was a bawdy farce. Sondheim promptly composed the zany "Comedy Tonight," which introduced the key characters and set the right tone from the get-go. From the moment this song was added, audience response shifted into high gear. *Forum* received the Tony Award for Best Musical, with additional prizes going to Mostel, Burns, Abbott, and the librettists. However, Sondheim's delightful score was not even nominated.

From this point on, Abbott's career was dogged by bad luck and questionable judgment. Carol Burnett won raves in Abbott's Hollywood spoof *Fade Out—Fade In* (1964, 271 performances), but her premature withdrawal from the cast turned a potential hit into a money loser. *Flora the Red Menace* (1965, 87 performances) marked the Broadway debut of powerhouse talent Liza Minnelli (1946–) and the first joint effort of composer John Kander (1927–) and lyricist Fred Ebb (1993–2004), but despite Abbott's best efforts, the story of an art student stumbling into involvement with the Communist Party was surprisingly unfunny and closed in a matter of weeks. The Wall Street send-up *How Now, Dow Jones* (1967, 220 performances) was a first-class treatment of a third-rate idea. Handsome Tony Roberts (1939–) made an impressive musical debut as an amoral stockbroker, and the score by movie composer Elmer Bernstein and lyricist Carolyn Leigh included the popular march "Step to the Rear," but nothing could overcome the moronic plot involving an announcer who sets off a panic by proclaiming a falsely inflated Dow Jones average—all so her boyfriend will marry her. Abbott's future original musicals were outright flops, but revivals of old hits kept him active until well past his hundredth birthday.

Big Singing: "Out of the Commonplace into the Rare"

The organic musical had essentially eclipsed the need for operetta, but there was still a demand for musicals with big emotions and big singing. The Los Angeles Civic Light Opera Company became a bastion of operetta, staging revivals of classics and spawning a string of new shows in the romantic tradition. Their biggest success was an adaptation of the old Edward Knoblock potboiler *Kismet* (1953, 583 performances). In a male variation of the Cinderella story, Baghdad's beggar poet Hajj (Alfred Drake) manages in one day to obtain wealth, win the hand of the Wazir's voluptuous wife Lalume, and even see his daughter Marsinah (Doretta Morrow) married to the Caliph. Hajj sees it all as "kismet," an Arabic word for "fate." George Forrest and Robert Wright adapted melodies by Alexander Borodin, creating songs that ranged from the bawdy to the sublime, right in tune with a humorous libretto by Charles Lederer and Luther Davis. As Lalume, soprano Joan Diener (1930–2006), with her death defying vocals, hourglass figure, and leering delivery of suggestive dialogue, made a superb match for Drake, who gave a bravura performance. Their witty comic interplay provided a crucial anchor for a production that talked like a musical comedy, sang like an operetta, and strutted its stuff like a burlesque show. As the Caliph, Richard Kiley (1922–1999) joined Morrow to introduce "Stranger in Paradise," which became a major hit. *Kismet* had the seeming misfortune to open during a newspaper strike, but this turned out to be a stroke of luck. By the time its mixed reviews were published, jubilant word of mouth had already translated into long lines at the box office.

Wish You Were Here (1952, 598 performances) thrived thanks to extensive post-opening rewrites and pop singer Eddie Fisher's million-selling single of Harold Rome's sentimental title song. It also helped that director Joshua Logan went so far as to install an in-ground swimming pool on stage at the Imperial Theatre, keeping the ensemble splashing about in skimpy bathing suits that provided plenty of male and female eye candy. The score was on the light side, giving no clue of what Rome would unleash in the semi-operatic *Fanny* (1954, 888 performances). Based on a trilogy by French playwright Marcel Pagnol, it is the story of a Marseille girl played by petite soprano Florence Henderson (1934–). Fanny loves the restless Marius (William Tabbert), who heads off to sail the world, not realizing that he has left Fanny pregnant. Gentle sail maker Panisse (Walter Slezak) marries Fanny and raises her son as his own. When Marius returns, his father Cesar (Ezio Pinza) prevents his reuniting with Fanny. Years later, Panisse dies comforted by the knowledge that Marius will care for Fanny and the boy. Pinza was perfectly cast to handle the demands of Rome's score, as was fellow *South Pacific* alumni Tabbert, who introduced the sweeping title song. *Fanny* was the first musical produced by attorney David Merrick, who would play a major role in musical theatre for the next four decades.

Thereafter, Rome dedicated his talents to musical comedy, including the aforementioned *Destry Rides Again*. His *I Can Get It for You Wholesale* (1962, 300 performances) starred Elliott Gould as a ruthless up-and-comer in New York's garment industry, but is primarily remembered for the Broadway debut of vocalist Barbra Streisand (1942–) as the long-suffering secretary "Miss Marmelstein." Rome continued writing through the 1970s, but did not have another Broadway hit. His last noteworthy work was a musical version of *Gone with the Wind* that had runs in London and Tokyo but never reached New York.

While Leonard Bernstein was working on the score for *West Side Story*, he took a glorious stumble by collaborating with playwright Lillian Hellman on *Candide* (1953, 73 performances), a comic operetta based on Voltaire's controversial 1759 novel spoofing the folly of naïve optimism. Despite good reviews, there proved to be little audience for a satirical operetta, and the show closed in two months. A cast recording preserved highlights of Bernstein's score (with lyrics by Richard Wilbur, John La Touche, and Dorothy Parker), including the ensemble "We'll Make Our Garden Grow," and the hilarious coloratura aria "Glitter and Be Gay," introduced by soprano Barbara Cook. Over time, that recording helped *Candide* develop a cult following, and inspired a series of concerts and revivals. In the 1970s, this show would have a triumphant, if radically revised, resurrection.

Resurrection has proven more elusive for *The Golden Apple* (1954, 124 performances), arguably the most highly praised musical failure of its time. With libretto by John La Touche and music by Jerome Moross, it reset the story of Homer's *Odyssey* in early-twentieth-century America. Helen (Kaye Ballard) is a sheriff's wife, stolen by a salesman named Paris (Jonathan Lucas). The good soldier Ulysses (Stephen Douglass) spends ten years searching for Helen, defeats Paris in a boxing match, and finally returns home to his incredibly patient wife Penelope (Anita Gillette). *The Golden Apple*'s run at the Phoenix Theatre was so enthusiastically received that it became the first musical to transfer from off-Broadway to on. Unfortunately, it did not draw a substantial audience and closed at a loss. Helen's ballad "Lazy Afternoon" won some attention, and although the cast recording only preserved part of the extensive score, it has been enough to win this quirky show new generations of admirers. In fairness, that recording has left some theatre buffs shrugging in confusion.

Only a few dozen theatres on the island of Manhattan are officially recognized as Broadway venues. Beyond the main theatre district, there are many more theatres of varied sizes, most far smaller than those on or near what gossip columnists once called the Rialto. By the 1950s, off-Broadway was home to everything from revived classics to experimental new works. At the intimate Theatre de Lys in Greenwich Village, Marc Blitzstein's translation of *The Threepenny Opera* (1955, 2,611 performances) turned a limited run into a record-setting redis-covery of the Brecht-Weill masterpiece, with Weill's widow Lotte Lenya in her original role as Jenny. During the six-year run, such future stars as Bea Arthur, Charlotte Rae, Jo Sullivan, Jerry Orbach, Edward Asner, and Estelle Parsons appeared in the cast. On a lighter note, a compact restaging of the old Kern-Wodehouse-Bolton hit *Leave It to Jane* (1959, 928 performances) at the tiny Sheridan Square Theatre also helped alert producers to the new commercial possibili-ties of off-Broadway venues.

The most successful original off-Broadway musical of the 1950s was the operetta spoof *Little Mary Sunshine* (1959, 1,143 performances). Rick Besoyan single-handedly crafted this story of Rocky Mountain resort owner Mary Potts (Eileen Brennan) who loves forest ranger Captain "Big Jim" Warrington (William Graham) and must contend with simpering schoolgirls, a clever maid who dreams of being "Mata

Hari," and a treacherous native called Yellow Feather. One of Mary's guests is Mme. Ernestine Von Liebedich (Elizabeth Parrish) who asks, "Do You Ever Dream of Vienna?" Besoyan invoked the musical styles of Romberg, Friml, Lehar, Herbert, and more, packing the libretto with enough innocent fun to keep the little Orpheum Theatre packed for almost three years. Even people whose knowledge of operetta was limited to the films of Nelson Eddy and Jeanette MacDonald got the jokes; those who knew more laughed even harder. Besoyan's secret was that his clever pastiche songs were practically as good as what they were making fun of, and a small, gutsy production accompanied by two pianos added to the fun. When his next effort, *The Student Gypsy* (1963, 16 performances), opened on Broadway with a full cast and orchestra, it was so close to the real thing that the humor fell flat. Besoyan never wrote another hit, but *Little Mary Sunshine* became a longtime staple at regional and amateur theatres.

London: "Consider Yourself at Home"

Almost every Broadway musical hit played London during these years, but a handful of British tuners made the trip to New York. The longest running West End musical of the 1950s was *Salad Days* (1954, 2,283 performances), which involved a dour government minister trying to suppress a magical piano that makes everyone within earshot dance. A 1958 off-Broadway production folded after eighty performances. Two other U.K. originals managed to find a sizeable American audience during these years. They couldn't have been less alike, or more distinctly British.

Sandy Wilson's *The Boy Friend* (1954, 2,084 performances in London) simultaneously parodied and paid homage to the musical comedies of the 1920s. Polly Browne (Anne Rogers), an English heiress at a Riviera finishing school, risks her father's displeasure by falling in love with delivery boy Tony, only to find out in the final scene that her beau is actually the heir to a peerage. "A Room in Bloomsbury" echoes Noël Coward's "A Room with a View," and the show's title recalls Rodgers and Hart's *The Girl Friend*. Originally intended for a limited run at London's Player's Club, the production moved to Wyndham's Theatre and ran for more than five years. American producers Feuer and Martin brought a slightly expanded version of the show to New York, but Wilson was so insistent on revising the show that he was finally barred from the theatre. *The Boy Friend* did very well on Broadway (1954, 485 performances), where it marked the American debut of Julie Andrews (1935–), a fresh-faced nineteen-year-old British music hall veteran with crisp diction and a crystalline soprano voice. Less than three years after *The Boy Friend* closed on Broadway, a more intimate revival opened off-Broadway for an even longer run (1958, 763 performances).

Several stories by Charles Dickens have lent themselves to effective dramatization, but few theatregoers had high hopes for a musical version of *Oliver Twist* written single-handedly by unknown English-man Lionel Bart (1930–1999). The idea of singing orphan pickpockets, or the covetous Fagin kicking up his heels struck many as preposterous until they saw *Oliver* (1960, 2,618 performances in London). Ron Moody played Fagin as a loveable rogue, singing "You've Got to Pick a Pocket or Two" and the tour de force "Reviewing the Situation." Earthy Georgia Brown (1933–1992) introduced the joyous "Oom-Pah-Pah," and the torchy hit "As Long as He Needs Me." As Oliver, young Keith Hamshere sang the plaintive "Where Is Love," and as the Artful Dodger, Martin Horsey lead the ensemble in "Consider Yourself." With Bart's engaging score and director Peter Coe's double turntable production, *Oliver* became the longest running West End musical up to that time. David Merrick brought Coe's staging to Broadway (1963, 744 performances), with Brown repeating her success as Sally and with TV's future *Monkees* star David Jones as the Dodger. Moody played Fagin in the acclaimed 1968 screen version, the last musical of the twentieth century to win the Academy Award for Best Picture. Bart wrote several more musicals, and in an ill-advised move, sold off all his rights to *Oliver* to finance a massive flop. He spent his final years in near poverty, but was eventually hailed by Andrew Lloyd Webber as "the father of the modern British musical."

Working with fellow composer-lyricist Leslie Bricusse (1931–), British vocalist Anthony Newley (1931–1999) cowrote, directed, and starred in *Stop the World—I Want to Get Off* (1961, 485 performances in London), the story of Littlechap, a lower-class Englishman who defies the establishment and rises to wealth and fame. Newley's poignant rendition of "What Kind of Fool Am I?" helped make the show a hit, and David Merrick brought Newley and the show to Broadway for a successful run (1962, 555 performances). Newley then cowrote (with Bricusse), directed, and starred in Merrick's New York production *The Roar of the Greasepaint—The Smell of the Crowd* (1965, 231 performances). This time, he was Cocky, a little man who must play the game of life versus the powerful Sir, played by Cyril Ritchard. Newley's ballad "Who Can I Turn To" became a hit, as did Ritchard's "On a Wonderful Day Like Today." Newley's future stage efforts were mostly limited to British productions that did not make it "across the pond." Critics savaged a 1978 revival of *Stop the World* starring Sammy Davis Jr., leading many to speculate that Newley's shows were either past their time or ineffective without their author and original star.

Lerner and Loewe: "With a Little Bit of Luck"

Lyricist-librettist Alan Jay Lerner followed up the success of *Brigadoon* by writing screenplays for several MGM musicals, taking home an Academy Award for his work on *An American in Paris* (1951). He reteamed with composer Frederick Loewe for *Paint Your Wagon* (1951, 289 performances), a tale of romance set during the 1850s California gold rush. The popularity of "I Talk to the Trees" and "They Call the Wind Mariah" made this show a regular feature in regional and amateur productions for many years.

Lerner and Loewe were approached by Hungarian film producer Gabriel Pascal with a fascinating idea: turn George Bernard Shaw's comedy *Pygmalion* into a musical. Oscar Hammerstein warned them not to pursue the project, because he and Rodgers had tried adapting it and had given up, convinced it could not be done. *Pygmalion* was an anti–love story that Shaw had designed to undercut the audience's romantic expectations. Impoverished London flower girl Eliza Doolittle finally walks out on Henry Higgins, the phonetics professor who has taught her proper speech, enabling her to break through Edwardian society's linguistic boundaries. Would audiences accept a book musical with no love story? By the time Lerner and Loewe decided to attempt the project, Pascal had died. They kept writing even though there was no guarantee they would obtain the rights. Shaw had forbidden musical adaptations of his shows ever since his *Arms and the Man* became *The Chocolate Soldier*, but Shaw himself had died in 1950, and his estate was finally persuaded to grant Lerner and Loewe an option.

Lerner completed the libretto for *My Fair Lady* (1956, 2,717 performances) with at least some input from director Moss Hart. Retaining substantial portions of Shaw's dialogue, Lerner opened up the action and created several new scenes, in particular a sequence that culminates in Eliza cracking her cockney accent. After a grueling night of phonetic drills, Eliza is in tears. The usually gruff Higgins shows some sympathy, and expresses confidence that she will succeed. Eliza suddenly pronounces "The Rain in Spain (Stays Mainly in the Plain)" perfectly, setting off a merry celebration with Higgins and his sidekick, Colonel Pickering. Higgins and Eliza even dance a tango. Afterward, as the housekeeper and staff whisk Eliza to bed, she tells them that "I Could Have Danced All Night." Another standout moment comes when Higgins first sees Eliza in her sumptuous ball gown. As they depart for the ball, he suddenly offers Eliza his arm; the squashed cabbage leaf has completed her transformation and is treated like a lady. These scenes are completely Lerner's, and give the relationship between the two leads a new dimension. There is no mention of love, but each has at least some degree of feeling for the other. This sentiment is echoed in the final scenes when a furious Higgins admits to himself that "I've Grown Accustomed to Her Face." Without turning the story into a romance, Lerner's libretto gave the central characters an emotional depth they lacked in Shaw's play, while retaining the rich intellectual content that made *Pygmalion* a lasting hit.

Mary Martin turned down the role of Eliza, saying of the songwriters, "Those dear boys have lost their talent." After former film star Deanna Durbin also declined, the role went to Julie Andrews. She came perilously close to losing the part during rehearsals, but after a successful weekend of solo coaching, Moss Hart told his wife Kitty Carlisle, "She has the sort of strength that makes you wonder how the British ever lost India." Rex Harrison was the first choice to play Higgins, and although no singer, he gradually perfected a form of talking on pitch known as "sprechstimme" that effectively hid his vocal limitations. Robert Coote bumbled loveably as Pickering. Veteran British performer Stanley Holloway gave a knockout performance as Eliza's hard drinking father, Alfie, leading the rowdy ensemble numbers "With a Little Bit of Luck" and "Get Me to the Church On

Time." Cecil Beaton's costume designs were practically characters in their own right, giving the production so much authentic period atmosphere—especially in the "Ascot Gavotte" scene, done entirely in shades of black, gray, and white—that Lerner later wrote of Beaton, "It is difficult to know whether he designed the Edwardian era or the Edwardian era designed him."

My Fair Lady opened to unprecedented acclaim, eventually overtaking *Oklahoma!* to become the longest running Broadway musical. The production was recreated in loving detail in numerous international incarnations. The New York leads repeated their triumph at the Drury Lane Theatre a year later (1958, 2,281 performances), and both Harrison and Holloway appeared in the 1964 film version. The show has been successfully revived on both sides of the Atlantic and after more than half a century is still considered by many to be the greatest musical of Broadway's so-called "golden age."

The folks at Columbia Records took a major gamble by investing in *My Fair Lady* in return for the recording rights. It proved a very profitable move. The original Broadway and London cast recordings both became best-sellers, and Columbia eventually recorded several foreign language cast recordings. All told, the company made millions from its involvement with *My Fair Lady*, marking a peak in the popularity of original cast recordings.

After writing the exquisite original screen musical *Gigi* (MGM, 1957), Lerner and Loewe decided to dramatize T. H. White's Arthurian novel *The Once and Future King*. The legend of King Arthur (Richard Burton) and the forbidden affair between his wife Guinevere (Julie Andrews) and the once-saintly Sir Lancelot was perhaps too much story for any one musical. Loewe complained that it was not possible to write a successful musical about a cuckold, but they forged on, with Moss Hart once again directing. *Camelot* (1960, 873 performances) boasted a glorious score, some extremely witty scenes, a rich physical production, and a dream cast. Burton sang the pensive and condescending "How to Handle a Woman," as well as the sprightly title tune, which grew into a superb musical scene. Andrews sang "Before I Gaze at You Again," and shared "What Do the Simple Folk Do?" with Burton. Handsome baritone Robert Goulet (1933–2007) played Lancelot, introducing "If Ever I Would Leave You," a song he became permanently identified with.

Camelot opened in Toronto at more than four hours in length, beginning a nightmarish try-out tour that left Hart, Lerner, and Loewe hospitalized with heart ailments. The material suffered from an inherent contradiction: despite generous doses of comedy, it is at heart a tragedy. Arthur's inability to deal with Lancelot and Guinevere's romance destroys the Round Table, leading to a war no one will win. Taking a cue from White's novel, the musical ends with Arthur on the eve of what he knows will be a disastrous battle, knighting a young boy and sending him home to keep the story of the Round Table alive. Burton played the moment for all it was worth, sounding a note of defiant hope. On Broadway, dismissive critics missed the point, complaining that this show was no match for *My Fair Lady*. A few weeks into the run, Hart made extensive changes, and arranged for highlights to air on Ed Sullivan's popular TV show. Ticket sales rebounded, and the production racked up a very respectable run. A 1964 West End production starring Laurence Harvey ran for 518 performances, and a 1967 film version suffered from terminal bloat and inept direction by Josh Logan. Over time, *Camelot* attracted a broad fan base, and has been revived just as successfully as *My Fair Lady*.

Camelot was a beginning for Goulet. Andrews spent the next thirty-five years in Hollywood, and an ailing Frederick Loewe retired altogether from songwriting. Just months after rejuvenating the show, Moss Hart suffered a fatal heart attack. After closing, the show was unexpectedly connected to a national tragedy when President John F. Kennedy's widow Jackie told an interviewer that her husband had frequently listened to *Camelot*'s cast recording, particularly to Richard Burton's final reprise of the title song: "Don't let it be forgot that once there was a spot for one brief shining moment ..." Kennedy's presidency was thereafter dubbed "the Camelot years," forever linking it to Lerner and Loewe's last original stage musical.

With Kennedy's slaying, the optimism of the post–World War II era truly began to fade. Once again, in theatre and in the world at large, the times they were a-changing.

13

Rock Rolls In (1960–1970) — "Soon It's Gonna Rain"

There are times when history refuses to be neatly pigeonholed, which is why the periods covered by this chapter and its predecessor overlap by several years. As one set of influences was coming to an end, others came into play.

For example, the 1960s marked the reemergence of intimate musicals both on and off-Broadway. A disarming fable called *The Fantasticks* (1960, 17,162 performances) started life as a seven character one-act college musical by composer Harvey Schmidt (1929–) and lyricist-librettist Tom Jones (1928–). Expanded to two acts for its production at the 153-seat Sullivan Street Playhouse in Manhattan's Greenwich Village, it told the story of two well-meaning fathers who manipulate their idealistic children into a storybook romance, only to learn that "happily ever after" has its darker side. In the first of many starring roles, Jerry Orbach (1935–2004) played El Gallo, the flamboyant adventurer who both instigates and narrates this tale of lost innocence. He also introduced the beloved "Try to Remember," which urged listeners to recall their own innocence. The original production of *The Fantasticks* became an institution, running in the basement of its producer's townhouse for forty-one years. In that time, there were more than 11,800 other productions of the show worldwide. Occasional attempts to expand the piece for presentation in larger theatres have invariably failed, and the 1995 film version was a lifeless error. A warmly received revival reached a new off-Broadway Times Square venue in 2006, proving that this musical and its original staging had lost none of their magic.

Later in the decade, songwriter Clark Gesner got permission to adapt Charles Schulz's beloved comic strip *Peanuts* into a musical. Director Joseph Hardy gave a relatively inexperienced cast of six actors a collection of the strips and let them pick which ones to enact between Gesner's tuneful, charming songs. *You're a Good Man, Charlie Brown* (1967, 1,597 performances) opened at the tiny Theatre 80 on Manhattan's St. Mark's Place, and became an instant classic. The staging was simplicity itself—six actors performed in street clothes, using a few wooden cubes and the audience's imagination to enact a typical day in the life of Charlie Brown (Gary Burghoff) and his friends. Charlie's pet beagle Snoopy (Bill Hinnant) was allowed to speak and sing as a turtleneck-clad human being, stopping the show as he celebrated "Suppertime." The most well-known number in the score was the closing anthem to "Happiness." A charming sequel entitled *Snoopy* (1983, 152 performances) played off-Broadway decades later, but was by other songwriters and never matched the popularity of the original, which was performed by thousands of schools and amateur groups and would even have a revised (and short-lived) Broadway revival in 1999.

No off-Broadway theatre could hope to handle a full-sized spoof of Busby Berkeley's big-screen musical spectaculars, but the artful pastiche *Dames at Sea* (1968, 575 performances) did exactly that with a six-person cast, a three-piece orchestra, and abundant imagination. Newcomer Bernadette Peters (1948–) played the Ruby Keeler–esque chorus girl who understudies an egotistical star, plated by Tamara Long. The clichéd lines and artful production numbers were all there, along with a genuine affection for the originals being giggled at. With kewpie-doll looks and stellar charm, Peters became an immediate audience favorite, a position she would retain well into the next century.

Big musicals could be innovative too. In the wake of Oscar Hammerstein II's death, Richard Rodgers served as his own lyricist for *No Strings* (1962, 580 performances), the story of a romance between two expatriate Americans in Paris—a black high-fashion model (Diahann Carroll) and a white Pulitzer Prize–wining novelist (Richard Kiley). The couple eventually part, realizing that their love will never be accepted if they return to the States. Despite a full cast of thirty-five, director-choreographer Joe Layton (1931–1994) created a visual sense of intimacy, putting the orchestra—which used

no stringed instruments, of course—backstage, with musicians sometimes strolling among the cast. Many listeners took the bewitching
"The Sweetest Sounds (I'll Ever Hear Are Still Inside My Head)" as
reassurance that Rodgers would carry on, and so he did, composing
new works and supervising revivals of his old hits for the remaining
seventeen years of his life. His only other new stage musical in the
1960s was *Do I Hear a Waltz?* (1965, 220 performances), an adaptation of the Arthur Laurents comedy *The Time of the Cuckoo.* The
collaboration between Rodgers and lyricist Stephen Sondheim turned
so acrimonious that both men refrained from writing for Broadway again until the next decade. It is unfortunate that Rodgers and
Sondheim later spoke disparagingly of this score, because they both
did first-rate work. The story of an American spinster (Elizabeth
Allen) vacationing in Venice and sabotaging her own romance with a
handsome local (Sergio Franchi) was a downer, but classy and packed
with heart. Although a tough sell, this show awaits rediscovery by the
right set of talents.

Champion: "When the Sparklers Light the Sky"

After serving as the Tony-winning director-choreographer of the
1947 revue *Lend an Ear,* Gower Champion spent the next decade pursuing movie stardom at MGM with his wife and dance partner Marge.
The collapse of the studio system in the mid-1950s spelled the end
of original movie musicals, so Champion aimed for a new career as
a director in musical theatre. With a background in ballet and ballroom dancing, he helped make the director-choreographer the *auteur*
or primary storyteller of the musical stage. Every element not only
served the story, but did so in the context of the director's vision.
Robbins and Fosse had already begun this redefinition but Champion
took it to a new level with five consecutive innovative hits.

Bye Bye Birdie (1960, 607 performances) was a youthful farce
about the furor caused when Elvis-like rock star Conrad Birdie
(Dick Gautier) marks his induction into the army by giving one of
his teenage fans a farewell kiss on *The Ed Sullivan Show.* First time
librettist Michael Stewart (1929–1987) constructed a fast-paced script
brimming with fresh humor. With Conrad's "One Last Kiss" and
"Honestly Sincere," the new songwriting team of composer Charles

Strouse (1928–) and lyricist Lee Adams (1924–) brought the sound of early rock and roll to Broadway, framed in an otherwise traditional Broadway score. As the egotistical Conrad's neurotic manager Albert Peterson, Dick Van Dyke (1924–) introduced "Put on a Happy Face," and sang "Baby, Talk to Me" to Chita Rivera, who played his loving assistant-girlfriend. Aside from dealing with Conrad, Albert must learn how to stand up to his overbearing mother, played with relish by Kaye Medford. As the girl who wins the chance to kiss Conrad, ingénue Susan Watson (1938–) sang "One Boy" and became an immediate Broadway favorite. Champion put the youthful ensemble into action in "The Telephone Hour," capturing teen after-school gossip in the pre–cell phone age. The show and Champion received Tonys, as did Van Dyke, who repeated his role in a 1963 film version that turned into a vehicle for teen movie star Ann Margaret.

Champion and Stewart took a very different approach with *Carnival* (1961, 719 performances), which borrowed its heartwarming story of a naïve girl learning about love and life while working as the human costar of a puppet show in a rundown French circus from MGM's 1953 film *Lili*. There was a simple unit set, eliminating the need for conventional set changes and allowing a continuous, almost cinematic flow of action. By sending roustabouts and circus performers into the audience, Champion turned the entire auditorium into a performing area. As Lili, petite soprano Anna Maria Alberghetti required the then-unprecedented assistance of electronic amplification, but she made Lili's crucial interplay with the puppets believable, and her performance of "Love Makes the World Go Round" was a musical highlight of composer-lyricist Bob Merrill's (1921–1998) score. As Paul, the embittered puppeteer who falls in love with Lili, Jerry Orbach made his Broadway debut, introducing the lyrical ballad "Her Face."

Carnival marked Champion's first collaboration with producer David Merrick, a frequently contentious relationship that both men realized was to their mutual advantage. They also worked together on *Hello, Dolly!* (1964, 2,884 performances), a musical version of Thornton Wilder's comedy *The Matchmaker* with a book by Stewart and score by composer-lyricist Jerry Herman (1931–). Herman's songs had a fresh, contemporary Broadway sound deftly laced with 1890s period flavor. Impoverished widow Dolly Gallagher Levi is a professional busybody, arranging the lives of others for a fee. She decides to rearrange her own life by marrying the gruff but wealthy widower Horace Vandergelder (David Burns), and manages to simultaneously marry off Vanderguilder's niece and shop assistants. With its resourceful widow, multiple couples, and a climactic sequence in a big city restaurant, this material bore a superficial resemblance to its 1890s ancestor *A Trip to Chinatown*.

This project was originally conceived as a vehicle for Ethel Merman, but after suffering a burst blood vessel in her throat during *Gypsy*, she would not take on another demanding role. Carol Channing gave a career-defining performance as Dolly Gallagher Levi, the manipulative widow who brings together various couples while plotting her own marriage to millionaire widower Horace Vandergelder (David Burns). Charles Nelson Reilly played Vandergelder's shop assistant Cornelius, introducing "It Only Takes a Moment" and the ensemble "Put on Your Sunday Clothes." Channing led the cast in "Before the Parade Passes By," which Champion used to fill the stage with the panoply of a Victorian parade. Every person and object was choreographed, including the set pieces, all synchronized to give the show a smooth cinematic flow.

Champion's staging of the title song took the art of manipulating audience reaction to new heights. The wait staff of the elegant Harmonia Gardens Restaurant, informed that their beloved Dolly is returning after an absence of several years, bursts into a dizzy "Waiter's Gallop" featuring whirling tables, flying roasts, and dueling shish kebabs. With the excitement at fever pitch, a brassy fanfare brings Dolly down a central staircase, greeting the boys by name. They take up the chorus of "Hello, Dolly," crowing "it's so nice to have you back where you belong." Dolly leads the celebration out onto a semicircular runway surrounding the orchestra pit, reaching beyond the proscenium to bring the action into the auditorium. Over the years many ladies would star in Champion's staging, and the results would be amazingly consistent. As the number proceeded from a solo strut to a group cakewalk, each variation drew applause as if on cue. The number ends with the leading lady in mid-runway, the waiters arranged in a tableaux of adoration. It was perhaps the most surefire showstopper of all time, one that would work with any star so long as the choreography remained. Even the dullest audiences hollered for an encore, which Champion staged to segue right back into Dolly's pursuit of Vandergelder.

Merrick took malicious pleasure in tormenting his creative teams, and *Hello, Dolly!*'s troubled tryout found him at his most malevolent. Arguments flared, firings were threatened, and other composers were brought in to augment the score—Bob Merrill is said to have contributed "Elegance," and Charles Strouse and Lee Adams had at least some hand in "Before the Parade Passes By." But Champion pulled the pieces together, and the show opened to rave reviews. Jazz legend Louis Armstrong released a chart-topping single of the title song, adding to the demand for tickets. *Hello, Dolly!* won the Tony for Best Musical, with Channing honored as Best Actress in a Musical and Champion winning for his direction and choreography. For leading ladies "of a certain age," Dolly was a dream come true. Channing was followed by Ginger Rogers, Betty Grable, Martha Raye, and others before Merrick recast the show as an all-black production with Pearl Bailey in the lead. With the civil rights controversies of the 1960s at their peak, this was seen as a bold move, and it paid off handsomely as Bailey's jazzy, improvisational style packed the St. James for almost two years. At one point, Merrick wanted Jack Benny as a drag Dolly with George Burns as Horace, a bizarre yet tantalizing possibility that never got beyond the discussion stage. Ethel Merman finally stepped in to the role originally written for her, extending her stay until *Hello, Dolly!* became the longest running Broadway musical—a distinction it would hold for less than a year. It even outlived an overblown 1969 film version starring a miscast Barbra Streisand. Channing starred in a series of national tours, keeping Champion's original staging before the public through 1997 and by her own count racking up more than 5,000 performances in the role.

Gower Champion teamed up with the creators of *The Fantasticks* for a comparatively simple project with one set and a cast of two. Since the two performers were Mary Martin and Robert Preston, *I Do! I Do!* (1966, 560 performances) merited national attention. Based on the hit play *The Fourposter*, it was the story of a couple living through a long marriage, all set in a simple bedroom. The musical added a warm and amusing score by Harvey Schmidt and Tom Jones. Martin later wrote in her autobiography, "Gower plotted that production like a wartime invasion—every movement, every prop, every second." A swirl of accessories and activity kept the single set alive with color and movement, and Champion even had the bed zoom about in one number. But it was Martin and Preston who made the show. Whether glowing with affection in

"My Cup Runneth Over," bickering in "The Honeymoon Is Over" or improvising a gleeful saxophone-violin duet while contemplating what life will be like "When the Kids are Married," the two stars were at their peak. Preston won a Tony, and Champion proved he could work magic even on an intimate scale. The two stars even made the cover of *Life* magazine doing a barefoot soft-shoe. However, while *I Do! I Do!* was a clear-cut hit, there was no film version, and none of the songs made it onto the pop charts. The once-automatic results of success on Broadway were no longer to be taken for granted.

Also-Rans of the Early 1960s

A number of successful Broadway musicals faced the same fate in the early to mid-1960s—no top-selling songs and no film version. Before *I Do! I Do!*, Schmidt and Jones had already reached Broadway with *110 in the Shade* (1963, 331 performances), a musical version of N. Richard Nash's play *The Rainmaker* that cast Inga Swenson as Lizzie, the spinster torn between her feelings for the reliable Sheriff File (Stephen Douglass) and the charismatic con man Starbuck (Robert Horton), who simultaneously offers romance and a magical cure for a crippling drought. An outstanding score overcame the sometimes dreary setting, and although the production had a profitable run, *110 in the Shade* never got the widespread attention it deserved. A 2007 Broadway revival made questionable changes—as originally written, the show is a gem.

Jule Styne reteamed with frequent collaborators Betty Comden and Adolph Green for *Do Re Mi* (1960, 400 performances), a straight-forward musical comedy about crooks trying for big bucks in the pop music industry. Phil Silvers played a small-time hoodlum, and Nancy Walker played his long-suffering wife—a duo guaranteed to win laughs, which they did in scene after hilarious scene. The score was a winner, including the romantic hit "Make Someone Happy" introduced by handsome baritone John Reardon. Silvers got the musical tour de force of his career in the schizophrenic "Late, Late Show," and Walker assured her husband that she enjoyed their life of "Adventure." But big laughs, great reviews, and a nearly yearlong run were not enough to pull this one into the profit column. Producers were discovering that ever-increasing weekly running costs could financially sink a high quality project.

Producer Harold Prince had spent years as George Abbott's assistant, so it came as no surprise when Prince chose to both produce and direct *She Loves Me* (1963, 302 performances), a musical based on a European play that MGM had already turned into the 1940 film comedy *The Shop Around the Corner* and the 1947 screen musical *In the Good Old Summertime*. Joe Masteroff's libretto set the action in 1930s Budapest, where perfumery shop manager Georg Nowack (Daniel Massey) and clerk Amalia Balash (Barbara Cook) feud constantly, unaware that each is the other's treasured secret pen pal. Composer Jerry Bock and lyricist Sheldon Harnick evoked the period while capturing exquisite character moments, such as the giddy title song and Cook's soprano showpiece "Ice Cream." Mostly excellent reviews and a healthy run were not enough, and this charmer closed at a loss. A favorite with college and regional theatres, *She Loves Me* developed a devoted fan base and has enjoyed acclaimed revivals on Broadway and the West End—but inexplicably remains "caviar to the million."

Noël Coward worked on three frustrating projects in fairly quick succession. He designed *Sail Away* (1961, 167 performances) as a throwback to the lighthearted musical comedies of an earlier time, with the acerbic Elaine Stritch (1925–) starring as cruise director of a luxury liner. Witty songs like "Why Do the Wrong People Travel (When the Right People Stay Back Home?)" could not make up for uneven casting and a libretto that never really jelled. A somewhat revised 1962 West End version did only slightly better, running 252 performances. *The Girl Who Came to Supper* (1963, 112 performances) was an adaptation of Terrence Rattigan's comedy *The Sleeping Prince*, with José Ferrer as a Grand Duke romancing an American chorus girl (Florence Henderson) in London during George V's coronation festivities in 1912. The show was thrown off balance by a music hall–style medley that hefty comedienne Tessie O'Shea turned into a showstopper. Superficial similarities to *My Fair Lady* led to unfortunate comparisons, and the production closed at a steep loss. The cast recording preserves Coward's fine score, as does his private demo recording, which has been available in various formats.

Although others adapted Coward's *Blithe Spirit* into the musical *High Spirits* (1964, 376 performances), he was so pleased with the results that he agreed to direct. The sheer physical demands of

musical theatre had changed since Coward's musical heyday, so
Gower Champion had to be called in to bring the production up to
speed. Tammy Grimes won praise as the ghostly Elvira, and Bea Lillie
delighted her many fans as the eccentric psychic Madame Arcati, but
the costly production failed to pay off its investors. Coward never
worked on another new musical, but spent his remaining years enjoying well-deserved praise for his contributions to the theatre. Within
a few years, Lillie suffered a series of debilitating strokes. Unable to
walk or speak, this brilliant comedienne endured for more than two
wordless decades before dying in 1989 at age 94.

Just how long could a Broadway show run and still lose money?
That all depended on how the money was handled. *Golden Boy* (1964,
569 performances) had been a 1937 play by Clifford Odets about a
musician becoming a prizefighter in order to support his family. Casting the popular Sammy Davis Jr. (1925–1990) in the title role guaranteed publicity and box office appeal, so a chilly critical reception
did not prevent a year-plus run. But inexperienced producers failed
to keep a watchful eye on operating costs, and *Golden Boy* did not
return its investment. This was another musical caught in the pattern
of a good run, no hit songs, and no movie adaptation.

Alan Jay Lerner had found the years after *Camelot* difficult. A serial
husband (married eight times) and a prescription drug addict plagued by
insecurity, he found it increasingly difficult to launch new projects. He
began collaborating with Richard Rodgers on a musical about a girl with
ESP, but endless postponements led Rodgers to withdraw. Burton Lane
stepped in. He had worked with Lerner in Hollywood years before, and
knew that Alan went through contrasting periods of relentless dedication and maddening inactivity while writing a new score. Two years
later, Lerner and Lane's *On a Clear Day You Can See Forever* (1965, 273
performances) began a tortured pre-Broadway tryout. The long delay
had forced other talents to drop out, including Gower Champion. Robert Lewis, who had directed the original *Brigadoon*, took over, bringing
little imagination to the project. Barbara Harris triumphed as a girl with
extrasensory powers, and movie star Louis Jourdan was her amorous
therapist. When it became clear that Jourdan was not up to the musical
demands, he was replaced by John Cullum (1930–), whose powerful
baritone made the title song a highlight. The score dazzled but Lerner's
libretto didn't, and he was not up to fixing it. The critics shrugged, and

a delightful cast recording eventually perpetuated the mistaken belief that this show was an underrated jewel. Subsequent productions and a muddled 1970 film version starring Barbra Streisand have verified that *On a Clear Day* is better heard and not seen.

A steady stream of new musicals were coming in, doing reasonably well, and then fading away. Such middling successes had once enjoyed a long life after Broadway. Had something changed in American popular culture?

Sunrise, Sunset: A Glorious Finale

Things were most certainly changing, but in the mid-1960s Broadway was still too busy to notice. Between 1964 and 1966, six new American musical blockbusters appeared. Each ran for more than a thousand performances and became a lasting international favorite. Beginning with the aforementioned *Hello, Dolly!*, all six centered on irrepressible characters who carry on with life despite all odds. It was not until a few years had passed that anyone realized this unprecedented whirlwind of profitable creativity had actually been the artistic sunset of the post-*Oklahoma!* era.

Three months after the triumph of *Hello, Dolly!*, producer Herbert Ross was struggling with a musical based on the life of his mother-in-law, the late Fanny Brice. As previews went badly, members of the creative team came and went, and the insecure temperament of leading lady Barbra Streisand led to ugly scenes both on and off stage. In the end it took an uncredited Jerome Robbins to get *Funny Girl* (1964, 1,348 performances) into working order. The tempestuous love story of Brice and con man Nick Arnstein had to be toned down because the real Arnstein was still alive and ready to sue, but the show did manage to evoke the glory of Ziegfeld's *Follies* and enshrine Brice's legend. It also proved a star-making vehicle for the mercurial Streisand, who seemed incapable of giving the same caliber of performance from one night to the next. The show's success was secured by its wonderful Jule Styne–Bob Merrill score, which was packed with winners, including the Streisand solos "Don't Rain on My Parade" and "People." The latter did poorly in early previews, but as Streisand's soulful single of it climbed the charts, it gradually became a showstopper. Kay Medford won acclaim as Brice's wry Jewish mother. As Nick, Sydney Chaplin had such a miserable experience costarring with Streisand (there were rumors of a roller-coaster offstage affair) that he never appeared on Broadway again. The 1968 screen version brought Streisand an Academy Award and movie stardom, as well as the lasting enmity of costar Omar Sharif (there were rumors of a roller-coaster offscreen affair).

In the months following the successful doctoring of *Funny Girl*, Robbins worked on a musical based on Sholom Aleichem's stories of Tevye, an Orthodox Jewish milkman trying to raise a family and survive oppression in a Tsarist Russian ghetto, or *shtetl*. Although many feared that *Fiddler on the Roof* (1964, 3,242 performances) would prove "too Jewish" for general audiences, Joseph Stein's masterful character-specific libretto struck a universal chord. Jerry Bock's music rooted the score in ethnic color, and Sheldon Harnick's lyrics expressed sentiments common to all, such as the bittersweet emotions of parents seeing their children grow up in "Sunrise, Sunset," or impoverished young girls accepting the blunt truth behind their romantic dreams in "Matchmaker, Matchmaker." Robbins created striking choreographic images, beginning with the title character, a Fiddler who plays a tune while precariously balancing on a slanted rooftop, much as the villagers of Anatevka live precariously beneath the constant threat of oppression. In a perfect blend of staging and song, "Tradition" introduced all of the players in this saga, dancing in a circle that embodies their little community, which is their only world. After a traditional orthodox wedding, the men join in a frenzied dance of celebration, balancing wine bottles on their hats—a thrilling moment that would be recreated in all future professional and amateur productions. As the irrepressible Tevya, Zero Mostel gave a towering performance, but his comic instincts led to so much disruptive, unrepentant scene-stealing during the first few months of the run that producer Hal Prince did not renew Mostel's contract. The show thrived without its original star, its writing more potent than any actor's ego. In 1971, it surpassed *Hello, Dolly!* and the comedy *Life with Father* to become the longest running Broadway production of any kind. That same year, it reached the big screen in a handsome adaptation starring Israeli actor Chaim Topol, who had played Tevya in the acclaimed London production and would continue appearing in revivals right into the next century.

The appeal of *Fiddler on the Roof* knows no boundaries and no time limits. Wherever it has been produced in the decades since its premiere, audiences have relished Tevya's "If I Were a Rich Man," empathized with his troubles, and found inspiration in his constant refusal to give up. In the final scene, Robbins had the circle of Anatevka form and disband for the final time, and as Tevya led the remnants of his family on the long trek to America, the enigmatic Fiddler followed. Some see the Fiddler as a symbol of tradition, but he actually represents the indomitable human spirit that keeps Tevya going in the face of whatever difficulties life throws his way. Everyone might like to have a friend like Dolly Levi, but prays that they can have the strength of Tevya. That is why *Fiddler on the Roof* has served as a mirror in which people from many cultures see reflections of their own unique experiences. On its opening night in Tokyo, a young man expressed surprise to librettist Joseph Stein that the show had succeeded in America, saying, "It's so Japanese."

Don Quixote has been the basis for ballets, grand operas, operettas, plays, and films, but no adaptation has matched the popularity of *Man of La Mancha* (1965, 2,328 performances). Librettist Dale Wasserman, composer Mitch Leigh, and lyricist Joe Darion set this one-act musical drama in the dungeon of the Spanish Inquisition, where Miguel De Cervantes (Richard Kiley) must convince his fellow prisoners not to destroy the manuscript of his novel, so he enacts it, with their help. Cervantes dons full makeup and becomes Alonso, an aging seventeenth-century country squire who convinces himself that he is Don Quixote, a medieval knight. His perceives an inn to be a castle, and proclaims its slovenly kitchen slut Aldonza (Joan Diener) to be a lady he calls "Dulcinea." Forced back into reality by family and friends, Quixote dies with his dream of a better world, but not until that dream has been instilled in others. Kiley gave a searing performance, including a soaring rendition of "The Impossible Dream." Diener's sexy physique and operatic vocals made her the ideal Aldonza, and she repeated the role in various international productions, at least in part because she was married to director Albert Marre, whose dark, energetic staging became closely identified with the show. Both stars would appear in Broadway revivals, but audiences embraced this show with any capable cast. Tonys went to Kiley, Marre, the composers, set designer Howard Bay, and the show itself for Best Musical. Critics have consistently attacked this show for being a meager echo of its source material. However valid those complaints may be, *Man of La Mancha* has been an inspiration and source of pleasure to millions of theatregoers, and is still frequently performed—this despite an egregious 1972 film version.

Patrick Dennis (a.k.a. Edward Everett Tanner III) struck gold with his best-selling comic novel *Auntie Mame*, but had no involvement in the successful dramatization by Jerome Lawrence and Robert E. Lee, which gave the title character more of a heart and proved a potent 1950s stage and screen vehicle for Rosalind Russell. The playwrights had Russell in mind when they began work on a musical adaptation, but Jerry Herman's score for *Mame* (1966, 1,508 performances) required a much stronger singer. The composer hoped to hire Judy Garland, but by that time her emotional and chemical dependencies made appearing in a prolonged Broadway run unthinkable. Herman then set his hopes on Angela Lansbury (1925–), a respected Hollywood character actress with solid stage credentials. It took several auditions to convince the producers that Lansbury was the best choice. She became a top rank musical star playing the unflappable eccentric who liberates her orphaned nephew Patrick from a stodgy upbringing, urging him to always embrace the unconventional and celebrate the banquet of life. Herman's title tune, brilliantly choreographed by Onna White, became an immediate hit, as did Mame's remorseful ballad "If He Walked into My Life." Director Gene Saks (1921–) staged the complex story with refreshing clarity, and uneven reviews did nothing to dampen audience enthusiasm for the show and its vibrant score. Beatrice Arthur (1923–) triumphed as Mame's best friend, the acidic actress Vera Charles, sharing the showstopper "Bosom Buddies" with Lansbury. Both actresses received Tony awards, as did ten-year-old Frankie Michaels, whose scene-stealing performance as little Patrick made him the youngest person ever to win a Tony. Lucille Ball was a disastrous choice to star in the 1974 film version, which is partially saved by a strong supporting cast, including the formidably hilarious Arthur. Like *Man of La Mancha*, *Mame* has suffered the scorn of critics, but has proven a solid audience pleaser for more than four decades.

Jerry Herman has not exactly been scorned by critics, but he has often been taken for granted. Herman has classified his own work as "the simple, hum-able showtune," and it is true that he is heir to a long tradition that Irving Berlin inherited from George M. Cohan, who had picked it up from Harrigan and Braham. Herman's real strength is in using conventional theatrical song forms to express a character's emotions. Audiences enjoy these songs to the extent that they recognize the feelings in question: welcoming a long lost friend ("Hello, Dolly"), dressing for a night on the town ("Put on Your Sunday Clothes"), introducing someone to a world of wonder ("Open a New Window"), or second guessing the raising of a child ("If He Walked into My Life"). Herman is, first and foremost, a musical dramatist. This gifted songwriter would never try to reform the musical theatre; he settled for creating some of its most tuneful, heartfelt expressions of the human condition. There has always been a snobbish element that views melody and sentiment with suspicion. Happily, that element has never been able to overrule the tens of millions of people who have enjoyed *Hello, Dolly!*; *Mame*; and the rest of Herman's best.

The final title in Broadway's mid-1960's blockbuster sextet is *Cabaret* (1966, 1,165 performances). Librettist Joe Masteroff worked closely with composer John Kander and lyricist Fred Ebb to adapt Christopher Isherwood's drama *I Am a Camera*, the story of a young American writer who falls in love with a cabaret singer and encounters raffish chorus girls, Nazi storm troopers, and other members of Berlin's demimonde in the early 1930s. Kander and Ebb's score was solid Broadway gold, including the riotous opening number "Wilkommen" and the hit title song. The often harsh material was in many ways ahead of its time, but director-producer Harold Prince's polished production gave the show tremendous appeal. Lotte Lenya was on hand as Fraulein Schneider, a landlady caught between her love for a Jewish shopkeeper and the rise of the Nazis. Altogether, *Cabaret* won eight Tonys, including best musical, score, director, and choreographer. Diminutive tenor Joel Grey (1932–) gave an electrifying performance as the leering Master of Ceremonies, a role he repeated in the acclaimed 1972 film version—joining Yul Brynner and Rex Harrison as the only actors to receive both a Tony and an Academy Award for the same musical role. In that film, director Bob Fosse focused the audience's attention on the Emcee and Sally Bowles, making a dark show into an even darker film. This interpretation would color all future revivals on both sides of the Atlantic, including a radical and acclaimed reassessment of the show at the century's end.

Kander and Ebb's compositions are often classified by one of their later song titles, "Razzle Dazzle." They certainly understood the sound and feeling of "show biz," which is so much a part of their work in *Cabaret*. But this team used show business as a metaphor for life, and turned razzmatazz into a means of expressing and rising above ugly realities. The catchy, up-tempo "Cabaret" is delivered by a woman who has just endured a painful abortion and a shattered romance, and damn it all she's going to keep singing even as her world sinks into Nazi oppression. Over the course of a forty-year collaboration, Kander and Ebb would write many songs that kept characters vamping through bittersweet moments. As their frequent interpreter Liza Minnelli put it, "The greatest thing about Kander and Ebb? You sing their songs, and you feel better."

A seventh show that became a lasting part of the international repertory but did not break the 1,000-performance mark was *Sweet Charity* (1966, 608 performances), adapted from Federico Fellini's film *Nights of Cabiria*. Gwen Verdon starred as a dance hall girl who keeps getting burned in her search for love, but by curtain fall is living "hopefully ever after." The Cy Coleman–Dorothy Fields score managed a tuneful combination of mid-1960s rock and the traditional showtune sound, and Bob Fosse's Tony-winning choreography turned several numbers into iconic moments: Charity's jubilant strut during "If They Could See Me Now," the raunchy poses of the dance hall girls calling out "Hey, Big Spender (Spend a Little Time with Me)," and the pompous pretension of the "Rich Man's Frug." Fosse re-created his dances for a 1969 screen version starring Shirley MacLaine, and the show would be revived regularly in years to come. Its lasting popularity is due to Fosse, as well as a fine comic libretto by Neil Simon. But *Sweet Charity* did something none of the members of "The 1000+ Performance Club" could claim—it recognized the existence of rock music.

It is no wonder that decades later these shows remain among the most frequently performed stage musicals. They speak to the heart of human experience: unique personalities seeking love in a harsh world, overcoming societal barriers, and ultimately affirming the triumph of the human spirit. They were the last great accomplishments of a fading era.

The World Turned Upside Down

For more than a decade, most Broadway composers had valiantly ignored rock and roll, convinced that it was a passing phase. And pass it did, followed by more vociferous variations. By the mid-1960s, young people were grooving to a pounding hard-rock beat, and Broadway, "The Main Stem" of popular entertainment, suddenly found itself demoted to being a cultural side street. There was no single dramatic event to mark the change. Some noticed it when pop radio music stations began switching to an all-rock format, making it virtually impossible for songs from hit musicals to reach a widespread listening audience. Many performers certainly noticed the change when musical theatre jobs became scarce. The days when anyone with good health, a dependable professional reputation, and a fair dose of talent could count on regular theatrical employment evaporated, and actors who occasionally worked as waiters turned into waiters who occasionally took time off to act. By 1968, Jack Poggi's study of *Theatre in America* (Cornell University Press) calculated that only three percent of New York City's professional actors were earning more than $2,500 a year from stage work.

The change really hit home when major Broadway musicals became no more than local news for New Yorkers. *The Happy Time* (1968, 286 performances) brought together the director-choreographer of *Hello, Dolly!*, one of the stars of *Camelot*, and the composers of *Cabaret* to tell the story of a world-famous photographer who causes an uproar when he visits his family in a small French Canadian town. Gower Champion used blown-up photographic backdrops to frame the action in an innovative high-tech production, and Robert Goulet bathed an evocative Kander and Ebb score in his black velvet baritone. But the songs were rarely heard anywhere outside of the show's theatre, and critics refused to overlook a terminally dull libretto. Despite Tony awards for Champion and Goulet, the costly show closed after running seven unprofitable months. *Darling of the Day* (1968, 31 performances) opened that same month to mostly positive reviews, boasting an exceptional score by Jule Styne, brilliant lyrics by E. Y. Harburg, and movie star Vincent Price as an Edwardian artist masquerading as a valet to escape unwelcome adulation. British soprano Patricia Routledge gave such a brilliant comic performance that she received the Tony for Best Actress in a Musical, but the production came and went within five weeks. Angela Lansbury returned to Broadway in *Dear World* (1969, 132 performances), a musical adaptation of Giradoux's comedy *The Madwoman of Chaillot* with music and lyrics by the creators of *Mame*. Lansbury won a second Tony for Best Actress in a Musical, but the only people who knew it were the ones watching the Tony award broadcast. Lambasted by the critics for a weak book that tried to make a quirky, intimate French play into a big Broadway musical, *Dear World* quickly ran through its advance sale and closed at a loss.

Only a few years before, the success or failure of these high-profile musicals would have commanded international attention. By the late 1960s, almost no one outside of the New York metropolitan area got to hear about them. The front page of *Life* magazine now touted the latest rock stars or covered America's deepening, ill-advised involvement in Vietnam's long civil war. That war gradually polarized the nation, digging an irrevocable chasm between generations. Popular music now focused on a youthful audience that disapproved of the war and expressed their displeasure through radical fashions and music filled with a spirit of protest. With Broadway no longer a source of hit songs, musicals became non-news, the occasional entertainment of an older generation.

Now and then a show managed to rate widespread interest. When the most famous actress in the English-speaking world announced that she was going to make her musical debut in *Coco* (1969, 332 performances), attention was paid. Katharine Hepburn played real-life fashion legend Coco Chanel, talk-singing her songs with a gutsy brio. The plot was set in 1953, with the aging designer looking back on her colorful life while trying to restart her stalled career. Alan Jay Lerner's book and lyrics provided some stellar moments, but the basic story proved less than compelling, as did most of Andre Previn's melodies. René Auberjonois won a Tony as Coco's effeminate assistant Sebastian, and audiences flocked to cheer Hepburn's bravura performance. Investors saw a small profit, but the show closed weeks after Hepburn left the cast and has not been professionally produced since. There were no other stars quite like Kate the Great; without her on hand, who or what would make this uniquely tailored vehicle worth seeing?

"The Age of Aquarius"

Broadway's old guard may have lost their milieu, but they still had their sense of humor. When confronted by a hippie protestor on a college campus, veteran lyricist-librettist P. G. Wodehouse quipped,

"Why don't you get a haircut? You look like a chrysanthemum." But it took more than quips to fill theatres, and with established directors and authors uncertain about how to reach their once-adoring public, the way was open for new talent and new ideas. Since old ideas about what was good no longer applied, being new was enough to merit professional attention.

The first rock musical hits were born off-Broadway. *Your Own Thing* (1968, 933 performances) reworked the gender-switching plot of Shakespeare's comedy *Twelfth Night*, telling the story of a rock band named "Apocalypse." After two and a half years at the Lower East Side's tiny Orpheum Theatre, the show toured and soon sank into oblivion.

A far more influential hit had made its first bow two months earlier at the New York Shakespeare Theatre Festival. Large numbers of young Americans "hip" enough to oppose the war and who expressed their dissent through casual fashions, hard-rock music, experimental drug use, open sexual attitudes, and long hair were being labeled as "hippies." *Hair* was an "American Tribal-Love Rock Musical," a free-form, definition-smashing celebration of the hippie counterculture. Librettist-lyricists Gerome Ragni and James Rado came up with a shadow of a plot involving a young man who revels in rock and rebellion until he gets a draft notice from the army. He falls in with a tribe-like group of hippies that sings about such pointed social issues as poverty, race relations, illegal drugs, Vietnam, and free love—and that's it. An explosion of anger, protest, and profanity, this "happening" had the advantage of a varied and melodious score by composer Galt MacDermot (1928–). After eight weeks, the production moved uptown to an abandoned discotheque, then underwent extensive revisions before moving to Broadway's Biltmore Theatre (1968, 1,750 performances). Much of the negligible plot was excised, and new songs were added, along with a nude scene that had most of the "tribe" doff their clothes for a matter of seconds. The promise of nudity brought in the customers, most of whom were either bemused or disarmed. "Good Morning, Starshine" and "Let the Sunshine In" became chart-topping hits, and "Aquarius" became an anthem for the times, proclaiming a peaceful new age "when love will steer the stars." As *Hair* became a sold-out hit, Broadway's establishment, in the parlance of the time, "freaked out." Shut out by the Tonys and most other major awards (MacDermot's score received a Drama Desk nod), the show ran for nearly five years and sent "tribes" touring across the United States and Europe. For a precious if somewhat noisy moment, Broadway and popular music were once more on common ground. For better or worse, it didn't last.

At least the show that beat out *Hair* for the Tony was a Pulitzer Prize–winning phenomenon in its own right. Few saw any commercial possibilities in a musical based on the debates that led to the signing of the Declaration of Independence, but former history teacher Sherman Edwards's dramatic score for *1776* (1969, 1,217 performances) melded perfectly with a libretto by Peter Stone (1930–2003). While some liberties were taken with strict fact, the show presented familiar historical events and icons in a heated, compelling clash of ideas and personalities. America's founding fathers, long enshrined on currency and in textbooks, were depicted as passionate, fallible human beings. William Daniels led the cast as determined rebel John Adams, with Ken Howard (1944–) as a tall, pensive Thomas Jefferson and the great Howard Da Silva as a beguiling Ben Franklin. As Jefferson's wife Martha, Texas native Betty Buckley (1947–) made an exciting Broadway debut, singing "He Plays the Violin" with a powerful belt that would become familiar to musical theatre lovers over the next few decades. With the exception of Buckley, most of the leads appeared in the excellent 1972 film version.

David Merrick offered a more conventional response to the changing times. Emulating the great producers of days gone by, he picked a likely comic source—the hit 1960 motion picture *The Apartment*—and then hired top talents to adapt it. Comic playwright Neil Simon wrote the libretto, and popular songwriters Burt Bacharach and Hal David handled the music and lyrics. The result was *Promises, Promises* (1968, 1,281 performances), which starred Jerry Orbach as Chuck, an ambitious bachelor who loans his apartment to his bosses for extramarital trysts in exchange for quick corporate promotions. When Fran (Jill O'Hara), a waitress in the company restaurant, is romantically dumped by one of the executives, she attempts suicide in Chuck's apartment—and this unlikely introduction leads to love. To capture the latest pop music sound, Bacharach got Merrick to install the first sophisticated sound system (equalizers, echo chambers, etc.) used in a Broadway musical. The score included "What Do You Get

When You Fall in Love," which became a chart-topping hit. Orbach's charismatic performance earned rave reviews and a Tony for Best Actor in a Musical. Choreographer Michael Bennett (1943–1987) won attention with his energetic musical staging, most notably a rocking dance routine for "Turkey Lurkey Time."

While some theatre professionals found reassurance in these main-stream hits, neither *1776* nor *Promises, Promises* ran as long as *Oh! Calcutta!* (1968, 1,922 performances), a small off-Broadway revue that moved uptown and ran for more than four years thanks to lots of nudity. Few would ever quote the skits written by such notables as Samuel Beckett, John Lennon, and Sam Shepard, and even fewer paid any attention to the music by the Open Window, a rock group that included the future creator of P. D. Q. Bach, Peter Schickele. Ticket buyers who were too timid to visit Times Square's seedy porn par-lors could feel perfectly respectable watching comely Equity actors drop their robes and display their naughty bits. (The ghosts of those who had once condemned *The Black Crook* or Lydia Thompson must have been howling in their graves!) Devised by theatre critic Ken-neth Tynan, *Oh! Calcutta!* did not to take itself too seriously. During one particularly bouncy scene, a cast member proclaimed, "Gee, this makes *Hair* look like *The Sound of Music*!" Four years after the origi-nal production of *Oh! Calcutta!* closed, a revival settled in at the Edi-son Theatre for an astounding 5,959 performances. It didn't amount to much as a musical, but it raked in millions.

With the theatregoing public sending contradictory signals, most stage composers had no idea what to try next. The inevitable crop of doom merchants insisted that the Broadway musical was dead. Luck-ily, the 1970s would bring more than a few "Little Things" that would prove to be "Singular Sensations." (If these allusions make you say, "God, I think I got it," bravo! If not, fear not—you soon will.) The Broadway musical wasn't dead; it was just preparing for war.

14

New Directions (1970–1979) — "Vary My Days"

By the 1970s, the Times Square theatre district had become saturated with seedy strip clubs, adult bookshops, illegal drugs, and prostitution. Those who worked in the area rubbed elbows with the dregs of society. The buildings were poorly maintained, the sidewalks grimy, the once-vaunted theatres of 42nd Street all serving as shabby movie grind houses. Within the mold-covered walls of the New Amsterdam, a shifting crowd of winos, addicts, and truant teens watched a continuous program of second run kung fu films. Next door, a dollar bought a one-on-one session with a go-go girl, who kept going as long as the tips kept flowing. On the streets just to the north where most of the active legitimate theatres stood, violent crime was a daily occurrence—muggings, stabbings, and worse. Vagrants slept in unused doorways, and trash was everywhere, creating a nauseating stench in hot weather. Going to a Broadway show now involved an element of very real danger. Theatregoers returned to the safety of their homes or hotels without lingering. Each night after the final curtain, the Times Square district swiftly became a ghost town.

Broadway's landlords used their own resources to keep the neighborhood alive. The remaining members of the Shubert family had lost control of their theatres to their onetime attorneys, Gerald Schoenfeld and Bernard B. Jacobs. The newly formed Shubert Organization took a page from the company's past and became a proactive producer of plays and musicals. The other major theatre-owning entity, the Messrs. Nederlander, followed suit. At the same time, both companies changed the standard theatre rental agreements, taking a larger share of the dwindling proceeds from the swiftly thinning ranks of independent producers. In Hamlet's words, it was "as if increase of appetite had grown by what it fed on."

In 1973, the newly formed Theatre Development Fund set up a temporary trailer in the middle of Times Square to sell unused tickets at half-price on the day of performance, making it possible for the general public to purchase an orchestra seat for less than ten dollars. The TKTS trailer became a permanent fixture, and theatregoers kept coming—not only because of such incentives, but because Broadway remained a hotbed of creativity. As of this writing, TKTS charges more than fifty dollars for a typical orchestra seat, and its sales account for a hefty percentage of Broadway's annual income.

The 1970s saw a heated three-way battle for stylistic dominance in the musical theatre among rock musicals, concept musicals, and the conventional post-*Oklahoma!* book show. All three subgenres had their strengths and flaws, and each had its champions, with some staggering new talents coming to the forefront. However tough the times were, it turned out from an artistic standpoint to be one of the most exciting decades the musical theatre has known. And in the kind of plot twist most librettists would kill for, just when it seemed that the three-way conflict was settled, yet another type of musical came from across the Atlantic and proved so popular that it wound up dominating Broadway in the final two decades of the twentieth century.

Rock Musicals: "Do You Think You're What You Say You Are?"

Many in the Broadway community had tried to ignore *Hair*, and they might have gotten away with it had it not been for *New York Times* theatre critic Clive Barnes. With a background in dance criticism, Barnes led a new school of theatre critics who were no longer content with commenting on an art form; instead, he wanted to take an active hand in shaping its future. Barnes acclaimed *Hair* as "the first Broadway musical in some time to have the authentic voice of today rather than that of the day before yesterday," and made it his mission to encourage more of the same. The trouble was that *Hair* was so unique, so lacking in formula that it proved impossible for others to follow its example.

Hair's composer Galt MacDermot took a very different tack with *Two Gentlemen of Verona* (1971, 627 performances), a multiracial rock version of Shakespeare's comedy. The book and lyrics by playwright John Guare veered playfully between Elizabethan poetry and pop verse. Like *Hair*, this show was nurtured by Joseph Papp's New York Shakespeare Theatre Festival. After a limited open-air run in Central Park, the show moved to Broadway and received the Tony for Best Musical. Charming in its day, this material has not aged well, and the show is rarely staged today.

MacDermot reunited with librettist Gerome Ragni for *Dude* (1972, 16 performances), a free-form musical that followed ... well, truth be told, it didn't follow much of anything; not even the "happening" format of *Hair*. *Dude*'s title character, jointly portrayed by an adult and an eleven-year-old boy, was seen traveling "the highway of life" without ever really getting anywhere or doing much. The Broadway Theatre was gutted to create an environmental performance space, with the audience sectioned into valleys, foothills, mountains, trees, and treetops. Such gimmicks crossed the fine line between the cool and the pretentious. With preview audiences booing, *Hair* director Tom O'Horgan was called in to take over and, just to be different, he deleted the nude scenes. Critics and audiences reacted with outrage, and the show folded in two weeks. Five weeks after that debacle, MacDermot's *Via Galactica* (1972, 7 performances) proved to be an even quicker and more expensive fiasco. Director Peter Hall from Britain's National Theatre tried to enliven this "space-age musical" about interplanetary travel with a hydraulic spacecraft, trampolines to simulate antigravity, and a curtain made of 375,000 ping-pong balls. Between them, *Dude* and *Via Galactica* lost $1.8 million and, in effect, ended MacDermot's Broadway career. He did try a surprisingly conventional adaptation of William Saroyan's *The Human Comedy* in 1984, which folded after thirteen performances.

It was up to others to successfully exploit the possibilities of the rock musical. Composer Gary Friedman and lyricist Will Holt worked with a team of librettists to build an off-Broadway revue based on poems and essays written by underprivileged ghetto kids. Most of the critics were unimpressed by *The Me Nobody Knows* (1970), but straightforward choreography by Patricia Birch and a rave from Clive Barnes kept the show packed for 208 performances at the Orpheum.

The production then moved to Broadway for an additional 378 performances. With dozens of real-life stories to tell, this show remains a fascinating document of its time, but is so of that time that there is little audience interest in it today.

Director John-Michael Tebelak first conceived a revue-style adaptation of the Christian gospels to fulfill his degree requirement at Carnegie-Mellon. Producers Edgar Lansbury (Angela's brother) and Joseph Beruh commissioned a tuneful rock score by songwriter Stephen Schwartz (1948–), and *Godspell* (1971, 2,645 performances) opened to cool reviews and several years' worth of packed houses. It depicted Christ as a loving, clown-like teacher leading a youthful troupe of disciples through lessons in life and faith. Instead of inspiring controversy, the show was widely embraced for its inoffensive simplicity. "Day by Day" and "Turn Back, O Man" became pop hits, and the opening anthem "Prepare Ye the Way of the Lord" became a fixture in the liturgies of various denominations. Schwartz also included a sweet dose of vaudeville in "All for the Best," a counterpoint showstopper for Jesus (Stephen Nathan) and Judas Iscariot (David Haskell). A pleasant 1973 film version starring Victor Garber did no harm to ticket sales. After 2,118 performances, the producers made the surprising decision to move to Broadway's Broadhurst Theatre in 1976, winning a new round of unimpressed reviews and chalking up an additional 527 performances. Simple to stage, *Godspell* became a budget-friendly favorite at schools, community theatres, and church groups.

Five months after *Godspell*'s successful off-Broadway premiere, director Tom O'Horgan brought a far more elaborate musical version of Christ's passion and death to Broadway. *Jesus Christ Superstar* (1971, 711 performances) was a rock opera by the British songwriting team of composer Andrew Lloyd Webber (1948–) and Tim Rice (1944–). First heard as a best-selling studio concept recording, the score included the hit "I Don't Know How to Love Him," sung by Yvonne Elliman as Mary Magdelene. She repeated her performance in O'Horgan's staging, which used elaborate effects to flesh out the action. The director prefaced the crucifixion by elevating the tortured Christ (Jeff Fenholt) skyward clad in a massive gold lamé cloak that enveloped the entire stage. African-American actor Ben Vereen (1946–) wowed audiences with his fiery portrayal of Judas Iscariot, and the production enjoyed a profitable run. But producer Robert Stigwood (1934–) was not satisfied, and brought a very different staging to London the following season, where it enjoyed a record-setting run of 3,358 performances. Ignored by the Tonys and other major American awards, Lloyd Webber, Rice, and their new form of book musical would be back.

Stephen Schwartz's first Broadway score was for *Pippin* (1972, 1,944 performances), which again blended contemporary sounds with more traditional song forms, including a minstrel cakewalk. In the fanciful book by Roger O. Hirson, Emperor Charlemagne's eldest son tries to find an identity beyond his father's shadow, eventually finding that war, sex, and other popular enticements are no match for the simple joy of raising a family. Ben Vereen served as a narrator whose attempts to lead Pippin through life took on an increasingly menacing tone as the action progressed. In the title role, dramatic actor John Rubenstein (1946–) sang the yearning "Corner of the Sky," and veteran comedienne Irene Ryan closed out a long career leading audiences in a sing-along of "It's Time to Start Living." *Pippin* marked director-choreographer Bob Fosse's return to Broadway after six years devoted to filmmaking. He used dance and minimal settings to create a cinematic flow of action, and his dance numbers included a steamy orgy sequence that raised—at the very least—eyebrows. The show got mostly good reviews, but it took a simple television ad in which Vereen and two dancers offered a smiling soft-shoe routine to inspire heavy ticket sales—the joke being that in performance, that pleasant dance served as an ironic counterpoint to a grisly battle scene. Schwartz and Hirson complained that Fosse took too many liberties with their material, but future productions that adhered to the authors' preferences could not match the imagination or the entertainment value packed into Fosse's conception.

Schwartz's score was not the main attraction of *The Magic Show* (1974, 1,920 performances), and few paid attention to the plot involving an embittered old magician getting outfoxed by a talented newcomer. Rather, the entire production was a vehicle for the brilliant Doug Henning (1947–2000), who could neither sing nor act, but whose inventive magic tricks delighted audiences of all ages. Henning went on to star in a series of popular television specials, and Schwartz became the only theatrical composer who could boast three new musicals that ran beyond 1,900 performances in the 1970s. It would be some time before this versatile composer wrote another hit, but he remained a major figure in musical theatre into the next century.

The most successful rock musical of the decade was *Grease* (1972, 3,388 performances), a traditional musical comedy that revisited the rock and roll sounds of the 1950s. Cocreated by actors Jim Jacobs and Warren Casey, it involved a high school romance between super-pure Sandy Dumbrowski (Carole Demas) and white trash hunk Danny Zukow, played by sexy tenor Barry Bostwick (1946–). The score included the he said/she said ensemble "Summer Nights," the graphic teen boy's car fantasy "Greased Lightning," and the lingo-packed "We Go Together" ("like rama-lama-lama, ka-dingidy-ding-a-dong"). Director Tom Moore and choreographer Patricia Birch created a boisterous, energetic staging. A run at off-Broadway's Eden Theatre did not impress the critics, but audience response led to a quick move to Broadway. Invoking memories of leather jackets, slick-backed hair, and peer pressure to "go all the way," *Grease* had a raunchy, joyous, and surprising multigenerational appeal. The incredibly popular 1978 film version starring Olivia Newton-John and John Travolta actually gave the Broadway box office a boost, and the production ran profitably until 1980, setting a new long-run record. There have been thousands of community and high school productions (many using a bowdlerized version), as well as successful professional revivals on both sides of the Atlantic.

There was a brief vogue of new black musicals with pop/rock-flavored scores. *Purlie* (1970, 690 performances) was an adaptation of Ossie Davis's 1961 comedy about a black preacher finding love and fighting bigotry in the old south. The score was by composer Gary Geld and lyricist Peter Udell—who coauthored the libretto with Davis and Philip Rose. Cleavon Little was irresistible in the title role, and Melba Moore won raves as his beloved Lutiebelle with some death-defying vocal pyrotechnics—both performers received Tonys. *Raisin* (1973, 847 performances) was a faithful adaptation of Lorraine Hansberry's 1959 drama *Raisin in the Sun*. The polished Judd Woldin–Robert Brittan score was less than memorable, but the story of an inner-city black family trying to balance ambition with integrity retained its power. The show earned the Tony for Best Musical, with a well-deserved Best Actress award for the show's indomitable mamma, Virginia Capers. Despite decent runs, both of these productions proved unprofitable. Things turned out far better for *The Wiz* (1975, 1,672 performances), an all-black retelling of *The Wizard of*

Oz. The score by Charlie Smalls brimmed with the urban rhythms of rock and soul, including the infectious "Ease on Down the Road" and the inspirational "Believe in Yourself." Geoffrey Holder's direction and inventive costumes added delightful visual humor, and the cast included Stephanie Mills as Dorothy and the charismatic André De Shields (1946–) in the title role. Ray Bolger was among the present-ers when *The Wiz* walked off with seven Tony awards, including Best Musical. A dreary 1978 movie version starring Diana Ross killed off much of the material's charm, as did a low-budget 1984 revival.

By mid-decade, the rock musical wave collapsed as major projects succumbed to a lack of stagecraft and/or poorly chosen subject matter. *The Lieutenant* (1975, 9 performances) was an American rock opera about the horrific 1968 massacre of 347 Vietnamese civilians at My Lai. This blunt indictment of the dehumanizing effects of war could not attract an audience despite some strong critical support. The most spectacular rock flop was *Rockabye Hamlet* (1976, 7 performances), which staged Shakespeare's tragedy about a fictional Danish prince avenging his royal father's death as a rock concert. The score by Cliff Jones included "He Got It in the Ear," "Your Daddy's Gone Away," and "The Rosencrantz and Guildenstern Boogie." Disgruntled audi-ences laughed when the despairing Ophelia strangled herself with a microphone cord. Bad rock and bad theatre, it closed in a matter of days. The shocker was that this abomination was directed and cho-reographed by Gower Champion. We'll discuss how he came to this bizarre pass a bit later in this chapter.

One rock musical got beyond Broadway failure to become a cultural phenomenon. Richard O'Brien's *The Rocky Horror Show* opened in a London cinema (1973, 2,960 performances), spoofing science-fiction films with an uncompromising hard-rock score. A Broadway pro-duction (1975, 45 performances) got an ice-cold critical reception, but American and British teens turned the 1976 film version into a cult classic, appearing in costume and performing "The Time Warp" and other numbers along with the film during special midnight screenings. The late 1990s brought a slew of revivals, culminating in a high-energy 2000 Broadway staging that ran for a healthy 437 performances.

Another production proved a massive hit by defying convention, and by taking advantage of a new Broadway convention: previews. With pre-Broadway tryout tours becoming prohibitively expensive, many productions now opted to play anywhere from a week to a month's worth of tryout previews in New York. Such was the plan for *Beatlemania* (1977, 1,001 performances). The Beatles had broken up in 1970, and despite tremendous public pressure, John, Paul, George, and Ringo refused to reunite. So someone had the novel idea of staging a Beatles concert using lookalike/soundalike stand-ins. Ads proclaimed it was "Not the Beatles, but an INCREDIBLE simulation!" The results delighted audiences in previews, and the producers, expecting the worst from critics, kept postponing the official opening. When months passed with no premiere, critics published scathing reviews, which had no effect on ticket sales. Altogether, the production ran for 1,011 performances, and touring versions traveled the world until 1983, when the real Beatles took legal action to collect overdue royalties and prevent any further performances. Theatre professionals bristled at *Beatlemania!*, calling it a "tourist attraction"—which it was, to its tremendous profit. But a stage show built out of recycled pop-rock songs? Broadway was not a jukebox, for gosh sakes—at least, not yet.

Concept Musicals: "A Spark to Pierce the Dark"

Five years after Stephen Sondheim's disappointing experience with *Do I Hear a Waltz?* he made his return to Broadway as a composer-lyricist, linked in a creative partnership with producer-director Harold Prince. Both men had extensive experience with the conventional post-*Oklahoma!* musical—central love plot plus auxiliary love plot—and they wanted to try a new approach, focusing on musicals built around a central issue, event, or theme: the single life vs. commitment, a bittersweet reunion, a weekend in the country, a historic culture clash. These "concept musicals" went beyond traditional narrative, breaking the limitations of time, place, and action to simultaneously examine numerous individuals and relationships. Every character has a story to tell, and all of them can comment on and/or illustrate different aspects of the concept. In later years, Prince expressed displeasure with the concept musical label, insisting that the six shows that he did with Sondheim were "unified" or "integrated": accurate terms, but they can be applied to the work of many others, from Offenbach onward. Historian Foster Hirsch has offered another classification, calling the Sondheim-Prince musicals "self-reflexive." Indeed, these shows all involve characters questioning themselves. By any name, these shows offered a new vision at a time when the Broadway musical desperately needed one. In the first two of these shows, they had an important collaborator who would soon take concept musicals even further—choreographer Michael Bennett.

The Prince-Sondheim partnership began with *Company* (1970, 706 performances). Librettist George Furth came up with an original story about Bobby (Dean Jones), a thirty-something bachelor in Manhattan, a city of strangers where "Another Hundred People" just got off of the train. His only close relationships are with five "good and crazy" married couples. They assure him that it's "The Little Things You Do Together" that make relationships work—the tactics you employ, neighbors you annoy, and children you destroy... together. Bobby's thirty-fifth birthday forces him to realize that having many otherwise-attached friends is no replacement for taking the risk of loving one person intensely. He finally resolves to find someone who will make "Being Alive" worthwhile. Playing a man struggling with the idea of marriage proved to be harrowing for Jones, who was undergoing a real-life divorce, and one month into the run he left the show and was replaced by Larry Kert. In an unusually strong ensemble cast, Elaine Stritch was a standout as the cynical alcoholic Joanne, toasting "The Ladies Who Lunch," those jaded women who use a blur of activity to obscure the emptiness of their lives. Michael Bennett's choreography captured the often frenzied pace of life in New York, from the forced jollity of a surprise party to the passion of coitus. As the audience overheard Bobby having a one-night stand with a stewardess, Donna McKechnie danced out "Tick Tock," a one-person lovemaking ballet.

Most critics raved, and *Company* received six Tony awards, including Best Musical and awards for Sondheim, Furth, Prince, and set designer Boris Aronson. Some critics complained that Bobby's character was not completely fleshed out, and the show took a dim view of marriage. Few could argue about the show's artistic caliber. Sondheim's combination of wit and heart was a vibrant continuation of what Berlin, Porter, Ira Gershwin, and Oscar Hammerstein II (Sondheim's mentor) had done in earlier eras, but his lyrics spoke for a generation in the midst of a cultural and sexual revolution. As no one else before or since, he gave uncertainty and self-exploration a voice.

As the only important producer-director in musical theatre, Prince faced a dilemma. In show business, artistic concerns must always be balanced against financial realities. Normally, it is the director's job to dream, and the producer's job to keep those dreams from breaking the production budget. But when one person fills both roles, there is no one to say "no." By allowing his inner artist to overrule his inner businessman, Prince created wonderful productions that had little if any chance of turning a profit.

Prince and Sondheim had been contemplating a project called *The Girls Upstairs* for several years, working with playwright James Goldman on an evolving libretto about people confronting the ghosts of their past. It became *Follies* (1971, 522 performances), the story of two former showgirls attending a reunion at their old theatre on the night before it is to be demolished. Phyllis (Alexis Smith) has married the successful politician Ben (John McMartin), and they have learned to loathe each other. Sally (Dorothy Collins) always wanted Ben, but settled for Buddy (Gene Nelson), a salesman who keeps a mistress in another town. All four are burdened with regret about past choices, and all have their pretensions shattered in the course of the reunion party, where recollections of the past haunt the present. As old-timers get up to perform, their ghosts are never far behind, providing a poignant contrast of then and now. By morning, as the theatre begins to come down, the two couples are shaken but still together, ready to release the ghosts of the past and face a more honest future. Sondheim's score was an homage to his predecessors, from Herbert to Kern to Porter. The former showgirls paraded on to the tenor serenade "Beautiful Girls," which captured the spirit of Berlin's "A Pretty Girl Is Like a Melody" without stooping to pastiche. Real-life Ziegfeld veteran Ethel Shutta belted "Broadway Baby" with gusto, and former movie starlet Yvonne De Carlo echoed her real-life roller-coaster career singing "I'm Still Here." Bennett's staging of "Who's That Woman?" had the aging showgirls stumble through an old dance routine while their ghosts performed behind them in the flawless haze of memory. In recognition of Bennett's extraordinary contribution, he shared directorial credit and the resulting Tony award with Prince. The most powerful songs went to the four leads: Nelson's tongue-twisting "Buddy's Blues," McMartin's chilling "Live, Laugh, Love," Smith's bitchy "Leave You," and Collins's heartbreaking "Losing My Mind." The reviews for *Follies* were mixed. Some theatregoers hated the show, praising the score but condemning the book for its sad, uncertain ending. The show won seven Tony awards—losing Best Musical to *Two Gentlemen of Verona*—and ran for more than a year. Even so, with its lavish production and large cast, *Follies* was a costly experiment, and closed at a loss. Thanks to a glorious score, *Follies* would be frequently restaged and recorded in years to come.

A Little Night Music (1973, 600 performances) was inspired by Swedish filmmaker Ingmar Bergman's comedy *Smiles of a Summer Night*. Set in turn-of-the-century Sweden, it has a central love story that draws together a network of varied characters. Len Cariou (1939–) played attorney Fredrik Egerman, a decent man whose unconsummated marriage to a second wife half his age leaves him vulnerable when he reconnects an old flame, actress Desiree Armfeldt, played by Glynis Johns (1923–). After years of "tearing around" on tour, and tired of her ongoing affair with the pompous Count Carl-Magnus (Laurence Guittard), Desiree finds the prospect of a real relationship appealing, even if it may require a bit of homewrecking. She invites the Egerman family to a weekend at her mother's country villa. Egerman brings his wife, his adult son Henrik (Mark Lambert) who secretly yearns for his stepmother, and the promiscuous housemaid Petra (D'Jamin Bartlett) who yearns for any man within reach. The jealous Carl Magnus appears uninvited and heavily armed, his devoted but waspish wife Charlotte (Patricia Elliott) in tow. All of these characters are supremely selfish people, each wanting their way regardless of the cost to others. The elderly Madame Armfeldt (Hermoine Gingold) tells Desiree's teenage daughter that the summer night will "smile" three times, and it does: once for the young, as Egerman's wife and son run off together; once more for the middle aged, as Frederick and Desiree find each other; and finally for the old, as Madame slips quietly into eternity.

With its period setting and aristocratic characters, *A Little Night Music* had the look and feel of an operetta. Sondheim decided to accent this by setting his entire score in variations of three-quarter time. There was plenty of "big" singing, including the epic first-act finale "A Weekend in the Country," and operatic commentary provided by an elegantly dressed quintet. Glynis Johns had a small vocal range, so her pivotal "Send in the Clowns" was designed accordingly, and she delivered it with such bittersweet dramatic power that few minded her limitations as a singer.

Bartlett's housemaid sang in a belt style, explaining in "The Miller's Son" that a girl has to "celebrate what passes by," and Gingold talk-sang while bemoaning the loss of romantic "Liaisons." Waltzes, sex, deceit, forbidden desire, duels, death, and salvation, all set to richly melodic music—it had something for damn near everyone, and did handsomely at the box office. Tonys went to the show, score, book, direction, costumes, and both Johns and Elliott for their performances. A 1975 London production starring Jean Simmons ran for 406 performances, and the show became a lasting favorite with regional theatres and opera companies on both sides of the Atlantic. A hit recording by Judy Collins made "Send in the Clowns" the most popular individual song with words and music by Sondheim.

Sondheim, Prince, and first time librettist John Weidman pushed the envelope further with *Pacific Overtures* (1976, 193 performances). The story followed a broad array of characters to dramatize how Japan's ancient culture was effected when the United States forced the isolated "floating kingdom" to open itself to international trade in 1853. The highlights of the score were several extended musical scenes, each so carefully crafted that they could stand alone as mini-masterworks. "Chrysanthemum Tea" had the Emperor's mother poisoning her indecisive royal son; "Please Hello!" depicted world powers pressuring Japan into unwelcome trade agreements; and "Bowler Hat" followed one man's gradual conversion from eastern to western ways of thinking. Sondheim's personal favorite was "Someone in a Tree," in which everyday people who witnessed negotiations between Japanese and American officials tell what they saw and heard. Japanese actor Mako led a mostly Asian cast, and the physical production made selective use of Japanese theatrical conventions, such as having female roles played by men in drag. Beautiful to both eye and ear, *Pacific Overtures* covered events that took place over the course of more than a hundred years, so there were no central characters to give a readily definable emotional focus. Unable to find an audience, the production folded at a tremendous loss. This show has maintained a staunch cult of admirers, but high-quality revivals have failed to kindle general interest in this still-challenging show.

The next Prince-Sondheim collaboration will be covered presently. First, let's look at some of the other talents who created concept musicals in the 1970s.

Fosse and "All That Jazz"

Few could match the extraordinary success director Bob Fosse enjoyed in 1972, winning an Academy Award for the film version of *Cabaret*, an Emmy for the television special *Liza with a Z*, and a Tony for the aforementioned *Pippin*. Like Sondheim and Prince, Fosse was a veteran of the well-built conventional musicals of the 1950s, and was anxious to take the art form forward. In 1973, he approached *Cabaret* songwriters John Kander and Fred Ebb with the idea for *Chicago* (1975, 898 performances), a musical adaptation of a 1926 play involving two scandalous husband-killing murderesses using headlines to manipulate a society hungry for sensation. Fosse's directorial vision took precedence over the book and score, an approach some coworkers referred to as "Fosse Uber Alles," but his working style inspired total devotion from performers. The cast included Chita Rivera as Velma Kelly, Gwen Verdon as Roxy Hart, and Jerry Orbach as shyster defense attorney Billy Flynn. Years of chain-smoking and alcohol and drug abuse caught up with Fosse when he suffered a massive heart attack during early rehearsals. After bypass surgery and an additional heart attack, he returned to work, slowly pulling the show together during a rocky out of town tryout. He framed the action in a vaudeville format, expanding a fairly traditional narrative into a concept musical. The Kander and Ebb score gave all three stars ample opportunities. Rivera set a hot pace in the opening ensemble "All That Jazz," and shared the folksy "Nowadays" with Verdon. Orbach's nononsense rendition of "Razzle Dazzle" captured the central point of the show—"keep 'em way off balance" with showmanship, and you can get away with anything, including murder. *Chicago* got a mixed critical reception and received no awards on Tony night, but it had a solid profitable run. Fosse's production was so packed with style that it almost overwhelmed the material. It would take thirty years and a more straightforward staging for this show to get the kind of reception it deserved in its smash hit 1996 revival.

Weary of collaboration, Fosse took the concept musical a step further and conceived an evening of dance numbers that required no story, no writers, no composers—just a cast executing his choreographic designs. *Dancin'* (1978, 1,744 performances) relied on preexisting music, like Benny Goodman's jazz classic "Sing, Sing, Sing."

The first all-dance Broadway musical, it became one of Fosse's most profitable productions. Not everyone was thrilled. Alan Jay Lerner wired the director, "Congratulations. You finally did it. You got rid of the author." The downside to such a project was that it had no life beyond its Broadway run and national tour. It was all about Fosse's dances, which smaller theatres and amateurs groups could never hope to recreate. Although his career was far from over, this was his last original Broadway hit.

Michael Bennett: "Singular Sensation"

After making a vital contribution to two Sondheim-Prince musicals, Michael Bennett was ready to start developing new works of his own. His first opportunity came when *Seesaw* (1973, 296 performances) ran into major trouble during try outs in Detroit. Following the Champion-Fosse model of director as auteur, Bennett took full control and completely revamped the show, with help from a six-foot-six-inch dancer from Texas, Tommy Tune (1939–). Tune also joined the cast, staging and performing the showstopping "It's Not Where You Start," backed by a full chorus clad in inexpensive tights, balloons, and streamers. Impossibly long, lean, and effeminate, he endeared himself to audiences and colleagues. Bennett and his team got the show into presentable shape for a Broadway run, although its costly try out made a profitable run almost impossible. Michelle Lee starred as a New York actress in love with visiting Omaha businessman Ken Howard. Bennett won his second Tony for choreography, and Tune picked up one as featured actor.

Bennett was approached by two chorus dancers interested in developing a musical based on the real-life experiences of their colleagues. Claiming he had been contemplating just such a project, Bennett brought together a group of dancers for a bull session, sharing memories from their careers as a cassette recorder captured it all. Soon afterward, Joseph Papp, founder of the New York Shakespeare Festival, offered Bennett a budget and rehearsal space to "workshop" his project. This was an altogether new idea, and Bennett made the most of it. He gathered a gifted creative team, with playwright James Kirkwood (1924–1989) and former dancer Nicholas Dante (1942–1991) assembling the book, Academy Award–winner Marvin Hamlisch (1944–)

composing the music, and the relatively unknown Edward Kleban (1939–1987) writing the lyrics. The score blended contemporary pop with traditional show biz razzmatazz, and it was rumored that Neil Simon helped polish the powerful libretto. Instead of a linear plotline, the show was built around an event: at a Broadway chorus audition, a director demands that dancers desperate for a job share their most private memories and inner demons.

Glorifying the individual fulfillment that can be found in ensemble efforts, *A Chorus Line* (1975, 6,137 performances) was a triumph on all levels, but Bennett's staging demanded and got the lion's share of the attention. "I Hope I Get It" involved a platoon of dancers being narrowed down to seventeen, who then form a line across the front of the stage, holding their formal headshots in front of their faces. Several of the women recall how they found a refuge from childhood's disappointments "At the Ballet." The fictional director's former lover Cassie (Donna McKechnie) wants to return to the anonymity of the chorus after a frustrating shot at solo stardom, and begs for the reassurance of "The Music and the Mirror." When one of the dancers is injured, the others share their fear of the inevitable day when dancing will end in "What I Did for Love." After the final cut is made, all the dancers return in "One," a spectacular finale-cum-curtain call in which Bennett utilized every eye-popping trick in the Broadway chorus repertory. His smiling ensemble danced in a circle, a pyramid, and wound up in a prolonged kick line. As a mirror on stage reflected an image of the audience, the lights finally dimmed. As Bennett explained, "There are no bows. I don't believe in bows, just the fade out. That's what a dancer's life is."

Previews at Papp's downtown theatre ignited unprecedented word of mouth, and the original cast soon moved to the Shubert Theatre. The hottest ticket in years, the show became such a phenomenon that the national media paid attention as in days gone by. *A Chorus Line* received every major award, including the Pulitzer Prize for Drama and nine Tony awards, including Best Musical, Direction, and Choreography. Donna McKechnie was honored as Best Actress, and during the run married Michael Bennett, fully aware that he was actively bisexual. Within a year, this ill-starred match was over, but the show ran on, with touring companies and foreign productions by the score. McKechnie and other dancers who helped create the piece had signed over all rights to Bennett, who made a fortune in royalties while they were only paid as performers—and only while they remained in the cast. On September 29, 1983, Bennett brought together 338 alumni for the show's record-breaking 3,389th performance—again, winning national attention. For theatre lovers who came of age in the 1970s and 80s, *A Chorus Line* was the musical of their generation. It ran for fifteen years, its flashing sign becoming a theatre district landmark.

The Revival Craze: "I Want to Be Happy"

Broadway had seen revivals since its earliest years, but they had become rare occurrences in the busy post-*Oklahoma!* era. When an epidemic of nostalgia swept all areas of popular culture in the early 1970s, it inspired a lasting wave of revivals. Ranging from reverential restagings to radical revisions, these old titles appealed to those who felt alienated by the cultural changes taking place around them. This trend began with the triumphant return of the 1925 hit *No, No, Nanette* (1971, 861 performances). An aging Busby Berkeley was credited as production supervisor, but it was director Burt Shevelove and choreographer Donald Saddler who turned the production into a perky dance-fest, overhauling the original book and interpolating material from other shows. Theatregoers welcomed *Nanette*'s tap-dancing chorus and former Berkeley movie star Ruby Keeler with an almost delirious sense of relief. Aside from a healthy Broadway run, it made millions from tours, foreign productions, and amateur rights.

The race was suddenly on, as producers scrambled to find old movie stars and old vehicles worth revisiting. But it was soon apparent that revivals were not guaranteed moneymakers. Gower Champion stepped in to save a heavily rewritten and troubled revival of *Irene* (1973, 605 performances), turning it into a solid crowd-pleaser for Debbie Reynolds, but the tryout revisions cost so much that the production was unable to return its investment despite a healthy run. A revised version of *Good News* (1974, 16 performances) starring Alice Faye profitably toured for two years before reaching Broadway, where painful reviews shut it down in two weeks.

Most producers got the hint and stuck to stars with solid stage credentials. In most cases, these productions made brief stops on Broadway and cleaned up on tour:

- *Lorelei* (1974, 320 performances) was a revised *Gentlemen Prefer Blondes* with original star Carol Channing, who toured in it for more than two years.
- *Gypsy* (1974, 124 performances) brought Angela Lansbury her third Tony for Best Actress in a Musical. She toured in the role for several years.
- *My Fair Lady* (1976, 384 performances) had the original designs and staging and featured veteran character actor George Rose (1920–1988) in a Tony-winning performance as Alfie Doolittle. The massive sets precluded plans for a tour.
- *Hello, Dolly!* returned in Champion's staging, first in an integrated production starring Pearl Bailey (1975, 45 performances) and then in a Houston Opera staging starring Carol Channing (1978, 152 performances). Both productions made fortunes on the road.
- Zero Mostel made his final Broadway appearance in a faithful re-creation of *Fiddler on the Roof* (1976, 168 performances).
- Faithful replicas of the original *Man of La Mancha* starring Richard Kiley returned in 1970 (140 performances) and 1977 (127 performances).
- Sandy Duncan became the longest-running *Peter Pan* (1979, 550 performances) in theatrical history, bringing a new staging and spirit to the 1954 version.
- *Oklahoma!* (1979, 301 performances) preserved the DeMille choreography but was otherwise given a fresh staging, coming to Broadway after a smash tour.

The most acclaimed revivals of the decade took a fresh look at existing works, but even those could be financially tricky. Harold Prince called in Stephen Sondheim and librettist Hugh Wheeler to revise Leonard Bernstein's 1956 flop *Candide* (1977, 740 performances). The music took backseat to the comedy in a street theatre-style environmental staging, with performing areas scattered around the audience at downtown's 180-seat Chelsea Center Theatre. The same arrangement was used in the Broadway Theatre (previously gutted for *Dude*), but although this arrangement reduced the seating to 900, the musicians and stagehands unions demanded the same staff minimums required when that house seats its full 1,600. Despite a long run under expert management, the production lost money.

On an even smaller scale, David Merrick brought a thoroughly revised version of the 1915 hit *Very Good Eddie* (1975, 307 performances) down from Connecticut's Goodspeed Opera House, reminding theatregoers that there was more to Jerome Kern than *Show Boat*. With no major stars and a score augmented with outstanding numbers from other Princess Theatre musicals, it ran the better part of a year and made a solid profit. For several years this show enjoyed new popularity in schools and regional productions.

The longest running and most profitable Broadway revival of the 1970s was *The King and I* (1977, 807 performances) starring Yul Brynner, who was now the right age to play the king. This production kept the Jerome Robbins choreography but had fresh direction and a sumptuous newly designed physical production. Capturing all the excitement of a new musical, this revival packed the 1,933-seat Uris Theatre for almost two years. Brynner proceeded to tour the world in this show, racking up more than 4,000 performances as the king with a succession of leading ladies. Diagnosed with lung cancer, he kept performing while undergoing treatment. By the time Brynner made a farewell return to Broadway (1985, 191 performances), his long illness and a tour-weary production took some of the power out of Rodgers and Hammerstein's classic, but audiences cheered the old lion no matter how hoarse his roar. He died several months after his final performance.

Traditional Forms: "What Is It That We're Living For? Applause!"

There were still plenty of talented people creating conventional book musicals. Heading the old guard was no less than Richard Rodgers, who was plagued by poor health, but continued composing, with frustrating results. *Two by Two* (1970, 343 performances) told the biblical story of Noah and boasted a tuneful score with fine lyrics by former chorus dancer Martin Charnin (1934–), but Danny Kaye's attention-grabbing stage shenanigans made for a bumpy run. Shakespearean actor Nicol Williamson had the voice and presence to play England's blood-soaked Henry VIII in *Rex* (1976, 48 performances), but sweet tunes by Rodgers and masterly lyrics by Sheldon Harnick could not make the royal beheader of wives an appealing character. Williamson's

temperamental behavior both on and off stage—which included slap-
ping another actor during curtain calls—kept gossip columns busy
during the nine-week run, the shortest ever for a new Rodgers musical. *I Remember Mama* (1979, 148 performances) offered film star
Liv Ullman as a Scandinavian immigrant using love and ingenuity
to raise her family in the early 1900s. Preview audiences cheered this
warm and well-crafted show, but the material was short on excitement, and after critics dismissed it as corny and old-fashioned, ticket
sales petered out. With hit revivals of *The King and I* and *Oklahoma!*
running strong, Rodgers finally lost a two-decade battle with cancer
and died on December 30, 1979. It had been sixty years since his music
was first heard on Broadway, and in the interim he had become one of
the greatest musical theatre composers. The 46th Street Theatre was
renamed the Richard Rodgers in 1990. Decades after his death, his
music remains popular, and his best musicals are still among the most
popular stage and screen works of all time.

Alan Jay Lerner and Frederick Loewe reunited briefly to adapt their
1958 screen hit *Gigi* (1973, 110 performances) for Broadway. Despite
some brilliant new lyrics and the stellar presence of Alfred Drake as
the roguish Honoré, the production suffered from pedestrian direction and lost a fortune. Lerner had even worse luck when he teamed
with composer Burton Lane and librettist Joseph Stein for *Carmelina*
(1979, 28 performances), which starred Georgia Brown as an Italian
mother who has convinced three American World War II veterans
that each was the wartime father of her child. What should have been
a romantic comedy played like an operetta, but as critics dismissed
the show they admired the score, particularly a ravishing trio for the
old vets, "One More Walk Around the Garden."

Jerry Herman saw two promising projects suffer disappointing fates. *Mack and Mabel* (1974, 69 performances) featured Robert
Preston and Bernadette Peters in the title roles, and Herman's exceptional score included Peters's devastating ballad "Time Heals Everything." But the true-life love story of silent screen director Mack
Sennett and comedienne Mabel Normand ends with her tragic death,
a downer that Herman, librettist Michael Stewart, and director Gower
Champion could not overcome. Damaged by too much tinkering during try outs, this promising reunion of *Hello, Dolly!*'s creative team
lasted barely three months on Broadway. It was this failure that sent

Champion into a creative midlife crisis that resulted in his directing the ghastly *Rockabye Hamlet*. The ultimate director-choreographer withdrew from the musical theatre, swearing he would not return. He might have been helpful with Herman's *The Grand Tour* (1979, 61 performances), which starred Joel Grey and Ron Holgate as refugees fleeing the Nazis in war-torn France. Although Champion and Herman were down, Broadway would hear more from each of them.

Charles Strouse and Lee Adams, who had proven with *Bye Bye Birdie* and *Golden Boy* that they could comfortably blend rock elements into an essentially traditional Broadway sound, did the same for *Applause* (1970, 900 performances). Librettists Betty Comden and Adolph Green updated the backstabbing plot of the acclaimed 1950 film *All About Eve*, moving it into the theatrical world of 1970. This time, rock rhythms and orchestrations gave a "mod" sound to traditional showtunes, and the presence of 1940s movie legend Lauren Bacall (1924–) cemented the show's success. She couldn't sing worth a damn, but she radiated star power in her musical debut as Margo Channing, the established theatre diva who finds her life and career being co-opted by her deceptively unassuming assistant, Eve Harrington (Penny Fuller). Tonys went to Bacall, director-choreographer Ron Field, and the show itself as Best Musical. Field had first won notice with his choreography for the original production of *Cabaret*, but although he remained active in the business until his death in 1989, he never helmed another original hit.

Strouse's next project got him tangled up with an orphan girl and a scruffy dog. It began when lyricist Martin Charnin bought an anthology of *Little Orphan Annie* comic strips as a gift for a friend. Enchanted by the book, he thought it might form the basis for a musical. Librettist Thomas Meehan came up with a story of how the little tyke met and captured the heart of Daddy Warbucks (Reid Shelton) in 1930s New York City, finding love, adventure, and a loveable mutt named Sandy along the way. On the surface, *Annie* (1976, 2,337 performances) was a shamelessly old-fashioned, well-built musical comedy. But it was also a call to honest virtues in an age saddled by political corruption and public disillusionment. After a rocky start at the Goodspeed Opera House, the show was picked up by producer Mike Nichols, the admired director of several Neil Simon hits. Polished on a brief road tour, it opened to valentine reviews and became the biggest sensation since *A Chorus Line*. Thirteen-year-old Andrea McArdle (1963–) gave a disarming performance in the title role, belting the anthem-like "Tomorrow," which Strouse set to a subtle rock-era beat. Dorothy Loudon (1933–2003) mugged her way to glory as the harried orphanage director Miss Hannigan, bemoaning a life filled with "Little Girls," and plotting with her brother Rooster (Robert Fitch) and his girlfriend Lily (Barbara Erwin) to deceive Warbucks and make their way to "Easy Street." A kicking chorus of six orphans delivered the surefire showstopper "You're Never Fully Dressed without a Smile," a nostalgic spoof of period radio broadcasts. Offering solid entertainment for audiences of all ages, *Annie* received six Tonys, including Best Musical and honors for the book, the score, and Loudon. There were dozens of international productions. After a seven year Broadway run, the show was frequently toured and revived, becoming a staple in regional and amateur theatres. Produced for approximately $650,000, it eventually earned over $100 million, not counting receipts for an ill-conceived 1982 big-screen version starring Carol Burnett as Hannigan.

Through the end of the decade, several traditional-format musicals did well enough to top the 1,000-performance mark:

- *Shenandoah* (1975, 1,050 performances) was based on a classic film about a Virginia farmer and his family facing the nightmare of the American Civil War. It had a handsome TV campaign, the catchy tune "Freedom," and a Tony award–winning performance by John Cullum (1930–) as the warmhearted *pater familias*. Despite a long run, the production never returned its original investment.
- *The Best Little Whorehouse in Texas* (1978, 1,703 performances) was inspired by the real-life political brouhaha that forced the closing of an infamous Lone Star State bordello. Native Texan Tommy Tune's energetic staging, a bawdy libretto, and catchy country-style songs by Carol Hall made the show a solid hit in New York. A London production played the Drury Lane.
- *Ain't Misbehavin'* (1978, 1,604 performances) revitalized the revue format with beguiling vignettes built around the songs written or performed by jazz great Fats Waller. Created by lyricist-director Richard Maltby (1937–), it brought stardom to the charismatic and amply proportioned Nell Carter. She and Maltby received Tonys, and the show won for Best Musical.

- Neil Simon's hilarious book *They're Playing Our Song* (1979, 1,082 performances) was a conventional but funny comedy inspired by a real-life romance between composer Marvin Hamlisch and lyricist Carol Bayer Sager—who provided a delightful score infused with the rhythms of late-70s pop.
- MGM veterans Mickey Rooney and Ann Miller scored a surprise smash with *Sugar Babies* (1979, 1,208 performances), a mildly risqué revue of burlesque skits and songs that evinced a razzle-dazzle glamour that old burlesque never had.

Since Broadway hits were raking in millions, few were willing to notice that the musical theatre was operating in a cultural vacuum. Rock and disco were the predominant pop sounds, and neither had more than a token presence in most stage scores. The potential sales for cast albums fell so low that major labels stopped recording them. At the same time, Broadway production costs soared. A musical that could be mounted for $250,000 in 1970 cost $1 million or more by 1979, and operating expenses rose so high that even a two-year run could not guarantee a profit. Some blamed the volatile economy, but Broadway was the only place where inflation ran at a rate of 400 percent.

In this unsettled environment, two important musicals came to represent the forces that would compete for the soul of musical theatre in the decade to come. They had a lot in common, but their inherent differences indicated the gap between where the Broadway musical had been and where it was headed.

Sondheim vs. Lloyd Webber: Round One

While Hugh Wheeler's libretto for *Sweeney Todd* (1979, 557 performances) used the conventional plot structure of a Victorian melodrama, its operatic score was the most ambitious that Stephen Sondheim had yet attempted. This tale of an unjustly persecuted barber's all-consuming quest for revenge explored emotional territory no musical had ever touched. Not since Shakespeare had stage writers taken such an unflinching look into the darkest corners of the human soul. Len Cariou played the title role with manic intensity, and Angela Lansbury countered with an over-the-top comic performance as his amorous-murderous landlady, Mrs. Lovett. Deciding to grind their victims into meat for pies, the two villains concluded the first act by speculating on the flavors of flesh they would soon offer, including "A Little Priest"—a maniacal waltz that ended with Lansbury and Cariou respectively raising their rolling pin and silver razor to the skies. In the second act, audiences laughed uneasily as blood flew and bodies fell. After Sweeney's rampage ended in his own death, the ensemble pointed at members of the audience, asking if they too had a murderous hate like Sweeney's hiding inside them. Prince gave this risky material a costly staging, utilizing hydraulic catwalks within the walls and ceiling of an abandoned factory trucked in from Rhode Island. The show ran for more than a year, with Dorothy Loudon and George Hearn (1934–) taking over the leads, but the budget was such that a healthy run could not turn a profit.

A far different musical came from England with advance hoopla that Gilbert and Sullivan might have envied. Following the pattern that they had initiated with *Jesus Christ Superstar*, composer Andrew Lloyd Webber and librettist Tim Rice launched their stage biography of Argentina's 1940s First Lady Eva Peron as a double LP. With Harold Prince as director, they refined the piece on stage in London, sharpening the book's focus, toning down the rock elements, and adding a touch of disco to expand the score's commercial possibilities. Elaine Paige (1951–) became an immediate star in the original West End staging of *Evita* (1978, 2,900 performances). It reached Broadway a year later (1979, 1,567 performances) as a slick and stylish smash hit, with breakthrough performances by Patti Lupone (1949–) in the title role and Mandy Patinkin (1952–) as unlikely narrator Che Guevara. A disco version of the big ballad "Don't Cry for Me Argentina" became a hit single. *Evita* was a calculated triumph of stagecraft and technology, undeniably entertaining but in some ways as vapid as Ziegfeld's *Follies*. Webber and Rice depicted Eva as a whore with flair and ruthless ambition, offering no clue as to what made her complex character tick. Meaningful or not, people enjoyed it. Running three times longer than *Sweeney Todd*, it made a massive profit from productions all over the world. With this flashy victory of matter over mind, the *megamusical* was born. The key characteristics of this form include:

- Megamusicals are sung through, with little if any dialogue.
- The songs and emotions are big, loud, and bombastic.

- Characterization is often explained rather than dramatized: characters tell you who they are rather than showing who they are by their actions.
- The music is rock-pop, but can incorporate various styles; it does not reflect the sound of any particular era.
- The plots are melodramatic, with minimal humor.
- All major professional stagings are carbon copies.

Substance took a backseat to spectacle, lush melody, and soap opera–style sentiment. In megamusicals, star performers were unnecessary—the production was the star, making these shows attractions regardless of who was in the cast.

Both *Sweeney* and *Evita* were expensive productions with stunning stage direction by Harold Prince. Both won seven Tony awards, including Best Musical, in adjoining seasons. The key difference: *Sweeney Todd* made theatrical history but lost money, while *Evita* left history to its own devices and made gobs of money. This was not lost on producers and investors. It is easy to advocate artistic merit over financial concerns, but answer this: If you were investing $100,000 or more of your own money, would you prefer to lose it or make a profit? The inevitable answer to that question set the uneasy course of the Broadway musical for the remainder of the twentieth century.

15

Spectacles and Boardrooms— "As If We Never Said Goodbye"

I t had been years since producer David Merrick and director Gower Champion had an original hit musical. Burying old hatchets, they set to work on an adaptation of *42nd Street* (1980, 3,486 performances), the 1933 film about stage director Julian Marsh (Jerry Orbach) trying to save a Depression-era musical by putting on untried understudy Peggy Sawyer (Wanda Richert) when temperamental star Dorothy Brock (Tammy Grimes) breaks her ankle. This classic backstager had already become a much-spoofed show business cliché, as had the director's line to the understudy, "You're going out there a nobody, but you've got to come back a star!" Instead of trying to reproduce the film, Champion reenvisioned the material in purely theatrical terms, interpolating additional songs by composer Harry Warren and replacing Busby Berkeley's kaleidoscopic musical sequences with brilliant new dance routines. Because Champion had a limited knowledge of tap dancing, he worked closely with dance assistant Randy Skinner.

Merrick generated publicity by taunting the public with postponements and cancelled previews, but *42nd Street* finally opened at the Winter Garden on August 23, 1980. The cheering began the moment the curtain rose on nearly fifty pairs of tap-dancing feet. The audience "oohed" at Champion's creative lighting effects during "The Shadow Waltz," "aahed" his Ziegfeld-style parade of chorines in "Dames," and roared for a joyous tap-a-thon on giant coins during "We're in the Money." Before leading the ensemble in a radiant "Lullaby of

Broadway," Orbach won a cheer proclaiming, "Think of 'musical comedy,' the two most glorious words in the English language!" The title number became a tap ballet co-choreographed by Randy Skinner. Six years after the humiliation of *Rockabye Hamlet*, Champion was back with the biggest hit of his career. After tumultuous curtain calls, David Merrick came on stage scowling, his hand on his chin. "This is a very tragic moment," he said, inspiring a burst of laughter. "No, no, no, no, you don't understand," Merrick said. "I have to tell you, Gower Champion is dead." After months of combating a rare blood disease, the director had succumbed earlier that day, and Merrick had sworn Champion's doctors to secrecy and cut the cast off from all outside communications. Richert, who was involved personally with Champion at the time, collapsed into tears as Merrick embraced her. With the audience gasping and the cast frozen in shock, Orbach called for the curtain to be lowered.

It was a moment of real-life tragedy, and Merrick had played it for all it was worth, knowing full well that a battery of television cameras and reporters was capturing every moment of his announcement. It received headline coverage all across the country, guaranteeing that practically everyone who might care would hear about *42nd Street*. The show became a solid sell-out, and the following June received the Tony for Best Musical, with Champion receiving the award for choreography. The production became a living tribute to his memory, so fans were infuriated when the producer removed Champion's name from the ads and started calling it "David Merrick's *42nd Street*." Life, death, and ruthless showmanship—and the decade was just beginning.

The 1980s saw another, more far-reaching tragedy with the outbreak of Acquired Immunodeficiency Syndrome, or AIDS. First seen almost exclusively among gay men, this deadly disease was initially labeled "the gay cancer." It would have a profound effect on the musical theatre, not only killing off many talents in the prime of life, but also wiping out thousands of dedicated theatre lovers. The theatrical community responded with its typical generosity, most notably the formation of two organizations that eventually joined as one—Broadway Cares and Equity Fights Aids. Their efforts raised millions of dollars and did much to raise public awareness of a disease that the government and major media tried to ignore. Such events as the Easter Bonnet Competition and Broadway Bares became regular highlights of the theatrical year for professionals and fans alike. But the initial terror, as a legion of friends and colleagues died terrible deaths, left a lasting impression on all who were part of show business at that time.

New Hits: "Come Follow the Band"

The usual crepe hangers howled that the professional theatre was in terminal condition, but new musicals were still plentiful, with seventeen musical productions coming to Broadway in 1980, twenty the following year. Some were authored by seasoned professionals, some, by exciting newcomers, and some called off-Broadway home—all were reassuring signs that the American musical theatre was thriving.

- *Barnum* (1980, 854 performances) was a rousing and largely fictional circus-style bio musical of showman P. T. Barnum. The Cy Coleman–Michael Stewart score and leading man Jim Dale (1935–) won raves, as did director-choreographer Joe Layton, and as Mrs. Barnum, Glenn Close (1947–) got her first taste of stardom. "The Colors of My Life" delighted audiences, but the pop music world no longer had much interest in Broadway.
- *Woman of the Year* (1981, 770 performances) boasted a fine John Kander–Fred Ebb score and Lauren Bacall in the title role. However, the most memorable thing in this sophisticated musical comedy was Marilyn Cooper, who won a Tony playing a mousy housewife who shared the hilarious duet "The Grass Is Always Greener" with the glamorous Bacall.
- *Dreamgirls* (1981, 1,552 performances) told the story of a Motown girl group's rise to fame. While there was much to admire in Henry Kreiger's score and Tom Eyen's book and lyrics, the triumph belonged to Michael Bennett, who infused the show with a visual drive that kept things pumping from start to finish. Jennifer Holliday had a moment of glory singing the exhausting "And I Am Telling You I Am Not Going." A 2007 film version would reignite interest in this crowd-pleaser.
- *Little Shop of Horrors* (1982, 2,209 performances) was a hilarious off-Broadway sci-fi spoof based on Roger Corman's low-budget 1960 film about a man-eating plant from outer space. Composer Alan Menken and lyricist-librettist Howard Ashman created a fresh,

kitschy, nostalgic hit that toured for years and became a standard part of the musical theatre repertory. The comic ballad "Suddenly Seymour" remained a favorite in piano bars for years to come.

- *Nine* (1982, 732 performances) was a musical version of Fellini's semi-autobiographical cinematic masterpiece *8½*. Composer/lyricist Maury Yeston won acclaim for a sophisticated score. Tommy Tune's innovative production cast Raul Julia as a womanizing Italian director trying to make a film while facing his midlife crisis. *Nine* won all the major Tonys, including one for Liliane Montevecchi, who stopped the show with an irrelevant but seductive paean to the "Folies Bergère."

- *My One and Only* (1983, 767 performances) set vintage songs by the Gershwins in a plot about a 1920s aviator romancing an aquacade star. The show almost collapsed in Boston, but star Tommy Tune took over the direction with an assist from *A Chorus Line* alumnus Thommie Walsh (1950–2007). After exhaustive revisions and rocky Broadway previews, the show opened to surprise raves. Audiences cheered as Tune and Twiggy splashed through a watery barefoot version of "S'Wonderful," and legendary tap star Charles "Honi" Coles won a Tony as the whimsical Mr. Magix. It proved even more popular on national tour.

But there were warning signs that something was amiss. As successful as the above shows were, none of their cast recordings reached the bestseller charts—not even *42nd Street*. And running costs were making it harder to define success. *Woman of the Year* ran the better part of two seasons and still closed at a loss. Now that Broadway musical budgets were rising into the millions, the cost of survival was high, and the cost of failure was becoming staggering. The day-to-day costs of running a show were now so high that with low advance sales and bad reviews, it made more sense to close. Producers could no longer afford to keep a show open in hopes that it would build an audience. *Onward Victoria* (1980, 1 performance) told the story of Victoria Woodhull, a scandal-prone feminist stockbroker who ran for president in the 1870s. While the premise had potential, a lifeless score, a humorless book, and lack of a major star left the show floundering from the outset. A relatively inexperienced creative team made few changes, and the costly period production opened and closed in one night. Seasoned pros could stumble just as badly. When the librettist of *My Fair Lady* (Alan Jay Lerner) and the composer of *Annie* (Charles Strouse) collaborated on a musical version of the anti-war play *Idiot's Delight*, hopes were high, but *Dance a Little Closer* (1983, 1 performance) was a poorly focused work left to die on a cold, oversized set. There was no second performance, and wags referred to the show as "Close a Little Faster." It proved to be a final bow for Lerner, whose death three years later ended a quarter century of post-*Camelot* creative frustration.

The team of Stephen Sondheim and Harold Prince had kept hope alive through the 1970s, but their collaboration hit a wall with *Merrily We Roll Along* (1981, 16 performances), an adaptation of a 1934 Kaufman and Hart comedy that told of a man selling out his moral convictions to achieve success. The trick was that the story was told in reverse, a trick that didn't work all that well in the original play, and proved functionally impossible for a musical. The strange thing was that instead of taking audiences more deeply into the characters, Sondheim and librettist George Furth pulled back, telling less despite a frequently luminescent score. Prince's production wasn't just bad—it was irritating, with an ugly set and a young, inexperienced cast. Firing the lead and extending previews for almost two months did not help, and vituperative word of mouth practically sealed the show's fate before the critics did. To those who thought Sondheim and Prince could do no wrong, *Merrily* was an unhappy revelation. The partnership that had resulted in so many fine, adventurous musicals ended here as the two men went their separate creative ways. *Merrily*'s many fans have refused to let it rest, primarily because of the score, but numerous restagings and revisions have not been able to make this unworkable idea commercially viable.

Cats: The Megamusical Triumphant

After Tim Rice cordially went off to work on projects of his own, Andrew Lloyd Webber teamed with Royal Shakespeare Company artistic director Trevor Nunn to convert T. S. Eliot's *Old Possum's Book of Practical Cats* into a musical. They framed the disconnected poems in a vague situation: a collection of cats gather in an alley, and after each tells his story, one will be allowed to shuffle off this feline coil and go to kitty heaven. Lloyd Webber's music was mostly pop with side trips to vaudeville and opera. Almost all of the words were Eliot's, the most notable exception being "Memory," a lyric that Lloyd Webber and Nunn pieced together for a character of their own making: Grizabella (Elaine Paige), a once glamorous beauty now fallen on hard times. After she sings her expression of lost hope, grandfatherly Old Deuteronomy (Brian Blessed) leads her onto a used car tire that flies off through the ceiling to "the heavy-side layer." Designer John Napier turned the interior of the New London Theatre into an alley filled with oversized trash. The British had never gotten the hang of using dance as a dramatically coherent element in musical theatre, but choreographer Gillian Lynne (1927–) impressed the masses with dances that were somewhere between gymnastic floor routines and aerobic workouts. *Cats* (1981, 8,949 performances) enjoyed a twenty-one-year run, breaking all previous records for West End musicals.

42nd Street was going strong at Broadway's Winter Garden, but when Lloyd Webber and producing partner Cameron Mackintosh (1946–) expressed interest in putting *Cats* into that theatre, the Shubert Organization pounced on the opportunity, moved *42nd Street* over to the Majestic, and gutted the recently renovated interior of the Winter Garden to make way for Napier's funky back alley accoutrements. Betty Buckley played Grizzabella, Ken Page greeted audience members on stage during intermission as Old Deuteronomy, and the ensemble included future leading men Harry Groener (1951–) and Terrence V. Mann (1951–). New York's critics gave a collective grumble, while *Cats* (1982, 7,485 performances) racked up the largest advance sale in Broadway history. More a revue than a book musical, the first fifteen minutes were so dazzling—with performers prancing through the audience, a sort of *Hellzapoppin'* with fur—that few complained about the two tedious hours that yawned before the hydraulic finale. *Cats* brought seven Tonys home to adorn its litter box, including one for the show, another for the long-dead Eliot, and a Best Featured Actress disk going to Buckley.

The most revolutionary thing about *Cats* was the marketing. Before this show, most musicals limited their souvenirs to photo programs, songbooks, and T-shirts. *Cats* splashed its distinctive logo (two yellow-green feline eyes with dancer-shaped irises) on coffee mugs, music boxes, figurines, books, greeting cards, baseball caps, satin jackets, Christmas ornaments, stackable storage tins, stuffed toys, matchboxes, umbrellas, key chains, pins, and more. Those glowing yellow-green eyes were damn near everywhere, and not just in London and New York. Like a theatrical cancer, *Cats* spread across the globe. In Vienna, Buenos Aires, and Minneapolis, dancers in furry spandex and garish makeup proved that "Jellicles can and Jellicles do" rake in a fortune, and that auxiliary marketing can boost a show's profits by millions of dollars. *Cats* was also that increasing rarity, a musical that one could take children to. The tykes might die from vapidity poisoning, but at least there was no danger of them being exposed to anything dangerous, like an idea. Whatever one thought of *Cats*, it entertained millions of theatregoers. By the time the New York production closed in 2000, it was the longest running Broadway production of all time.

Cats marked the rise of the megamusical form first established by *Evita*. Few noticed that these British and French megamusicals were pop-flavored descendants of a form thought long-dead: operetta. It was no accident that megamusicals often replaced their pop-voiced original casts with singers who had operatic training. No one else could deliver the big melodies and gushing emotions eight times a week.

A prime example of the best and worst aspects of the megamusical trend was Willy Russell's *Blood Brothers* (1983). It told the story of twin brothers separated when one is given up for adoption—one is raised in wealth, the other in poverty. They become friends as schoolboys, unaware that they are related. Class differences lead one to political power, the other to bitter failure, and their final meeting is tragic. Throughout the show, the characters explain who they are, telling rather than showing. The result is a series of self-revelatory ballads, long on talk but short on drama. Because of theatre booking issues, the original West End production closed after six months. A touring production returned to London five years later (1988, 8,300+ performances), and is still running as of this writing two decades later. *Blood Brothers* took its time getting to Broadway (1993, 840 performances), where it lasted for two years, thanks to the stubbornness of its producers, who never recouped their costs.

It would be several years before more megamusicals landed on Broadway. In the meantime, the American theatre responded to the

British "meow" with a glorious roar. The 1983–84 season brought a clash of Broadway titans, as five hits vied for top honors:

- Lyricist-librettist Richard Maltby and composer David Shire's *Baby* (1983, 276 performances) was an underrated concept musical about three couples whose lives are altered by the challenge of having a baby.
- Composer Henry Krieger and lyricist Robert Lorick scored with *The Tap Dance Kid* (1984, 669 performances), an original story about an African-American teenager who dreams of a dance career despite his father's disapproval. Danny Daniels won a Tony for his energetic choreography.
- Kander and Ebb's *The Rink* (1983, 233 performances) paired Chita Rivera and Liza Minnelli as a mother and daughter battling over the sale of their roller skating rink, with stories of rape and heartbreak leading to their eventual reconciliation. Rivera received a long-overdue Tony for Best Actress in a Musical, but the show closed soon after Minnelli left for her first stint in rehab.
- Stephen Sondheim's initial collaboration with director-librettist James Lupine (1949–) was *Sunday in the Park with George* (1984, 604 performances), which examined the commercial and emotional challenges of being an artist. Pointillist painter Georges Seurat (Mandy Patinkin) struggles to create his "Sunday Afternoon on the Island of the Grand Jatte," with his lover Dot (Bernadette Peters) appearing in life and in the painting. Audiences cheered for a breathtaking first-act finale that recreated Seurat's painting while the cast sang the ravishing "Sunday." The action then moves to modern times, where Seurat's grandson faces the same issues while an aged Dot urges him on.
- *La Cage aux Folles* (1983, 1,761 performances) was defiantly old-fashioned in its melodic Jerry Herman score but daring in its focus on a gay couple dealing with their son's marriage to the daughter of ultra-rightist, homophobic parents. Playwright Harvey Fierstein provided a hilarious book, and Arthur Laurents helmed the best musical comedy Broadway had seen in years. Tony awards for Best Musical and Score ended years of creative frustration for the composer of *Hello, Dolly!* and *Mame*. George Hearn won a well-deserved Tony for his performance as the loveable drag queen Albin, and won

cheers with his renditions of "I Am What I Am" and "The Best of Times Is Now."

This heady season ended all too soon. By the mid-1980s, it took several years to bring a new project from the page to the stage, so it would be some time before any of these creative talents would return to Broadway. The following season brought only one hit. *Big River* (1985, 1,005 performances) was a refreshing version of Mark Twain's *Huckleberry Finn* with a tuneful, eloquent score by country-western composer Roger Miller. With no effective competition, it won most of the major musical Tonys, ran for three years, and became a favorite with school groups and regional theatres. In 2003, a partially signed revival by Deaf West Theatre brought this show back to Broadway for a brief but acclaimed run.

Then there was a sudden, chilling change of pace. For the first time since *Oklahoma!*, a full decade would go by before a new American musical would pass the 1,000-performance mark on Broadway. After years of ignoring changes in popular culture, Broadway had become a small subculture routinely ignored by mainstream media and the general public. With top ticket prices soaring to thirty-five dollars, it became difficult to get the public to notice anything but each season's biggest hit. Even then, it was a struggle to sell a show that lacked a star. And while no one discussed it at the time, the rise in ticket prices killed off walk-in business, which had kept many a show alive over the years. Theatre became something one planned to do, rather than a spontaneous act. Several major composers—including Herman—and veteran producers left the field, either from exhaustion or frustration. In their wake, inexperienced newcomers brought in a series of expensive, ill-advised disasters.

Redefining Failure

Misconceived projects have always found ways to reach Broadway, but they now involved millions of dollars and proved infuriating to paying audiences. Consider these monumental mistakes:

- The producer of *The Magic Show* brought back Doug Henning as the ultimate magician, *Merlin* (1983, 199 performances). With preview audiences cheering and little hope of pleasing the critics, the producer followed *Beatlemania*'s example and kept postponing the opening for three months. The critics snuck in, the reviews were blunt, and the show's one lasting legacy was that it marked the musical debut of Nathan Lane (1956–), who would prove to be the most gifted comic star of his generation. According to rumor, investors lost a whopping $6 million.

- No one with an ounce of theatrical common sense would have wasted energy on a musical about an atheistic scientist finding faith as he examines the Shroud of Turin. *Into the Light* (1986, 6 performances) promised high-tech effects that turned out to be cheap projections. Audiences found little solace in a campy chorus of tap dancing priests and nuns, and a preachy, incoherent libretto.

- Even living legends can mess up if there isn't someone with the power to rein them in. For *Big Deal* (1986, 77 performances), Bob Fosse dispensed with collaborators, writing his own book and using a catalog of classic Depression-era songs to tell a tale of bungling bank robbers. No one involved with the show had the nerve to tell Fosse it wasn't working, but critics and the public soon made it clear that a few brilliant dance numbers could not redeem a tedious libretto and unattractive physical production.

- With a large cast, complicated physical production, and an ambitious Charles Strouse and Stephen Schwartz score, *Rags* (1986, 4 performances) told the epic story of Jewish immigrants coming to America in the early 1900s. Metropolitan Opera diva Teresa Stratas sounded spectacular in the lead, but Joseph Stein's wideranging libretto required a slightly tighter focus and far stronger direction than it received. *Rags* closed the same weekend that it opened, an impressive, heartbreaking muddle.

- Australian-born pop star Peter Allen was a favorite in nightclubs with no theatrical experience, but producers allowed him to simultaneously compose and star in *Legs Diamond* (1988, 64 performances). The score was surprisingly uninspired, and Allen was no actor. The flamboyance that made his club acts sizzle made him the worst possible choice to play a deadly 1920s gangster. After his character was supposedly murdered, Allen leapt on top of a coffin to announce, "No one can kill me except a critic." Truer words were never spoken, and unanimous pans bumped off the show in eight weeks.

Mega Musicals: "The Inside Might Be as Black as the Night"

Andrew Lloyd Webber and Tim Rice had written *Joseph and the Amazing Technicolor Dreamcoat* (1982, 747 performances) back in 1968 as a cantata for children's choirs, but fully staged adaptations had been around for some time before Tony Tanner's disarming production reached Broadway. Powerhouse singer Laurie Beechman (1954–1998) wowed audiences as the narrator, and no one seemed to notice that the biblical tale of Joseph and his brothers was told without any mention of God. In the 1990s, a souped-up revival toured the U.K., the U.S.A., and Canada with a succession of pop stars in the lead. A good deal noisier, it reached Broadway (1933, 231 performances) with none of the previous production's charm.

The European-based megamusical trend literally picked up speed with Andrew Lloyd Webber's *Starlight Express* (1984, 3,000+ performances in London). Initially intended as an intimate children's musical about anthropomorphic train cars, designer John Napier lavished it with hydraulic ramps that sent rollerskating actors careening through the Apollo Victoria Theatre. There was no real plotline, just "two hours of speed, spectacle, excitement, and energy!" Revivals and tours kept this show before an adoring British public through the start of the next century. It did not fare as well on Broadway (1987, 761 performances), where publicity about the set's fifty-plus miles of electrical wiring led critics to dismiss it as overproduced. Like the Hippodrome shows of the early 1900s, this lighthearted musical roller derby was all about the spectacle. *Starlight Express* had several runs in Las Vegas, and as of this writing has been seen by more than 20 million people.

Lloyd Webber took a very different tack with *Song and Dance*, an intimate "song cycle" that developed in a series of concert and television productions before reaching the West End (1982, 781 performances) with Marti Webb in the one-woman first act and dancer Wayne Sleep leading an ensemble in the all-dance second act. For the Broadway staging (1985, 474 performances), Richard Maltby Jr. added to Don Black's original lyrics, and Bernadette Peters won a long overdue Tony as Best Actress in a Musical.

Cameron Mackintosh was intrigued to hear about a musical adaptation of Victor Hugo's epic novel *Les Misérables* by composer Claude-Michel

Schönberg and librettist Alain Boublil (1941–). First staged at the Palais des Sports in Paris, it used a sung-through pop-style score—in effect, a pop opera. Mackintosh cosponsored a Royal Shakespeare Company production that had been co-adapted and staged by John Caird and company director Trevor Nunn. On a wave of praise, it moved from the Barbican Arts Centre to the West End (1985, 9,600+ performances), where it was still running more than twenty-three years later, having overtaken *Cats* as London's long-running musical champ. Herbert Kretzmer's English lyrics were part translation, part reinterpretation, and new music was written to accommodate the changes. The translation was no work of art, but it milked as much schmaltz as possible out of the tale of Jean Valjean (Colm Wilkinson), a petty criminal who turns respectable but is doggedly pursued by small-minded policeman Javert (Roger Allam). Valjean becomes foster father to Cossette (Rebecca Caine), whose mother Fantine (Patti LuPone) was forced into a life of prostitution. Cosette's lover Marius (Michael Ball) is among the young rebels who barricade the streets of Paris in 1843, only to see their efforts end in rivers of wasted blood.

The strong plot and hydraulic sets wowed most theatregoers, and the logo of little rag-clad Cosette set against the French tricolor became familiar on every imaginable sort of souvenir, including overpriced reprints of Hugo's novel. While hype and hydraulics may have drawn some into the theatre, once they were there *Les Misérables* offered them a touching theatrical experience. The Broadway production (1987, 6,680 performances) opened to tepid reviews but received eight Tony awards, including Best Musical. Wilkinson repeated his performance as Valjean, with Terrence Mann as Javert and Randy Graff as Fantine. Hoards of tourists and dedicated fans kept *Les Miz*'s turntable stages whirling well into the next century on both sides of the Atlantic. The New York production closed in 2003, but within three years a revival using the original staging opened to healthy ticket sales.

Tim Rice collaborated with Björn Ulvaeus and Benny Andersson, two former members of the Swedish pop group Abba to create *Chess*, a musical that used a high-pressure chess championship to illustrate the cold war tensions between America and the Soviet Union. A successful concept recording led to a popular West End production (1986, 1,102 performances). The show had less luck in a revised, bloated American version (1988, 68 performances in New York) directed by Trevor Nunn. Fans of the ballad-heavy, Euro-pop score, which included the hits "One Night in Bangkok" and "I Know Him So Well," were shocked, but subsequent concerts and an off-Broadway revival have not changed this show's standing in the United States. Things might have been different if original plans had held and Michael Bennett had directed the Broadway version, but he was diagnosed with AIDS at a time when that illness amounted to a swift death sentence, and was forced to withdraw from the project. As Bennett lay dying, producer Joe Papp asked if he had any message for the kids in the still-running *A Chorus Line*. His reply: "Tell them no show runs forever." Not long afterward, Bennett was dead at age forty-four.

European-born megamusicals were a force to be reckoned with, and for a time they appeared to be critic-proof. Then one proved to be the most infamous flop musical of its time, one whose title remains a byword for theatrical disaster—*Carrie* (1988). Stephen King's bestselling horror novel had already inspired a 1976 film, and Terry Hands of the Royal Shakespeare Company decided to produce and direct a megamusical adaptation. The plot: Teenager Carrie White (Linzi Hateley), ostracized at school for being different and tormented at home by a judgmental mother (Barbara Cook), discovers she has destructive telekinetic powers. When vicious classmates humiliate Carrie at the prom, her rage sets off walls of flame that bring the gym crashing down in a holocaust of death, and a final showdown with her mother leaves both women dead. The inexperienced team of librettist Lawrence D. Cohen (screenwriter for the film), composer Michael Gore, and lyricist Dean Pitchford did some impressive writing. The scenes between mother and daughter were a stunningly beautiful two-person pop opera, but the scenes involving Carrie's high school classmates seemed to take place in another world—and at the very least, in another musical. Experienced New York producers refused to touch this inconsistent project, but after several years, Hands and the show's writers decided to team up with the RSC and an inexperienced American producer.

Hands staged *Carrie*'s premiere in England at the RSC, where it went so badly that Cook—whose involvement was the main reason many musical theatre fans were interested in the show—withdrew from the project. The producers ignored all warning signs and brought the show to Broadway with only minimal revisions. In a bizarre move, the auditorium of the Virginia Theatre (the historic former home of the Theatre Guild) was painted black, making the sizeable 1,261-seat space feel oppressive—especially with the stage boxed in glaring white. Betty Buckley, who had played a teacher in the non-musical film, now played mother to Hateley's Carrie. The resulting duets were haunting and powerful, making the high school scenes seem all the more moronic, including "Out for Blood," which had Carrie's enemies collecting pork blood and chanting "Kill the pig" while recorded pig squeals played over the sound system. With no previous experience directing musicals, Hands had no idea how to finesse this uneven material, and his tacky staging made these scenes seem nonsensical to the point of being offensive. Megamusicals almost always have a painfully basic point to make: poverty is bad (*Les Misérables*), losing your looks is bad (*Cats*), or even America is bad (*Miss Saigon*). *Carrie*'s point was not so obvious—bullies are bad? Be careful who you pick on 'cause you might get burned?

As *Carrie*'s two weeks of previews passed by, word of mouth spread that this one was too ghastly to miss. People attended *expecting* to hate it. The show's resolute lack of intentional humor made it unintentionally seem all the funnier. As a blood-soaked Carrie dripped her way down a long, impossibly white staircase, a moment designed to evoke terror left many audience members laughing out loud. A few customers were so offended that they walked out hollering imprecations at the stage. When the reviews came out, some fine material went unnoticed as the critics engaged in a feeding frenzy. With its few plausible characters lost in a clumsily produced explosion of laser lights and synthetic blood, *Carrie* closed after five official performances. That should have been the end of it, but it wasn't. More than two decades later, this show retains its fascination. *Carrie*'s playbills, window cards, pirated performance tapes, and scripts are prized by theatre buffs. Ken Mandelbaum cemented the show's mystique when he entitled his popular chronicle of musical flops *Not Since Carrie*. Yes, it was a flop, and much of the subject matter simply did not sing. But those "in the know" who laughed as they walked out of *Carrie* made the mistake of dismissing the large part of the audience that did not walk out. Some of them actually liked the show; not just the powerful mother-daughter scenes, but the schlock parts too. These people clearly didn't know squat about the musical theatre—and it turned out they were the future.

Sondheim vs. Webber: Round Two

The same season brought new works from the British and American schools of musical theatre. The West End debut of Andrew Lloyd Webber's *The Phantom of the Opera* (1986, still running) unleashed a wave of expectation in the United States, where theatre buffs snapped up copies of the recording and admired the ambitious score.

Lloyd Webber insisted that the Majestic was the only theatre in New York appropriate for his new work—and only if the mezzanine was reshaped first. Just as *Cats* had forced *42nd Street* to evacuate the Winter Garden six years before, *Phantom of the Opera* now pushed *42nd Street* out of the Majestic Theatre and over to the St. James. Literally and figuratively, the American musical was in a forced retreat. In an interview, coproducer Cameron Mackintosh quipped that Broadway was "just another stop on the American tour." The British were not only back on top; they were downright cocky about it.

After an almost two-year wait, the Broadway production of *Phantom of the Opera* (1988, still running) opened to a record advance ticket sale, accompanied by a new record high ticket price of forty-five dollars. The lush score featured uninspired, babbling lyrics by unknown lyricist Charles Hart, who had set words to Lloyd Webber's prewritten pop-operetta melodies with an assist from Richard Stilgoe. The plot was pure soap opera, with the mysterious Phantom terrorizing an 1880s Parisian opera company and controlling the simple-minded but vocally gifted soprano Christine Daae. Stellar performances by Michael Crawford (1942–) and Sarah Brightman (Mrs. Lloyd Webber at the time) helped, but it was Harold Prince's lavish production that made the show another triumph of form over function. Massive sets suggested the baroque glory of the Paris Opera House, including a grand chandelier that rose into the auditorium during the opening scene and crashed to the stage at the end of the first act. Many theatregoers added to their ticket price by taking home *Phantom* music boxes, mugs, sweatshirts, holiday ornaments, and masks. The marketing blitz made the Phantom's white mask as familiar as any other corporate logo.

Stephen Sondheim and director-librettist James Lapine collaborated on *Into the Woods* (1987, 769 performances), combining revised versions of several classic fairy tales to illustrate that nothing goes happily ever after, but also assuring audiences that "No one is alone."

One subplot had Bernadette Peters as a wicked witch manipulating her neighbors, a baker and his wife played by Chip Zien (1947–) and Joanna Gleason (1950–)—the latter received a Tony. Although Sondheim and Lapine were able to relish that season's Tonys for Best Score and Book, *Phantom* walked off with the award for Best Musical. What mattered most was the verdict of the ticket buying public. *Into the Woods* closed after running just shy of two years. Two decades later, *Phantom of the Opera* would still be running on Broadway, having set a new long-run record—and would still be going strong in London too. It even survived the release of an inept 2004 film version.

It's not that Sondheim had lost his touch. In fact, his technique was at its sharpest, his work still packed with emotional depth and intellectual insight. That sort of thing pleased serious theatregoers, running about as long as Sondheim's 1970s hits. Lloyd-Webber's bombastic, sentimental style made no attempts at depth or insight, but it went down easily. One did not need previous theatregoing experience, cultural background, or a refined sense of humor to enjoy a megamusical—one merely had to show up, just as at any other tourist attraction. Instead of making intellectual demands, megamusicals urge audiences to lie back while the show does all the work. The plots could be followed by any person with healthy physical senses and the I.Q. of an eight-year-old. The good guys are always tenors; the bad guys (or gals) always sing with a harsh edge. The pretty melodies are all love songs, and since there are no comic songs, there are few laughs to miss out on—so even language is no barrier.

Musical theatre as tourist attraction drew in millions of paying customers, including many who normally never went to the theatre. Successful megamusicals ran for decades, not just a few years. Traditionalists grumbled and tried to dismiss this as a passing trend. And pass it would—on to more of the same, with kid appeal thrown in.

From the Home Team

As the invasion of foreign-born musicals rolled on, American writers and producers were hard pressed for fresh ideas, but two Broadway musicals broke through to popular success.

Grand Hotel (1989, 1,077 performances) was a George Forrest and Robert Wright project that had closed on the road in 1958, and was now resurrected by Tommy Tune. Based on the classic novel and MGM film, it told of the intertwined fates of guests at a Berlin hotel in 1928. To the dismay of the original composers, director Tune called in Maury Yeston to replace half of the score. Tune set the action in a gleaming unit set by Tony Walton, keeping the action in a continuous flow that limited applause. The revised, intermission-less show got mixed reviews, but limited competition, good word of mouth, and strong marketing kept it running for several years. Big-name cast replacements (including movie legend Cyd Charisse) helped make *Grand Hotel* the first American musical since *La Cage aux Folles* to top a thousand performances on Broadway.

City of Angels (1989, 878 performances) won the 1989 Tony for Best Musical thanks to its hilarious Larry Gelbart script. Gregg Edelman (1958–) played a screenwriter who interacts with one of the characters in his latest script, a detective played by James Naughton (1945–). The Cy Coleman–David Zippel score was pleasant, but some of the songs echoed numbers from previous Coleman shows.

When these American hits had come and gone, *Les Miserables* and *Phantom of the Opera* were still playing to capacity, with multiple companies worldwide. So the 1980s were very much the decade when the Brits "got a little of their own back." Americans would soon outdo the British megamusical at its own game, but a cure can be worse than the sickness.

The 1990s: "The American Dream"

In 1990, the only memorable new musical appearing on Broadway was *Once on This Island* (1990, 469 performances), the story of a native girl (La Chanze) in the French Antilles whose love life is shaped by the intervention of the local gods. The rich, colorful score was by a pair of promising newcomers, composer Stephen Flaherty (1960–) and lyricist-librettist Lynn Ahrens (1948–). Delightful as this show was, theatre lovers were dismayed by the lack of new quality musicals. The world at large did not notice. Less than five percent of the American public attended the theatre on a regular basis, and many people went for years without hearing a showtune. There was a core group of regular theatregoers, consisting of aging suburbanites, tourists, and gay men. At sixty dollars a ticket, no one else had the disposable cash required. Students often had access to discounted tickets, so their enthusiasm could fill seats. The most successful American hits of the early 1990s were aimed at one or more segments of this core audience.

- *The Will Rogers Follies* (1991, 983 performances) had a muddled book, but Tommy Tune's ingenious production numbers and a disarming performance by Keith Carradine in the title role kept folks smiling between yawns. Carradine and a line of chorus girls won cheers with a synchronized minstrel-style tambourine routine during "Favorite Son."
- Gays and students kept more adventurous shows running until word of mouth brought them a wider audience. Their favorites included *Secret Garden* (1991, 709 performances), an emotional and visually stunning adaptation of the classic children's tale with music by Lucy Simon, book and lyrics by playwright Marsha Norman, and direction by Susan H. Schulman.
- William Finn (1952–) saw two of his off-Broadway shows combined into *Falsettos* (1992, 489 performances), which gave a musical voice to the ongoing AIDS crisis. Producers hedged their bets with a carefully planned pre-Broadway tour that covered all production expenses. Many expected this subject impossible to sell on mainstream Broadway, but Tonys for book and score, a slew of rave reviews, and shrewd management led to a profitable run.
- *Jelly's Last Jam* (1992, 569 performances) used the life story of composer Jelly Roll Morton to take a frank look at racial attitudes within the black community. It gave tap master Gregory Hines (1946–2003) the greatest role of his stage career, and brought him the Tony for Best Actor in a Musical.
- Theatregoers seeking a familiar product flocked to stylish revivals of *Guys and Dolls* (1992, 1,144 performances), *Carousel* (1994, 368 performances), and *Show Boat* (1994, 946 performances).
- *Crazy for You* (1992, 1,622 performances) reworked the bare bones of *Girl Crazy* into a giddy new musical comedy with sensational choreography by Susan Stroman (1954–) and a Gershwin score. Most of the credit went to director Mike Ockrent (1946–1999), who pulled it all together with style. Harry Groener played a New York playboy banished to a Nevada backwater, where he falls in love

with postmistress Jodi Benson. Despite a Tony for Best Musical and a run of almost four years, it took tours and foreign productions for this show's investors to see a profit.

- Kander and Ebb's *Kiss of the Spider Woman* (1993, 922 performances) mixed the showbiz dazzle of Chita Rivera with a gritty tale of homosexual love in a South American prison. It won the Tony for Best Musical but tied for Best Score with the Who's *Tommy* (1993, 927 performances), a stylish high-tech staging of the popular 1969 rock opera.
- Nothing could keep Stephen Sondheim's somber *Passion* (1994, 280) running for more than a few months. This ambitious look into the sometimes tragic price of obsession won several Tony awards (including Best Musical) but closed within weeks of the ceremony.

The British brought in more megamusicals, all offering the requisite doses of bombast and melodrama. *Miss Saigon* (1989, 4,264 performances in London; 1991, 4,097 performances in New York) took the plot of *Madame Butterfly* and moved it to Vietnam, where an American soldier falls in love with a prostitute in the days before Saigon fell to communist forces in 1974. With the assistance of American colyricist Richard Maltby, Schoenberg and Boublil turned out the most coherent and dramatically moving megamusical to date. The production did not skimp on spectacle, most notably a military helicopter that landed and took off in full view of the audience. It took some convoluted storytelling to save this effect for the second act, but audiences did not mind. Philippine actress Lea Salonga created the title role in both London and New York. The Broadway production was prefaced by a ridiculous Actor's Equity fracas over casting British actor Jonathan Pryce as a Vietnamese pimp. The union was eventually mollified and Pryce's brilliant performance earned a Tony for Best Actor in a Musical. *Miss Saigon* toured the planet and sold mountains of souvenirs. In the United States, suburbanites and tourists lapped up the lavish effects and tearjerker love story. This megamusical is the last one so far to be nurtured by Cameron Mackintosh, who sensed a change in the pop-culture mindset and has since concentrated his efforts on musical comedies and revivals.

Hints of change were certainly in the theatrical air. Andrew Lloyd Webber served as sole producer for his tedious soap opera *Aspects of Love* (1989, 1,325 performances in London; 1990, 377 performances in

New York), which ran well on the West End but according to rumor lost more than $8 million during its forced Broadway run. Lloyd Webber's $11 million adaptation of *Sunset Boulevard* (1993, 1,529 performances in London; 1994, 977 performances in New York) was arguably his weakest dramatic effort so far, despite taking its plot from Billy Wilder's classic 1950 film about a young screenwriter's (Kevin Anderson) relationship with fictional ex-movie goddess Norma Desmond (Patti LuPone). Critics complained that too much effort had been lavished on the mammoth sets but not enough on the libretto. Rather than admit to flaws in the material, Lloyd Webber fired leading lady LuPone, whose resulting lawsuit was settled out of court for a supposedly astronomical amount. Glenn Close took the show to New York and received a Tony for Best Actress in a Musical. Thanks to a lack of competition, *Sunset Boulevard* swept the 1995 Tonys, but it was a hollow victory. Although Broadway audiences worshipped when divas Betty Buckley and Elaine Paige took turns as Desmond, the production had such a high running cost—the electrical bill rivaled that of some small towns—that even a run of two and a half years could not turn a profit.

The British couldn't get enough of this schlock, but other London-born mega-productions either died in London or on the pre-Broadway road (*Martin Guerre*, *Whistle Down the Wind*). Expensive attempts to copy the British mega-style consistently failed on Broadway:

- Poland's *Metro* (1992, 13 performances)
- Holland's *Cyrano* (1993, 137 performances)
- America's *Shogun* (1990, 72 performances)
- America's *The Red Shoes* (1993, 5 performances)

The American public had seen too many lavish spectacles that took themselves too seriously, and wanted something lighter. Not necessarily smarter—just less gloomy. It was only a matter of time before someone would create the supply to meet this demand, and who better to do it than the folks who brought us Mickey Mouse?

The Corporate Musical: "Put Our Service to the Test"

The season following *Sunset Boulevard* saw change arrive on Broadway in the form of *Beauty and the Beast* (1994, 5,464 performances and

46 previews), the first stage effort of Walt Disney Productions. Helmed by theme park talents, this show was no match for the acclaimed animated film that it was based on, but whatever it lacked in finesse, it more than made up for in box office appeal. People with no interest in the theatre happily paid top dollar to bring their children to *Beast*. If the price tag added up to a few hundred dollars, no problem—it was still cheaper than taking the family to a Disney theme park. True to form, the Broadway community pretended with all its might that nothing important was happening. *Beast* was pooh-poohed by the critics and saw all the major Tonys go to *Passion*. But a seasoned entertainment corporation with massive economic clout was out to show the old pros a new way of doing things. *Beauty and the Beast* was replicated in cities all over the world, with actors giving careful imitations of the original Broadway cast in a rainbow of languages. Kids who loved the animated movie were delighted, parents were relieved to find a clean show, and billions rolled in. Souvenirs became a bigger moneymaker than ever. If the British wrote the book on auxiliary marketing, Disney built the library.

Disney had invented the *corporate musical*, a genre of shows built, produced, and managed by multifunctional entertainment corporations. These shows may begin as the idea of a composer or writer, but their development is corporate approved and sponsored. The distinctive stamp of creative individuals has little chance when key decisions are made in boardrooms. As a result, corporate musicals have the clean and anonymous efficiency of a department store. They look impressive, flow with ease, and provide a steady supply of pop ballads. They can even make audiences smile, which is more than most British mega-musicals ever did. Once they are up and running, corporate musicals can be efficiently reproduced for foreign or touring productions with matching sets and anonymous casts—no need for high-priced stars. What's missing is the joy, the vitality, the spontaneous humanity that a corporate consciousness cannot provide.

The triumph was complete by the time Disney's *The Lion King* (1997, 4,000+ performances) came to Broadway. It premiered in the New Amsterdam Theatre, one-time home of Ziegfeld's legendary *Follies*. The Disney Corporation purchased and restored this venerable theatre, opened a large retail shop next door, and planned an ultra-modern Disney hotel just up the block. So what if *The Lion King*'s score was forgettable and the whole production little more than a $12 million puppet show? It was the biggest hit of the 1990s. No one cared who was in the cast—the show was its own star. While some still pretend that *Rent* was groundbreaking, it was *The Lion King* that had a revolutionary (albeit disquieting) impact on Broadway.

People lined up for *The Lion King*, and even a price hike to eighty dollars a seat didn't prevent the show from selling out for more than a year in advance. This time, the Tony awards kowtowed to the new regime, giving *The Lion King* six Tony awards, including Best Musical (despite the fact that Best Score and Book went to *Ragtime*). Disney was triumphant and hit-hungry; Broadway was in no mood to argue. London soon had an identical production, and *The Lion King* became the most desired ticket on both Broadway and the West End until well into the next decade.

When the Pulitzer Was Up for *Rent*

By the late 1990s, almost every show that made it to Broadway was either a corporate product or the joint effort of numerous independent producers. With musical budgets running over $8 million, it took a lot of people to finance a show, and they all wanted some say in the production. This situation left no room for amateurs or rebels.

Even the much ballyhooed *Rent* (1996, 4,500+ performances) was nurtured by a New York–based company that booked and produced national tours. I was an assistant in their office during the two years leading up to *Rent*'s professional premiere. These producers had vision and took a genuine risk, but it was a risk informed by years of business experience. They guided composer-lyricist Jonathan Larson (1960–1996) through extensive rewriting in the months before the show opened off-Broadway at the New York Theatre Workshop, and told me that they would have encouraged further revisions had Larson lived. As it was, the thirty-six-year-old Larson's unexpected death on the night of the dress rehearsal made *Rent* a cultural cause célèbre. Because he had no health insurance, two hospital emergency rooms had misdiagnosed his symptoms as minor. While heating water for a cup of tea, he collapsed in his kitchen, the victim of a terminal embolism. As a national wave of sympathetic publicity carried the show to Broadway, no commercial opportunity was wasted. Long before arranging foreign productions, the producers authorized a *Rent* clothing department at

Bloomingdales. The Broadway opening was hailed as a new beginning for musical theatre, and since it was produced at less than a quarter of the cost of most musicals, hefty profits were assured.

It had been a lean season for Broadway musicals. The other contenders were adaptations of films—a genial rethinking of Rodgers and Hammerstein's *State Fair* (1996, 126 performances), and Maltby and Shire's surprisingly uninspired version of the comedy *Big* (1996, 192 performances). Nathan Lane won a long-awaited Tony starring in a revival of *A Funny Thing Happened on the Way to the Forum* (1996, 750 performances), and the rest of that year's news was about *Rent*. Having already received the Pulitzer Prize for Drama, it garnered the Tony award for Best Musical, with Larson receiving posthumous honors for his book and score, and Wilson Jermaine Heredia was named Best Featured Actor for his performance as the drag queen Angel. A younger Generation X audience flocked to see *Rent*, embracing its confused, self-pitying characters as a realistic reflection of their time. Few had the guts to point out that by letting Mimi live and killing off one of the gay characters in her place, Larson and those who praised him had set back the art of playwrighting by several decades. For all the fuss over Larson's contemporary score, no songs from the show ever made it to the pop charts, but the original cast recording did sell better than most cast CDs of its time.

As with corporate musicals, the independently developed *Rent* was reproduced worldwide with the precision of a photocopy. Its generic set, bargain-basement costuming and rudimentary staging were scrupulously recreated from New York to Tokyo, as bleached blonde Rogers wrapped their bare biceps around curly haired Mimis, their head mikes meeting in an identical kiss. *Next* magazine columnist Ron Lasko commented: "I have nightmares every time I see the new ad campaign for *Rent* that features an entirely new cast of actors that look and act exactly like the original cast; it's like some B-Horror movie version of itself, *Invasion of the Rent People*." *Rent* was an outright failure in London, where critics and audiences were less susceptible to the poignant publicity surrounding the author's death. The 2005 film version was a commercial and artistic disappointment, but the New York production lived on as a tourist must-see, and was still running as of this writing, low overhead keeping the show profitable at less than sixty percent of capacity.

In a way, *Rent* marked the end of an era. Some of its characters are identified as HIV positive, and when Larson was writing the show, such a diagnosis was still a death sentence. Medications could buy patients time, but full-blown AIDS would inevitably set in and prove fatal. In 1996, new treatments became available that would allow those with HIV to live long, functional lives. The AIDS crisis was nowhere near over, but its terrifying death toll slowed considerably.

With far less fanfare but a more hardcore rock score, the bizarre and daring *Hedwig and the Angry Inch* (1998, 857 performances) opened off-Broadway and slowly found a dedicated following. Librettist John Cameron Mitchell (1963–) starred as the title character, a transsexual punk rocker whose operation was botched and whose ex has stolen his/her songs—an unlikely premise for a musical, but young audiences embraced it. Mitchell starred in a 1981 big screen version that captured the anger and energy of the original and brought *Hedwig* to an international audience.

"Fortune's Winds Sing Godspeed"

Two well-known Kander and Ebb musicals returned to Broadway in the mid-1990s in stagings that gave them as much impact as new hits:

- A five-performance City Center *Encores!* concert version of *Chicago* (1996, 4,500+ performances) was such a sensation that it moved to Broadway. Codirectors Walter Bobbie and Ann Reinking respected the late Bob Fosse's original intentions, but they trusted the material more, creating a simpler, streamlined staging that made this cynical look at fame and American pop culture seem even timelier than it had in 1975. The revival was still running strong in New York and London a decade later, by far the longest running revival in theatrical history.
- In 1998, the Roundabout Theatre Company brought over the hard-edged British Donmar Warehouse revival of *Cabaret* (1998, 2,306 performances in New York) that rankled traditionalists but delighted many others. Director Sam Mendes further darkened the action, which now ended with the Master of Ceremonies—played with bisexual glee by Scottish actor Alan Cumming (965–)—appearing in a striped

concentration camp uniform. Thanks to rave reviews and a succession of stellar replacement casts, this revival outran the original.

The most successful black musical of the 1990s was *Bring in Da' Noise, Bring in Da' Funk* (1996, 1,148 performances), which used a series of contemporary tap numbers to dramatize and reflect on the history of Africans in America. The score was new, but the key issue was the dancing, which expressed every emotion from despair to rage to triumph. Savion Glover headed a spitfire cast and received a Tony for his groundbreaking contemporary tap choreography.

One of the few new American songwriters to find success on Broadway in the 1990s was Frank Wildhorn. His turgid adaptation of *Jekyll & Hyde* (1997, 1,543 performances) developed a dedicated cult following, greatly helped by handsome tenor Robert Cuccioli's (1958–) soaring rendition of "This Is the Moment." Wildhorn's entertaining *The Scarlet Pimpernel* (1997, 772 performances) was revised twice during its run, but never managed to find enough audience to turn a profit. The songwriter made a noisy misstep with *The Civil War* (1999, 61 performances), an incoherent attempt to present America's national nightmare in a semi-revue format. But there was no question that Wildhorn's works appealed to a dedicated, if limited, repeat audience who made history by organizing and encouraging each other via the Internet.

Side Show (1997, 91 performances) had a great cast and composer Henry Kreiger's richest score to date, but the story of real-life Siamese twins Violet (Alice Ripley) and Daisy Hilton (Emily Skinner) seeking fame and love in the world of show business proved to be a hard sell. Some blamed unadventurous audiences for not embracing this show, but in all honesty, when would a serious musical about Siamese twins have had widespread appeal?

The best musicals of the late 1990s came from producers who aimed for artistic integrity as well as profit. Composer/lyricist Maury Yeston (*Nine, Grand Hotel*) and librettist Peter Stone (*1776*) had built their reputations on making unlikely projects sing. Many laughed at their plans to write a musical inspired by the greatest maritime disaster of all time, and a *New York Times* editorial even ridiculed the project days before its premier. When *Titanic* (1997, 804 performances) won rave reviews and sailed off with five Tonys, including Best Musical, the theatrical community was caught off guard. With the best new American stage score in over a decade, this concept musical put creative aspects ahead of marketing concerns. Those accustomed to megamusical pap were turned off, but many serious theatregoers rejoiced. Over a dozen key characters were defined through songs that invoked various period or ethnic styles: the hopeful immigrants dreaming of life "In America," the Gilbert and Sullivan–style arrogance of the rich exclaiming "What a Remarkable Age This Is," and the Herbert-style heartbreaking affirmation of the elderly Mr. and Mrs. Strauss that they "Still" love each other as they face imminent death on the sinking liner. A stronger director or solo producer might have sharpened the dramatic focus, but corporate thinking let matters lie. Whatever its imperfections, *Titanic* deserved its success.

Ragtime (1998, 861 performances) was another example of the corporate musical at its best, thanks to a spectacular score by Lynn Ahrens and Stephen Flaherty, and an unusually strong libretto by playwright Terrence McNally (1939–). The epic story told of a crumbling family, a black man seeking justice, and a Jewish immigrant fulfilling the American dream for himself and his child, all set in the first turbulent decade of the twentieth century. As with *Titanic*, a huge cast of characters was brought into focus by a score that invoked period musical styles and a book that wove disparate lives into a common pattern— the concept musical blown up to epic proportions. *Ragtime*'s opening title song was a landmark event in its own right, possibly the finest example of plot and character exposition yet attempted on the musical stage. Ahrens and Flaherty were not afraid to use satire ("Crime of the Century") or ribald humor ("What a Game") along with ensembles, rags, and soaring ballads. When Brian Stokes Mitchell (1957–) as musician Coalhouse Walker and Audra McDonald (1970–) as his beloved Sarah sang of how they would ride into the future "On the Wheels of a Dream," it was potent musical theatre. Though overproduced and underdirected, *Ragtime* was a musical with brains, heart, a touch of courage, and more than a little excitement.

Century's End: Old and New

The 1998–99 season was filled with disappointments for musical theatre fans. The few new Broadway musicals suffered from serious flaws.

- A stage adaptation of the film *Footloose* (1998, 737 performances) had enthusiasm but reeked of professional ineptitude, repulsing critics even as it drew strong ticket sales, thanks to tourists and suburbanites.
- A bloodless adaptation of the film *Saturday Night Fever* (1999, 500 performances) was dismissed by the critics, but still racked up a fourteen million dollar advance, proving yet again that there is no underestimating the taste of casual ticket buyers.
- Despite composer Michael John LaChiusa's insistence that his *Marie Christine* (1999, 44 performances) was a musical, it was a didactic modern opera version of *Medea*, inaccessible to most audiences.
- Jason Robert Brown's *Parade* (1998, 84 performances) was a somber history lesson with little audience appeal, given a handsome production by director Harold Prince. The true story of a bigoted Southern mob lynching a Jewish man for a crime that he didn't commit, this show had few admirers until after it closed. When people realized that this was the only book musical competing with *Footloose*, their opinions changed, and *Parade* copped Tonys for Best Book and Score.
- *Fosse* (1999, 1,108 performances), a compendium of the late choreographer's finest dances, was the season's longest running hit. Consisting of previously seen material, *Fosse* was only new in form, but it won the Best Musical Tony. Codirected by Richard Maltby Jr. and Ann Reinking, with special assistance by Fosse's widow Gwen Verdon, it offered a wide-ranging look at what this "razzle dazzle" genius had accomplished.

A revised *Annie Get Your Gun* (1999, 1,046 performances) gave the radiant Bernadette Peters one of her strongest vehicles to date and her second Tony as Best Actress in a Musical. Despite some clumsy cuts, Irving Berlin's stage score still delighted audiences. The highlight of late 1999 was a revival of *Kiss Me Kate* (1999, 885 performances), a glorious production that that gave Brian Stokes Mitchell his first Tony as Best Actor in a Musical and stood out all the more in an era when new shows were marked by intellectual vapidity and a terminal shortage of humor. Audiences were amazed to hear themselves laugh out loud at lyrics for the first time in years, proving Cole Porter's genius was indeed timeless.

Musical theatre professionals and aficionados had good reason to wonder what the next century might bring. After flourishing for more than a hundred and fifty years, the Broadway musical was in uncertain condition. Shows that appealed to the lowest common cultural denominator thrived, while wit and melody were reserved for revivals. But those revivals were doing big business. After years of megamusical flummery, could it be that theatregoers were hungry for musical comedy? What an absurd notion! Musical comedy was a dead and buried dinosaur—wasn't it?

16

Musical Comedy Returns (The 2000s) — "Where Did We Go Right?"

T he eyes of the world turned to Times Square on New Year's Eve 1999 as a ball of light descended a flagpole, igniting a sign that proclaimed the birth of a new millennium. But the year 2000 found the Broadway community unsure of what the future of musical theatre could be. The first Broadway musical of the twenty-first century was James Joyce's *The Dead* (2000, 111 performances), written by men with no experience creating musicals. It showed. The plot: after sharing a subtext-laden Christmas celebration with friends, a Dublin couple realizes that their longstanding marriage is a loveless sham. The fact that a cast of musical stage and screen veterans took part in such a dull project was symbolic of how desperate actors had become for a chance to appear in a new Broadway musical.

Disney scored a tremendous commercial hit with *Aida* (2000, 1,852 performances). Audiences flocked to this reworking of the classic Verdi opera, with a slave princess and a war hero sharing romance, death, and a vertical swimming pool in ancient Egypt. However, the Elton John–Tim Rice pop-rock score had little substance to back up the glitzy high-tech production. Dance remained a dominant force on Broadway. After sell-out runs at Radio City Music Hall, the Irish step dancing revue *Riverdance* (2000, 605 performances) came to Broadway for a healthy run. But top honors for the season went to Susan Stroman's *Contact* (2000, 1,008 performances), a trio of dance pieces that wowed the critics and swept the Tonys, including one for Best Musical. Unions and theatrical purists protested that a show with no orchestra, no singing, and no book was not really a musical—and they had a point. If this was a musical, so was every offering of the New York City Ballet. But ticket buyers packed Lincoln Center's Vivian Beaumont Theatre for more than two years to see ravishing Deborah Yates as "The Girl in the Yellow Dress" who taunted the handsome but clueless Boyd Gaines. Like other all-dance musicals, *Contact*'s demanding routines could not be easily replicated, so the show had no life in regional or amateur theatre.

The following season got off to a promising start as critics raved for *The Full Monty* (2000, 768 performances), based on the hit 1997 film about a group of unemployed men who try to make a few bucks stripping for ladies night in a local club. David Yazbek's pop-infused score was no match for Terrence McNally's witty book, and business was far from sell-out level. Amid a slew of revivals and ill-conceived new shows, filmmaker Mel Brooks brought in the long-threatened musical adaptation of his 1967 screen classic *The Producers* (2001, 2,502 performances). Nathan Lane played manic producer Max Bialystock, who hopes to make millions staging a Broadway flop, assisted by Matthew Broderick as the nebbishy accountant Leo Bloom. Staged by Susan Stroman, it picked up a record-setting fourteen Tony awards. The full-sized, shameless Broadway musical comedy, long considered extinct, was back and roaring. The sore point was that, for all its laughs, *The Producers* had almost no genuine sentiment, and won its laughs by ridiculing the theatre and those silly enough to love it. When the producers of *The Producers* went beyond the top ticket price of a hundred dollars and started selling their best seats at a chilling $485, it was hard to say which was more frightening—the greed of those willing to charge such an amount, or the stupidity of those willing to pay it. The good news was that with *Full Monty, The Producers,* and a sensational revival of *42nd Street* (2001, 1,525 performances) running strong, American-made musical comedy was once again the dominant force on Broadway.

This resurgence of American musical comedy coincided with a period of creative stasis in London's West End. A musical comedy based on the hit film *The Witches of Eastwick* (2000, 510 performances) and Andrew Lloyd Webber's British football musical *The Beautiful Game* (2000, 391 performances) had their admirers but did not find an international audience. The ball was once again very much in America's court, and Broadway did its damnedest to keep it that way, even after a nightmare event that redefined New York City's way of life for years to come.

Dark Times, Fresh Humor

When terrorists commandeered commercial airliners and destroyed the World Trade Center towers on September 11, 2001, every theatre on Broadway went dark for two days. New York was a battleground for the first time since the British drove out Washington's troops 225 years earlier. While many wondered what this calamity meant for the future, the theatrical community did its best to regroup and carry on. Tourism took a sharp plunge for several months, providing a painful reminder of how heavily Broadway now relied on tourist dollars.

Just ten days after the attacks, the outrageous musical satire *Urinetown* (2001, 965 performances) opened on Broadway to rave reviews, reaching sell-out status and reaffirming that meaningful theatre would go on. The surrealistic plot involved a drought-plagued city where the impoverished populace confronts a monolithic corporation controlling waste management—yes, a musical about the right to tinkle! John Cullum won fresh acclaim as the amoral head of that corporation, who warned his naïve daughter that this is a world full of wolves, so "Don't Be the Bunny." Staged as a Brechtian send-up of various theatrical conventions, *Urinetown* became the sleeper hit of the season and proved that playful satire still had commercial possibilities on Broadway. Audiences were so busy laughing that they didn't balk when the show chided "that their way of life is unsustainable." Like the great musical comedies of an earlier age, *Urinetown* succeeded by offering humor with an intelligent edge, or "serious fun."

The London-born *Mamma Mia* (which opened in London in 1999) roared into town weeks later, offering a familiar comic plot already seen in the film *Buona Sera Mrs. Campbell* and the musical *Carmelina*—a mother must confront the three men who might be her daughter's father—rebuilt around old hit songs by the Swedish pop group ABBA. Critics were underwhelmed, but enthusiastic audiences kept the Winter Garden sold out for years. On Broadway and on tour, *Mamma Mia* proved that pure joy and deafening bubble-gum rock could sell a heck of a lot of tickets, and in 2005, it became the first book musical to top one thousand performances in Las Vegas. This show was the first in a wave of *jukebox musicals* (also known as "pop-sicals")—new musicals built around existing pop songs. Some of these shows were revues, but most were book musicals. They kept a few key features of the megamusical age—cookie-cutter international productions, a heavy stress on marketing, and lookalike/soundalike casting.

For musical buffs, few thrills could match the return of Broadway legend Elaine Stritch in a one-woman triumph, *At Liberty* (2002, 69 performances). The limited-run hit brought Stritch the Tony she had waited half a century for, albeit a special award, not a Best Actress trophy. That honor went to newcomer Sutton Foster (1975–) for her performance of the title role in *Thoroughly Modern Millie* (2002, 903 performances), a tap-happy adaptation of the 1967 movie musical. The new songs were mediocre, but vintage showstoppers from Gilbert and Sullivan's *Ruddigore* and Victor Herbert's *Naughty Marietta* combined with sensational choreography by Rob Ashford (1959–) to earn several Tonys, including Best Musical.

Many enjoyed *Movin' Out* (2002, 1,202 performances), Twyla Tharpe's dance musical built around the pop songs of Billy Joel. Baz Luhrmann's updated Australian Opera production of Puccini's opera *La Bohème* (2002, 228 performances) won justified raves but lost millions of dollars during its brief run. Bernadette Peters starred in a minimalist revival of *Gypsy* (2003, 451 performances), but did not rate as much of a publicity fuss as movie star Antonio Banderas did making his Broadway debut in a badly staged revival of *Nine* (2003, 285 performances), which also boasted Jane Krakowski (1968–) making an electrifying "Call from the Vatican" suspended in midair clad in nothing more than a sheet. Two musicals based on old movies were the most spectacular disasters of the season. The long-awaited German hit *Dance of the Vampires* (2002, 56 performances plus previews) offered Michael Crawford in an incoherent blend of misfired comedy and passionless romance, and a well-intentioned but bland stage version of *Urban Cowboy* (2003, 60 performances) soon two-stepped its way into obscurity.

On the other hand, the new musical comedy trend rocked on with the arrival of *Hairspray* (2002). Based on a popular 1988 film by John Walters, it told the story of Tracy Turnblad (Marissa Jaret Winokur), an overweight Baltimore teen whose dreams of a singing career led to romance, stardom, and racial integration on a local TV show in the early 1960s. With a hilarious book by Thomas Meehan and Mark O'Donnell and a giddy period-flavored score by Marc Shaiman and Scott Wittman, *Hairspray* delighted critics and audiences and gave Harvey Fierstein a chance to camp his way to glory as Tracy's mama Edna. *Hairspray* became the third American musical comedy in a row to win the Tony for Best Musical—and all three had been based on decades-old movies.

Wizards, Puppets, and Jukeboxes

Exactly one hundred years after *The Wizard of Oz* debuted on Broadway, along came a lavish musical adaptation of *Wicked* (2003), the best-selling novel that retells the same story from the Wicked Witch's point of view, providing a reminder that history is told and distorted by the so-called "winners." Veteran composer-lyricist Stephen Schwartz offered that increasingly rare thing, a deceptively simple, well-crafted score that benefits from rehearing. *Wicked* was considered a frontrunner for the Tonys, but it was eclipsed by *Avenue Q* (2003), an intimate, low-budget musical comedy about life among struggling thirty-somethings in New York's outer boroughs. With Muppet-style puppets, some mild naughtiness (coy ads promised "full puppet nudity"), and an irreverent sense of humor, *Avenue Q* quickly moved from off-Broadway (adopted by the producers of *Rent*) to win rave reviews and Tonys for Best Book, Score, and Musical. Of course, it helped that the Tony committee classified Stephen Sondheim's brilliant *Assassins* (2004, 101 performances) as a "revival," despite the fact that the show qualified as a new show under existing eligibility guidelines. This daring production had to settle for winning Best Revival and Best Director of a Musical for Joe Mantello, who had also helmed *Wicked*. The same season saw Australian film hunk Hugh Jackman (1968–) play fellow countryman Peter Allen in *The Boy from Oz* (2003, 365 performances), which was no masterpiece, but Jackman's sexy, charismatic performance won a Tony and made him the hottest star on Broadway.

The following season saw the zany *Monty Python's Spamalot* (2005, 1,000+ performances) win the Tony for Best Musical over the toughest competition of the decade. Freely adapted from the 1975 film comedy *Monty Python and the Holy Grail*, it pleased dedicated fans of the old British comedy troupe by dumbing down an already silly spoof of the Arthurian legend. That same season saw three other shows that all enjoyed prolonged and profitable runs, proving that there was still a diverse audience for quality Broadway musicals.

- *Dirty Rotten Scoundrels* (2005, 666 performances) was an adaptation of a hit 1988 film, enlivened by David Yazbek's solid musical comedy score, a sharp libretto by first-timer Jeffrey Lane, and stellar performances by John Lithgow and Norbert Leo Butz as competing con men joining forces to fleece the unknowing. The producers showed their own sense of humor by ending the run at a neodemonic 666 performances.
- *A Light in the Piazza* (2005, 504 performances) was an adaptation of a 1962 MGM comedy, with a sensitive libretto by Craig Lucas and an almost operatic Tony-winning score by Adam Guettel (1965–), grandson of Richard Rodgers. Victoria Clark starred as mother of a retarded young woman (Kelli O'Hara) who falls in love with a handsome Italian (Matthew Morrison) during a trip to Venice.
- William Finn's original *The 25th Annual Putnam County Spelling Bee* (2005, 1,136 performances) took a humorous look at one of America's scholastic institutions, giving several quirky contestants a chance to shine. It did not take a crystal ball to predict that this witty, inexpensive project would have a tremendous future in regional and amateur theatre.

Many felt less than ecstatic when the charming *Jersey Boys* (2005, 850+ performances), a dramatized collection of pop hits introduced by Frankie Valli and the Four Seasons, became the first jukebox musical to win the Tony for Best Musical in 2006. Its main rival was *The Drowsy Chaperone* (2006, 500+ performances), a spoof of 1920s musicals that bore little resemblance to the real thing but won laughs from an unknowing public. A handsome adaptation of the hit novel and film *The Color Purple* (2005, 800+ performances) was overpacked with plot, but a promising score and generous publicity (courtesy of producer Oprah Winfrey's popular daytime talk show) helped keep the show running strong. British director John Doyle won acclaim and a Tony with a gimmick-laden revival of *Sweeney Todd* (2005, 349 performances) that had the actors serve as their own orchestra. With no orchestra to pay, the production made a small profit. The Tonys ignored Disney's *Tarzan* (2006, 486 performances), which nevertheless drew a year's worth of tots and ill-advised parents with its vine-swinging antics and mind-numbing score.

As the decade passed its midpoint, faithful restagings of *A Chorus Line* (2006) and *Les Misérables* (2006) opened to very profitable houses. Schönberg and Boublil did not do nearly as well with *The Pirate Queen* (2007, 85 performances), which suggested that while Americans audiences might welcome back an old European megamusical, they were in no mood for a new one. John Doyle fell back on his actors-as-orchestra trick in a revival of *Company* (2006, 247 performances) that wound up losing much of its investment due to resolute audience disinterest. Disney had a hard time selling tickets to a loud but painfully saccharine adaptation of *Mary Poppins* (2006). Although Fred Ebb died in 2003, John Kander continued to develop several of their late collaborative projects, and with the assistance of Rupert Holmes brought the charming murder mystery spoof *Curtains* (2007) to Broadway earning cheers from traditionalists but shrugs from industry insiders.

That season, two musicals that began life off-Broadway provided most of the excitement. *Grey Gardens* (2006, 308 performences) was based on a disturbing 1979 documentary about two wealthy eccentrics who wound up losing their minds and sharing their crumbling Long Island mansion with a legion of cats. Christine Ebersole gave an epochal Tony-winning performance playing "Little" Edie Beale and (in flashbacks) her own mother, Edith Bouvier Beale—relatives of former First Lady Jacqueline Bouvier Kennedy.

But far more buzz surrounded *Spring Awakening* (2006), which took its plot from a 115-year-old play about teenagers coming of age in 1890s Germany. Melchior (Jonathan Groff) discovers the joy of sex with his girlfriend Wendla (Lea Michele), then writes a sex manual for his repressed best friend Moritz (John Gallagher Jr.). When Moritz commits suicide, Melchior's manual is discovered, and he is sent to reform school, where he is gang-raped by his fellow inmates. When Wendla discovers that she is pregnant, her mother forces her into an abortion that proves fatal. On Melchior's release, he discovers Wendla's grave, providing a tragic ending to a bleak, angry tale. Pop composer Duncan Shiek's songs were staged in contemporary rock concert style, with the cast stepping out of character and picking up microphones. The use of obscenity-laced lyrics and mosh pit dancing helped to make each number a complete stylistic departure from the libretto. Theatre-loving teens enthusiastically embraced this unintegrated musical, which offered a clear break from the parade of megamusicals and revivals dominating Broadway. *New York Times* reviewer Charles Isherwood went so far as to suggest that "Broadway, with its often puerile sophistication and its sterile romanticism, may never be the same." Even those who did not like the show could not deny its extraordinary energy. One retiree was overheard saying, "I didn't care for the songs or the sex, but it was the most exciting musical I've seen all year." *Spring Awakening* received eight Tony awards, with thirty-six producers coming onstage to accept the Best Musical accolade.

The State of the Art: "Who Are You Now?"

On May 26, 2006, chief *New York Times* theatre critic Ben Brantley published an article entitled "The Day the Musical Died," making him the latest in a long line of doom merchants who declared the musical theatre a dead art form. He stated that in the Broadway season that just ended, "this once lively art seemed finally to have crossed the border that divides flesh from ectoplasm." By the article's end he hedges, in the sort of self-contradiction that allows the indecisive to avoid saying anything of real substance. But his headline captured his premise—and his premise was as false now as when others made the same statement countless times before.

There are no dependable means of divining the future, so whenever someone tells you that they know what lies ahead for the theatre, you can count on them being wrong—particularly boneheaded critics who use such clichés as "Broadway will never be the same" when praising the latest hit. However, we can say some reasonable things about where musical theatre is at the start of the twenty-first century, and about the forces that seem likely to affect its future course.

Are musicals dead? Nonsense. Even if the Broadway musical were to die—which is still not likely—the musical theatre is not just an

American art form; it is a world art form with a 2,500-year history, one that America has played a leading part in for only one and a half centuries. There is no denying that certain statistics are disheartening. Broadway used to greet forty or fifty new musicals per season, and now sees fewer than a dozen. With production costs averaging more than ten million dollars, and with a relatively small percentage of the population attending the theatre regularly, there is no reason to believe that figure will soar in the near future. On the other hand, a study by the New York League of Theatres and Producers revealed that in 2005, $769 million were spent on Broadway theatre tickets—and nine out of every ten of those dollars were spent on tickets to musicals. So there is still a lot of money to be made in musical theatre, enough to keep new productions coming for as long as anyone can guess. But that same study pointed out a fascinating demographic. For many years, it was assumed that Broadway audiences consisted mainly of New Yorkers and residents of adjacent suburbs. However, as of 2005, the League study revealed that a typical Broadway audience consisted of:

- New Yorkers: 16.7%
- Suburbanites: 22.9%
- Tourists: 60%

So it is no exaggeration to say that the Broadway musical is now a tourist attraction, relying on out of towners for almost two thirds of its income. This is a key reason why corporate megamusicals currently dominate the scene. These are musicals for the masses, as accessible as any other tourist attraction.

Based on more than two thousand years of historical precedent, we can safely predict this much: so long as musical theatre remains dependent on audience support, it will develop along whatever lines public taste dictates. Several factors will probably play key roles in that process:

- The swift erosion of historical and cultural literacy in America's general population. Audiences addicted to action films, video games, and popular songs that glorify violence are going to be looking for something other than *My Fair Lady* when paying top ticket prices.

- The banishment of music and theatre from most elementary and high schools means that a growing percentage of Americans are entering adulthood without any exposure to music or theatre.
- The replacement of a predominantly European-descent population with a population that is mostly of Latin American descent will shift the focus of popular culture. Current estimates suggest that the twenty-first century will see Latinos become the largest ethnic group in the United States. To date, this population has displayed little active interest in musical theatre. Unless this particular trend shifts, the commercial viability of stage musicals in the United States will be in doubt.

At one time, the above list would have included the ongoing erosion of New York City's dominance as the world's premiere theatrical capital. Most new musicals are now being developed at regional theatres beyond New York's influence. However, in the last few years, the swift shrinkage of America's aging theatre-going population has led to the disappearance of several major regional theatres, with many others struggling for survival as never before. If these trends continue, it is likely that musical theatre in America will go the way of grand opera, becoming the provenance of a few companies specializing in revivals and catering to an elite urban audience.

From 1943 to the mid-1960s, Broadway musicals could be mounted for under $250,000, and a well-managed production could turn a solid profit in less than a year. Now physically simple productions like *Rent* can cost $3 million or more, while *The Producers* cost well over $10 million. According to League statistics, nineteen of the thirty shows that opened during the 2005–2006 season closed without recouping investments, posting an aggregate loss of $96 million. Even with ticket prices topping $110, shows can run for several years and still close at a loss. The combined effects of inflation and too many people demanding a bigger share of potential profits take a mounting toll, so that a large-scale Broadway musical must spend $700,000 or more per week just to keep running. At the same time, the core audience of musical theatre lovers is shrinking. CD producers currently limit cast recording releases to 5,000 copies because that's how many collectors are out there—not even enough bodies to constitute one full Tony awards audience at Radio City Music Hall.

When *Rent* proved a bona fide sensation in 1996, some critics said that it pointed the way to Broadway's musical future. Well, after more than a decade, it is clear that these pronouncements were misfires. With amateurish production values, lust labeled as love, and bathos where a plot should be, *Rent* was less a signpost than a stumble. It spawned no trends. The 2007 appearance of *Spring Awakening* has ignited the same sort of hype—all for an antique flop play interrupted for contemporary concert sequences. If style, romance, melody, and joy are things of the past, what is the point of a musical? Why not just go to a rock concert?

The Producers, Thoroughly Modern Millie, Urinetown, and *Hairspray* succeeded by doing what great musical comedies have always done—approaching material in fresh and funny ways that no one has attempted before. (Male strippers, singing Nazis, bathroom politics, and interracial romance would have been unthinkable in the so-called classic musicals of the 1950s!) At the same time, several Broadway revivals have taken new approaches to well-known material, infusing classics with fresh energy.

Is this really a new springtime for musical comedy on Broadway, or just a momentary thaw? Only time will tell. For this trend to last, we need an informed audience large enough to make the results profitable, and an army of new talents to keep new hits coming. One wonders how many creative people will be willing to attempt the costly, high-risk process of creating musicals for Broadway in years to come, especially when film and television offer far more lucrative employment. A hit musical takes years to pay its creators anything like the six figure income a sitcom writer earns in just one season. New producers face the increasingly daunting demands of the various unions, as well as the unbridled greed of theatre owners who charge horrifying rental rates.

There is also the ongoing trend of jukebox musicals. These range from plot-based book shows (*Mamma Mia, All Shook Up*) to essentially plotless semi-revues or dance musicals (*Movin' Out*). *Contact* truly pushed the envelope by mixing classical and pop recordings, dispensing with songwriters, live musicians, and singers—and managed (in a feeble season) to win the Tony for Best Musical. While traditionalists may not be happy with jukebox musicals, it is hard to deny that the best of them sell lots of tickets. So long as the money keeps flowing in, this trend will continue. One can only hope that it does not reach the point where Broadway turns into Las Vegas East.

Although regional and nonprofit theatres face financial challenges, they remain the best source of new, exciting musical theatre. From *Rent* to *Urinetown* to *Spring Awakening*, the most artistically ambitious musicals of recent years have almost exclusively begun life thanks to such companies. At present, most nonprofit theatre companies develop musicals on a limited basis. The only company in New York City—and one of a very few in the world—that makes a full-time commitment to developing new musicals and resurrecting promising works from the past is the York Theatre. In a typical year, the York presents more than thirty developmental readings of musicals "in progress," allowing writers and composers to get feedback from the general public. Such shows as *Avenue Q* and the off-Broadway cult favorite [title of show] saw their first audiences as York readings. The York also presents two or three new musicals in full off-Broadway productions with Equity casts. Stressing content over spectacle, these are not the sort of musicals that would appeal to a corporate board, but they are among the most intelligent and adventurous new works in any New York theatrical season.

What corporate board would present a musical about Leopold and Loeb, the infamous 1920s thrill killers? Worse yet, it was written by a first-time composer-lyricist! The York did exactly that with Stephen Dolginoff's *Thrill Me*, which received a sheaf of rave reviews in the spring of 2005. The run faced so many extensions that Dolginoff himself eventually joined the cast to play Nathan Leopold, whom many historians have considered the dupe of the more diabolical Richard Loeb. *Thrill Me* plays on that popular perception, and then turns it on its ear, suggesting that it is not always obvious who the manipulator is, even in an abusive relationship. It is also a reminder of how attractive evil can seem. Working from the historical record, Dolginoff paints a complicated, fascinating interplay between the popular, cruel Loeb and the nerdy, dependent Leopold. Their early acts of vandalism include setting a warehouse ablaze and then making passionate love because there's "Nothing Like a Fire." Convincing each other that they are the sort of "Superior" supermen defined by Nietzsche, they set out to commit the ultimate crime, a murder that no one can solve. But the killing of a neighborhood boy is swiftly unraveled by investigators, and as the partners face "Life Plus 99 Years," it becomes clear that one of them planned it to work out that way.

George M. Cohan could never have conceived of such a dark topic for a musical—neither would the Gershwins, Cole Porter, or even Rodgers and Hammerstein. All were revolutionaries, but could only go where their era allowed. It has taken an ongoing evolution to bring the musical theatre to the point where something as dark as the Leopold and Loeb story could sing. Since its York production, *Thrill Me* has had acclaimed regional productions all across the United States, as well as successful stagings in London, Seoul, and other foreign cities.

The musical has been changing ever since Offenbach did his first rewrite in the 1850s, and change is the clearest sign that the musical is still a living, growing genre. Will we ever return to the so-called "golden age," with musicals at the center of popular culture? Who knows? Public taste has often undergone fundamental changes, and the commercial arts can only flow where the paying public allows. The musical will survive and occasionally thrive by adapting to changes in artistic and commercial expectations. But change often comes at a price. The new century will take musical theatre and film to places we could no more imagine than the people of the early 1900s could have foreseen the technology of *The Jazz Singer* or the subject matter of *Hedwig and the Angry Inch*. As it moves forward, the musical will go places some of us will not care to follow. But so long as a song helps to tell a story, musicals will be around.

We opened this book with a definition of the musical, and now we close with another, courtesy of Oscar Hammerstein II:

> It is nonsense to say what a musical should or should not be. It should be anything it wants to be, and if you don't like it you don't have to go to it. There is only one absolutely indispensable element that a musical must have. It must have music. And there is only one thing that it has to be—it has to be good.

Granted, in the current environment, only a crazed fool would invest the years of thankless effort required to get a musical to either Broadway or the West End. But as Mr. Hammerstein also observed, "the world is full of crazies and fools," and thanks to them "impossible things are happening every day."

SUGGESTED READING:
AN ANNOTATED BIBLIOGRAPHY

Many of the books and websites listed here were referred to in the course of preparing this volume. All will be of interest to those looking to do further reading on the history of musical theatre.

Abbott, George. *Mister Abbott*. New York: Random House, 1963. An entertaining and frank autobiography from the dean of Broadway directors. Only drawback: some of his most important musical projects get the barest mention.

Allen, Robert C. *Horrible Prettiness: Burlesque and American Culture*. Chapel Hill: University of North Carolina Press, 1991. A first-rate study of burlesque and its place in American culture during the nineteenth and twentieth centuries.

Alpert, Hollis. *The Life and Times of Porgy and Bess: The Story of an American Classic*. New York: Alfred A. Knopf, 1990. An exhaustive and engrossing history of a masterpiece, with detailed coverage of all major productions up to 1990.

Altman, Richard, and Mervyn Kaufman. *The Making of a Musical: Fiddler on the Roof*. New York: Crown Publishers, 1971. A fascinating behind-the-scenes look at the major stage and screen incarnations of a beloved classic.

Astaire, Fred. *Steps in Time: An Autobiography*. New York: Cooper Square Press, 2000. Astaire was far too classy to write an unkind word about anyone, but his memories of life in vaudeville, on Broadway, and in Hollywood offer some fun firsthand insights.

Ayre, Leslie. *The Gilbert & Sullivan Companion*. London: Papermac, 1985. A helpful dictionary covering Gilbert and Sullivan operas and related history.

Baral, Robert. *Revue: A Nostalgic Reprise of the Great Broadway Period.* New York: Fleet Publishing Company, 1962. A veteran *Variety* columnist spent ten years compiling one of the first serious attempts to document classic Broadway revues.

Barry, John M. *The Great Influenza.* New York: Viking, 2004. Detailed and well-researched investigation of a long ignored topic.

Beckerman, Bernard, and Howard Siegman, eds. *On Stage: Selected Theatre Reviews from the New York Times, 1920–1970.* New York: Arno Press, 1973. A fine overview of *New York Times* criticism during the Broadway musical's so-called "golden age."

Beddow, Margery. *Bob Fosse's Broadway.* Portsmouth, New Hampshire: Heinemann, 1996. A Fosse dancer's intimate and loving perspective on the man and his work.

Bernheim, Alfred L. *The Business of the Theatre: An Economic History of the American Theatre, 1750–1932.* New York: Benjamin Blom, Inc., 1964. Prepared for the Actor's Equity Association in 1932, this book remains a fascinating record of stage economics.

Block, Geoffrey. *Enchanted Evenings: The Broadway Musical From Show Boat to Sondheim.* New York: Oxford University Press, 1997. A musicologist looks at the way music is used as a dramatic tool in some of Broadway's greatest twentieth-century musicals.

———. *The Richard Rodgers Reader.* New York: Oxford University Press, 2002. It would take months, if not years, to track down all the materials gathered in this fascinating resource.

Bordman, Gerald. *American Musical Theatre: A Chronicle.* New York: Oxford University Press, 1978 (new edition 1992). Still the most comprehensive single-volume history of the American stage musical.

———. *American Operetta.* New York: Oxford University Press, 1981. A fine look at the beginnings of the musical in America. My only quibble is that Bordman may go a bit far to qualify certain shows as operettas.

———. *Jerome Kern: His Life and Music.* New York: Oxford University Press, 1980. The definitive resource on Kern and his work.

Bratton, J. S., ed. *Music Hall Performance and Style.* Philadelphia: Open University Press, 1986. An interesting, if limited, collection of essays.

Burke, Billie. *With a Feather on My Nose.* New York: Appleton-Century-Crofts, 1948. From wife of Ziegfeld to her performance as Glinda, a lighthearted memoir.

Carlyou, David. *Dan Rice: The Most Famous Man You've Never Heard Of.* New York: Public Affairs Press, 2001. Long overdue look at early show business in the United States. Valuable insights into the prehistory of minstrelsy and musical comedy.

Chapin, Ted. *Everything Was Possible: The Birth of the Musical Follies.* New York: Alfred A. Knopf, 2003. An absorbing behind-the-scenes look at the development of a controversial masterwork.

Cheshire, D. F. *Music Hall in Britain.* Rutherford, New Jersey: Fairleigh Dickenson University Press, 1974. Concise and insightful history of British variety, one of the clearest and most rewarding books on the subject.

Coward, Noël. *Play Parade.* New York: Doubleday, 1933. Coward's first collection of hits, including *Bittersweet.* Playwrights (and theatre lovers) still have much to learn from "The Master."

Davis, Lee. *Scandals and Follies: The Rise and Fall of the Great Broadway Revue.* New York: Limelight Editions, 2000. An entertaining if sometimes stretched overview of the legendary Broadway revues of the early twentieth century.

Disher, M. Willson. *Music Hall Parade.* London: Charles Scribners Sons, 1938. A celebration of music hall history, with some fascinating illustrations.

Dunn, Don. *The Making of No, No, Nanette.* Secaucus, New Jersey: Citadel Press, 1972. Although hard to find, this is the dishiest book ever on the madness involved in putting a Broadway musical together.

Ewen, David. *American Musical Theatre.* New York: Holt, Rinehart & Winston, 1970. Underrated and now out of print, this is a thorough encyclopedia of important American musicals up to 1970.

Feuer, Cy. *I Got the Show Right Here.* New York: Simon & Schuster, 2003. Fast-paced, entertaining memoir from the producer of *Guys and Dolls* and many other hit musicals.

Fields, Armond, and Marc Fields. *From the Bowery to Broadway: Lew Fields and the Roots of American Popular Theatre.* New York: Oxford University Press, 1993. I live to find books like this! Evocative, well researched, and a pleasure to read.

Filichia, Peter. *Let's Put on a Musical: How to Choose the Right Show for Your Theatre.* New York: Watson-Guptill, 1997. A treasure! Lists the key production requirements for all the major musicals. Aimed to help your group pick the perfect show.

Flinn, Denny Martin. *Musical!: A Grand Tour.* New York: Schirmer Books, 1997. A wide-ranging and eloquent look at the history of the musical, with some inaccuracies.

Fordin, Hugh. *Getting to Know Him: Oscar Hammerstein II.* New York: Ungar Publishing Co., 1977. Sensitive and superb biography of a gentle giant.

Frank, Rusty E. *Tap!: The Greatest Tap Dance Stars and Their Stories, 1900–1955.* New York: DaCapo Publications, 1994. A much needed book on an all too rarely covered subject. It gives the rarified art form of tap a human face.

Furia, Philip. *Irving Berlin: A Life in Song.* New York: Shirmer Books, 1998. Delightful biography, written with great insight into Berlin's life and career.

Ganzl, Kurt. *The Encyclopedia of Musical Theatre.* 3 vols. New York: Schirmer Books, 2001. Only serious research libraries carry this set listing thousands of shows and individuals. The best source to date on European musicals, with solid U.S. coverage too.

———. *Lydia Thompson: Queen of Burlesque.* New York and London: Routledge, 2002. Detailed and thoroughly researched, this long overdue biography of a burlesque legend offers a fascinating glimpse into a lost theatrical era.

———. *Musicals.* London: Carlton Books, 2001. Few people have covered the subject of musicals with such a strong international perspective. Handsomely illustrated and, as is always the case with Ganzl's writings, a pleasure to read.

Garland, Robert. *Daily Life of the Ancient Greeks.* New York: Greenwood Press, 1998. Thorough and enjoyable overview, with an excellent section on Athenian theatre.

Gilbert, Douglas. *American Vaudeville: Its Life and Times.* New York: Dover Publications, 1963. The first serious attempt to tell vaudeville's story, and still one of the best books on the subject.

Goldman, Howard. *Fanny Brice: The Original Funny Girl.* New York: Oxford University Press, 1992. A well-researched and readable biography of the woman who inspired *Funny Girl.* Great insights into the show business world of the early twentieth century.

———. *Jolson: The Legend Comes to Life.* New York: Oxford University Press, 1988. One of the best theatrical biographies ever; astounding research.

Goldstein, Malcolm. *George S. Kaufman: His Life, His Theatre.* New York: Oxford University Press, 1979. The best Kaufman biography to date: detailed, humorous, and very readable.

Green, Stanley. *Encyclopedia of the Musical.* London: Cassell & Company, 1976. A priceless resource covering New York and London productions up to the mid-1970s.

———. *Ring Bells, Sing Songs: Broadway Musicals of the 1930s.* New Rochelle, New York: Galahad Books, 1971. Lavishly illustrated and packed with detailed info on every musical that played the Main Stem during this turbulent decade. A joy to read.

———. *The World of Musical Comedy.* New York: A. S. Barnes & Co., 1960 (and later editions). Focuses on major composers. Appendix has production stats and discography.

Grubb, Kevin Boyd. *Razzle Dazzle: The Life and Work of Bob Fosse.* New York: St. Martin's Press, 1989. Entertaining and thorough, with many rare Fosse photos.

Grun, Bernard. *Gold and Silver: The Life and Times of Franz Lehar.* New York: David McKay Co., 1970. Charming and informative.

Hanson, Bruce. *The Peter Pan Chronicles.* New York: Birch Lane Press, 1993. Every incarnation of *Peter Pan* is chronicled with affection and solid research.

Harris, Warren G. *The Other Marilyn: A Biography of Marilyn Miller.* New York: Arbor House, 1985. Good biography of this once legendary star; not nearly thorough enough.

Haskins, Jim, and M. R. Mitgang. *Mr. Bojangles: The Biography of Bill Robinson.* New York: William Morrow & Company, 1988. Straightforward, well researched.

Henderson, Mary C. *The City and the Theatre: The History of New York Playhouses* (second edition). New York: James T. White & Co., 1973. New York: Back Stage Books, 2004. The most important—and most quoted—history of New York theatres.

Herman, Jerry. *Showtune.* New York: Donald I. Fine Books, 1996. A master composer/lyricist reviews his life in a book filled with sentiment and optimism.

Hirsch, Foster. *The Boys From Syracuse: The Shuberts' Theatrical Empire.* Carbondale: Southern Illinois University Press, 1998. A frank and thorough chronicle of the most powerful and hated dynasty in American theatre.

——. *Harold Prince and the American Musical Theatre.* New York: Oxford University Press, 1989. A detailed look at Prince's directorial work up to *Phantom of the Opera.* Plenty of useful facts and observations for serious students of these works.

Horne, Alistair. *Seven Ages of Paris.* New York: Vintage, 2004. An engrossing history of Paris, with extensive information on the changes that marked the city during the reign of Napoleon III.

Jablonski, Edward. *Irving Berlin: American Troubadour.* New York: Henry Holt & Co., 1999. The best biography of Berlin to date, thoroughly researched and a pleasure to read.

——. *Gershwin: A Biography.* New York: Doubleday, 1987. There are many books on George Gershwin, but this is the best to date.

Jackson, Henry T., ed. *The Encyclopedia of New York City.* New Haven, Connecticut: Yale University Press, 1995. Over 1,300 informative pages covering the history of New York, theatrical and otherwise. A priceless resource.

Jones, John Bush. *Our Musicals, Ourselves: A Social History of the American Musical Theatre.* Lebanon, New Hampshire: Brandeis University Press, 2003.

An examination of the way Broadway musicals reflect and promote social change. Essential reading for all serious students of musical theatre history.

Kahn, E. J. *The Merry Partners: The Age and Stage of Harrigan and Hart.* New York: Random House, 1955. One of the best theatrical histories ever written, this book brings a long-lost Broadway world to vibrant life.

Krasner, David. *A Beautiful Pageant: African-American Theatre, Drama, and Performance in the Harlem Renaissance, 1910–1927.* New York: Palgrave MacMillan, 2002. Noteworthy for its coverage of the landmark hit *Shuffle Along*.

Kruger, Miles. *Show Boat: The Story of a Classic American Musical.* New York: Oxford University Press, 1977. Updated as a soft cover edition. New York: Da Capo, 1990. The complete history of *Show Boat*, a model of scholarly research blended with passion for the musical theatre.

Lahr, John. *Notes on a Cowardly Lion.* New York: Limelight Editions, 1984. Bert Lahr's son takes a frank, moving look into the life and heart of his father.

Larkin, Colin. *The Virgin Encyclopedia of Stage and Film Musicals.* London: Virgin Books, 1999. This hefty volume gives ample coverage to both American and British musicals. A sensational reference.

Lerner, Alan Jay. *The Musical Theatre: A Celebration.* New York: McGraw Hill, 1986. Written at the end of Lerner's life, a perceptive overview of musical theatre history.

———. *The Street Where I Live.* New York: W. W. Norton & Company, 1978. Delicious entertainment! This magical autobiography by a master lyricist/librettist is worth reading again and again—of course, some of it should be taken with a grain of salt.

Logan, Joshua. *Josh.* New York: Delacorte Press, 1976. Fascinating memoir from a playwright-director.

Magraw, Roger. *France 1800–1914: A Social History.* London: Longman/ Pearson, 2002. Fine collection of essays covering nineteenth-century France.

Mandelbaum, Ken. *A Chorus Line and the Musicals of Michael Bennett.* New York: St. Martins Press, 1989. The definitive book on the subject. Well-researched, lovingly and energetically written, based on countless interviews.

———. *Not Since Carrie.* New York: St. Martin's Press, 1991. A witty and joyous valentine to flop musicals; required reading for all serious musical theatre buffs.

Martin, Mary. *My Heart Belongs.* New York: Morrow & Co., 1976. A warmhearted autobiography, packed with great anecdotes.

Marx, Samuel, and Jan Clayton. *Rodgers & Hart: Bewitched, Bothered, and Bewildered.* New York: G. P. Putnam's Sons, 1976. Long overdue, well researched, a great read.

Mates, Julian. *The American Musical Stage Before 1800*. New Brunswick, New Jersey: Rutgers University Press, 1962. A well-researched look at a neglected subject.

McBrien, William. *Cole Porter: A Biography*. New York: Knopf, 1998. Informative, frank, and well written, this is the definitive Porter bio.

McCabe, John. *George M. Cohan: The Man Who Owned Broadway*. New York: Doubleday & Co., 1973. A solid biography that brings Cohan's era to life.

Merman, Ethel (with George Eells). *Merman: An Autobiography*. New York: Simon and Schuster, 1978. Broadway's beloved musical superstar turned out an enjoyable book.

Meyerson, Harold, and Ernie Harburg. *Who Put the Rainbow in The Wizard of Oz?: Yip Harburgh, Lyricist*. Ann Arbor: University of Michigan Press, 1993. Celebration of Harburg's life and career, filled with entertaining detail.

Miller, Scott. *Deconstructing Harold Hill: An Insiders Guide to Musical Theatre*. Portsmouth, New Hampshire: Heinemann, 2000. Continuation of the influential, insightful series.

———. *From Assassins to West Side Story: The Director's Guide to Musical Theatre*. Portsmouth, New Hampshire: Heinemann, 1996. The first in a series of revealing books on the ways classic musicals can be reinterpreted for today's audiences. All of Miller's books are highly recommended.

Mizejewski, Linda. *Ziegfeld Girl: Image and Icon in Culture and Cinema*. Durham, North Carolina: Duke University Press, 1999. A serious academic approach meets with readable text in this insightful examination of how the Ziegfeld legacy spread through pop culture.

Moody, Richard. *Ned Harrigan: From Corlear's Hook to Herald Square*. Chicago: Nelson Hall, 1980. Detailed and informative, this biography of the inventor of Broadway musical comedy will please any serious student of the period.

Mordden, Ethan. *Beautiful Morning: The Broadway Musical in the 1940s*. New York: Oxford University Press, 1999.

———. *Coming Up Roses: The Broadway Musical in the 1950s*. New York: Oxford University Press, 1998.

———. *The Happiest Corpse I've Ever Seen: The Last 25 Years of the Broadway Musical*. New York: Palgrave MacMillan, 2004.

———. *Make Believe: The Broadway Musical in the 1920s*. Oxford University Press, New York, 1998.

———. *One More Kiss: The Broadway Musical in the 1970s*. New York: Palgrave MacMillan, 2003.

———. *Open a New Window: The Broadway Musical in the 1960s*. New York: Palgrave for St. Martin's Press, 2001.

———. *Sing for Your Supper: The Broadway Musical in the 1930s.* New York: Palgrave MacMillan, 2005. In this detailed decade-by-decade series, Mordden takes a passionate and opinionated look at musical theatre. You may not always agree with Mordden, but you can count on being entertained and informed.

Morely, Sheridan. *Spread a Little Happiness: The First Hundred Years of the British Musical.* New York: Thames and Hudson, 1987. The British musical after Gilbert and Sullivan gets its due here in a loving and lavishly illustrated volume.

Nardo, Don, ed. *Greek Drama.* San Diego: Greenhaven Press, 2000. Useful collection of critical articles on the conventions and literary aspects of ancient Greek drama.

Nolan, Frederick. *Lorenz Hart: A Poet on Broadway.* New York: Oxford University Press, 1996. A highly readable biography.

———. *The Sound of Their Music: The Story of Rodgers and Hammerstein.* New York: Walker and Company, 1978. A superb book, with great photos and a wonderful appendix outlining the Rodgers and Hammerstein years.

Norton, Richard C. *A Chronology of American Musical Theatre.* 3 vols. New York: Oxford University Press, 2002. A massive chronology, listing songs, casts, and creative staff for every Broadway musical from 1750 to 2001. Fantastic resource.

Poggi, Jack. *Theatre in America: The Impact of Economic Forces 1870–1967.* Ithaca, New York: Cornell University Press, 1968. How the "business" of show business developed, with facts and figures placed in a well-considered perspective.

Porter, Susan L. *With an Air Debonair: Musical Theatre in America 1785–1815.* Washington, D.C.: Smithsonian Institution Press, 1991. The most comprehensive review of musical theatre in early America, scholarly yet readable.

Raymond, Jack. *Show Music on Record: From the 1890s to the 1980s.* New York: Frederick Ungar Press, 1982. A detailed catalog of commercial recordings of stage and screen musical scores up to 1981. From *Robin Hood* to *Cats*, an awesome effort.

Rosenberg, Deena. *Fascinating Rhythm: The Collaboration of George and Ira Gershwin.* London: Lime Tree, 1991. One of the few books to examine the collaboration between lyricist and composer, based on extensive interviews with Ira.

Sante, Luc. *Low Life: Lures and Snares of Old New York.* New York: Farrar, Strauss & Giroux, 1991. An entertaining and engrossing look at lower class life and entertainment in New York from the 1840s through World War I.

Secrest, Meryle. *Somewhere for Me: A Biography of Richard Rodgers.* New York: Alfred A. Knopf, 2001. A detailed look back at one of the greatest figures in this genre.

————. *Stephen Sondheim: A Life.* London: Bloomsbury, 1998. Sondheim cooperated with this author, which makes her occasional inaccuracies annoying.

Senelick, Laurence. *The Age and Stage of George L. Fox 1825–1877.* Lebanon, New Hampshire: University Press of New England, 1988. Expanded as a paperback edition. Iowa City: University of Iowa Press, 1999. Well-researched, readable, and fascinating.

Singer, Barry. *Ever After: The Last Years of Musical Theatre and Beyond.* New York: Applause, 2004. Although I disagree with some of Singer's opinions, he offers a well-informed firsthand look at musical theatre from 1975 to the early 2000s.

Slide, Anthony. *The Encyclopedia of Vaudeville.* Westport, Connecticut: Greenwood Press, 1994. The best resource on vaudeville—period. A lifetime of love and research went into this book, which includes detailed biographies of hundreds of performers.

Sommerstein, Alan H. *Greek Drama and Dramatists.* New York: Routledge, 2002. A clear and accessible examination of the social and artistic function that theatre filled in ancient Greece.

Smith, Cecil, and Litton, Glenn. *Musical Comedy in America.* New York: Theatre Arts Books, 1950/1981. The first book on musicals. Still a winner. Smith's look at early musicals remains fresh and perceptive after half a century.

Snyder, Robert W. *The Voice of the City.* New York: Oxford University Press, 1989. A delightful and well-researched look at the history of vaudeville and popular culture in New York City. Superb.

Stagg, Jerry. *The Shubert Brothers.* New York: Random House, 1968. An entertaining and informative look at the men who built America's largest theatrical empire.

Stedman, Jane. *W. W. S. Gilbert: A Classic Victorian & His Theatre.* New York: Oxford University Press, 1996. An excellent academic review of Gilbert's life and times.

Stein, Charles, ed. *American Vaudeville.* New York: Da Capo Press, 1984. A fascinating collection of vintage articles, essays, and other resources written during vaudeville's heyday. Those with a serious interest in vaudeville will love this one.

Steyn, Mark. *Broadway Babies Say Goodnight.* New York: Routledge Books, 1997. Sometimes entertaining but more often a tiresome collection of misinformed, bigoted opinions. The bitchy homophobia speaks for itself.

Stratyner, Barbara. *Ned Wayburn and the Dance Routine: From Vaudeville to the Ziegfeld Follies. Studies in Dance History, No. 13.* Madison, Wisconsin: Society of Dance History Scholars, 1996. An insightful look at the career of the first important dance director in American show business. A first-rate resource for dance aficionados.

Strausbaugh, John. *Black Like You: Blackface, Whiteface, Insult & Imitation in American Popular Culture.* New York: Jeremy T. Parcher/Penguin, 2006. A sane, eloquent, and well-researched examination of a sensitive and complex topic.

Suskin, Stephen. *More Opening Nights on Broadway.* New York: Schirmer Books, 1997. Original reviews for most of the musicals that opened between 1965 and 1981, with a special section for important road shows that never made it to New York.

———. *Opening Night on Broadway.* New York: Schirmer Books, 1990. I adore this book! The original newspaper reviews for most of the musicals that opened between 1943 and 1964, with perceptive and dishy commentary.

———. *Show Tunes 1905–1991: The Songs, Shows, and Careers of Broadway's Major Composers.* New York: Limelight Editions, 1992. Suskin strikes again with an exhaustive catalog of who wrote what and when. Spectacular!

Toll, Robert. *Blacking Up.* New York: Oxford University Press, 1974. This detailed academic chronicle of minstrel shows remains the definitive study of minstrelsy—crucial reading for anyone interested in the topic.

Traub, James. *The Devil's Playground: A Century of Pleasure and Profit in Times Square.* New York: Random House, 2004. A readable and insightful look at Times Square's reign as New York's cultural hub.

Traubner, Richard. *Operetta: A Theatrical History.* Garden City, New York: Doubleday & Company, 1983. The ultimate love letter to operetta, with superb scholarship throughout. A new paperback edition appeared in 2003.

Viagas, Robert, Baayork Lee, and Thommie Walsh, with the Entire Original Cast. *On the Line.* New York: William Morrow & Company, 1990. They have a lot to say and hold no punches. All the highlights and low points of ACL's production process.

Waterfield, Robin. *Athens: A History, From Ancient Ideal to Modern City.* New York: Basic Books, 2004. Readable and thoroughly researched discussion of the rise, fall, and resurrection of the city that gave birth to western civilization.

Wilk, Max. *OK! The Story of Oklahoma!* New York: Grove Press, 1993. A detailed and fascinating look back at the gestation of Rodgers and Hammerstein's landmark hit.

Willis, John, and Daniel Blum, eds. *Theatre World.* 1943–present. New York: Chilton, Crown, 1981. New York: Applause Books, 2007. Cast lists, photos, and performance statistics. Still the definitive print source on who played in what and when.

Wodehouse, P. G., and Guy Bolton. *Bring on the Girls!: The Improbable Story of Our Life in Musical Comedy, With Pictures to Prove It.* New York: Simon & Schuster, 1953. A delicious joint memoir by the co-librettists of the Princess Theatre shows.

Woll, Allen. *Black Musical Theatre: From Coontown to Dreamgirls.* Baton Rouge: Lousiana State University Press, 1989. A long overlooked part of theatre history got its first (and still most thorough) treatment here.

Zadan, Craig. *Sondheim & Co.* New York: Harper & Row, 1974, 1986. A fascinating behind the scenes look at how Sondheim's shows were created.

Ziegfeld, Richard, and Paulette. *The Ziegfeld Touch: The Life and Times of Florenz Ziegfeld, Jr.* New York: Harry N. Abrams Inc., 1993. A lavish compendium of photos and data with cast lists, plots, etc.

RECOMMENDED WEB RESOURCES

Cast Album Database (http://www.castalbumdb.com). A comprehensive listing of all existing cast recordings, with extensive support data.

The Gilbert & Sullivan Archive (http://math.boisestate.edu/gas/). Complete librettos for all of the Gilbert and Sullivan canon, plus articles, sound files, etc. A blessing for fans and students.

The Internet Broadway Database (http://www.ibdb.com). The place to check stats on any Broadway production, performer, or creative talent.

The Internet Movie Database (http://www.imdb.com). Data on film and television productions and talents.

Musicals101.com (http://www.musicals101.com). Ancestor to this book, the cyber encyclopedia of musical theatre, film, and television.

Playbill.com (http://www.playbill.com). The world's premiere source for theatre-related news and statistics; includes a massive list of theatre-related links.

Index